TELLING GOD'S STORY

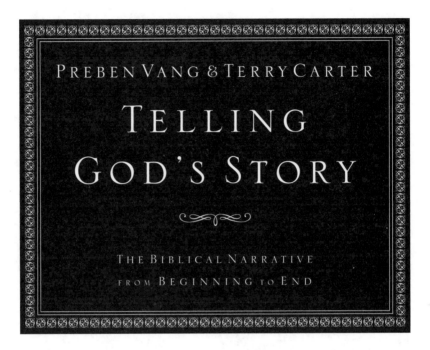

PREBEN VANG & TERRY CARTER

TELLING GOD'S STORY

THE BIBLICAL NARRATIVE
FROM BEGINNING TO END

PUBLISHING GROUP

NASHVILLE, TENNESSEE

ISBN: 978–0–8054–3282–4

Published by Broadman & Holman Publishers
Nashville, Tennessee

Dewey Decimal Classification: 234.3

Subject Heading: SALVATION—HISTORY
ATONEMENT—CHRISTIANITY
BIBLE—HISTORY OF BIBLICAL EVENTS

4 5 6 7 8 9 10 11 12 15 16 • 15 14 13 12 11 10 09
LB

Dedication of Preben Vang

*To my children, Signe and Andreas, who so evidently allow
God's Story to direct their lives.*

Dedication of Terry Carter

To Kathy

Contents

Preface xi
The Bible Story: An Overview 1
Background to the Bible Story 11

EPISODE ONE
CREATION

ACT 1
The Story Begins 23
ACT 2
Humans Reject God's Plan. 31

EPISODE TWO
THE PLAN OF REDEMPTION

ACT 1
The Covenant and Promise. 43
ACT 2
Isaac, Jacob, and Joseph. 50

EPISODE THREE
THE FORMING OF A NATION: GOD'S PEOPLE AND THE LAW

ACT 1
Moses and the Deliverance. 61
ACT 2
The Sinai Experience 71

ACT 3
    The Wilderness Experience 79

EPISODE FOUR
THE PROMISED LAND AND SIN'S POWER

ACT 1
    The Conquest and the Judges 85

ACT 2
    The Period of the Judges 93

EPISODE FIVE
ISRAEL GETS A KING

ACT 1
    Samuel and Saul 103

ACT 2
    David the King 108

EPISODE SIX
REBELLION, JUDGMENT, AND FUTURE HOPE

ACT 1
    Solomon and the Demise of the Unified Kingdom 117
    A Note on the Prophets 124

ACT 2
    The Demise of the Northern Kingdom 127

ACT 3
    The Southern Kingdom Slides 136

EPISODE SEVEN
CAPTIVITY AND RETURN

ACT 1
    The Judgment 145

ACT 2
    The Captivity 151

ACT 3
    The Return from Exile and the Rebuilding of the Temple 155

ACT 4
    Rebuilding Jerusalem 158

ACT 5
    Wisdom: Finding God's Way 163

EPISODE EIGHT
Unto Us a Child Is Born

ACT 1
God Sends His Promised Messiah 173
ACT 2
Incarnation and the Two Natures of Jesus 179

EPISODE NINE
The Ministry of Jesus

ACT 1
Jesus Begins His Ministry 189
ACT 2
Jesus' Message and Methods 198
ACT 3
Jesus' Miracles and Ministry 210

EPISODE TEN
"A Prophet Must Die in Jerusalem"

ACT 1
Jesus' Entry into Jerusalem 219
ACT 2
Jesus' Last Supper and His Crucifixion 225

EPISODE ELEVEN
The Grave Could Not Hold Him

ACT 1
Jesus' Burial and Resurrection 239
ACT 2
Jesus' Postresurrection Appearances and Ascension 246

EPISODE TWELVE
This Gospel Shall Be for All People

ACT 1
A Sound as of a Rushing Wind 257
ACT 2
The Church in Jerusalem and the Early Spread of the Gospel 265
ACT 3
Paul's First and Second Missionary Journeys 272
ACT 4
Paul's Third Missionary Journey, His Arrest and Final Days 278

EPISODE THIRTEEN
CHURCH GROWTH AND CHURCH STRUGGLES

ACT 1
  Church Struggles and the Examples from 1 Corinthians 289
ACT 2
  Church Struggles and Christian Thinking 296
ACT 3
  Church Struggles and Issues of Faith 303

EPISODE FOURTEEN
LOOKING FOR A CITY

ACT 1
  God's Future for His People 313
ACT 2
  God Brings His Story to Its Climactic End 319
  Last Thoughts: The Meaning of the Story in the 21st Century 329

PREFACE

I magine attending an English literature class focusing on Mark Twain's *Tom Sawyer*. You buy the book, but you wait for the teacher to give you the class reading schedule. When you come to class, you find that the teacher, rather than asking you to read the book from cover to cover, wants you to engage the story in a different way. The teacher enjoys the various smaller stories within the story, especially the episodes that reveal certain principles about life he finds specifically relevant and applicable to the students. As a result, his teaching plan consists of picking and choosing different substories. This approach allows the teacher to focus on themes from the story and to emphasize issues of special interest to him.

You feel this approach is innovative and exciting, and you agree with the teacher that it will make the book relevant and able to speak to issues you are thinking about. You have no problem jumping from one part of the story to another, and you like the idea of investigating how Mark Twain develops and explains Tom Sawyer's life. You find the class stimulating, the discussions lively, and you are picking up good information.

As the time for the big exam approaches, you feel you are ready for it. You have been to every class and have taken notes on every theme from Tom Sawyer's life covered by the teacher. You have not read the book from cover to cover, but you have studied so many themes from Sawyer's life that you feel you know him well.

The first question on the exam fills you with a sense of shock: *Retell the story of Tom Sawyer in your own words from beginning to end.* What are you to do?

Although you have studied many interesting aspects of Sawyer's life, you have no real understanding of the totality of his life story. The second question is almost as shocking: *What is the purpose of the story?* You never asked that question or concerned yourself with it. The class had focused on several independent insights from Tom Sawyer's life which the professor felt significant and helpful for class discussions.

To students of the Bible, this scenario is not as strange as it appears. In fact, many have grown up with such an approach to Scripture. Week after week they have heard and seen ministers stand in the pulpit, Sunday school teachers sit before classes, and youth ministers lead Bible studies using such an approach. Each of these Bible teachers shared only small vignettes of the story told in the Bible—elements from the big story they felt were relevant for their students.

Those listening find the information helpful and enjoyable, something that speaks to the immediate issues of their lives. Over time they learn that this is how one should handle the biblical story. The Bible is not a book to be read as much as a depository of truth statements to be studied one by one. It follows that the normal approach to Scripture is to pull out smaller stories from their context and draw conclusions about their meaning that may not have much to do with the purpose of the larger story. The result of this approach has been that many people read the Bible with little idea of its whole message and purpose, guided only by their current interests and immediate needs.

At the university where we teach, we discovered the above described problem with incoming students. Students who had grown up under the ministry of great pastors and good Sunday school teachers, many who also spent time daily reading the Bible on their own, were unable to retell the story and explain its meaning. Furthermore, when we asked them to place a section of the Bible into the sequence of the full story of Scripture, they were unable to do so. Most were even unsure how the major events and names, like Abraham, Moses, David, Jesus, and Paul, fit into the Bible's story line.

This realization forced us to rethink the way we taught the Bible to incoming freshmen. In the past we offered two traditional courses—Old Testament and New Testament surveys. These classes tried to cover the various books of the Bible and peruse its history. We talked about authorship, dates, purposes, and recipients of each book. In the end, however, we found we had failed to help students make the connection between the individual biblical books and, even more so, between the two testaments. Students did not see the story of the Bible as one story beginning with Genesis and ending with Revelation.

Since all students at the university, regardless of their major, take six hours of Bible classes as a part of their liberal arts core, we rethought our strategy. We were more interested in getting the students to know and understand the biblical story itself than to have them learn facts about individual biblical books. We found the students were better helped if we walked them through the Bible episode by episode than by discussing the historical background of 1 Kings, for example.

This book is the result of this change in teaching philosophy. *Telling God's Story* serves as a text for a course that takes students through the entire biblical story helping them learn and understand the Bible as one story. Having field-tested this approach for several years now, our experience confirms that this method of placing smaller sections of the biblical story in their context helps students avoid poor interpretations of individual biblical passages. In addition, we are convinced this makes them better church members who hear sermons more clearly and explain the Bible to others more effectively.

                                                          Preben Vang and Terry Carter

THE BIBLE STORY:
AN OVERVIEW

The story of the Bible begins with God. In the beginning, God created the universe. God was not a part of the universe as a mere power but as a separate and independent Creator who willfully and deliberately created everything that exists. Being an expression of God's own beauty, love, and relational character, creation belongs to God. Everything in creation, therefore, from the smallest and seemingly most insignificant to the crowning work, the human being, finds its meaning and reason for existence in the relationship between the Creator and his creation.

To express his love, God decided to give to creation an expression of his own image—the human being. He created the human being as man and woman and gave them managerial power over the rest of creation. They were to live in a close and loving relationship with their Creator and conduct their lives as an expression of that relationship. Human beings, however, decided that they could live on their own without God. This decision destroyed the intimacy of their relationship with the Creator; and as this relationship deteriorated, the image of God faded; and humans lost the true quality of their humanity.

Outside God's presence human beings experienced the results of the destroyed fellowship with God. Blessing had been exchanged for curse. Envy, pain, and evil (even to the point of murder) became the rule of the day. Humans proved that the goodness and love that came from the presence of God were annihilated by their own desire to put themselves first. Sin, which in its essence is the rebellion of humans against God, had become the governing quality of humankind. Evil grew and covered the earth; God was forgotten.

The never-ending grace of God, however, would not let go of the crowning work of the creation. Rather than withdrawing, God established a new covenantal relationship with humankind. A man named Abraham, later called the

Father of Faith because of his unwavering trust in God, received a promise that his numerous descendants would be blessed. In fact, blessing would come to the whole earth through them. Because of this covenant promise given to Abraham, all the people of the earth would have the opportunity to experience the blessing of God's presence once again.

The promise to Abraham was a unilateral promise; that is, it was a promise from God with no condition placed on man. It was an expression of pure grace; God placed it solely upon himself to reestablish the relationship with the rebellious creatures he originally had created in his own image. This Abrahamic covenant thus became the basis for the salvation of human beings. Again and again, in spite of the repeated attempts by humans to destroy their relationship with the Creator, God remembered his covenant with Abraham and opened a door for humans to find a way back into his presence.

At first it looked as if God's promise was empty; Abraham was without children. But in Abraham's old age, God granted him a son of promise, Isaac, who in turn became the father of a son, Jacob. Jacob, whom God later renamed Israel, became the father of twelve sons whose names would later give rise to the names of Israel's twelve tribes. God had created for himself a people called Israel. This people, also called the Hebrews, were to be recognized and characterized by their trust in the one God, the Creator of heaven and earth.

Famine came upon the land, and the family of Jacob went to Egypt to find food. In Egypt the people of Israel increased in number; and as time passed, the Egyptian rulers, called pharaohs, worried that the Israelites would become too powerful. To counter this threat, the pharaohs enslaved the Israelites. For four hundred years the faithful among the people cried to God for help in their misery. In these darkest of days, an Egyptian princess fell in love with one of the Israelite babies called Moses and took him as her son to be raised as an Egyptian prince. When he came of age, Moses realized his relationship with the people of Israel and left Egypt to live in the desert. Remembering his covenant with Abraham, God called Moses in the desert and charged him with the task of liberating his people from their bondage in Egypt. Moses refused, arguing that he did not even know the name of Israel's God. At a burning bush, God revealed himself to Moses as Yahweh, the I AM, the one who is always present with his people.

Moses returned to Egypt, imploring Pharaoh to let the Hebrews go, but Pharaoh would not listen. Plagues sent by God invaded the land, but Pharaoh did not listen—not even when God gave his last warning. Yahweh promised to send the angel of death to visit every household in Egypt and kill the firstborn of all families unless Pharaoh released Israel from slavery and allowed them to leave Egypt.

To avoid death in the families of Israel, God told his people to make a meal in haste. They took the blood of a lamb and smeared it on the door frames to let the angel of death know that he was to *pass over* their homes. God would save his people by the blood of the lamb.

After this final plague, Egypt let Israel go, even hurrying them along. Israel left and came to the sea of reeds.[1] By this time the Egyptians regretted their decision to release the slaves and sent out armies to take them back. The Hebrews were caught between the water and the Egyptian army. They were trapped; the only one way of escape went through the water—an impossible situation.

God kept his promise to Abraham, however, and opened the waters for them to cross to the other side. The Egyptians, close behind, drowned on the bottom of the sea as God closed the waters as soon as Israel passed through. God had rescued his people! He had created for them an *exodus*—a way out of slavery. They were now on their way to the land God had promised them, free to follow him and to live in his presence. He would guide them through the desert by a cloud during the day and a pillar of fire during the night.

A new situation had become a reality for Israel. Yahweh was in the midst of his people; the holy Creator God lived among humans. He dwelled among them in a tabernacle—a portable tent designed for worship, the celebration of God's presence.

How were people to live in this new situation? What guidelines should govern this new relationship? God called Moses to a mountaintop and gave him a set of rules consisting of Ten Commandments—Ten Commandments which became the foundation for a new bilateral covenant, called the Mosaic covenant. It was bilateral because demands were put on both parties in the relationship. Yahweh promised he would be their God, they would be his people, and he would dwell in their midst. They were to keep the Law expressed in the commandments. Beyond the Ten Commandments, other rules and regulations were written down to define how humans should live and worship the God in their midst. As a legal covenant the Mosaic covenant required man's obedience to the Law as its central feature. This was different from the Abrahamic covenant, which had God's faithfulness to his promise as its central feature.

As usual, God kept his end of the agreement. He led the people to the edge of the promised land; but when they arrived, they were afraid to take possession of the land. This lack of trust in God sent them back into the desert to wander for forty years. Only after that faithless generation had died off did Yahweh again lead them to enter the land. After Moses' death Joshua became the leader of the people, and he led them to victory after victory until they took possession of the land God had promised them.

Following Joshua's death in the promised land, a series of judges became leaders of the people. People like Gideon, Deborah, and Samson led Israel's armies and passed judgment on the people. This is sometimes considered the

---

[1] The original Hebrew text says *Yam Suph*, which means "sea of reeds." The reference is probably not to the Red Sea as we normally think of that body of water.

Dark Age of Hebrew history. Not only did many of the people stop worshipping Yahweh, but several of the judges were active in worshipping idols. It was a dark day for the relationship between God and his people. But as before, God ended the misery of his people. The time of the judges came to an end as Israel elected a king like the other peoples.

During the reign of the second of these kings, King David, the promise from God approached its fulfillment for the nation of Israel. The Abrahamic covenant—with its promise of land, blessing, and peace—came close to a complete fulfillment during David's reign. David was Yahweh's answer to the destitution caused by the period of the judges. He was a man after God's own heart, a shepherd boy whose greatest desire was to please God. Under David the kingdom grew to hitherto unknown size and greatness. David made Jerusalem the capital of Israel and sought to build Yahweh a temple. This task, however, fell to his son, Solomon.

Nonetheless, God was pleased with David's desire to build a temple for Yahweh's presence among his people and extended a covenant promise to David. God promised to make David's name great, grant an eternal place for his people, and establish a permanent dynasty in the Davidic line. This Davidic covenant, like the Abrahamic, was a unilateral covenant with no condition placed on humans for its fulfillment. It forms the basis for Israel's hope as later expressed by the prophets and most climactically underscored in the genealogies of Jesus.

Solomon, who followed his father David as king, became world renowned for his wisdom and incredible wealth. Out of this wealth he built Yahweh a temple in Jerusalem. Upon its completion, the Bible explains how God filled the temple with his presence. Solomon disobeyed God in other areas, however, and "did not have the heart of his father." Solomon's sin led to the split of the kingdom after his death. Ten tribes followed Jeroboam, a former general under Solomon who established the kingdom of Israel in the north; two tribes stayed with Rehoboam, Solomon's son, to establish the kingdom of Judah in the south. These two nations picked up where the judges left off and continued the destruction of their relationship with God. Even priests replaced the worship of Yahweh with the worship of Baal, a Canaanite god. The people seemed intent on breaking the Mosaic covenant!

During this time, the eighth century before Christ, prophets spoke out from both the North and the South, warning the people of the imminent judgment of God. The prophetic message proclaimed God's indictment on the people. God's people had violated the covenant by their idolatry, their social injustice, and their religious formalism. "You have broken the covenant," the prophets charged, "you must repent! If there is no repentance, judgment will come!" And judgment came! The Assyrians destroyed the Northern Kingdom of Israel in 721 BC; and Babylon destroyed Judah in 586 BC, forcing a large number of

Hebrews into exile in Babylon. The people had broken their covenantal relationship with God, and they now had to rely solely on the hope of restoration, which had always been part of the prophetic message.

During the exile the focus of the people changed. Prophets like Ezekiel (similar to Jeremiah before him) looked forward to a time when God's law no longer would be written on tablets of stone but on human hearts—a time when God's Spirit would indwell every member of God's family to ensure an internal drawing toward God's word and will. God will establish a new covenant with his people, they proclaimed. Daniel, a devout young man from Judah, who counseled the king of Babylon during the exile, saw a vision of someone like a Son of Man who possessed authority and who was to create an everlasting kingdom. People from all nations and all languages would come to worship this Son of Man. It was a time of renewed hope.

The Mosaic covenant was shattered, but the prophets were looking back to the unilateral covenants given to Abraham and David. God would no longer limit his presence to the temple in Jerusalem. Ezekiel shared a vision in which God's throne was on wheels moving in every direction. In the days to come, God would move with his people as in the days of old—not just among them as with the tabernacle but within them through his Spirit. The glory that had left the temple would be manifested through the people of the Spirit.

When Persia conquered Babylon, the Persians allowed the people of Israel to return. After seventy years of exile, Zerubbabel led God's people back to the promised land to rebuild the temple. The restoration of the wall around Jerusalem and the reestablishment of the full worship of Yahweh came later under the leadership of Ezra and Nehemiah. These leaders of Israel made great efforts to bring Israel back to preexilic times. But it never happened! Yahweh did not return to fill the temple as he did under Solomon. The nation of Israel did not become truly independent. The Mosaic covenant had been broken, and it would not be restored. The Law no longer defined the covenant relationship between God and his people; it functioned simply as a rigorous guideline for living. The period after the exile, the so-called postexilic period, functioned as an interim period between the judgment of the exile and the promise of a new covenant restoration where God once again would be visible among his people. This new covenant, which Jeremiah, Joel, and Ezekiel had prophesied about, was to be a covenant of the Spirit.

The people had broken the bilateral Mosaic covenant, but God remembered his covenant with Abraham and David. In the fullness of time, he sent his own Son in the form of a human to fulfill the promises of blessing to the world and eternal kingship on David's throne. The New Testament begins its story by placing this Son in the lineage of both David and Abraham.

An angel of God visited a priest named Zechariah while he was doing his ministry in the temple and told him that his wife Elizabeth would give birth to a son who would be great in the eyes of God. The child, John, who became known as John the Baptist, served as the forerunner to the Messiah. His purpose was to announce to the people that the new covenant relationship God had promised was at hand. John the Baptist, in other words, served as the bridge between the old and new covenants.

God's angel, Gabriel, visited a young girl from Judah named Mary and told her that God's own Spirit would overshadow her and make her pregnant. The child to come should be called Jesus, which means Savior. He would become the long-awaited Messiah whom the prophets had looked for to save the world.

Jesus was born in simple circumstances and grew in wisdom, stature, and favor with God and man. At about thirty years of age, Jesus came to the desert where John the Baptist was preaching and baptizing, and he asked John to baptize him. Coming up from the water, God initiated Jesus' ministry when the Holy Spirit descended upon him in the form of a dove; and God spoke the words: "You are my Son, whom I love; with you I am well pleased."

Everywhere he went, Jesus preached the message that God's kingdom had come near. For three years he walked and taught. His message was consistent in both word and deed. God's kingdom had come near. Some people were confused, however, because their expectations to the promised Messiah were so different from what they saw in Jesus. Even John the Baptist, who himself had looked forward to God's intervention, became confused and sent his disciples to ask Jesus if he was the one to come. Jesus sent these words back to John the Baptist: "Tell John what you have seen and heard. The blind receive sight, the lame walk, those with leprosy are cured, the deaf hear, the dead are raised, and the good news is preached to the poor."

The evidence was abundantly clear: God had come back to dwell among his people. His power overflowed, and the message of his presence was again proclaimed. The old prophetic indictment and warning that the people were destroying the covenant had been replaced by the proclamation that God was fulfilling his promise. Jesus' message sounded just as clear as the prophets' of old. God wants his people for himself; there is no room for idolatry. "You must repent," Jesus said. God has no pleasure in religious formalism; what matters, said Jesus, is the heart. New covenant worshippers will worship in Spirit and in truth. God still hates social injustice. Jesus came to preach good news to the poor and to release the oppressed.

For the Jewish leader this message served as a radical indictment of their lifestyle, beliefs, and position. They plotted to kill Jesus and put an end to his growing group of disciples. It all came to a head during a week of Passover celebration. Jesus assembled his twelve closest disciples in an upper room to celebrate the Jewish Passover. Knowing what was about to happen, he told them of his immanent death. Gathered around the Passover table for a meal to remember how God saved them from slavery in Egypt, Jesus changed the symbolic content of the typical Jewish Passover meal and made it a celebration of the new covenant. Jesus took the bread and broke it saying that it represented his body which was about to be broken for many. He also poured the wine saying that it represented his blood which was about to be shed for the forgiveness of sin.

Later that evening he went to the garden of Gethsemane to pray. As he was praying, the Jewish leaders, escorted by a large number of soldiers, came out and took him captive. After an illegal trial before the Jewish Sanhedrin, Jesus stood before Pilate for a Roman trial. The Romans found him not guilty, but they gave in to the pressure of the Jewish leaders who had stirred up the crowd against Jesus. Jesus was crucified on Friday—killed by the cruelest and most painful method of execution known to the Romans. That same day, when Jesus died, the pain of God, giving his own Son for the sins of humankind, became evident. The sun darkened and the temple's curtain, which separated the temple's holy area from its most holy area, tore from top to bottom. It was as if God had torn his clothes to express his own pain and suffering. At the same time, God had created open access into the place of his holy dwelling.

Jesus' death on the cross was not God's final word, however. By his sacrificial death, Jesus paid the price for the sins of humankind, opening the door for people again to enjoy the fellowship with God that sin had broken. Jesus died not just as a religious man but as the Son of God. God majestically and powerfully confirmed Jesus as his Son when Jesus rose from the dead on the third day. The resurrection qualified Jesus' death as an act of God. As Paul would later say, without the resurrection faith in Jesus would have been meaningless. But, as it is, because he *did* rise, faith in Jesus means everything. It reestablishes a saving relationship between God and humans who put their trust in him.

During a forty-day period after his resurrection, Jesus appeared to his disciples to ensure them of his continued presence and to give them instructions for the future. He would ascend to heaven, he explained; and while he was there, the disciples were to continue to spread his message. Jesus commissioned his followers to make disciples of all nations by baptizing and teaching them everything that he had taught. The ascension is necessary, Jesus continued, because "unless I go back to my Father, the Holy Spirit will not come to you" (see John 16:7).

The Spirit came ten days after the ascension of Jesus. It happened on the day that we now call Pentecost. The Spirit came with a power that enabled the ministry of Jesus to continue through his disciples. The Spirit brought the presence of God in a way that was unlimited by space and time. Through his Spirit, God could now be everywhere at the same time, granting his presence to all people who would commit their lives to him.

After God's Holy Spirit had descended upon each of Jesus' followers, he gave them a boldness to preach the gospel. The gospel is the good news about God's new covenant with all people. The first time the disciples preached, people from everywhere, who were assembled in Jerusalem for the Pentecost festival, heard the gospel and were moved to conversion—three thousand that first day. Before long the gospel spread far beyond Jerusalem, and the church became a powerful reality in the world.

This rapid growth of the church created a strong opposition. One of the primary opponents was a young Jew named Paul. In spite of his young age, he had gained great prominence among the Jewish leaders. One day, on his way to Damascus to track down and persecute more Christians, a powerful vision of the resurrected Jesus stopped him. This encounter radically convinced Paul of the truth of the Christian message, and it led him to conversion and baptism. After a season, a prominent church member named Barnabas, who was ministering in the church in Antioch, called on Paul to come and help him there.

This ministry in Antioch gave impetus to the conviction that God wanted the gospel to be preached to all people everywhere. Paul and Barnabas now left the church in Antioch to take a journey into Asia Minor to spread the good news. Coming back from this first journey, Paul and Barnabas found that some Pharisees, although they had acknowledged that Jesus had come from God, were vehemently opposed to their ministry. These so-called Judaizers preached that people could only become Christians if they also would keep the Law of Moses. Paul and Barnabas were infuriated! To them the new covenant was a covenant of Spirit and faith, not of Law and rituals. The so-called gospel of the Judaizers was no gospel at all.

To settle the matter, Paul and Barnabas went to talk to the leaders of the mother church in Jerusalem. In this meeting—after prayer, testimony, and conversation—it was determined that God did not require Gentiles (non-Jews) to become Jews before they could become Christians. By giving his Spirit to the Gentiles, God had already spoken on the matter, they concluded. Everyone who would trust in Jesus' death as atonement for human sin and who would recognize his resurrection as the manifestation of God's power over evil, belonged to God. The evidence that someone had become a Christian was the presence of God's Spirit, not the keeping of the Mosaic covenant. In this way the meeting in Jerusalem became the starting point for a powerful mission enterprise that would spread the gospel throughout the world with the speed of wildfire.

Paul made at least three missionary journeys, starting churches everywhere from the province of Galatia through Asia Minor to Europe. Beside his job as a leatherworker, Paul worked tirelessly day and night, preaching, teaching, and writing letters to help the churches stay on track and be strong in the face of opposition. Hostility was vehement from both within and without. Within the church false teachers and the pagan culture fired their malignant darts in an attempt to pull the infant church away from the gospel message Paul had preached. From outside the church, social and political pressures vouched to crush the new and struggling fellowships. Although the gospel message as a tremendous witness to God's power withstood this animosity, opposition finally caught up with Paul himself who consequently appealed to Rome to be tried as a Roman citizen before Caesar.

In Rome, Paul stayed under house arrest for two years where he was able to continue a teaching and writing ministry. After this imprisonment he was probably released for a little while before being taken captive again and martyred during a heavy persecution launched against all Christians by the Roman emperor Nero. This persecution did not stop the spread of the gospel, however. Even when the persecution increased about twenty years later under the Roman emperor Domitian, who demanded that Christians call him lord (a title they reserved for Jesus alone), Rome could not stop the gospel. Willing to pay with their lives for the good news about Jesus Christ, Christians continued to preach about the grace of God and the presence of his kingdom.

The last book of the Bible speaks to the suffering that God's people often face. At a time when Christians served as prey for wild animals for the amusement of thousands of people at the coliseum in Rome, the book of Revelation gave Christians a glimpse of what was to come. Suffering will not last forever! God will honor his promise and vindicate his people. He will create a new heaven and a new earth where all evil will be removed. Those who have received his Spirit and become a part of his people in this life will come to enjoy his full presence forever. The presence of God and the coming of his kingdom that is now experienced in part will then be experienced in full. Those who through faith in Jesus enjoy God's fellowship in this life will end up where humanity began, in the full presence of God where they will see him face-to-face. God will bring the crowning work of his creation back into his garden. The story will end where it began—God and humans together in close fellowship.

* * * * * * * * * *

Why tell this story? We tell this story because it is more than a story, even more than just a true story. It is *the* story! It is a story that better than any other story makes sense of life. It gives coherence and structure to our understanding of the universe. It gives meaning to our experiences and direction to our decisions. It is a story that has the power to reestablish the true quality of the humanness of life. It is a story that refuses apathy! It requests a hearing! It petitions to be internalized! It promises a life-changing encounter with God!

Our lives as human beings are made up of stories that have shaped, or are shaping, who we are. The story of the Bible has the power to make sense of all the other stories of your life. When it is internalized and it becomes *your* story, it gives meaning in the midst of meaninglessness and value in the midst of worthlessness. Your personal story will find grounding in creation, guidance in crises, re-formation in redemption, and direction in its destination. People become Christians when their own stories merge with, and are understood in the light of, God's story.

BACKGROUND TO THE BIBLE STORY

TESTAMENTS AND COVENANTS

The Bible consists of two testaments—the Old and the New. The designation *new* and *old* should not be overly pressed. It does not mean that the Old Testament is completely replaced by the New. Rather, old and new together reveal the covenantal relationship between God and his people. The last twenty-seven books of the Bible, which traditionally are called the New Testament, explain and describe the new covenant God has made with people from all places and of all races. The first thirty-nine books of the Bible, which traditionally are called the Old Testament, explain and describe the covenants God made from the beginning. Since God is not discontinuous, the two testaments are not disjointed either. The new covenant, which is the covenant God established through the death and resurrection of his Son Jesus Christ, results from the first promises God gave to Abraham and David.

The connection between the two sections of the Bible might be described in this way: God constituted his special relationship with humankind in the creation event itself. Humans, who were given a free will, chose to go their own way and reject God. What God created, humankind devastated! Still desiring a special relationship with humans, God covenanted to restore the fellowship between himself and his creation. The first covenant is described as the Abrahamic covenant. God promised Abraham, a man of extraordinary faith, that he, as the father of those who have faith in God, would become a great people. His numerous descendants would receive a land of promise and a life of blessing and peace. This is an unconditional promise. However, in spite of God's continuous expression of love, most prominently shown when he miraculously led his people out of their slavery in Egypt, people stubbornly persisted in their rejection of God. To give guidance to his people, God used Moses as the mediator of a legal covenant that based the relationship between God and humans on a conditional statement of Law. As long as the people kept the Law, God's presence and power would be present. However, the people neither could nor would keep the law, and they broke the conditional covenant mediated through Moses.

Humans could not, however, break the covenant promised to Abraham. The Abrahamic covenant came close to its fulfillment for the nation of Israel during the reign of David. A man after God's own heart, David received the promise that an eternal dynasty would be established in his lineage. This Davidic covenant found its complete fulfillment in the new covenant.

Ezekiel and Jeremiah prophesied concerning this new covenant that it was to be a covenant of the Spirit. Isaiah foresaw that God instituted a new covenant through his Suffering Servant who was to pay with his life for the sins of humankind. Bearing the pain himself, God sent his own Son to shed his blood for the forgiveness of sin. After the death, resurrection, and ascension of God's Son, God sent his Holy Spirit to convert and convince humans from within about God's desire for relationship. Given to people of faith, this Spirit of the new covenant realizes the promise of the old covenants given to Abraham and David.

THE BIBLE AND ITS BOOKS

Beyond the two major divisions of the Bible, each of the testaments contains different sections. The *Hebrew* Bible, the books belonging to the Old Testament, falls into three major categories: the Law (*Torah*), the Prophets (*Nᵉbi'im*), and the Writings (*Kᵉtubim*). Luke referenced this threefold division when he quoted Jesus saying, "Everything must be fulfilled that is written about me in the Law of Moses, the Prophets and the Psalms" (24:44). *Torah* refers to the Law of Moses, the first five books of the Bible, also called the Pentateuch. The Prophets (*Nᵉbi'im*) include both a section of what we traditionally call the historical books and the prophetic literature. The historical books from Joshua to 2 Kings are called the Former Prophets whereas what we traditionally call "prophetic literature," from Isaiah to Malachi, is called the Latter Prophets. The section called "Writings" (*Kᵉtubim*) contains books of poetry, wisdom literature, apocalypse (Daniel), and some of what we may traditionally consider history. The old church fathers called this section *Hagiographa,* sacred writings. Whatever is not placed in the first two divisions is found here.

In spite of these Hebrew categories, most English translations have a different way of organizing the Old Testament. Why is that? Most English editions follow the divisions of the Latin Vulgate (a translation of Scripture into the Latin language produced around AD 400 by the early church father, Jerome) rather than those of the Hebrew Bible. The reason for the Hebrew division is probably found in a different understanding of history, prophecy, and revelation. In Hebraic thinking there is not a sharp distinction between what we now call "historical" and "prophetic." God reveals himself in two principal ways—through mighty deeds and prophetic words. These two modes of revelation are moored inextricably together. Through both God communicates mercy and judgment. One affirms the other. The words of Moses, for example, are affirmed in the event of the Exodus much the same way as the significance of the Assyrian and Babylonian conquests were explained by words of the prophets.

Beyond the sixty-six canonical books, the early church made use of another set of writings relating to the Old Testament. These are called the Apocrypha and were considered helpful for private study and edification. They are apocryphal (i.e., hidden) because they are not approved for public reading. They are included in the Septuagint and in the Catholic translations but not in most Protestant translations.

THE DIVISIONS OF THE BOOKS
IN THE HEBREW BIBLE

LAW / TORAH	PROPHETS	WRITINGS
Genesis	**Former Prophets**	Psalms
Exodus	Joshua	Job
Leviticus	Judges	Proverbs
Numbers	Samuel (1 & 2)	Ruth
Deuteronomy	Kings (1 & 2)	Song of Solomon
		Ecclesiastes
	Latter Prophets	Lamentations
	Isaiah	Esther
	Jeremiah	Daniel
	Ezekiel	Ezra-Nehemiah
		Chronicles (1 & 2)
	Twelve Minor Prophets	
	Hosea, Joel, Amos,	
	Obadiah, Jonah, Micah,	
	Nahum, Habakkuk,	
	Zephaniah, Haggai,	
	Zechariah, Malachi	

THE DIVISIONS OF THE BOOKS IN THE CHRISTIAN OLD TESTAMENT

PENTATEUCH	HISTORICAL BOOKS	POETRY AND WISDOM	PROPHETIC BOOKS
Genesis	Joshua	Job	*Major Prophets*
Exodus	Judges	Psalms	Isaiah
Leviticus	Ruth	Proverbs	Jeremiah
Numbers	Samuel (1 & 2)	Ecclesiastes	Lamentations
Deuteronomy	Kings (1 & 2)	Song of	Ezekiel
	Chronicles	Solomon	Daniel
	(1 & 2)		
	Ezra		*Minor Prophets*
	Nehemiah		
	Esther		Hosea, Joel,
			Amos, Obadiah,
			Jonah, Micah,
			Nahum, Habakkuk,
			Zephaniah, Haggai,
			Zechariah, Malachi

APOCRYPHA

1 Esdras	2 Esdras	Tobit	Judith
Additions to Esther	Wisdom of Solomon	Ecclesiasticus	Baruch
Letter of Jeremiah	Song of the Three	Susanna	Bel and the Dragon
Prayer of Manasseh	1 Maccabees	2 Maccabees	Psalm 151

Although the material of the New Testament differs vastly from that of the Old Testament, there is still a clear pattern to its arrangement. Four types of literature give structure to the arrangement. The Gospels are a kind of historical/theological biography of Jesus in which biographical elements become launching pads for theological truth. Following the Gospels, Acts is a historical description of the spread of the early church and its message. The book of Acts recounts how the presence of God's Spirit (beginning with Acts 2) empowered the early disciples to accomplish the commission given them by Jesus (Acts 1:8). Therefore, beyond the mere recording of history, Luke set out to show the pattern for the work of the Spirit.

A series of letters follow Acts. Paul wrote the first thirteen of these, all of which are named according to their recipients (e.g., the letter to the Galatians). Paul's letters deal with problems and issues specific to the churches or people he wrote. The exception is the letter to the Romans, a church he had never visited when he wrote the letter. Romans, therefore, reads more like a theological treatise than do his other letters. Traditionally, Paul's letters are grouped into four categories: The Early Letters (Galatians, 1 and 2 Thessalonians), the Major Letters (Romans, 1 and 2 Corinthians), the Prison Letters (Philemon, Colossians, Ephesians, Philippians), and the Pastoral Letters (1 and 2 Timothy, Titus). The Early Letters are so called because they were written first. The Major Letters are the longest; the Prison letters were written during Paul's imprisonments, and the Pastoral Letters, written to two of his closest coworkers, address pastoral concerns.

The letters that follow Paul's are called the General Letters or the Catholic Letters. Rather than addressing the issues of specific churches, these letters predominantly give teaching on theological issues facing the early church in general. The General Letters receive their name from the author who wrote them. The exception here is Hebrews. Hebrews reads more like a sermon than a letter, and it purposes to show how the new covenant of Christ is better than the old covenant of the Law. The other General Letters are James, 1 and 2 Peter, 1, 2 and 3 John, and Jude. The final document in the New Testament is the book of Revelation. It is an apocalyptic piece (symbolic literature written during times of persecution), written in a style that closely resembles other apocalyptic material of that time. Revelation gives hope and promise to suffering Christians, showing that God will have the ultimate victory over the forces of evil.

THE DIVISIONS OF THE DOCUMENTS
IN THE NEW TESTAMENT

GOSPELS	THE ACTS OF THE APOSTLES	PAUL'S LETTERS	GENERAL LETTERS	THE BOOK OF REVELATION
Matthew Mark Luke John		*Early Letters* Galatians 1 & 2 Thessalonians *Major Letters* Romans 1 & 2 Corinthians *Prison Letters* Philemon Colossians Ephesians Philippians *Pastoral Letters* 1 & 2 Timothy Titus	Hebrews James 1 & 2 Peter 1, 2 & 3 John Jude	

The Gospels make up 47 percent of the New Testament; Acts, 13 percent; Paul's letters, 23 percent; the General Letters, 10 percent; and Revelation, 7 percent.

THE BIBLE AS CANON AND SCRIPTURE

The Bible is a book filled with accounts of God's dealings with people. It is not open-ended, however. Although God continues to interact with his creation and people continue to give account of these encounters, the function of the Bible as a guide for the relationship between God and people requires that it be protected against false teaching or theology. As Scripture, the Bible gives God's final, authoritative, and revelatory word about himself and his creation. That the Bible is a revelation from God means that it is both willed and informed by God. In other words, God inspired the human authors to write the manuscripts of the Bible in a way that completely and truthfully expresses what God desires to reveal. As completely trustworthy writing, the Bible functions as the enduring revelatory word from God to his people. Its quality as Scripture gives it the right to speak with authority and guiding power to human situations.

The process of protecting God's Word from false theology is canonization. Among a growing number of religious writings that all claimed the quality of inspiration, sixty-six books were selected as "canon," thirty-nine in the Old Testament and twenty-seven in the New Testament. The word *canon* comes from the Greek *kanōn,* which means "rule or standard." The word was used to denote that the books chosen were authoritative as a guide/rule for belief and behavior.

The canonization process itself was not smooth. Scholars have traditionally held that the collection of the Old Testament books now recognized as canonical was determined in Jamnia, AD 90. A rabbinical school, which was located in the town of Jamnia on the Mediterranean coast and which had taken over the legislative powers of the Sanhedrin after the fall of Jerusalem in AD 70, is claimed to have closed the Hebrew canon and given it status as the official Scripture for Israel. However, the continuing debate over the inspiration of books like Ecclesiastes, Song of Songs, and Esther shows that it is highly uncertain the meeting in Jamnia had the authority to make such a unilateral decision. Rather, Jamnia, in the attempt to curtail the ongoing discussion, simply affirmed the texts that were already broadly thought of as inspired. The actual acceptance of some manuscripts as inspired came in stages.

Israel considered some of their writings divinely inspired from early times. Moses, for example, wrote down everything Yahweh said (Exod. 24:7) and read to the people from the Book of the covenant (Exod. 24:7). Hilkiah, the high priest of king Josiah, found the Book of the Law and read it to the king and the people.

The reason for the *written* word, as opposed to the *spoken* word, may find part of its origin in the need to send God's message to other places (Jer. 29:1; 36:1–8; 2 Chron. 21:12). This is probably not the only reason, however. As the finding of the Law during the reign of Josiah shows, the uncertainty of the oral tradition was well-known to Israel. When Hilkiah read the Book of the Law, its teaching came as a great shock to the people, for it had been forgotten (2 Kings 22–23). The Canon, therefore, rises out of the realization that the more permanent form for God's message is the written form.

Most likely the Book of the Law, the Pentateuch, was the earliest collection of documents that was completed as a whole. The Pentateuch presents itself as the work of Moses who was one of the earliest and the greatest prophets of the Old Testament. The time for its final form is not certain, but it is possible that Moses finished it in his own lifetime and placed it in the ark of the covenant (Deut. 31:24–26). If so, it would be a practice that followed the traditional pattern of Near Eastern treaties. The section on Moses' death was then obviously added later.

The timing for the close of the prophetic books cannot be established with certainty either. But as early as 130 BC, Ben Sira's grandson refers to "the Law and the prophets," indicating that "The Prophets" were considered a unified piece with authority at the level of the Torah. Earlier references (165 BC) include 2 Maccabees 2:14, which records Judas Maccabeus's collection of the books during the time of the war. Whether Judas Maccabeus organized the Prophets and the Writings as we have them now is not certain but possible. At any rate, the Maccabees' awareness that the prophetic voice had ended (1 Macc. 9:27) gave them great impetus to zealously collect and arrange holy writ.

Although the road to canonization went through rugged terrain, the identification of these texts as sacred and inspired came quite early. As early as 250 BC, long before the references given above, these same Hebrew texts were translated into Greek and came to be called the Septuagint. Although biblical books were placed in a different sequence and even included texts the Hebrew Bible did not include, the Septuagint became Scripture for all Greek-speaking believers including Paul and the early church.

In the early church the necessity of canonization flowed directly from the need to protect the church from false teachers. As early as Paul's missionary journeys, forgeries were circulated that falsely claimed the authority of the apostles. Paul references this when at the end of his Galatian letter he writes: "See what large letters I use as I write to you with my own hand!" (Gal. 6:11). He signed with his own hand in order for the churches to distinguish his letters from other fraudulent letters.

As the church spread rapidly, itinerant teachers and preachers of various backgrounds and insight became the messengers of the Christian gospel. Churches were established in areas and by people with no background or relationship to the Judaic culture. Diversity flourished and, as the letters of the New Testament clearly show, guidance became mandatory. The diversity of the New Testament writings reflects the diverse situation of the early church.

Each of the New Testament documents first appeared as a separate document directed to a certain audience. Paul's letters are the oldest documents in the New Testament, and they all have a specific geographical destination. The Gospels likewise were written with the intention of making the story of Christ accessible and convincingly understandable to various audiences. The same holds true of the other New Testament letters, which, unlike Paul's, are named according to their author rather than their recipients.

Selecting and collecting the New Testament writings into what we now know as the canon was a slow process. The earliest references we have to the struggle of sorting the genuine documents from the fraudulent indicate that the early fathers gave different lists of authoritative writings. Paul's letters were recognized as inspired very early as, among other things, the reference in 2 Peter 3:15–16 shows. The earliest reference to all four of the canonical Gospels included in the New Testament comes from a letter written by Clement, a famous bishop in Rome, writing early in the second century. Although the final demarcation of the New Testament writings from other edifying material did not come until the fourth century, the second-century church leaders had already ranked Paul's letters, the four Gospels, and Acts as canonical. The general letters, especially Jude, 2 Peter, 2 and 3 John, and Revelation, were the latest to find general acceptance. The Syrian church still does not accept these five.

Three criteria were given for the selection of the twenty-seven books of the New Testament. First, it had to be written by an apostle or an eyewitness. Mark and Luke did not fulfill this criterion, but their close relationship with Peter and Paul respectively was considered sufficient. Second, it had to have been generally accepted either by a leading church or by the majority of the churches. By this criterion many of the apocrypha, and maybe even some genuine writings, were rejected. Third, it had to have spiritual integrity and practical value. That is, it had to be in accord with sound doctrine and bear the marks of divine inspiration. The doctrine concerning Jesus became center stage for this third criterion as many fraudulent writings presented a different Jesus from the Jesus presented in the four Gospels of Matthew, Mark, Luke, and John.

READING THE BIBLE

Everyone who reads a text does so with a set of presuppositions. There is no such thing as a completely open mind. This also holds true when a person reads the Bible. If they choose to reject its content even before they begin, they miss its point and will not experience its transforming power. To be open-minded means to give the biblical text a chance to address people on its own terms.

Broadly speaking, approaches to Bible reading have typically followed the lines of the following belief options.

BELIEF OPTIONS

Agnosticism
"I don't know if there is a God."

Belief
"I claim to know something."

Atheism
"I don't believe there is a God."

Theism
"I believe in some kind of God or gods."

Polytheism
"I believe in many gods."

Monotheism
"I believe in one God."

Pantheism
"I believe God is everything and everything is God."

Supernaturalism
"I believe in a God that is separate from creation, a transcendent God."

Deism
"I believe God is real but remote; he has not made himself known to us."

Revealed Theism
"I believe God is present and he has revealed himself to us."

Unitarianism
"I believe God is one person."

Trinitarianism
"I believe in one God who exists in three persons."

Historically, the left column reflects non-Christian options and the right column Christian belief options. Belief options leading to Christian faith often follow the progression:

belief $\rightarrow$ theism $\rightarrow$ monotheism $\rightarrow$ supernaturalism $\rightarrow$ revealed theism $\rightarrow$ trinitarianism.

The Bible itself takes the belief options of the right column to be self-evident and does not discuss these issues at length. To understand the Bible, one must read it with these presuppositions.

EPISODE ONE

CREATION

ACT 1

THE STORY BEGINS

E very story has a beginning, and God's is no exception. The beginning found
in Genesis 1–2 starts the biblical answer to the questions of where are we
and who are we. In other words, how did everything that exists get here?
Many ancient cultures tried to provide answers to that question. For instance, the
Babylonians wrote an account of beginnings called *Enuma Elish*. The Babylonian
story focused on polytheism with creation being the result of a sexual union between deities and gods behaving badly.[1] In contrast, the biblical story centers
around one true God who wills to create. Every event from that time on finds its
source in God. What do we find in the biblical story of beginnings?

GOD CREATES *EX NIHILO*

The biblical story tells us how all these things around us (light, dark, earth, sky,
water, land, fish, dogs, cats, us) came to be, but it doesn't say the same about the
main character—God. The Bible just assumes God exists. "In the beginning God"
(Gen. 1:1). He simply existed as the only being already in existence. That leads us
to an awesome conclusion. If God alone existed when he created, then he created
everything from nothing.[2] Theologians call this creation "ex nihilo." God simply
called or spoke everything into existence. So where are we? We are in a world created entirely by God. That is the biblical explanation for the beginning of life and
the world. God's story centers on God who by his nature and power speaks all that
is into being.

---

[1] Clyde T. Franscisco, *Introducing the Old Testament*, rev. ed. (Nashville: Broadman Press, 1977), 64.
[2] For more discussion on *ex nihilo*, see J. Philip, "Creation: The Biblical Doctrine" in *New Bible Dictionary*, 3rd
ed., ed. by I. H. Marshall, A. R. Millard, J. I. Packer, D. J. Wiseman (Downers Grove, Ill.: InterVarsity Press,
1996), 239.

What does that mean to us? First, all things including people owe their being and continued life to God. It means that the creating God is powerful beyond all imagination. He required nothing but himself to create. He created from his own resources and will. It completely belongs to God. He cares about and participates in the created world. God spoke into existence all things, relates to the creation, sustains it, and rules over all.

THE CREATION

According to the Bible, the process of God's creation followed a planned pattern. In what Genesis calls six days,[3] God unfolded the plan. The story says that on the first day God created light where before there was only darkness, and he separated the light from the darkness. "God saw that the light was good" (Gen. 1:4). God continued on the second day by speaking into existence the firmament or sky. The sky separated the earth from all other entities in the universe. Again God declared this creation good. On the third day God made the bodies of water, dry ground, and vegetation. "And God saw that it was good." On the fourth day God made the sun, moon, seasons, and days. "And God saw that it was good." God created fish for the bodies of water and birds to fill the sky each according to their own kind on the fifth day. "And God saw that it was good." And then on the sixth day he made animals each according to their own kind and finally the crown of creation—humans. "Then God said, 'Let us make man in our image, in our likeness, and let them rule. . . .' So God created man in his own image, in the image of God he created him; male and female he created them" (Gen. 1:26–27). The man and woman (humanity) were blessed and given the task of filling the earth and ruling over the other creatures. God gave them the garden as their place for living and the plants within it to sustain them. "And God saw everything that he had made and it was very good." God rested on the seventh day after his self-proclaimed good work. This description appears in the first section of God's creation story found in Genesis 1:1–2:3.

THE CROWN OF THE CREATION

God provides a more detailed explanation of human origins in Genesis 2:3–2:25. God fashioned the first man called Adam from the dust and "breathed into his nostrils the breath of life, and the man became a living being" (Gen. 2:7). Man was placed in a garden in the east with trees for food that were pleasing to the eyes. In the middle of the garden stood two unique trees, the tree of life and the tree of the knowledge of good and evil. God instructed Adam that he could eat of any tree except the tree of the knowledge of good and evil. To eat it was to die. Although Adam communicated with God and tended God's garden, he was the only human. Nothing among the created order corresponded with man as was the case with the

---

[3] The Hebrew word used here for day is *yom* and can mean a literal day or a period of time. More will be said about this later.

animals. God said, "It is not good for man to be alone. I will make a helper suitable for him" (Gen. 2:18). *Suitable* means "corresponding to or opposite him." It indicates the woman would be complementary, equal, and "even able to respond to him and even challenge him."[4] How did God create this woman? God caused Adam to fall into a deep sleep; and from one of his ribs, he made the first woman, Eve. As equal partners in humanity, they were commanded to be fruitful and multiply. With this action God established the first social unit of the creation, the family. Together Adam and Eve served God and communicated with him daily in the garden.

This story of God's creation of Adam and Eve means that all people on earth are connected to these two original humans. God related to them and created them, male and female, for relationship. Humans form families and are family in a larger sense. With the creation of Eve came the first marriage relationship and from that the first family. This formed the basic structure for society. "And the man said: This one, at last, is bone of my bone, and flesh of my flesh; this one will be called woman for she was taken from man. This is why a man leaves his father and mother and bonds with his wife, and they become one flesh" (Gen. 2:23–24 HCSB).

Woman became man's helpmeet or partner. She shared in the responsibility of filling the earth and overseeing the creation. God's wisdom recognized that two are better than one for they can help and relate to each other (Eccles. 4:7–9). The two multiplied and eventually filled the earth. They grew from family to nation to nations of people.

THE IMAGE OF GOD

Who are these humans? What made them so unique from the other animals created? Some argue that people are just more advanced animals, but the story says more. "Let us make man in our image, in our likeness" (Gen. 1:26). God created humans in the image of God, in his likeness. What could that mean? Certainly it doesn't refer merely to physical qualities or could it? John Calvin argued that "in man's body 'some sparks' of God's image glow."[5] But later the biblical story clearly states that God is Spirit. Some biblical scholars make a distinction between "image" and "likeness." *Likeness* indicates that man is not identical to God but reflects God. Interpretations vary on the image of God. What can we know about the biblical use of *image* and *likeness* in describing humans in the created order? First, mankind serves as viceroy over creation as God's choice for dominion. Second, people possess a filial relationship to God as part of his family and therefore have family likeness. Third, humans have a dignity and value connected to their unique relationship to God.[6]

---

[4] H. M. Wolf, "Eve" in *Evangelical Dictionary of Theology*, ed. by Walter A. Elwell (Grand Rapids: Baker Book House, 1984), 384.

[5] S. B. Ferguson, "Image of God" in *New Dictionary of Theology*, ed. by Sinclair Ferguson, David F. Wright, J. I. Packer (Downers Grove: InterVarsity Press, 1988), 328.

[6] Ibid., 328–29. See this source for more discussion on the image of God.

But what else does the image of God mean? On the more practical level some argue image relates to abilities that humans have. We reason more effectively than the other animals, or we are more intelligent. Without a doubt these observations prove true but may refer more to degree than to a unique possession. *Image* may refer to the ability to know right from wrong (conscience), while animals operate by mere instinct. But maybe a practical answer can be found in the fact that of all the creatures made by God, people alone walked with God in the garden and talked with him. They related personally to God. Perhaps the best practical option for the image of God is the ability to relate to God in a personal way. God breathed into man's nostrils, and he became a living soul. God endowed humans with spirit to relate to God who is also Spirit. We can know God, communicate with him, praise him, and serve him. Maybe the extra reason and intelligence we possess enhances that ability. Herein we also find some of the purpose of God's creation—to relate to the Creator. To miss that may be to miss what we were created for.

> The God who made the world and everything in it—He is Lord of heaven and earth and does not live in shrines made by hands. Neither is He served by human hands, as though He needed anything, since He Himself gives everyone life and breath and all things. From one man He has made every nation of men to live all over the earth and has determined their appointed times and the boundaries of where they live, so that they might seek God, and perhaps . . . find Him, though He is not far from each one of us. For in Him we live and move and exist, as even some of your own poets have said, "For we are also His offspring" (Acts 17:24–28 HCSB).

What else is included in this image concept? If we are created in the image of a God of freewill, then we also have the right to choose. Can there be true relationship outside of free choice? As God is a free agent who chooses to create and relate to his creation, humans as free agents choose freely. We are not puppets who only do what the Creator causes us to do. The next episode in the story makes that truth clear. Humans can choose God and relate to him or choose not to. We are created in his image and are free. This is humanity.

DOMINION

The special quality of humans becomes apparent one more time in the story. "And let them rule over the fish of the sea and the birds of the air, over the livestock, over all the earth, and over all the creatures that move along the ground" (Gen. 1:28). As the crown of God's creation, we receive dominion over all other parts of the creation. Now how do we understand the idea of rule or dominion? If we study the human track record for the past few millennia, it appears to mean we can do whatever we want with whatever we find in creation. As a result people have abused God's creation in unbelievable ways—depleted natural resources, abused other creatures and even other people. Our idea of dominion sometimes resembles unbridled freedom.

What does *dominion* mean? Perhaps if we ask some questions, we can find the meaning of this idea. Who is the Creator? Who does the creation belong to? The answer to these questions according to the biblical story is God. Dominion cannot mean the right to do whatever we please with what we find here on earth. Instead ruling over the creation demands that we seek what is best for God's creation and that we desire always to please God in the way we use it. It suggests we constantly keep in mind that all belongs to the Creator and we are merely the stewards. Maybe the best way to understand dominion is with that word *stewardship*. A steward manages things that belong to the master for the master's good and according to his desire. Dominion is more responsibility than privilege. Perhaps we need to revisit the beginning of the story often to be reminded of our role as stewards and servants of the Creator. So who are humans? Humans are creatures created in the image and likeness of the Creator God who exercise stewardship over all his creation.

THE SEQUENCE OF THE CREATION

Is there any significance to the sequence of the creation? What does it teach us? Of course, opinions vary. Some see a creative order designed to support each created thing in succession. Fish don't appear before water; and vegetation precedes animals, birds, and humans. Others argue a concept called "continuous creation" where God still creates. "God is regarded as both the originator of all being and the only cause of all natural effects in each successive moment. Thus sustenance or preservation is really continued creation."[7] In other words, God created and still creates what is necessary to preserve or sustain the creation. G. J. Wenham even suggests a parallel idea in the sequence when he notes that the first three days of the creation correspond respectively to the next three—day 1 to day 4, light to luminaries; day 2 to day 5, sky to birds; and day 3 to day 6, seas and land to animals and humans.[8] This may simply be a way to tell the story. Although we may never really know the significance of the sequence, clearly God worked according to a self-designated plan.

A newer approach to understanding creation is a movement called *intelligent design*. It doesn't overtly focus on God as Creator but argues that the created order and all living things exhibit qualities indicating they were created or resulted from an intelligent cause. This view insists matter and creatures didn't just come together naturally but some intelligent cause put them together. The creation itself, and perhaps its order of appearance, reflects intelligent design. This is the old argument that a design must have a designer. Of course, Christians proposing intelligent design conclude that the designer is the God of creation found in the biblical story.[9]

---

[7] M. H. Macdonald, "Creation, Continuous," in *Evangelical Dictionary of Theology*, 281.

[8] G. J. Wenham, "Creation: The Genesis Account" in *New Bible Dictionary*, 240.

[9] William A. Dembski, "The Intelligent Design Movement," Center for Science and Culture (March 1, 1998), Online: http://www.discovery.org. For more information on this theory and movement see the Web site or William A. Dembski, ed., *Mere Creation* (Downers Grove, Ill.: InterVarsity Press, 1998).

How Long Did Creation Take?

We know the biblical story says God created everything in six days and rested on the seventh, but many have questioned what is meant by a day. In fact, this is a major issue for many. Where is the confusion? The Hebrew word *yom*, most often translated "day," causes part of the confusion. It can mean daylight, a twenty-four-hour period, a time of unspecified duration, or even a generation. As a result many interpret the story differently. Some say it means six twenty-four-hour days in the same way we experience days. Others argue that a day may be thousands of years and so the process lasted longer than traditionally thought. Others even believe a day refers to how Moses, the human author receiving the creation story from God, obtained the information. For instance, this Revelational Day Theory would say that Moses received the information about human and animal creation on the sixth day that God spoke to him and wrote it down accordingly.[10] As you can see, these theories leave room for discussion. God could have taken as little or as much time as he wanted. Even though opinions vary, the more important issue is the theological truth that God created. The biblical story's intention was to tell all people that God created everything that is.

What Was the Method of Creation?

The time issue raises other questions in the story. Some who hold that the process took more than a literal seven days wonder if it happened in a way other than what the biblical record indicates. How did God create, or did he? The biblical story simply says that God spoke light, sky, and animals into existence. But opinions vary as to what that means. Of course, many Christians simply take the biblical story literally believing that the creation came to be when God willed it and said it.

Others think the time issues (science believes the world to be millions of years old) and the apparent complexity of creation demand other options. Some take God out of the picture completely, essentially nullifying the biblical account. This movement got its start when Charles Darwin's *Origin of Species* first appeared in 1859. It introduced an idea that species as entities may not be as unchangeable as most people thought. Darwin proposed the idea of "descent with modification," which was eventually taken by many to mean that animals came to be through an evolutionary process. Neo-Darwinian views hold that new species arise through this process. A simpler life form evolves and changes into a more complex life form. As such, God plays no part. All this occurs naturally when the right environment and elements come together to allow it. The idea centers around a chance occurrence of all the right elements for life to begin and evolve.

What about this theory of evolution? Most people agree that small changes occur allowing life forms to adapt to the environment (size, color, disease resis-

---

[10] For a broader discussion see Gleason Archer, *A Survey of Old Testament Introduction*, rev. ed. (Chicago: Moody Press, 1974), 184–87.

tance). This has been called micro-evolution.[11] However, more significant change from specie to specie or macro-evolution raises problems for those accepting the biblical story. Evolution as the primary explanation for how the world came to be is not without some key obstacles. First, how did the first life form begin? To argue for an almost accidental beginning when the right combination of materials and environment merged seems harder to accept than creation by God. In fact, this has not been reproduced in a lab today even with the right elements. Second, is there any evidence of a specie to specie development or from lower to higher forms? No clear evidence of that phenomenon exists. Scientists still seek the missing link that would show that development. Thus considering these two objections, a pure evolutionary explanation struggles for credibility.

But how can one explain the belief held by many (even Christians) that the world is perhaps millions of years old. Some Christians allow for evolution as God's method of creating. This theory, called Theistic Evolution, proposes God as the power that allows the first life to form (right elements and environment) and the movement from simpler to more complex life to occur (God orchestrated the jump from specie to specie). This means God created all but used evolution as his method. The main obstacle to this view is that the biblical story simply says God spoke and it became.

What should we focus on in the biblical story of creation? Duration? Method? What did God want to teach us in his story? The method of creation as well as the duration do not appear to be the main concern of the biblical story. What is the main concern? It is that God created everything that exists including people. He created all from nothing, sustains all, has a plan for it, and is the main character of the story. It is a theological story not a scientific story. *"In the beginning God."* The biblical explanation of the existence for everything that exists rests in God and his awesome power to speak matter into being.

MEANING IN THE STORY

The creation story begins God's story of relating to his creation and sets the stage for the rest of the biblical story. God shows himself as Creator and Sovereign of and over all that is. We see him as the creating God who desires to have relationship with the creation. He walks and talks with Adam and Eve, and they know him personally. The beginning gives us clues as to how the story should continue—God the Creator in relationship with the crown of his creation, man and woman.

The story also defines humans as those who are created in a special sense in the image of God. They possess the ability to choose, and they have a spirit that allows them to have close communion with God who is Spirit. God is separate from them but not separated from them. He is the always existing God, and they are finite creatures. He is a powerful God who made whatever exists out of nothing, and

---

[11] O. R. Barclay, "Creation: Evolution" in *New Dictionary of Theology*, 178. See this source for further discussion of evolution and creation.

humans are his stewards who are given dominion and responsibility over creation. They serve him as he is their God. The garden which God made for his creation is as it should be—God and his creation in harmony and relationship. Does the story continue so well? The next act reveals the answer to that question.

STUDY QUESTIONS

1. What does God create and how?
2. What does the "image of God" mean?
3. What are the practical implications of the idea of dominion in today's world?
4. What is the connection between man and woman, and what are their tasks?

ACT 2

HUMANS REJECT GOD'S PLAN

A ll things are in place, and God has declared his creation good. God walked in the garden daily and talked to Adam and Eve directly. And then the first crisis of history shook the creation and influenced events from that time on. According to Genesis 3, Adam and Eve encountered a serpent who tempted them to disobey God. In fact, when the serpent finished his work with Adam and Eve and they made their decision to disobey the Creator, everything and every subsequent event suffered under the weight of that fateful decision. So what did Adam, Eve, and the serpent do? The story continues.

TEMPTATION AND SIN

This part of the biblical story begins with one of God's creatures, a serpent, whom the text describes as shrewd. Even though the serpent sits as subordinate to Adam and Eve, he raises questions in the mind of the humans concerning the trustworthiness of the Creator. Later the story connects Satan, described as a deceiver and enemy of God, to the serpent. He indwelled the creature or simply used it to tempt Eve. Satan selected the serpent because of its craftiness. Later the harsh punishment meted out to the serpent for his role in this deceit and temptation will be directed toward Satan (Rom. 16:20; Rev. 12:9; 20:2).

In the biblical story the serpent tempted Eve. He set out to convince Eve to eat fruit from the tree of the knowledge of good and evil, which God had commanded them not to eat. The serpent used several methods to accomplish his purpose in temptation. He deceived Eve by making her believe that God really did not mean what he said about that tree. He lied to her by telling her that she surely would not die if she did eat the fruit. The serpent assured her that God wouldn't really do that. He misrepresented God by first recalling to Eve what God said but embellishing it: "You must not eat from *any* tree in the garden" (Gen. 3:1). Satan sowed a seed of doubt in the woman's heart by telling her the reason God told her not to eat of that particular tree: that fruit would result in Eve's becoming like God. She would know good from evil. The serpent made God sound like a selfish being who wanted all the power and knowledge to himself. To keep his uniqueness, God lied to Eve and deceived her according to the serpent. In order to tempt Eve, the serpent resorted to all kinds of deception, lies, and misdirection to accomplish his purpose. He caused Eve to question everything God commanded.

How could the serpent so successfully tempt a human? The serpent's greatest tool in temptation was Eve's own desire. The serpent's suggestion to be like God, to know good from evil, to be more than she was (even though she was the crown of God's creation) appealed to her. She wanted that. The serpent played on that desire. Here we see some of the nature of temptation. In the New Testament James offers a description of temptation. "But each one is tempted when, by his own evil desire, he is dragged away and enticed. Then, after desire has conceived, it gives birth to sin; and sin when it is full-grown, gives birth to death" (James 1:14–15). The temptation of Eve began with her desire to be more than she was, to be like God. The serpent took full advantage of that desire and tempted her to do what she was clearly told not to do. Because of human desire, temptation is a part of life. Although temptation itself is not sin, it can lead to sin. Eve did not sin in the mere temptation, but when she gave in to the desire and allowed the temptation to lead her to do something God had forbidden, sin was born. The biblical story makes clear that in Eve's case the temptation became sin.

When did sin conceive for Adam and Eve? "When the woman saw that the fruit of the tree was good for food and pleasing to the eye, and also desirable for gaining wisdom, she took some and ate it. She also gave some to her husband, who was with her, and he ate it" (Gen. 3:6). At this point we see the shift from ordinary, common temptation to sin. Sin is the open rebellion against God. It occurred when Eve said by action that what she wants is more important than what God wants. She crossed the line. Sin occurred. And she gave it to Adam, and he ate as well. They stood equally guilty since both did what God commanded against. Both chose their will over God's. That raises an important issue concerning humans. As seen earlier in the story, we were created with free will. From the beginning we possessed the ability to choose freely concerning any number of things we face in life. The most important free choice is whether to follow and obey God. Will we relate to him? Will we listen to him? Adam and Eve and every human since faced the same choice. They listened to their own desire and not God's. They rebelled and sinned. Everything changed in one instant. The fact that Adam and Eve rebelled against the Creator indicates they were not perfect and with the sin lost their innocence.

THE CONSEQUENCES OF SIN

With sin and rebellion came far-reaching consequences. Eve and Adam exercised free choice to disobey God, but they could not choose the consequences.

Neither could any other human since. With every choice come consequences. The biblical story explains that clearly. First, guilt accompanies sin and rebellion. Immediately Adam and Eve realized something changed with them and certainly between humans and God. Their eyes were opened. They felt shame. They realized their own nakedness and hid from God when he walked in the garden to talk with them. God forced an encounter. He called to them, and from their hiding place they responded. And guess what? They reacted to God's questions in a way that may sound familiar to us. Eve blamed the serpent, and Adam blamed Eve. All humans since have learned to blame others. Refusal to accept responsibility for wrong seems to be intricately related to sin. It is never our fault. But refusal to accept responsibility does not stop consequence.

God passed specific judgment on each of the participants in the fall. The serpent received the punishment of crawling on its belly for the rest of its existence. This implies that the original serpent stood on the ground either with two or four legs and did not crawl. This serpent lost that ability, and God destined it to eat dust the rest of his existence. The next verse in the story offers us a clue to the connection between Satan and the serpent. Genesis 3:15 explains, "And I will put enmity between you and the woman, and between your offspring and hers; he will crush your head and you will strike his heel."

Do not focus merely on the fact that the serpent will crawl and eat dust. A deeper theological issue seems to be in play here. Satan who indwelled or used the serpent to tempt Eve and Adam is being judged. It is Satan who will be crushed. Most evangelical scholars believe this verse to be the first messianic prophecy in Scripture. God's plan revolves around relationship with created humans. Adam and Eve rejected the relationship with God, and God started the plan of reconciliation with his people. Satan remains at odds with God and his people and does all he can to thwart the plan, including killing the most important offspring of woman, Jesus. But according to Genesis 3:15, God's plan of redemption cannot be thwarted. The cross experience of Jesus fulfills the prediction. Satan (the serpent) struck at the heel of Jesus (cross) but without permanently taking him out of the picture. Jesus will crush Satan and destroy him. The resurrection proved that Satan could not defeat Jesus.

In the fall account God gave us a glimpse of the end of the story. He provided a sign of hope in the midst of this tragic story of the fall of Adam and Eve and all other humans who sin and rebel against God. Sin carries consequence, but eventually God will offer the way to be reconciled. God's plan is already underway even in the beginning of the story. He will raise up a special human who will also be God (Jesus) and that man (Second Adam) will crush Satan. God controls the future of his creation even when people, Adam and Eve, chose to go their own way.

Eve received her verdict. From that time on Eve and all women experienced pain in childbirth. This punishment remains in effect, and in some cases the pain is excruciating. Remember the God-given task of multiplying and filling the earth with people. Well that task became painful due to the sin of Eve. She bore children and every time undoubtedly thought about her rebellion and the consequence.

Adam stood as guilty before God as did Eve. His sin resulted in a curse on the land which he must toil over. From that time the ground produced thorns and thistles, and Adam struggled to harness it to grow food for life. This outcome of sin gives us insight into the far-reaching effect of sin not only on the creatures initially involved (Eve, Adam, Serpent) but also on the earth itself. Adam and Eve lived out their days in a land cursed because of the sin they introduced into the creation. That land continues under the curse of sin. Even the earth itself groans. Later the apostle Paul explained this. In Romans 8:19–22 he said that the creation itself waits in eager expectation for God to take care of the sin problem finally and forever. The creation was subjected to frustration brought on by sin as a result of Adam and Eve's rebellion. Creation hopes for the liberation from sin's effect of bondage and decay. In the meantime it remains twisted and marred by sin. So Adam faced an uphill battle just trying to live on the earth due to sin's horrible influence.

This consequence offers a glimpse into the philosophical idea of evil and suffering. Often people ask why innocent people suffer in this world. How can this be? A theodicy is an argument which tries to reconcile the fact of a good, loving God with the reality of evil, pain, and suffering. Part of such an argument might focus on the effect of sin connected with Adam's consequence. Unfortunately all of creation was affected by the sin Adam and Eve introduced. That includes all people. Bad things happen to good people, and we ask why. Although not a complete answer, this part of the story gives us some clues. Every person from Adam on lives in a world twisted by sin and therefore a world which no longer cooperates with humans. Sometimes it rains when we don't need it while at other times there is drought when we need rain. Hurricanes, tsunamis, tornadoes, forest fires, mud slides, disease, and innumerable other things plague the world in which we live; and many suffer and die who really don't deserve it. Sin in the world causes pain for everyone. This remains true until the weight of sin is removed. But for now we live in a world deformed by sin. In other words, Adam no longer enjoyed the perfect setting of the garden, and neither do we. Sin changed everything.

The consequences included both Adam and Eve being expelled from the garden. Sin changed life as they knew it. To be expelled from the garden meant to be separated from God. They had daily communion with him before but no longer. Sin breached the relationship. We saw the first indication of that when guilt and shame caused Adam and Eve to hide from God, and now they are truly separated from him. Perhaps this represents the worst outcome of sin—to be estranged from the Creator puts the creature in the most difficult circumstance imaginable, to be alienated from the life source, the beginning, the core of existence. This was not what God desired for his creation; and yet because of Adam and Eve's exercise of free choice, people are in a condition of estrangement from the Creator.

As James 1:14–15 explains, sin always leads to its ultimate end—death. The last consequence was death. Adam and Eve would have lived forever with God, but sin resulted in death. They began to die physically and spiritually. They died because of separation from God. If the image of God in humans includes the ability to relate to him, then to be unrelated means to be dead spiritually. Death entered the world and wreaks havoc in every aspect. We die and we are dead. This part of the story addresses two of the key questions of life. Who are we? What is wrong with me and the world? We are people affected by sin and its consequence and living in a twisted creation. We stand in need of redemption from God. The rest of the story focuses on that problem and its solution.

What about the image of God after sin? The biblical story does not clearly state what happened to the image of God when sin entered humans. As with most interpretations, opinions vary. Three categories with variations seem possible. One option claims that sin destroyed the image of God, making it impossible for us even to choose good and requiring a miracle of God to again be related to him. This work of God comes through his grace and the word of his Spirit in the hearts of humans. Another option suggests that sin only marred the image of God so that it is hindered from full understanding and ability to choose right. God still must work in the heart to help such a person find reconciliation. The last option claims sin did not affect the image of God at all. It remains intact and possesses the ability to choose correctly and even to choose to relate to God.

SIN'S FUTURE INFLUENCE

What happened to Adam and Eve not only affected them but also surged through all of creation from the beginning until now. They died, and sin estranged them from God. Every person since lives in the same condition. When we think of people, we think of creatures with the ability to relate to God but who are separated and dead in sin. The consequences of that sin remain in all people at all times. All sinners share in the effects of sin. We need help. Here the biblical account has good news.

The rest of the story deals with the God of love and mercy orchestrating a plan for reconciling people to him. He desires that the chasm between Creator and the created caused by sin be spanned and relationship restored. That is why we must understand this part of the story. The rest of the biblical account is based on it. The loving, creating God created all; and then the crown of that creation rebelled against him. However, God's love for the creation endured. He seeks throughout the rest of the story to restore creation to himself. God's story is one of love, grace, and mercy. Based on Genesis 3, sin deserves punishment, but God cares for us and eventually provided the way to deal with that sin.

SIN LEADS TO GOD'S JUDGMENT—
FLOOD AND THE TOWER OF BABEL

Sin continued to worsen. Genesis 4–11 chronicles the seriousness of this sin problem as it manifested itself in the generations following Adam and Eve. Eve bore her first children, Cain and Abel; and because of Cain's unwillingness to honor God properly through his offerings while his brother Abel acted more honorably, disaster struck. Cain grew angry and his jealousy of his brother resulted in murder. Cain killed his own brother and then tried to cover up the sin. The effects of sin become more widespread as the story progresses. The evil nature of mankind continued to flourish, and finally God decided that he must start over using a flood to judge all those rebelling against his will. He selected Noah, instructing him to build an ark and collect pairs of all the animals on earth. Noah built the ark and obeyed God's instructions. Then God sent torrential rains for forty days to kill all those who had sinned. Noah's family survived and became a new beginning. God even established a covenant or agreement with Noah promising never to destroy the earth by water again. He placed a rainbow in the sky as a symbol of that promise.

With a new start one would think the sin issue would subside, but the next event shows that to be a false assumption. Genesis 11 records the story of the Tower of Babel. The people of Babel decided to build a tower all the way up to the heavens. It appears their motivation for this action corresponds to Eve's when she sinned— to be like God. They wanted to reach God himself. They sought to control their own destiny and become great. This pride and arrogance is nothing but a symptom of the sin that still characterizes all people in all places. God thwarted the plans by causing an unusual communication struggle. Before beginning the tower, all the people in Babel spoke the same language enabling them to plan, scheme, and build together. But God "confused" the languages. Instead of one language they spoke many, and communication slowed to a standstill. Imagine what it was like in the building process when one man asked another for a hammer and neither understood. This caused confusion, frustration, and evidently a desire to seek out those who could understand. People scattered over the earth in groupings according to language. The biblical story here offers an explanation of the different language groups in the world today.

Obviously sin, as evidenced by pride and arrogance, continued to cause problems. But remember, the rest of the biblical story deals with the sin issue and how God solves it. It is a story of reconciliation and redemption. By the way, this confusing of tongues and scattering will eventually be addressed by God in the New Testament part of the story. At Pentecost we see that even though the gathered crowd spoke different languages they all understood and received the one Spirit which connects instead of scatters. God does not give up or forsake but continues throughout the story to orchestrate the restoration of his creation.

SETTING THE STAGE

God created all that is, and it was good. He allowed humans, the highest form of created beings, the freedom of choice. Humans sought to be like God and rebelled against God. With that decision sin entered the creation and infected all people and all creation. God then set out to do something about this rift between him and his creation. The story from Genesis 12 on concerns God's activity in bringing all back into relationship with him. Now watch to see how God unfolds the plan and shows people the way to him.

THINGS TO CONSIDER

Look around at the world. You see a wonderful creation that the biblical story says God made. People are wonderfully made, and each one has the ability to relate to God. They were made for that relationship. However, we all realize something is wrong in us and in the world—selfishness, bigotry, hatred, violence, and pride. What is wrong? God's story explains it. He created people who chose to rebel. With that rebellion or sin came multiple issues and consequences. The world is twisted by sin, and people suffer because of it daily. The doctrines of creation, sin, and the problem of evil and suffering surface early in the story. God determined to remedy the problem. That is the rest of the story. This beginning of the biblical story sets the stage for what is to come.

STUDY QUESTIONS

1. What is the difference between temptation and sin?
2. What are the consequences of sin?
3. Is the world getting better or worse?
4. How do we see God's judgment and mercy when humans rebel?

OUTLINE HELP

The book started with an overview of the biblical story designed to help you see the big picture so the details would not overwhelm. Perhaps a good way to keep up with the progression of God's story would be a highlighted outline reminding you of where we are in the storytelling.

THE STORY OF THE BIBLE

Creation   **The story begins with God creating the world and human beings.**

Crisis   **Humans choose to rebel (or sin) against God. Sin brings consequences: pain, suffering, death, and separation from God. All people and all creation are affected.**

Covenant	God chooses Abraham and establishes a covenant with him so that he might become the leader of a group of people who will follow God and call other people to follow God. God delights in using his people to bring the rest of the world to himself.
Calling Out	Genesis tells the story of the patriarchs: Abraham, Isaac, Jacob (Israel), and Joseph, who ends up in Egypt. In Egypt the small group of Hebrews grows into a nation and ends up in slavery. God uses Moses to deliver his people through the exodus event.
Conquest	God uses Joshua to help his people take the promised land (Canaan). After the conquest during the Period of Judges, God rules through judges in various parts of the land. This is a dark time for the Hebrews accentuated with sin, idolatry, and oppression.
Kingdom	God's people acquire a king. Samuel is the link between the judges and the kings. Saul is the first king, followed by David and his son Solomon. God establishes a covenant with David, promising the Messiah will come through his family line and reign forever.
Kingdom Divided	After Solomon civil war breaks out leading to a division of the kingdom: Israel, the Northern Kingdom; Judah, the Southern Kingdom. There are numerous kings, some good but most bad.
Captivity	Israel (Northern Kingdom) is judged for the sin of breaking the covenant when Assyria conquers it in 722 BC, and Judah receives a similar judgment later when Babylon conquers it in 586 BC and takes Judah's people into exile.
Coming Home	The people return from Babylonian exile under Zerubbabel, Ezra, and Nehemiah. They rebuild the temple and focus on the law of God.
Christ	About four hundred years later, God sends his Son, Jesus the Christ, to save his people from their sins, fulfilling the promise given to Abraham. Jesus is crucified, dies, is raised from the dead, and ascends into heaven to return again later.

Church	Those who accept Jesus become part of the church, the people of God made up of both Jews and Gentiles. God continues to use his people to extend his offer of salvation to a sinful world.
Consummation	God closes history with a final victory over evil. Those who have rejected God will suffer his judgment while those who have received him will live with him in a new heaven and a new earth.[12]

---

[12] Adapted from an outline developed by J. Scott Duvall. Used by permission.

EPISODE TWO

THE PLAN OF REDEMPTION

ACT 1

The Covenant and Promise

What plan will God use to redeem people back to him? He began with Adam who through his rebellion became the door for sin and death to enter the creation. We know God did not give up on people altogether because he selected one man, Noah, to restart the population of the earth. In Genesis 12 we discover that God chose another man to begin the process of bringing humans back to relationship with the Creator. Obviously God decided to allow the people struggling with sin to participate in the plan of redemption. There is something refreshing and gracious in God's method. God involved humans in his work. Let's return to the biblical story of redemption.

The Call of Abraham and the Covenant

God began his plan by establishing a covenant with one man and through him creating a whole nation of people. That man was Abram. Abram lived in the city of Ur of the Chaldees, which today is in modern-day Iraq. We date Abram sometime around 2000 BC. This area around the Tigris and Euphrates we now call the "fertile crescent," an area favorable for early agricultural settlements. It stretched along the Tigris and Euphrates rivers. This land probably served as the setting for the beginning of civilization. Abram, who was undoubtedly a wealthy and well-known man, lived at the lower end of the region. Abram resided in the midst of a pagan society that paid little attention to Yahweh (or the God of the biblical story). The inhabitants of Ur worshipped deities such as Sin, the moon god. These religions involved pagan worship practices and sacrifices. The temples or ziggurats were large, flat-topped pyramids with stairs to the top. The rulers heavily involved themselves in the religious practices and were even considered deities. Out of this setting God elected and covenanted with a man named Abram. Why did God elect this man? Either in the midst of pagan worshippers Abram worshipped Yahweh or became a worshipper of God as a result of the call. As the Sovereign, God elects based on his will and choice.

How did God establish the covenant with Abram? God spoke to Abram and told him to take his family and servants and move to a place that God would reveal to him. Imagine the faith it required for Abram to pack up and leave his extended family and friends, land, and culture. Few people would move under such circumstances. In the encounter God established a covenant with Abram that in a sense directs the rest of the biblical story. In the ancient world there were numerous types of covenants. In the case of Abram, it was a unilateral or one-sided agreement between God and his servant. God made several promises to Abram, and Abram's role was to obey. Abram had to trust God. Even when Abram disobeyed God (i.e., passing off his wife Sarah as his sister in order to save his own neck), he still received God's blessing and protection. God took center stage in this covenant, and it was based on God's grace to deal with the sin issue introduced earlier in the story.

The ultimate result will be restoration of the relationship between humans and God. God works with people on the basis of covenant. Later God established a covenant with Moses but a two-sided or bilateral one requiring a great deal of human obligation in the form of obedience to the law. We will compare the two at that point in the biblical story. The covenant with Abram represents God's plan of restoring a wandering people back to himself.

THE ABRAHAMIC COVENANT

What were the elements of Yahweh's covenant with Abram? Genesis 12:1–9 provides the details. God spoke to Abram and called him to leave his country, people, and father's household and go to the land that God would show him. Then God made several significant promises.

God promised to make Abram into a great nation. God planned to use people to fulfill his goal of reconciliation. This people, known as the Hebrews or Israel, eventually rose from Abram. This promise included the birth of a son who would be the necessary beginning point of creating a nation. God also promised to bless Abram and his people. God provided for Abram and his family in every way. God pledged to make Abram's name great. Later in the story God changed Abram's name to Abraham meaning "father of a multitude"[1] and Sarai's (Abraham's wife) to Sarah meaning "mother of nations." The names reflected the covenant relationship.

How great is Abraham's name? People around the world refer to it thousands of years later. Three of the great religions of the world look back to Abraham— Judaism, Islam, and Christianity. God covenanted to bless those who bless Abraham and curse those who curse him. This represented a commitment to protect and care

---

[1] D. J. Wiseman, "Abraham" in *The Illustrated Bible Dictionary*.

for Abraham and his people. Abraham often experienced God's protection from enemies and circumstances. In addition, God vowed to bless all peoples on the earth through Abraham. This promise set the direction of the biblical story of redemption. The blessing passed through Abraham and the people of Abraham—the Hebrews. As we will see in the story, God produced from Abraham's seed one who blessed all people. With this blessing came responsibility for the Hebrews. As God's people they were to show others by lifestyle and proclamation how to be in relationship with God. Although they did not always take the responsibility seriously, God accomplished his blessing for the world through them in spite of their failures. Finally, God promised Abraham and his descendants a new land. Abraham must leave his home and land and go to a new place. God led him to Palestine, which to this day stands central in the covenant history—a new land for a new people.

This covenant ceremony indicated the seriousness of such an agreement. Although lacking excessive information concerning covenantal rites in Abraham's time, there are writings which speak of it. An animal was slaughtered and cut into two or three pieces. Part of it would be burned in honor of God and the rest eaten in a covenantal meal.[2] Genesis 15 records the ceremony Abraham performed to consecrate the covenant with Yahweh. According to God's instructions Abraham collected a heifer, a goat, a ram, a dove, and a young pigeon. He cut all in half and placed them opposite each other with the exception of the birds. God caused a smoking fire pot to appear and pass between the pieces and promised Abraham the land from the "river of Egypt to the great river, the Euphrates" (v. 18). Some of the ancient treaties required the vassal to return annually to renew the covenant with the king. The same custom was likely attached to this covenant. Abraham renewed it later, at which time he received a name change. Covenants were serious. To distinguish the agreement even more, God instructed Abraham to be circumcised. This covenant set the stage for the story of redemption and grace.

THE JOURNEY OF ABRAHAM

Abraham left Ur of the Chaldees (the lower portion of modern-day Iraq) and traveled northwest to Haran, located in the top portion of the fertile crescent. God led Abraham along the fertile land bordering the rivers instead of directly across the desolate desert toward Palestine. He took with him his extended family including his father. In Haran he buried his father, left part of the extended family, and moved southwest (through modern-day Syria) to the land God promised him (Canaan or Palestine). Included in Abraham's caravan were his wife Sarah, his nephew Lot, servants, and livestock. They arrived in the land located between the Jordan River and the Mediterranean where God appeared to Abraham and promised him the land of Canaan. "To your offspring I will give this land" (Gen. 12:7). Abraham and his family settled in the new land. During their time in Palestine a famine occurred.

---

[2] F. C. Fensham, "Covenant, Alliance" in *The Illustrated Bible Dictionary*.

Abraham moved his family to Egypt, which benefited from its fertile land along the Nile. Here they waited out the famine and then returned to the land God gave them. Abraham settled in Canaan, built altars to the Lord, and worshipped in a new land as God promised.

ABRAHAM'S LIFE

As Abraham followed God, his character became clear. He faithfully obeyed God and fulfilled the covenant. However, Abraham was human, and his humanity surfaced from time to time. Abraham was not perfect. The biblical story includes both sides of Abraham's life.

ABRAHAM'S FAITHFULNESS

Whether Abraham was a faithful follower of Yahweh before his election, he certainly took following God seriously after his call. As Abraham moved obediently at God's bidding and experienced divine protection and blessing, he always took the time to build altars and worship God. For instance, when God showed Abraham the land, Abraham built an altar by the great tree of Moreh at Shechem. From there he went to a place west of Bethel and built an altar there. After Abraham split the land with his nephew Lot, he moved to the great trees of Mamre at Hebron and built another altar to worship God. Abraham worshipped, followed, and trusted Yahweh. He remembered the covenant.

Abraham also exhibited a strong sense of fairness. Lot, his nephew, had traveled with him; and the two were evidently very close. When they reached the promised land, Lot's people and Abraham's people struggled to get along, so Abraham suggested a solution. He offered Lot a choice. "Let's not have any quarreling between you and me, or between your herdsmen and mine, for we are brothers. Is not the whole land before you? Let's part company. If you go to the left, I'll go to the right; if you go to the right, I'll go to the left" (Gen. 13:8–9).

This story gives us a clue into Abraham's character. Remember that the land was promised to Abraham if he obeyed. But Abraham offered Lot his choice of land. Lot looked at the plain of the Jordan, which appeared good to him, and chose it. Abraham took the land of Canaan. We see no arrogance on Abraham's part, no selfishness. He was a generous man who wanted what was best for his nephew. Without doubt Abraham knew that God would care for him in any case.

Lot's choice soon got him into trouble. Lot chose to live in the vicinity of Sodom and Gomorrah. War broke out between the kings of these cities and four kings from the north. They defeated Sodom and Gomorrah and took Lot as a captive. When Abraham received this news, he gathered 318 of his men and went to rescue Lot. Abraham routed the enemy and brought Lot back. He obviously went up against a larger force but still won the day. Abraham loved his family and risked much to save Lot.

The biblical account reveals the bravery and the trust Abraham placed in God. God promised to bless those who blessed Abraham and curse those who cursed him. God kept his promise. By the way, when Abraham returned from battle, Melchizedek, the priest, blessed him. "Blessed be Abram by God Most High, Creator of heaven and earth. And blessed be God Most High, who delivered your enemies into your hand" (Gen. 14:19–20). Abraham then gave a tithe to the priest. Once again he worshipped and honored God. Abraham faithfully followed God and proved to be a good choice for God's plan of creating a nation.

ABRAHAM'S HUMANITY

How did Abraham falter? Abraham's humanity surfaced on a few occasions in his life. Perhaps understanding this helps readers of the biblical story to identify with him and realize that God used an ordinary human being to accomplish his plan.

Even though God proved over and over his power, still in times of human weakness, Abraham sought to arrange his own security. Two times Abraham faced rulers who had ultimate power in their realms. Abraham feared these rulers would see the beauty of Sarah, take her, and kill him. He took precautions. The first encounter came in Egypt (Gen. 12:10–20). Fearing Pharaoh, Abraham instructed Sarah to say she was his sister. When Sarah followed this plan, she was taken into Pharaoh's house. However, Pharaoh's household suffered; and when he discovered the truth, he chided Abraham for lying to him. Later Abraham did the same thing when he came into contact with King Abimelech (Gen. 20:1–3). God threatened King Abimelech in a dream for taking a woman who was married. Abimelech had not touched her, and God told him to return her or die. In both cases it seems that Abraham forgot the power and protection of God. Although God promised protection in the covenant, Abraham took it upon himself to ensure his safety. What does this say about Abraham? Simply that he was human. God's plan of redemption used real, normal human beings who did the best they could for God.

This struggle to trust God reached into other areas of Abraham's life as well. Perhaps the greatest promise made by God in the covenant was to make a great nation out of Abraham. "A son coming from your own body will be your heir" (Gen. 15:4). This promise came to Abraham and Sarah who were already old and childless. The chances of having a baby were slim to none and grew worse as they aged. Abraham and Sarah decided to take matters into their own hands. Sarah owned a maidservant named Hagar who could bear children. She convinced Abraham to have relations with Hagar to gain an heir. Abraham agreed; and a baby boy, Ishmael, resulted from joining with Hagar. This moment of distrust by Abraham and Sarah resulted in two negatives—jealousy on the part of Sarah and a command from God to send the mother and child away. Abraham and Sarah had decided to shortcut the promise of God. They failed to wait for God. God commanded Abraham to send Hagar and Ishmael away, but God's mercy cared for them. Hagar procured a wife for Ishmael from Egypt, her homeland. Ishmael became the father of a nation. Abraham and Sarah then waited for God to fulfill the promise of a child to carry on the covenant.

Even though Abraham struggled to trust God in every situation, God continued to work through him to fulfill his ultimate will. God gave the child to Sarah, and the promise of a great nation started. Despite the moments of distrust, Abraham was honored later as a great man of faith (Heb. 11:8–19).

THE BIRTH OF ISAAC

God prepared Abraham for the promise to come. At ninety-nine Abraham was instructed to renew the covenant with all its promises. However, Abraham questioned the promise of a son. He laughed and asked how it could be possible for a man of one hundred with a wife of ninety to have a child. God assured him that a son would be born and his name would be Isaac, which means "laughter." God has a sense of humor as well. The mark of this covenant became circumcision (Gen. 17). At the renewal of the covenant, God changed Abram's name to Abraham and Sarai to Sarah. Then God confirmed the promise once again with Sarah in attendance. Three visitors came to them, and Abraham offered hospitality. During the meal one of the visitors told Abraham that by the same time the next year Sarah would have a son. Sarah overheard and laughed to herself, believing in her heart this was not possible (Gen. 18).

A promise is only as good as its fulfillment. God made his promise good, and Sarah gave birth to a son. Sarah declared that God brought her laughter, and his name was Isaac. This is a significant part of the story. God's plan of redemption began with one person who would grow into a nation and then bless the world. Isaac represented the first step in that plan. He became the joy of Abraham and Sarah, and eventually Abraham's seed became the joy of the world. God's plan of reconciliation was set in place; and as the story unfolds, God moves through his people to bring about a solution to the sin issue.

ABRAHAM'S TEST

In the biblical story Abraham had shown himself untrustworthy in a few difficult situations. God would test him one last time. Abraham needed to trust God completely even with Isaac, the promised child. When Isaac reached an age that would allow him to travel with Abraham, God issued a command. Take Isaac, go to the region of Moriah, and sacrifice him as a burnt offering (Gen. 22). The story records that Abraham got up early the next morning to fulfill this command.

Abraham must have had quite a night! It was a normal night for Sarah because like any savvy husband Abraham said nothing to her about this plan. Imagine Sarah's response had she known. The account does not indicate what Abraham told Sarah, but he took Isaac and some servants along with wood for the fire. Isaac questioned his father concerning the sacrificial lamb, but Abraham assured him that God would provide. Leaving the servants behind, they journeyed to the place designated by God and made preparations. Abraham bound Isaac and placed him on the altar and raised the knife to kill him. Only at the last second did God stop him.

God accepted that Abraham would obey and sacrifice Isaac. Abraham passed the exam. His faith in God was stronger than his love for his one and only son. Think about that! Abraham waited one hundred years to have a son and willingly offered him up to God. How is that possible? Why would Abraham do such a thing? Hebrews 11:19 gives us insight: "Abraham reasoned that God could raise the dead, and figuratively speaking, he did receive Isaac back from death." He believed God could bring Isaac back even from death. Abraham believed God could do anything. After all God did provide a one-hundred-year-old man and a ninety-year-old woman with a baby. This faith of Abraham set the stage for the means of redemption. It will come by faith.

One last question. What went through the mind of Isaac in this experience? He questioned the lack of a sacrificial animal, indicating things seemed strange. Then he watched his father raise a knife with full intention of killing him. If nothing else, certainly Isaac learned a lesson concerning the seriousness of faith in God and the covenant relationship. God is God. Abraham and Isaac had the obligation to obey. Abraham provided his son with a role model for that truth. Certainly this prepared Isaac to be a faithful follower as well.

SOME THEOLOGICAL THOUGHTS

God's covenant with Abraham is vitally important to understanding the rest of the story. It is the beginning of God's plan to provide a way to bring all people back into relationship with him. One man, Adam,[3] brought sin into the world, which separated humans from the Creator. Through Abraham's seed came one who healed the rift caused by sin and blessed all nations. This covenant passed on through Abraham's son, Isaac, and the nation to follow.

STUDY QUESTIONS

1. Explain the covenant God established with Abraham.
2. What part do Abraham, Sarah, Isaac, Hagar, and Ishmael play in the unfolding of God's plan?
3. How did Abraham fulfill his role in the covenant? What can we learn from his victories and failures?
4. How is God's awesome love evident in the story of Abraham and Sarah?

---

[3] In the New Testament Adam will be called the "first Adam" who brought sin and death into the world. Jesus will be called the "second Adam" who brings life.

ACT 2

ISAAC, JACOB, AND JOSEPH

The world of Abraham and Isaac was male centered, a patriarchal society. Men carried on the family name and received birthrights. They led the family and the tribe. As God covenanted with Abraham, he continued through the heir, Isaac. Ancient custom gave special rights to the firstborn son. Ishmael held that position in Abraham's family, but he was not the promised child. God blessed Ishmael, but Isaac carried on the covenant relationship with God. When Abraham died, his sons, Isaac and Ishmael, buried him in the cave of Machpelah next to Sarah. "God blessed his son Isaac, who then lived near Beer Lahai Roi" (Gen. 25:11).

ISAAC AND REBEKAH

Before Abraham's death, Isaac needed a wife. Abraham rejected the idea of a wife from the Canaanites, the original inhabitants of Palestine and pagan worshippers. Therefore, he commanded his servant to travel to Haran, where many of Abraham's extended family still lived, to find a wife for Isaac among relatives. Although this sounds strange, keep in mind the unusual circumstance. God is in the process of creating a people—unique, devoted, covenant people. The servant returned with Rebekah. The biblical story says that Isaac accepted her from the start. "Isaac brought her into the tent of his mother Sarah, and he married Rebekah. So she became his wife, and he loved her" (Gen. 24:67). Isaac's family continued the covenant relationship with God.

Isaac prayed for Rebekah because she was barren, and of course the biblical story clearly indicates the importance of a male heir. The value of a woman rested on giving birth to heirs. Barrenness ranked as one of the worst curses for a woman.

This issue surfaces often in the story, and more than once God miraculously intervenes. God answered Isaac's prayer, and Rebekah became pregnant with twin boys. Rebekah experienced some discomfort as the twins struggled and jostled in her womb. When she inquired of God why this was happening, she received a direct answer. "Two nations are in your womb, and two peoples from within you will be separated; one people will be stronger than the other, and the older will serve the younger" (Gen. 25:23). The word from God revealed to Rebekah that trouble and unusual situations lay ahead for her and her boys. Normally the older would rule, but God promised a variation in this case which no doubt caused strife.

THE BIRTH OF THE TWINS

When the twins were born, the oldest was named Esau and the youngest, Jacob. The birth itself revealed the future strife as Jacob held on to Esau's heel when they were born. The birth times were only seconds apart. The boys differed from the beginning. Esau's name means "red," and he had red hair all over his body. He became the father of the Edomites who dwelled in the red sandstone area of Petra. Their differences grew as they matured. Esau was a man's man with all the instincts we usually connect to boys. He hunted and loved the outdoors. Jacob loved staying close to home and remained quiet. Isaac favored Esau while Rebekah leaned toward Jacob. Rebekah no doubt remembered the word from God before the twins were born. Their character differed as well. Esau lived for the moment and cared little for things normally considered valuable. Jacob sought status and focused on such.

An incident in the biblical story reveals these differences. When Jacob was cooking some stew, Esau returned from a hunting trip famished. He wanted the lentil stew and demanded some of it. Jacob agreed on one condition—that Esau sell him the birthright. The birthright was important in patriarchal society. It included a double portion of the possessions and the right of leadership. It represented authority and power. Esau's character became clear. He agreed, and for a bowl of pea soup he sold his birthright. Jacob's true self came out in this encounter as well. Either he played on the weakness of Esau, or Rebekah informed him of his future, and he seized it. Jacob's action appears deceptive. This event lays the foundation for problems between the boys and their descendants.

THE BLESSING

Isaac reached the end of his life and prepared to pass on the blessing to Esau as the oldest son. Esau either forgot he sold it or just refused to keep the bargain. Isaac sent him out to kill wild game and prepare a meal for his aging father. Meanwhile Rebekah heard of the plan and conspired with Jacob to trick old, blind Isaac. They prepared a meal to taste like wild game, put hair on Jacob's arms, and fooled Isaac. Before Esau returned, the blessing had been given to Jacob, leaving Esau furious. Jacob fled north back to Rebekah's home and brother, Laban. How should this event be interpreted? Was Rebekah simply fulfilling God's promise that Jacob would rule? Did it require deceit and lies? One might argue that Rebekah did not trust God and tried to take things into her own hands. As Abraham lied about Sarah being his sister, Rebekah lied to ensure Jacob's birthright. Perhaps Rebekah simply did what God wanted before Isaac distorted the plan. In any case, God would have accomplished his will. Jacob had the blessing and would receive God's blessing.

RENEWAL OF THE COVENANT WITH JACOB

In route to Haran, God encountered Jacob in a dream. He saw a stairway to heaven with angels ascending and descending. At the top stood God, and he spoke to Jacob. *"I am the LORD, the God of your father Abraham and the God of Isaac. I will give you and your descendants the land on which you are lying. Your descendants will be like the dust of the earth, and you will spread out to the west and to the east, to the north and to the south. All peoples on earth will be blessed through your offspring"* (Gen. 28:13–14).

The biblical story focuses on covenant, and this event plays a key role in it. God established the covenant with Abraham promising him blessing, land, and a nation. This continued through Isaac and now is renewed with Jacob. God repeated the promises to Jacob—land, descendants as many as the dust, and all the earth blessed by his descendants. God made clear that he was intimately involved in Jacob's life and had a great plan for him. Jacob recognized the significance of this encounter and upon awaking declared the place to be awesome and "the house of God; this is the gate of heaven" (Gen. 28:17). He called it Bethel, which means "house of God." Jacob also vowed to God that he would follow and give a tenth of all he gained to God.

THE TIME IN HARAN

Jacob arrived in Haran to stay with and work for his mother's brother, Laban. Early on he encountered one of Laban's beautiful daughters, Rachel, and struck a bargain to marry her. He would work seven years for Laban for the right to marry Rachel. When the agreement was completed and the wedding day arrived, Laban tricked Jacob. He gave his daughter Leah in marriage to Jacob instead of the beautiful Rachel. Laban argued that the oldest must marry first. A new bargain was struck. Jacob gained Rachel for seven more years of labor. Laban recognized that Jacob was good for his business and wanted to keep him around. The story indicates that Jacob received Rachel as his bride at the end of the wedding week (a week after marrying Leah) and worked the seven years payment for her. Jacob had two wives and the beginning of a family whom God would use to build his nation.

God promised to bless Jacob, and wealth was part of it. Jacob worked for Laban, but Laban received most of the benefit. In an effort to convince Jacob to stay on and work, Laban allowed Jacob to name his wage. So it was Jacob's turn to trick his uncle. Jacob already knew the character of Laban and devised a rather deceptive plan himself. Jacob asked that all the speckled, spotted, and dark-colored lambs and goats be his wage. He would take all from the flock currently fitting that description and any born. It was agreed. As keeper of the flocks, Jacob led them to the watering hole. He took fresh-cut poplar, almond, and plane tree branches and peeled the bark off in stripes. He placed those branches in the watering troughs, and the sheep and goats drank. After mating at the watering holes containing the branches, the sheep and goats produced streaked, speckled, and spotted offspring. Jacob became a rich man. God miraculously intervened in the life of his servant to fulfill promises of blessing. Jacob, God's covenant choice, then returned to the promised land to fulfill his role.

THE RETURN HOME

The relationship between Laban and Jacob took a bad turn. Laban did not accept Jacob's fortune very well. God informed Jacob that it was time to return to Palestine. God also promised to be with Jacob at all times. Here again God pledged blessing and guidance. Jacob gathered all his wives, children, servants, and flocks and fled from Laban; but he faced a major obstacle—Esau. He had run for his life years ago, and Jacob feared Esau held a grudge. Jacob prepared a long line of gifts to greet Esau as a plan of appeasement. Flocks and herds with servants were sent ahead. Esau heard of Jacob's impending arrival and went out to greet him. In route Esau encountered the waves of appeasement gifts. But there was no worry. God blessed Esau as well with wealth and a large family. He had forgiven and even offered his protection to his brother. This biblical event represents a classic case of how much broken relationships hurt and what those suffering under them are willing to do for reconciliation. Jacob offered much of his wealth just to be in relationship again with his brother. God had prepared Esau ahead of time for the reconciliation.

Just prior to the reunion of brothers, God encountered Jacob again. At the Jabbok River, while Jacob was alone, a man came and wrestled with him all night long. The battle waged on, and eventually the man injured Jacob's hip, but still Jacob would not let go without a blessing. The man gave Jacob a new name, *Israel,* and he blessed him. Jacob had wrestled with God all night and survived. Jacob meant "he clutched," or "overtaker," referring to the way he was born clutching the heel of his brother Esau. But the new name signified the covenant God made with him. The name *Israel* means "God strives," for he struggled with God and survived. This name became the covenant name for God's people throughout the story and the reminder of God's covenant with Jacob, Isaac, and Abraham. Once again God offered a new name to the one with whom he established a covenant—Abram to

Abraham, now Jacob to Israel. These were changed men who became God's covenant bearers. Jacob realized he had wrestled with God and called the place Penuel (the face of God) because he had seen the face of God and survived. Jacob would be the father of the nation of Israel as fulfillment of the covenant. The biblical story is straightforward with God's plan: God will use this people Israel as the means to bring all people back to him.

THE FAMILY AND THE COVENANT BEARER

The family of Jacob grew. With his four wives Jacob had twelve sons and several daughters. Jacob played favorites. Rachel, his favorite wife, bore his two favorite sons, Joseph and Benjamin. She died giving birth to Benjamin. Even though Joseph was not the oldest, Jacob favored him above all others and gave him a richly ornamented coat, proving to the older brothers Joseph's favored position in the family. In a series of dreams, God revealed to Joseph his special role concerning the covenant people. In the first dream Joseph saw himself and his brothers in the field binding sheaves of grain. Joseph's sheaf rose up above the others, and they bowed and worshipped it. The second dream had the sun, moon, and eleven stars; and all bowed down to Joseph. These dreams occurred when Joseph was only seventeen. He was not mature enough to handle such information. He shared these dreams with his older brothers. "And they hated him all the more because of his dream and what he had said" (Gen. 37:8).

After this the brothers determined to get rid of Joseph. When Joseph went out to check on the brothers in the field, they conspired to kill him. Instead they sold him as a slave and told Jacob he had been killed by wild animals. They covered his beautiful coat with blood as evidence. Jacob was devastated, and Joseph was off to Egypt. Although a horrible event for Joseph and Jacob, God used it to prepare Joseph for his role. In Egypt he was sold to a powerful man, Potiphar, in Pharaoh's court. God blessed Joseph, and he rose to serve as head over household affairs. Potiphar prospered with Joseph's skill. Things went well until Potiphar's wife sought an intimate encounter with Joseph. He refused. In this we see the character of Joseph. He refused the advances made on him and declared that he could not. "How then could I do such a wicked thing and sin against God?" (Gen. 39:9). Joseph remained faithful to God and true to Potiphar. For his rejection Potiphar's wife accused him of attempted rape, and Joseph was thrown into jail.

Although the situation turned sour for Joseph, God's plan continued. The jail sentence put Joseph into a situation where he encountered some men with connections that aided him. In prison Joseph met a cupbearer and a baker, both of whom had been in Pharaoh's employ. While in prison each had a dream and needed an interpretation. Joseph possessed the ability to do so. Joseph interpreted the cupbearer's dream, saying that in three days he would be reinstated with Pharaoh. The baker's dream indicated a more negative future. In three days he would lose his head. Both came true. Joseph had been given a gift from God that would later impress Pharaoh. God worked in and through Joseph to accomplish his goals.

Pharaoh dreamed as well, and two dreams caused him concern. The first consisted of seven fat, healthy cows followed by seven gaunt, ugly cows. The skinny cows ate the healthy ones. The second dream sounded similar with seven healthy heads of grain followed by seven thin, scorched heads that devoured the first seven. Pharaoh anguished over the dreams and demanded they be interpreted. However, his wise men possessed no gift for such. Providentially the cupbearer remembered Joseph's ability and told Pharaoh.

Joseph explained to Pharaoh that only God could interpret dreams. Joseph's gift was from God. God used Joseph to interpret the dreams. The seven fat cows and heads of grain represented seven years of plenty in Egypt. Crops and life would flourish. The seven gaunt cows and scorched grain stood for seven years of famine to follow. Joseph through his God-given gift gave Pharaoh the interpretation and then advised him on a plan for dealing with the famine to come. Joseph told Pharaoh to look for a discerning man to supervise the good years in order to store up for the lean ones. Pharaoh took Joseph's advice and installed him as the man in charge of supervising the food storage and distribution.

Now think about it. God promised to carry on the covenant with Jacob. It was not Rueben, the oldest son, who would carry on the promises. Although the situation turned bad for Joseph, God chose to use him to bless his brothers and future generations. God used all the circumstances of Joseph's life to put him into the position where he could best serve. God prepared the way, cared for his servant in the worst of situations, and blessed him in ways Joseph could not imagine when he was a slave. God's sovereignty and power guided and directed his plan of redemption even when it seemed dismal to Joseph.

THE FAMILY BECAME A NATION

When the famine came to Egypt, it also affected Canaan. Jacob and his family suffered but heard that Egypt had prepared and stored grain. Jacob's sons minus Benjamin went to buy grain and, for the first time since selling him into slavery, encountered Joseph. Although they did not recognize him, Joseph recognized them. He sold them grain but orchestrated a plan (planted silver in their bags so they would be accused of thievery) to get his younger brother Benjamin to Egypt. Jacob feared he would lose Benjamin but finally agreed.

During the second visit to Egypt with Benjamin in tow, Joseph revealed his identity and assured the brothers of his forgiveness. They realized God's blessing on Joseph. He invited all the family to come and reside in Egypt until the famine eased. The brothers finally convinced Jacob, and the entire family moved to Egypt and settled in the land of Goshen, in the upper delta area of the Nile. Jacob died in Egypt, but his family thrived.

From one family God built a nation. The names of the tribes somewhat corresponded to Jacob's sons—Rueben, Judah, Simeon, Dan, Issachar, Zebulun, Naphtali, Asher, Gad, and Benjamin made up ten tribes. Levi and Joseph are missing from the list. God appointed Levi for a religious task to be explained later in the story. Joseph as the one carrying on God's promise got a double portion with his sons Manasseh and Ephraim becoming tribe leaders. By the time the Hebrews left Egypt four hundred years later, the families had grown to as many as three million. God's covenant with Abraham included the making of a nation. God created a nation to bless the world. The plan came together in Egypt, and out of these Hebrews came the promise of redemption. Remember the covenant; they will bless all the nations of the earth.

STUDY QUESTIONS

1. How did Isaac, Jacob, and Joseph reveal strengths and weaknesses as they followed God?
2. How are God's mercy, power, and compassion evident in the stories of Isaac, Jacob, and Joseph?
3. How does God pass down the covenant?
4. How did God create a nation of people out of one man, Abraham?

OUTLINE HELP

Let's look at the overarching outline to see where we are in the story.

THE STORY OF THE BIBLE

Creation	The story begins with God creating the world and human beings.
Crisis	Humans choose to rebel (or sin) against God. Sin brings consequences: pain, suffering, death, and separation from God. All people and all creation are affected.
Covenant	**God chooses Abraham and establishes a covenant with him so that he might become the leader of a group of people who will follow God and call other people to follow God. God delights in using his people to bring the rest of the world to himself.**
Calling Out	**Genesis tells the story of the patriarchs: Abraham, Isaac, Jacob (Israel), and Joseph, who ends up in Egypt. In Egypt the small group of Hebrews grows into a nation and ends up in slavery. God uses Moses to deliver his people through the exodus event.**

Conquest	God uses Joshua to help his people take the promised land (Canaan). After the conquest during the Period of Judges, God rules through judges in various parts of the land. This is a dark time for the Hebrews accentuated with sin, idolatry, and oppression.
Kingdom	God's people acquire a king. Samuel is the link between the judges and the kings. Saul is the first king, followed by David and his son Solomon. God establishes a covenant with David, promising the Messiah will come through his family line and reign forever.
Kingdom Divided	After Solomon civil war breaks out leading to a division of the kingdom: Israel, the Northern Kingdom; Judah, the Southern Kingdom. There are numerous kings, some good but most bad.
Captivity	Israel (Northern Kingdom) is judged for the sin of breaking the covenant when Assyria conquers it in 722 BC, and Judah receives a similar judgment later when Babylon conquers it in 586 BC and takes Judah's people into exile.
Coming Home	The people return from Babylonian exile under Zerubbabel, Ezra, and Nehemiah. They rebuild the temple and focus on the law of God.
Christ	About four hundred years later God sends his Son, Jesus the Christ, to save his people from their sins, fulfilling the promise given to Abraham. Jesus is crucified, dies, is raised from the dead, and ascends into heaven to return again later.
Church	Those who accept Jesus become part of the church, the people of God made up of both Jews and Gentiles. God continues to use his people to extend his offer of salvation to a sinful world.
Consummation	God closes history with a final victory over evil. Those who have rejected God will suffer his judgment while those who have received him will live with him in a new heaven and a new earth.

EPISODE THREE

THE FORMING OF A NATION: GOD'S PEOPLE AND THE LAW

ACT 1

MOSES AND THE DELIVERANCE

E xodus, the second book in the record of the biblical story, begins with Israel in Egypt. The Hebrews lived on prime land in Egypt due to Joseph's influence. They resided in the favorable land of Goshen in the delta region of the Nile. It was well suited for flocks and herds. In the years following the move to Egypt, the family grew to be a large nation of people—some estimate as many as three million. God's covenant promise to Abraham and Jacob to make a great nation from their seed became reality. No doubt the Hebrews also grew wealthy and took a position of prominence in Egypt. However, their growth eventually threatened the Egyptians. Exodus continues the biblical story citing this crisis and the resulting difficulty for the Hebrews.

A PHARAOH WHO KNEW NOT JOSEPH

Unusual circumstances allowed for the rise of a Semitic Hebrew, Joseph, to a prominent position in Egypt. It may have even caused a stir among native Egyptians. How could this happen? An odd statement is found in Exodus 1:8: "Then a new king, who did not know about Joseph, came to power in Egypt." Joseph had passed from the scene centuries earlier, but history still recorded his significant contributions. So how can there be a pharaoh who did not know him? This statement could simply refer to the fact that the Hebrews had become a threat and the pharaoh desired to subdue them. However, some understanding of Egyptian political history at this time helps us interpret the statement. Evidence confirms that at one time in Egyptian history a group of invaders from the north took over the country for a period of time. These people are sometimes referred to as Hyksos kings; they ruled around 1750 to 1570 BC.[1] Two theories concerning Joseph's rise to power connect to this group. One theory claims they were Semitic peoples similar to Joseph in background. They would have seen no problem in honoring a fellow Semite with a position of power. Eventually the Hyksos kings were expelled by an Egyptian pharaoh who then turned against the Hebrews. A second theory argues the opposite. An Egyptian pharaoh installed Joseph in the prestigious position; and then when the Hyksos kings arrived, they enslaved the Hebrews. Of course by this time Joseph has long been dead. However it happened, the Hebrew people suffered under this new pharaoh's wrath.

This discussion also impacts the dating of the exodus event. When did Joseph and his brothers enter Egypt? This is important because Exodus 12:40–41 claims that the Hebrews spent exactly 430 years in Egypt. "Now the length of time the Israelite people lived in Egypt was 430 years. At the end of the 430 years, to the very day, all the LORD's divisions left Egypt." Abraham had received a prediction that his descendants would "be strangers in a country not their own, and they will be enslaved and mistreated four hundred years" (Gen. 15:13). Consider these biblical statements with the dating of the Hyksos rule. The date of the Hyksos rule is fairly well established as between 1750 and 1570 BC, give or take a few years.[2] So, if a Semitic, Hyksos king raised Joseph to a position of authority, then Joseph entered Egypt somewhere around the late 1700s BC. If we take seriously the four hundred years, then the exodus dates around 1300 to 1250. Some have even suggested that the four hundred years is not to be taken literally, and therefore the exodus may have occurred earlier. Others argue that Joseph entered Egypt earlier than the Hyksos reign (in the previous dynasty 1991–1786 BC) and an Egyptian pharaoh endowed him with authority. When the Hyksos arrived, they did not know Joseph or his people and enslaved them. If we take the four hundred-year stay literally, then we offer an earlier date of around 1450 BC for the exodus. No final certainty can be established for an exodus date. Dating depends on when Joseph entered Egypt and how one interprets the 400–430 year statement concerning the duration of the Hebrew inhabitation of Egypt. The most likely option is that Semitic Hyksos kings put Joseph into his prominent position and four hundred years later (1290–1250) the exodus occurred under Moses.[3]

The dynasty change affected the Hebrews dramatically. Due to the large numbers of Hebrews, Pharaoh feared them. He decided to enslave them for his build-

---

[1] James I. Packer, Merrill C. Tenney, and William White, *The Bible Almanac* (Nashville: Thomas Nelson Publishers, 1980), 99–100.

[2] Thomas Brisco, *Holman Bible Atlas* (Nashville: Broadman & Holman Publishers, 1998), 51–52.

[3] K. A. Kitchen and T. C. Mitchell argue that the Hebrews worked on the cities of Pithom and Ramses during Moses' time. These were built by Sethos or Ramses II who ruled from 1304 BC. This means the exodus had to occur after 1300 BC. The archeological evidence at Jericho which served as the first target of the invading Hebrew army just forty years after leaving Egypt is scant although some believe there is no evidence of the existence of Jericho earlier than the thirteenth century BC. If that is true, the post-1300 BC date for the exodus sounds correct. See K. A. Kitchen and T. C. Mitchell, "Chronology of the Old Testament" in *The Illustrated Bible Dictionary*, ed. by J. D. Douglas (Wheaton: Tyndale House Publishers, 1980), 270, 275. The date of the arrival and enslavement of Israel in Egypt and the exodus from Egypt remains a point of debate.

ing purposes and keep them under control. They built Egyptian cities and were op-pressed. However, the numbers continued to increase, and Pharaoh decided to curb that growth with a hideous plan to kill all new baby boys by throwing them into the Nile. In a patriarchal society Pharaoh struck at the heart of the Hebrew fam-ily while at the same time ensuring a smaller number of Hebrew males to fight if rebellion occurred. One of the Hebrew women gave birth to a son described as "a fine child" and hid him for three months. She devised a dangerous plan when hid-ing him became too risky. She built a papyrus basket and covered it with pitch to allow it to float and placed the baby boy in it. She launched the boy and makeshift boat into the Nile; and his older sister, Miriam, watched to see what would happen. While Pharaoh's daughter bathed in the Nile, she noticed the basket and saved the baby. Miriam offered to find a Hebrew woman to act as nursemaid, and the prin-cess agreed. Miriam returned with the baby's Hebrew mother. Pharaoh's daughter took the baby to be her own and called him Moses because she drew him out of the water. So Moses, a Hebrew child condemned to die by order of Pharaoh, ended up being saved by an Egyptian princess; and the baby grew up in the palace. God's hand in this situation seems clear. Moses rose to lead the people out of slavery; but to accomplish that feat he had to deal with the pharaoh and his court, a place familiar to him from childhood. Later we'll see more of God's unique preparation of Moses for his providential task.

MOSES DISCOVERS REALITY

Being protected by the princess and raised in court provided Moses with all the advantages of any son of a princess. His education (Egyptian history, lan-guage, culture, and military strategy), experience (with court protocol and skills for leadership), and contacts prepared him for many tasks in the future. He felt comfortable in the royal setting. Eventually Moses became aware of his ethnic background, which led him to commit a rash act. Moses witnessed an Egyptian abusing a Hebrew slave. He killed the Egyptian overseer and hid his body. Later Moses broke up a fight between two Hebrews who feared he would kill them too. Obviously Moses' previous act of murder produced witnesses. To keep from being discovered, he fled into the desert, giving up his life in Egypt. Moses settled on the Sinai Peninsula in the Median desert.

The desert also served well to prepare Moses for the task ahead. He met Jethro, a priest, and married one of his daughters. Moses learned how to live and survive in the desert and stayed for forty years. He supported himself as a shepherd. Later Moses would spend an extended time wandering in the desert with the Hebrews as they made their way to the promised land in Canaan.

THE BURNING BUSH EXPERIENCE

One day while Moses tended sheep, he happened upon a strange phenomenon—a burning bush that refused to burn up. Moses investigated, and out of the bush God spoke to him. God instructed him not to come closer to the bush but to take off his shoes since the ground was holy with the presence of God. Then he informed Moses of the reason for the encounter.

> The LORD said, "I have seen the misery of my people in Egypt. I have heard them crying out because of their slave drivers, and I am concerned about their suffering. So I have come down to rescue them from the hand of the Egyptians and to bring them up out of that land into a good and spacious land, a land flowing with milk and honey. . . . And now the cry of the Israelites has reached me, and I have seen the way the Egyptians are oppressing them. So now, go. I am sending you to Pharaoh to bring my people the Israelites out of Egypt" (Exod. 3:7–10).

Moses hesitated to accept the invitation to join God in his activity. In fact, Moses gave every excuse he could think of. He wondered how the people would actually know that God sent him. God promised he would be with him and that when Israel left Egypt they would worship on the same mountain Moses now stood on. Moses continued to waffle. How would the people respond to such a story? What name should Moses give when the Hebrews asked who sent him? God said tell them, "I Am Who I Am" sent you—Yahweh, the God of Abraham, Isaac, and Jacob. The name of God becomes important to the biblical story, the covenant, and the Hebrew people. The basic name for God was *El,* which simply meant "God" or "god." In Exodus 3:6, God said to Moses that he is the God (*Elohim*) of his father Abraham. But from this story the Hebrews focus on the name "Yahweh" for God. Names were highly significant, representing the personality of the one to whom it belonged. Therefore, the Hebrews felt that God's name was too sacred to pronounce and used the word *Adonai* (my Lord) with the consonants of Yahweh resulting in Jehovah. However, Yahweh is the covenant name for God in the strictest sense.[4] In Exodus 3:15, when God spoke to Moses, he said that his name is "Yahweh, the God of your Fathers, the God of Abraham, the God of Isaac, and the God of Jacob. . . . This is my name forever; this is how I am to be remembered in every generation." Yahweh became the covenant name for God.

Moses remained reluctant. He argued that he possessed no authority which would encourage Pharaoh to listen to him. So God gave Moses a sign. He commanded Moses to throw his staff on the ground. God changed it into a viper. Then God told him to pick up the snake. Moses did as God said, and the snake turned into a staff again. God gave him a second sign. He instructed Moses to put his hand into his cloak. Upon removal Moses discovered it to be leprous. God instructed

---

[4] G. T. Manley and F. F. Bruce, "Names of God" in *The Illustrated Bible Dictionary.*

him to put it into his cloak again, and it was healed. God used these two miracles to exhibit to Moses his power to take care of him and duly impress both the Israelites and the Egyptians. Moses was not convinced and persisted in offering excuses. He complained to God that his speaking ability would not fit the task. God offered Moses' brother, Aaron, as the spokesman, and the discussion was over.

In the encounter we see God revealed. He is a powerful God, able to do whatever he wills. He is a holy God whose presence demands acts of reverence such as removal of shoes. God showed his compassion: he saw the misery of his people and had a plan for their good. He is a God of promise who promised Moses his power, presence, and direction in everything to be done. He is a present God evidenced both by his presence with Moses in the burning bush and his promise to be with Moses and the people throughout the entire ordeal to come. God is a holy, powerful, loving, and willful God who is able to use a man even as unwilling as Moses to accomplish miraculous things for the people of Israel. On the other hand we see Moses revealed as well. He was a man of excuses. He was a man who realized his own inadequacy for the task. But in the end he was a faithful servant. In spite of his excuses, he submitted to God and fulfilled his role. God once again used an ordinary, inadequate human being to carry out his awesome plan for salvation and redemption.

THE ENCOUNTER WITH PHARAOH

Moses obediently made the trek back to Egypt and met his brother Aaron on the way. Together they journeyed to Pharaoh's palace to present God's request. Pharaoh was obstinate and responded that he did not know the God of Israel. In retaliation for this bold request, Pharaoh increased the difficulty for Hebrew slaves by forcing them to supply their own straw for the mud bricks. Moses and Aaron returned to Pharaoh and exercised the power of God by demonstrating how the staff could turn into a snake. Pharaoh remained unimpressed with this trick since his own sorcerers appeared to duplicate it even though God's snake swallowed up their snakes. Pharaoh remained obstinate and refused to let the people go. God then used Moses to teach the Egyptians an important theological point: the God of Abraham, Isaac, Jacob, Joseph, and now Moses was God over all and would have his way. God sent plagues to the land of Egypt to convince them to let the Israelites go. Ten plagues came, and all were significant: the Nile turned to blood; frogs invaded the land; and gnats, flies, death of livestock, boils on people and animals, hail, locusts, darkness over all the land except on the land of Goshen where the Hebrews lived. The last plague, the killing of the firstborn son in every family, proved to be the most devastating. Some of these may seem to be just nuisances while others are extreme, but all proved to Egypt and Israel the power of God. Pharaoh earlier asked an important question, and in the plagues God answered it. "Who is the Lord that I should obey him?" (Exod. 5:2 HCSB). God revealed who he is in the plagues.

The Egyptian religious world centered on a complex polytheistic system. They worshipped everything from the Nile to animals to the sun. Can you see what God is doing through the plagues? God dealt with every deity the Egyptians held dear and proved his power over them. In the ancient world strict monotheism was rare. The ancients believed in many gods, and even war was a test of whose god was strongest. In this battle the God of Moses proved his mettle. He ruled and demanded the release of his people. But notice in the biblical account the Hebrews escaped the crushing blow of the plagues. Exodus 9:6 states that all the livestock of the Egyptians died, but not one of the Hebrew livestock died. God blotted out the sun for three days in all of Egypt, yet "all the Israelites had light in the places where they lived" (Exod. 10:23). The cause of these plagues was no doubt tied closely to the enslaved Hebrews.

But how about that last plague? Does it also deal with the polytheistic beliefs of Egypt? Yes, it does. The Egyptians also believed Pharaoh was divine and that the heir to the throne, the firstborn son, was as well. Remember that Pharaoh ordered all the firstborn male children of the Hebrews to be killed. God shows his power. Who is Yahweh that Pharaoh should listen to him? The taking of the firstborn son of Pharaoh settled that question.

THE PASSOVER, GOD'S SALVATION

The last plague ultimately revealed God's salvation for the Israelites. The means for killing the firstborn of the Egyptians was a death angel. The angel would pass over each house, and those that were not protected by God's rule would suffer the loss of the firstborn son. But how would the angel recognize God's people? God provided Moses with instructions for the Hebrews. Each man was to take a lamb for his household. The lambs must be one year old and without defect. They were to slaughter them at twilight and paint some of the blood on the sides and tops of the door frames of the houses. Then they were to prepare the lamb and eat it as a meal inside the home. God explained that at night the death angel would pass over all the homes with the blood on the doorposts. By doing this the Hebrews saved their firstborn. Only those who trusted and obeyed God by applying the blood to the doorposts were saved. This event became a symbol for God's wonderful provision of salvation for Israel. Later Jesus associated himself with the Passover lamb and the symbol of salvation. The blood of the lamb brought salvation to the Hebrews; and later the blood of the lamb, Jesus, would bring salvation to all.

It is clear that God orchestrated all the events surrounding the release of his people from slavery. His sovereignty and power were undeniable. We see how the plagues and other events taught the Israelites and the Egyptians who God is and just how powerful he is. After four hundred years of slavery, Israel had forgotten God. They required a time of reeducation before they would be willing to follow Moses into the wilderness, and that education began in Egypt.

The Escape from Egypt

The last plague proved to be the decisive blow for Pharaoh. "At midnight the Lord struck down all the firstborn in Egypt, from the firstborn of Pharaoh, who sat on the throne, to the firstborn of the prisoner, who was in the dungeon" (Exod. 12:29). Wailing could be heard throughout Egypt. "During the night Pharaoh summoned Moses and Aaron and said, 'Up! Leave my people, you and the Israelites! Go, worship the Lord as you have requested'" (Exod. 12:31).

The Egyptian people urged the Israelites to leave. The Hebrews grabbed their possessions and dough for bread before the yeast was even added and left. Before they departed, God told Moses to ask the Egyptians for articles of silver and gold as well as clothing. The Egyptians complied and gave the Israelites valuable items for the journey. These items God will use later in his tent of worship. The Israelites left after 430 years of residing in Egypt to return to the land God originally promised Abraham when he called him out of Ur of the Chaldees. God's plan of redemption continued. He orchestrated it perfectly to get Israel back to Canaan. But the time in Egypt was not wasted. God used it to grow a large nation of people, as many as three million; and they began the return journey to possess the promised land.

One More Saving Act, the Red Sea

The escape from Egypt was not yet complete. Pharaoh allowed their departure during his time of deep grief and pain. But in time, anger coupled with the pain of loss caused him to seek revenge. Pharaoh decided to go after the Hebrews to enslave them again. The Egyptians loaded up the chariots and pursued the Hebrews. Moses followed God's guidance and took the people to the edge of the Red Sea[5] where they camped. God led them with a pillar of fire by night and a cloud by day. Then word came that the Egyptian army neared.

We get the first clue of the nature of the Hebrews and the difficulty they provided for Moses on the journey. They immediately complained. "What have you done to us by bringing us out of Egypt? Didn't we say to you in Egypt, 'Leave us alone; let us serve the Egyptians'? It would have been better for us to serve the Egyptians than to die in the desert!" (Exod. 14:11–12).

Moses exercised his role as leader. He assured them that they need not fear. God would deliver. And God did. God commanded Moses to raise his staff and stretch it out over the sea. When Moses raised his staff, a strong east wind split the water; and the people walked over dry land to the other side. God held the Egyptian army back with a pillar of fire until this was accomplished. Imagine how long it might take to move millions of people across the sea. When the Israelites reached the other side, Moses stretched his hand over the sea again; and the waters returned

---

[5] The name used for the body of water was "Yam Suph" which is literally translated "reed sea." Some feel that the Hebrews did not cross the Red Sea but a smaller body of water. It is also possible that Yam Suph was a name used for the Red Sea. This issue is debated, but the biblical story makes clear that God caused the water to split, saving the Israelites from destruction.

crushing Pharaoh's pursuing army. God won the victory. "And when the Israelites saw the great power the LORD displayed against the Egyptians, the people feared the LORD and put their trust in him and in Moses his servant" (Exod. 14:31). Surely this event marks a beginning of the relationship of God with his people. That relationship ebbed and flowed as the people trusted and distrusted, but God remained faithful throughout the entire journey and story.

A SALVATION STORY

Often the biblical story of God's redemption is called *Heilsgeschichte* or salvation history. Certainly the exodus story centers on two salvation events that bookend the work of God. Both have significance for later portions of God's story. They are pictures of what God intended to do later. The first was the Passover event or the night the death angel passed over those who obeyed God. God used the blood of the lamb to save the Israelites from the death angel. Later God used Jesus' blood to provide salvation to all who would believe in him. Passover is a picture of the cross of Jesus to come.

In the second event, the parting of the Red Sea, God provided a picture of salvation as well. In the water experience the people find their freedom. Later the baptism experience symbolized the freedom from sin that people experience through Jesus. These two miracles rank as two of the most significant in Hebrew history. The entire event is a story of salvation: God saved his people from that which oppressed them.

A WORD ABOUT MIRACLES

Miracles take center stage in this part of the story, from staffs turning to snakes to plagues to the parting of the Red Sea. How significant are they, and what do they tell us about God's power to save? Some people struggle with the miraculous and seek to explain it away. Some argue that these events surrounding Moses' life were not really miracles but can be explained in natural terms. For instance, one might argue the parting of the Red Sea resulted from an earthquake in the middle of the sea which sucked all the water away leaving dry land and then closed again (squirting the water out of the hole) to cover the dry land and the Egyptians. One could suggest that the turning of the Nile into blood was merely an infestation of amoeba which turned the water rusty red and then polluted it to the point of killing fish and making it unfit for consumption.

Even if natural events caused the emptying of the sea or the turning of water to blood, would that make the events nonmiracles? Perhaps answering a few questions will help us understand. Who is God, and what is a miracle? First, we already know from the biblical story that God created all that is—all nature and all the systems of nature. He is the architect. No one in the universe understands nature more than God. God as Creator can work within nature or outside of it. We must also admit that most of us, even the most educated and intelligent, do not understand everything about nature and the things of nature. We live with unknowns. Therefore, if God chose to use natural forces to perform the miracles, that would not make them nonmiracles. God alone is capable of causing an unusual act of nature such as turning water into blood. From our perspective all miracles appear supernatural. In fact, we define miracles in terms of the supernatural since they "always run counter to the observed processes of nature."[6] We are bound by our minimal understanding. However, regardless of God's method, miracles require his intervention. He causes them to occur. Miracles require an act of God.

Another important factor in the miraculous concerns timing. When do these events occur? They happened when they were needed, and God caused them. When did the Nile turn to blood? When did the other plagues come? When did the Red Sea part? These all occurred when God commanded them and when the Israelites desperately needed an intervention. The Egyptian army rushed toward them, and God caused the sea to part, allowing their escape, and to close, defeating Pharaoh's army. Even if someone insists on an earthquake, it happened when God said it should happen. The biblical story explicitly says an east wind forced the water back. The wind is a part of nature, but God commanded the wind at the time it was needed, and a miracle resulted. In other words, timing plays an important role in the concept of miracles. God's power moves the events at the right time.

One last thought. Many of the miracles could not possibly be explained by natural causes. For instance, the death angel would be a hard one to connect to a natural occurrence. Perhaps death could come to many people on a given night, but how could anyone explain that it took only the firstborn son of all the Egyptians and their animals but did not harm the Israelites. That kind of specific killing defies natural explanation. We are left with one conclusion. The Passover (death angel) is a miracle requiring God's intervention and power. God performs miracles in his way (using natural or supernatural means), in his time and with his power, which is the only power capable of such.

THINGS TO CONSIDER

Act one of this episode revealed to us numerous theological truths about God and people. God loved his people and never forgot them. He expressed his compassion by providing the means of their salvation through his awesome power. His ultimate and sovereign power provided for a leader and the miracles necessary for the escape from Egypt. God revealed himself to Moses as holy, powerful, and compassionate. He revealed himself to Pharaoh as the one and only God whose plan for his people cannot be thwarted by any human ruler. God showed a divine patience which expressed mercy and compassion even to an obstinate and ungrateful

---

[6] J. D. Spiceland, "Miracles" in *Evangelical Dictionary of the Bible,* 723. For a larger discussion of miracles, see this article.

people. The exodus moved the covenant people toward the reclaiming of the land promised to Abraham.

STUDY QUESTIONS

1. What can we learn about God and Moses from the burning bush experience?
2. How did God prepare Moses for the difficult task given him?
3. How did God deal with the Egyptian religious system in convincing Pharaoh to let the Hebrews go?
4. What were the two key miracles God performed to allow the salvation of the Hebrews?

ACT 2

THE SINAI EXPERIENCE

Having escaped Egypt and Pharaoh's army, the Hebrews traveled southeastward toward the mountain where God first encountered Moses. But life in the desert presented problems and obstacles. Water ranked as the number-one need, and the lack of it caused complaints. God proved himself faithful; and when the caravan of around three million reached Marah, they found water; but it was bitter and not fit to drink. The people grumbled. Moses prayed to God and was instructed to throw a piece of wood into the water. This action changed the bitter water into sweet water, and they all drank. God provided miraculously. Consider the magnitude of this miracle. If the people numbered only one million, the amount of water required to quench their thirst boggles the mind. How much would a city of one million need for drinking water for just one day? The Hebrew people realized the power of Yahweh.

God took the opportunity at this first miracle in the wilderness to set down a rule of life for the Hebrews. "There the LORD made a decree and a law for them, and there he tested them. He said, 'If you listen carefully to the voice of the LORD your God and do what is right in his eyes, if you pay attention to his commands and keep all his decrees, I will not bring on you any of the diseases I brought on the Egyptians, for I am the LORD, who heals you'" (Exod. 15:25–26).

God laid a beginning foundation for the covenant and law he would give to them at Sinai. They would be his people, follow and obey him; and he would care for them. Immediately after this God led them to camp at a place called Elim where there were twelve springs and seventy palm trees. His provision equaled their need.

GOD'S PROVISION

The nature and character of the Hebrew nation surfaced frequently in the desert, and Moses endured their grumbling voices regularly. After receiving needed water, the reluctant followers of God complained about the lack of food. "In the desert the whole community grumbled against Moses and Aaron" (Exod. 16:2). Once again consider how much food it would take to feed such a large constituency. This time the Israelites compared the ample supplies of food in Egypt to the lack of food in the desert. God stepped up and delivered. In the evening God sent quail to the people so they would have meat to eat. The following morning he rained down manna (a sort of bread) from heaven which covered the ground like dew.

God gave specific instructions for this manna. Every family was to collect enough manna for that day only and then on the day before the Sabbath enough for two days. If they failed to follow the instructions, the manna would rot with maggots. What was God trying to teach these people? He wanted them to trust him every day for all their needs. They seemed to have an issue with trust so training was in order. In the evening the quail came, and in the morning the manna covered the ground. God was in the early stages of developing a covenant people who must learn to follow his instructions and trust his power. They had to learn to consider him as the one and only God.

GOD'S PROTECTION

Sooner or later the large group of Hebrews had to encounter other tribes living in the desert. As there was little in the desert to support large numbers of people, natural resources like water attained premium importance. The Hebrews eventually clashed with the Amalekites over the use of an oasis critical to survival of both. It was time again for God to prove his unmatched strength against the enemies of his people. The encounter occurred at Rephidim. Joshua led the forces on the ground while Moses, already an old man, stood on the top of the hill above the battleground. Moses held up his hands; and as long as he did, the Israelites won. But when he grew tired and his hands dropped, the battle turned against the Hebrews. Aaron and Hur helped by holding Moses' arms to support his hands, and God's people proved victorious.

What significance did Moses' action on the hill have, and what was God trying to teach his people? The lifting of hands was more than a symbol. When we pray, we often bow our heads and in serious prayer may even get on our knees. But in Moses' time it was common to lift hands in prayer. Moses intervened through prayer over the battle, calling down God's power and strength for his people. As long as the intervention continued, the Hebrews prevailed; but when it ceased, they failed. God proved who was vital to the battle. It was his victory and his power that counted. As long as the people remembered and depended on Yahweh, they would be successful. God soon would promise them the land of Abraham as their own.

Battles would need to be fought. They realized early on against the Egyptians and then the Amalekites that God is capable. He ensured their victory and would again. It was God's plan and his purpose for the redemption of his people.

MOUNT SINAI AND THE COVENANT

God established a covenant with Moses and the Hebrews at Sinai. God told Moses that the people would worship at the same place where he encountered the burning bush. This location marked the spot of the beginning of much of what came to be called Judaism. Here God bestowed his expectation on the people in the form of laws, regulations for life, and religious ceremony. These served as the distinctions that would distinguish Israel from all other peoples of the region, the most important distinction being that these people would serve only one god—Yahweh. With the establishment of the covenant, Moses and the Hebrews became covenant people. The key phrase of the covenant was: "I will be your God; you will be my people, and I will dwell in your midst." In the Mosaic covenant God demanded that the people obey and follow a certain lifestyle. This lifestyle was spelled out in the law given at Sinai.

The Ten Commandments represented the heart of what God expected from his people—how the Hebrews should relate to God and to other people. They were written on stone tablets and given to the people through Moses.

1. You shall have no other gods before me.
2. You shall not make for yourself an idol.
3. You shall not misuse the name of the Lord your God.
4. Remember the Sabbath.
5. Honor your father and your mother.
6. You shall not murder.
7. You shall not commit adultery.
8. You shall not steal.
9. You shall not give false testimony.
10. You shall not covet ... anything that belongs to your neighbor (Exod. 20:1–17).

Notice that instructions concerning the relationship to God preceded those for relationships with people. Why? Obviously, the relationship with God took priority. The first four commandments specifically reveal to the Hebrews significant theological truths. God is the only God, teaching them a monotheistic faith. God is Spirit, and he cannot be depicted in an image of stone or wood. God is much too great and awesome for that. God is holy and worthy of all reverence, even when speaking his name. God deserves worship and honor every day, but a Sabbath day should be recognized weekly.

A proper relationship with God sets the stage for all other relationships in life. The biblical story is one of reconciliation and redemption to God. When God's people have a good relationship with the Creator, then other relationships fall into place. The Hebrews were to give God his rightful place in their life and community for society to work as it should. The last six commandments related to others. Honor your father and mother and don't commit adultery. The family was the cornerstone of human society from the beginning. God's law protected the family and gave it due honor. Treating parents properly and protecting the marriage relationship ensured the health of the family. Don't murder, steal, lie, or covet. God created humans in his image and therefore with dignity and worth. People deserve to be treated properly, and God's special people were commanded to be models of respect and proper action. The commandments taught the people that God wanted them to honor another's name and reputation, property, family, and integrity. The last six commandments corresponded to other legal codes of the day (notably the Code of Hammurabi). However, when combined with the four commandments concerning God, they stand as unique. God's law provided the foundation for creating a special and unusual monotheistic, moral people—his people.

In other words, the people of God were to be people grounded in the belief in one God; and that belief was to serve as the source of all thought and action. As they lived out that belief, they would be unique among people. They would be God's people as promised to Abraham, and through them God would bless the world. A new covenant came into play at Sinai.

The people readily agreed to follow God. However, shortly they had forgotten him and turned to the practices learned in Egypt. The Egyptians worshipped many animals including the bull. While Moses lingered on the mountain receiving the law from God, the people persuaded Aaron to craft for them a calf made from the gold plundered from the Egyptians at their departure from Egypt. Aaron consented, and the people worshipped an idol. Obviously they broke the first laws God set out for them. God judged many of the guilty people with death, but once again his mercy and patience saved the Hebrews. God's compassion never failed them.

ABRAHAMIC COVENANT VERSUS MOSAIC COVENANT

As already mentioned covenant took priority in the biblical story. The two most significant to this point are God's covenant with Abraham and the covenant with Moses. Significant differences in the covenants represent a shift in the story line. God's ultimate plan of redemption works through both, but the Mosaic serves a particular purpose. A comparison of the two at this point serves to clarify God's intention.

Moses addressed a people who were the seed of Abraham and the covenant people. However, the covenant made at Sinai differed from the one made with Abraham. The promises to Abraham remained in effect—great name, great nation, blessing of all nations, protection, and land. However, with the Mosaic covenant

God intended to create a unique people who lived according to a
God. They were to stand out as God's covenant people. Note th

ABRAHAMIC	MOS
one-sided, unilateral	two-sided, bilateral
"divine commitment" covenant	"human obligation" covenant
feature: God's promise	feature: man's obedience
result: restoration	result: judgment
NT term: grace	NT term: law

In the covenant between Abraham and God, God made the commitment
and promises. It was a unilateral covenant that God would fulfill regardless of
Abraham's faithfulness. The ultimate aim was to take care of the sin issue with a
plan based solely on God's grace and mercy. People did not deserve redemption,
but God would through Abraham's seed provide it. While Abraham obeyed, the
focus of his commitment was God's commitment. In the Mosaic covenant God
made promises, but the people made promises as well. It was a bilateral covenant
between a superior with his followers. The Israelites had an obligation to obey the
law that God spelled out at Sinai. To refuse to do so meant judgment as we will
see in the story.

Later, just before Moses died, he restated the covenant to the people. This is
recorded in Deuteronomy, which means "second or repeated law." Moses wanted
desperately for the Hebrews to know how serious the covenant was for their life
and future. If the Israelites took the covenant seriously, then God's blessing followed them. If they rejected it, they would suffer God's judgment. In fact, Moses
listed a series of blessings and curses connected to the covenant. The prophets
later reminded the people of the Deuteronomic covenant and called them to return
to God. Usually the breaking of the covenant involved worshipping idols (as the
Hebrews did at the base of Mt. Sinai), social injustice (ignoring the last six commandments), and immorality. Curses and blessings were determined by the faithfulness of the Hebrews.

THE LAW AND SACRIFICES

A reading of the Law and the regulations God gave at Sinai appears detailed
and in some cases odd. Why would God require such things? What was the purpose of the Law? This remains an important question even into the New Testament
part of the story. God had a purpose. God's goal centered on developing a people
unique in character and action which would distinguish them from all others as

---

[7] Chart used by permission of J. Daniel Hays.

ₑers of the one true God. The Law revealed what God desired for their
nd therefore represented God's will for his people.[8] The lifestyle represented
ᵤe law was a good one that God approved of for his people.

What about the sacrifices required by the Law? How did they benefit the
Hebrews? The greatest need of all humans dates back to the beginning of the biblical story. In Genesis 3 Adam and Eve rebelled against God and disobeyed his
command. As already discussed, sin entered the world and affected everything.
That event set up the rest of the story as God unfolded his plan to redeem people
back to him. In other words, God had a plan to deal with the sin issue. Sacrifice
became part of that plan. Sacrifices in the ancient world were not uncommon,
and the Hebrews did not stand out on that account. However, the purpose of the
Israelite sacrifices concerned the sin issue. God required a blood sacrifice of animals to deal with sin. Why? God made clear in Leviticus 17:11 that the life of a
being is connected to the blood and it is blood that atones for sin. He forbade them
from eating blood because of its significance and reserved it for sacrifices at the
altar. Sacrificing the life force of an animal because of sin showed dependency on
God for both physical and spiritual life. Sin led to and required death (Gen. 3), so
through the death of a sacrificial animal, atonement for sin became possible. God
wanted the Hebrews to realize the seriousness of sin. It was costly, and something
or someone paid a price. It also provided a way for the sinner to approach God after
committing sin. Sacrifices represented the repentance necessary for forgiveness.
To offer a sacrifice for sin at God's altar was to admit the sin and realize the need
for God's forgiveness. God is a holy God as Moses discovered at the burning bush.
How can a sinner come to a holy God? A sacrifice atoned for the sin and allowed
the approach. Significantly, the sacrificial system also foreshadowed the ultimate
sacrifice which dealt with sin completely and finally—the death of Jesus on the
cross. God made provision for the sin of the covenant people.

GOD'S PRESENCE

The focal point of all God's Law and regulations at Sinai was God's presence with
his people. God made his presence known to them from the beginning through the
plagues and then leading them out of Egypt in the day by a cloud and at night with a
pillar of fire. The people could simply look and know that God resided with them and
had not abandoned them. But with the law God provided for a dwelling place for his
presence that the people would construct, use for worship, and carry with them. The
presence of God closely connected to the covenant: I will be your God. That presence marked the people as covenant people. Several events in Hebrew history will be
defined by God's presence among them or by his absence from them. The Hebrews
bound in slavery experienced freedom with the presence of God in their midst. To
reject God's presence would prove devastating for the Hebrew nation.

---

[8] For more information on the Law and its significance to covenant and Hebrew life, see G. J. Wenham, "Law"
in *New Bible Dictionary,* 672–75.

God instructed the building of a portable tent of worship to be taken wherever the people traveled. This tent of worship became known as the tabernacle. God provided specific instructions on the construction including size, materials, design, its use, and maintenance. The tabernacle was built with many of the precious materials given by the Egyptians when the Hebrews escaped. The courtyard of the tabernacle contained an altar for burnt offerings where the priests offered sacrifices to God and lavers or water bowls for ceremonial washing. A tent was erected inside the enclosure consisting of two main rooms for priestly activity. The first room was called the holy place and contained three pieces of furniture. A table of shewbread held twelve loaves of bread representing the twelve tribes of Israel. A candlestick, better known as a menorah, held seven candles and represented the light of God. An altar of incense, from which smoke rose representing the prayers of the people lifted to God, sat in front of the massive curtain or veil separating the two rooms. Many priests worked in this room to care for the spiritual needs of the people. The room behind the curtain took the name holy of holies and contained the most sacred items. When the tabernacle was constructed in the middle of the camp, God's cloud and pillar of fire descended and dwelt in the holy of holies. The Israelites visibly saw his presence among them. In this room an ark was placed on a platform called the mercy seat. In the ark of the covenant, Moses placed some of the manna, tablets of the law, and his staff.

This room was used only once a year by one person, the high priest. On that one day, the Day of Atonement, the high priest sacrificed a goat and sprinkled the blood of the goat on the mercy seat as a propitiation for the sins of Israel. *Propitiation*

means "a covering." The blood of the sacrifice covered the sins of all Israel. Then the high priest went out to the people and placed his hands on another goat, and the sins of all Israel transferred to the goat. This goat or scapegoat was taken into the desert bearing away the sins of the people. God's presence in the holy of holies and the blood sacrifice became the heart of the redemption plan at this time and the foreshadowing of future redemption. The presence of God in his Son Jesus and his sacrifice on the cross ultimately fulfilled that covering and forgiving of sin. The tabernacle served as the centerpiece for Israel's faith and would continue until the temple was built.

Remember the twelve tribes—ten of Jacob's sons and Joseph's two sons. The tribe of Levi (another son of Jacob) did not receive land but took on a special role in the worship practices of Israel. God set aside Levi's tribe for service in the tabernacle to construct it, transport it, and camp around it as guardians. Later they performed similar duties in the temple. In the promised land they will be scattered throughout and occupy refuge cities for those in need. The priests and the high priest came from Aaron's family. The priests offered sacrifices and served as bridges from God to the people through the laws and regulations. This system continued for the Hebrews well into the first century AD.

THINGS TO CONSIDER

In this portion of the biblical story God taught his people, Israel, some important lessons. First, God's presence holds the secret to their fulfillment both corporately and individually. God made himself known to a people void of his saving presence for four hundred years. That presence and power saved them, released them, and redeemed them. He showed himself as provider by giving food, water, protection, and guidance. At Sinai God gave his Law for the purpose of making the Hebrews into a unique nation of people—God's people. This made it possible for the Israelites to know how to live in God's presence. His provisions provided for them physically and spiritually. God made provision for sin through the sacrificial system—a system which indicated the seriousness and costliness of sin. Sin required a blood sacrifice, and God instructed the priests to carry it out. Israel needed that provision. God's power, strength, love, mercy, compassion, and patience became the basis for Israel's hope. Without it they had little chance.

STUDY QUESTIONS

1. How did God provide for the Hebrews in the desert?
2. How would you compare the Mosaic and the Abrahamic covenants?
3. How did God reveal his presence constantly to the Israelites?
4. What do the Ten Commandments and the sacrificial system do for the Hebrews?

ACT 3

THE WILDERNESS EXPERIENCE

A fter leaving Mount Sinai with the instructions from God, the Hebrew nation headed toward the land promised to Abraham, Isaac, Jacob, and now to Moses and the people. As the people departed, God organized them into an order for marching with the tabernacle in the middle and the ark in the front. When they camped, the tabernacle was placed in the middle with each of the tribes surrounding it. God led them by fire at night and a cloud by day. Finally they reached the entrance to the promised land, Kadesh Barnea. At this location the Israelites made a decision that drastically affected them for the next forty years.

KADESH BARNEA

The book of Numbers places the total number of Hebrews that reached the border of the promised land at Kadesh Barnea at 603,550 men who were twenty years old or able to serve in the army. This figure leads many to estimate the total number with women and children at three million or more. God commanded Moses to send out some men to explore Canaan in preparation for the invasion. Moses selected twelve men, one from each of the tribes. They were to go through all the land surveying the people (strength and size) and the land itself. When they returned, the report caused dissension. Ten of the spies gave reports of giants living in large, fortified cities. They discouraged invading because the inhabitants were just too strong. However, two spies disagreed. Caleb and Joshua (the military commander in the earlier battle against the Amalekites) issued a report based on optimism and faith in God. "We must go up and take possession of the land because we can certainly conquer it" (Num. 13:30 HCSB). They were convinced of God's power and ability and theirs to follow. However, as is normally the case, the Israelites went with the majority of the spies and refused to enter the land God had prepared for them, the land God gave Abraham and promised the Hebrews. This decision may rank as one of the worst in Hebrew history. The people rebelled and grumbled against Moses, Aaron, and God. They reasoned that it would be better to return to slavery in Egypt and suggested the selection of a new leader to take them there. They even talked about stoning Moses, Aaron, Joshua, and Caleb. They turned their back on God, his plan, and his leaders.

God determined to strike them all down with a plague. "How long will these people despise Me? How long will they not trust in Me despite all the signs I have performed among them? I will strike them with a plague and destroy them" (Num. 14:11–12 HCSB). Moses intervened, counting on the character and nature of God. Moses described God as "slow to anger, abounding in love and forgiving sin and rebellion." In other words Moses' prayer of intercession was based on God's character and nature, not that of the Hebrews.

God agreed and forgave the Hebrews, but justice would still be meted out. God promised that "not one of the men who saw my glory and the miraculous signs I performed in Egypt and in the desert but who disobeyed me . . . not one of them will ever see the land I promised on oath to their forefathers" (Num. 14:22–23). Those who had witnessed God's powerful plagues and the miracles at the Red Sea and in the desert should have believed God. Because of the rebellion God's people wandered in the Arabian Desert for forty years while the rebellious were judged. However, God showed both his mercy and grace in this event. He could simply have killed them all. He instead allowed them to live but without entering Canaan. During this time of wandering, the older generation, those who distrusted God and rejected his promise, died of various causes. This event served as an illustration of God's promises concerning keeping or rejecting of the covenant and the consequences.

ISRAEL IN THE DESERT

Moses continued to lead the rebellious people and continued to love them and seek their best interest. However, his patience grew short as they continued to grumble and reject his leadership and God. When the people reached the Desert of Zin, they found no water and turned on Moses. They suggested again that it would have been better to stay in Egypt, a favorite theme for the Hebrews in the wilderness. Moses and Aaron prayed to God who instructed Moses to take the staff (representing God's authority and power) and speak to a certain rock and it would pour forth water for the people. But when Moses stood in front of the people, his anger and impatience got the best of him. He addressed the people as rebels asking them harshly, "Must we bring water out of this rock" (Num. 20:10). Then instead of speaking to the rock, he struck it with the staff. The water gushed out, but Moses had obviously disobeyed God's instructions. The judgment of God came immediately. "Because you did not trust in Me to show My holiness in the sight of the Israelites, you will not bring this assembly into the land I have given them" (Num. 20:12 HCSB). Moses—who at the age of eighty went into Egypt and brought the people out, led them to Sinai, interceded for them, and put up with all the grumbling and rebellion—would not be allowed to enter the promised land.

This seems a bit harsh to a reader of the biblical story. After all Moses had done for God and for the people, could one mistake keep him out of the land? Why would God judge his most faithful servant so harshly? Perhaps it was simply because Moses was the leader, and leaders are held to a higher standard than all the others. Psalm 106:32–33 indicates that "rash words came from Moses' lips." Maybe Moses' statement before striking the rock gave the impression that he and Aaron were giving them water. This would mean Moses put himself in God's place. Certainly that would be sin. What is certain is that Moses did not obey God's instructions. As a result of this one event, Moses only saw Canaan from afar, but he did not enter. Moses served at God's pleasure and accepted God's judgment and will. Surely the people recognized the seriousness of following God's way and will because of this experience. God would be their God, and they were to be his obedient servants.

POISONOUS SNAKES IN THE DESERT

Just a few weeks after God had powerfully defeated the Canaanite king Arad in battle, the Hebrews once again grew impatient of traveling in the wilderness and grumbled against God. Aaron had recently died and was no longer subjected to the complaints, but Moses endured the onslaught again. The people complained: "Why have you led us up from Egypt to die in the wilderness? There is no bread or water, and we detest this wretched food!" (Num. 21:5 HCSB). For this rebellion the Lord sent a judgment in the form of venomous snakes—vipers. They bit the people, and many died. In repentance and fear the people came to Moses and asked him to intervene. They confessed their sin and asked for mercy. God instructed Moses to fashion a bronze snake and place it on the top of a pole in the camp. When bitten, the people could look at the bronze snake and live.

Here God provided an unusual solution to a serious problem. The people were bitten by deadly snakes, sometimes referred to as fiery serpents. We know that vipers marked by a red patch on their head lived in the Arabian Desert. Their venom caused a harsh burning sensation as the poison coursed through the body and eventually killed. But how would looking at a snake on a stick help that situation? God provided a way for powerful healing to take place in their bodies. He only required obedience. Look at the bronze snake. Their judgment came from rejecting God's way and disobeying. The solution consisted of obedience to God. The only way to live if bitten was to take advantage of God's provision. Hebrews who experienced the serpent's bite and then refused God's provision died. God provided the only way of salvation from the snakebites.

Throughout the biblical story God alone provides for salvation. Later Jesus even declared to the disciples that just as Moses lifted up the snake in the wilderness so must the son of man be lifted up. God offered all the solutions for sin and its consequence. Rebellious sinners must depend on God because without his work sin cannot be dealt with. Remember the whole story is the story of redemption and salvation. God was teaching the Hebrews that he was and will be the only solution to the spiritual issues of life. Sin brings death and God gives life.

THE NATION

The book of Numbers records the account of the wandering in the desert for forty years. At the beginning of the journey, the census indicated 603,550 fighting men among the Hebrews. After failing to trust God and invade Canaan at Kadesh Barnea, God judged the older generation by disallowing their entry into the promised land. God judged them, and they died over the forty years after Kadesh Barnea. At the end of the wandering another census occurred. The number of fighting men was 601,730. A nation of people still existed. God created a nation out of Abraham's seed, and that nation would occupy the land promised to Abraham. He had blessed those who aided Israel and cursed those who opposed them. God remained faithful to the covenant even when the people were not.

THINGS TO CONSIDER

God fulfilled his promises. He led them to the promised land and promised to give it to them. Then God judged them when they refused to obey. No matter how often God provided, blessed, protected, and led the people, they still rebelled against him. How well did the Hebrews learn to be God's people? The next episode answers that question.

STUDY QUESTIONS

1. Why did the Hebrews refuse to enter the promised land at Kadesh Barnea?
2. How is God's merciful nature revealed in the story of the wandering?
3. How does the wandering in the wilderness reveal the nature of people?
4. How is the fiery serpent event similar to the crucifixion of Christ?

THE PROMISED LAND AND SIN'S POWER

ACT 1

THE CONQUEST AND THE JUDGES

T he Hebrews reached the entrance to the promised land at the Jordan near Jericho. Moses could not enter because of God's judgment. He climbed Mount Nebo above the plains of Moab, and the Lord showed him the land. "This is the land I promised Abraham, Isaac, and Jacob, 'I will give it to your descendants.' I have let you see it with your own eyes, but you will not cross into it" (Deut. 34:4 HCSB). Moses did not protest. He died in the land of Moab as the people stood at the entrance to Canaan. God buried him in an unknown grave. He was 120 years old when he died, and the Israelites wept and mourned for thirty days. Moses was praised in the story. "He was unparalleled for all the signs and wonders the LORD sent him to do against the land of Egypt—to Pharaoh, to all his officials, and to all his land, and for all the mighty acts of power and terrifying deeds that Moses performed in the sight of all Israel" (Deut. 34:11–12 HCSB).

Before his death Moses selected Joshua as his successor, and God filled Joshua with his Spirit's power to fulfill the task of leadership. He would lead the armies of Israel into the promised land. The journey from Egypt probably began around 1290 to 1250 BC and took a long forty years. A new generation prepared to receive the promise given to Abraham. But how would the conquest be accomplished? Could it be done by the sheer power and numbers of the Hebrews? God answered that question at the Jordan River, the first obstacle between his people and the promised land.

THE MIRACLE AT THE JORDAN

Normally the Jordan River posed little problem for crossing, but in flood stage it presented a menacing wall before Canaan. The Hebrews reached it at flood stage. Three million people needed to ford this river to begin the conquest of the promised land. How could this be accomplished? God performed another miracle. Remember how the Hebrews were finally saved from Pharaoh? As they arrived at the Red Sea, Pharaoh pursued them. With backs against the sea, they had no options except God's power. God acted in a miraculous way parting the sea for them to cross on dry land and using the same sea to crush the enemy. That began their journey into the desert. Now faced with another water barrier, a flooded Jordan, God acted again. This time he stopped the flow of the Jordan, and the people crossed on dry ground. The first miracle proved God's awesome power to the old generation, but they perished in the desert. Now God exhibited his power to the new generation. They came to Canaan to conquer it but needed a powerful God to rely on. God proved himself powerful at the outset of the invasion. The two miracles, the Red Sea and the Jordan, served as bookends of God's salvation for the people he now called his own. Who could doubt him?

Just as a good teacher emphasizes an important point, God took the time at the Jordan River to highlight his message. He instructed Joshua to recruit twelve men, one from each of the tribes, to perform an unusual task. "Take 12 stones from this place in the middle of the Jordan where the priests' feet are standing, carry them with you, and set them down at the place where you spend the night" (Josh. 4:3). When they camped, they built a memorial with the stones as a historical marker. Why did God require this memorial, and what purpose could it serve in the future? "In the future, when your children ask you, 'What do these stones mean to you?' you should tell them, 'The waters of the Jordan were cut off in front of the ark of the LORD's covenant.' . . . Therefore, these stones will always be a memorial for the Israelites" (Josh. 4:6–7 HCSB). The stones acted as conversation starters in the future. The children would inquire as to the purpose of a pile of stones; and the answer entailed the wonderful story of God's power, provision, and care for his people. It was the covenant story.

God not only desired Israel to remember his power and provision, but he also expected them to pass it along to the next generation. Some people believe the study or knowledge of history amounts to wasted time. God disagreed. He counted it as important that his people not only know their history but also teach it to their children and then to their children in turn. When asked, the Hebrew parents would tell even more than the Jordan miracle. No doubt they recounted the plagues which released them from Egypt; the parting of the Red Sea; manna, water, and quail in the desert; the victory over the Amalekites; and God's provision and his presence with them in the desert. In other words, they would recount how God's powerful hand moved through them as a nation.

The Law and the worship practices established by God at Sinai served as "remembrances" of God's salvation as well. The Hebrews were commanded to celebrate Passover annually to remember the salvation act of God. Worship and celebration of the people of God served as one way to remember God's deeds. In the repeating of the Law before his death, Moses commanded the passing down of God's story to the next generation. "These commandments I give you today are to be upon your hearts. Impress them on your children. Talk about them when you sit at home and when you walk along the road, when you lie down and when you get up. Tie them as symbols on your hands and bind them on your foreheads. Write them on the doorframes of your houses and on your gates" (Deut. 6:6–9).

Remembrance and history became a vital part of the covenant worship of God's people. God required it. God's people were to be covenant people, but that was possible only if they remembered God and his powerful salvation.

JOSHUA AND JERICHO

The Israelites entered the promised land and started the road to conquest. The first city to conquer was Jericho. Jericho was a strategic oasis city near an important crossing place on the Jordan. Although archaeological information concerning the city during this period is meager due to erosion, evidence indicates that Jericho was a small city of approximately ten acres with walls. The routes from Jericho into the central highlands provided the Hebrews with an entry for the conquest.[1]

Joshua proved himself to be the consummate general making all the right preparations including reconnaissance work. He dispatched spies into Jericho to gather vital military information prior to the attack. The spies barely escaped with their lives and only because of the bravery and cunning of a prostitute named Rahab. She risked her own life to hide them and arrange for their escape over the city walls. Because of her heroism and faith, Rahab became an important figure in Hebrew history. She and her entire family survived the destruction of Jericho for this act of faith. In the Hebrew world at this time, the idea of corporate personality prevailed. For Rahab's act her entire family benefited with salvation. Rahab became incorporated into the Israelite nation and married a Hebrew man. Her children played an important role in God's plan, for from her line the Messiah eventually came. She is mentioned in Matthew 1:5 in the genealogy of Jesus and in Hebrews 11 in the list of heroes of the faith.

God provided the battle plan for Jericho, and certainly it must have seemed strange to the Hebrews.

> The LORD said to Joshua, "Look, I have handed Jericho, its king, and its fighting men over to you. March around the city with all the men of war, circling the city one time. Do this for six days. Have seven priests carry seven ram's-horn trumpets in front of the ark. But on the seventh day, march around the city seven times, while the priests blow the trumpets. When there is a prolonged blast of the horn and you hear its sound, have all the people give a mighty shout. Then the

---

[1] Thomas Briscoe, *The Holman Bible Atlas* (Nashville: Broadman & Holman Publishers, 1998), 77–78.

city wall will collapse, and the people will advance, each man straight ahead" (Josh. 6:2–5 HCSB).

What must the Israelites have thought when Joshua presented this battle strategy to them? Talk about unconventional warfare! Why this way? What was God trying to convey to his people and to the inhabitants of Jericho? Jericho was the first battle and as a result was critical to the attitude and confidence of the Hebrews for the rest of the conquest. By doing things God's way, the people learned certainly that God's strength and wisdom would ensure victory in Canaan. The conquest required dependence and trust in God. The Hebrews possessed impressive numbers, but their size would not take Canaan. It would be God. God also commanded the Hebrews to destroy everything in Jericho including all the people. However, all silver, gold, and valuable materials would go into the Lord's treasury for future use.

Joshua followed God's commands. The fighting men marched around Jericho on the first day one time and then went home. They repeated that each day up to the seventh. What went through the minds of the Hebrews in the processional? What are we doing? How can this possibly work? What about the conversations within the city of Jericho? They must have thought the Israelites had lost their minds. What are they doing? How can this plan possibly defeat us? The seventh day came, and the Israelite warriors kept marching until the end of the seventh round, and then the trumpet sounded, the people shouted, and the wall came down. With such exposure Jericho had little chance of survival. Israel routed and destroyed the city. God won the day for the Hebrews—his way, his plan, his strength. The lesson delivered, the word spread across Canaan of this formidable force called Israel.

ACHAN'S DISOBEDIENCE—CORPORATE JUDGMENT?

With this victory Israel moved to the next objective. The city of Ai stood in the way, and the Hebrews marched against it. However, a strange turn of events resulted in a sound defeat of the Hebrew forces. Joshua and the army reeled in confusion and questions. Why the loss? What happened? The culprit in this disaster was a man named Achan. The story says he was "unfaithful regarding the things set apart for destruction" (Josh. 7:1 HCSB). Achan took some of the silver and gold from Jericho. Even though one man stole God's treasures and broke the command, God informed Joshua that Israel had sinned. They violated the covenant and stole and deceived. The language makes clear that when one breaks the rules, all break the rules in God's eyes. As a result people died in the battle against Ai, and the Hebrews lost. It was judgment for the sin of Achan, and all suffered because of it. Just as an act of faith resulted in all of Rahab's family being saved and blessed, the idea of corporate personality applied in judgment to all of Israel as the family of God.

Why would many be punished for one man's sin? For most Westerners this story provides a real dilemma. Immediately we react with concern for fairness. We argue it is not right that others should be affected by the sin of one. However, we must understand the communal mindset of the Hebrews. With the concept of corporate personality, the Hebrews saw "self-awareness, moral and legal responsibility, blessing and trouble, reward and punishment" as both individual and corporate realities. Often the fate of families and nations was bound together even affecting the next generation. The Hebrews could use "I" and "we" interchangeably in some cases.[2] They were a nation, the family of God; and what one did affected all. They saw the group as one. God acted within this concept of corporate identity and responsibility. They would be blessed together and judged together. They were responsible for each other. This same idea applied to the cross as Jesus died for many, and his act dealt with the sins of the world. Corporate personality lays the background for the substitutionary atonement Jesus offered the world, one man paying for the sins of many. Personal responsibility existed in the world of Joshua as well. When the truth came to light, Achan was judged and killed. However, that judgment contained the corporate idea. All of his sons and daughters died as well. Maybe they were aware of the disobedience, or maybe they were punished for being part of the sinner's family—corporate responsibility.

THE DEFEAT OF AI

Joshua rebounded well and proved his prowess as a military commander in the ensuing battle at Ai. He devised a plan using the confidence given to Ai by their victory. Joshua sent thirty thousand men out at night to station them behind Ai, and the city inhabitants were unaware of this move. The thirty thousand waited for an ambush to be set up. Joshua took a force of five thousand to the city for a frontal attack and at the right time pretended to be in retreat due to losses. When the king of Ai saw the retreat, he ordered his men to open the city gates and pursue the Israelites. He wanted to deal with them once and for all. However, the opening of the gate and the evacuation of many of the fighting men gave the thirty thousand Israelites behind the city opportunity to enter the city and rout it. When their job was finished, they came out and sandwiched the army of Ai. Ai lost thousands, and the battle belonged to the Hebrews. The total number of the enemy that fell that day numbered twelve thousand, and the city was destroyed. God's people again celebrated victory.

Joshua followed this battle with the building of an altar to God on Mount Ebal. He built it according to God's directions, "an altar of uncut stones on which no iron tool has been used" (Josh. 8:31 HCSB). The people worshipped at the altar, offering burnt sacrifices and fellowship offerings. On the stones Joshua copied the Law of Moses received at Sinai. The ark of the covenant was placed in the midst with the priests, elders, officers, and judges on both sides. Joshua read every single word from the law including the blessings and curses. This event connected the conquest closely to the worship of God. God won the first battle for them as they followed his instructions. In worship Joshua intended the people to know that the entire invasion (including the victory at Ai) was guided by, empowered by, directed by

---

[2] J. Goldingay, "Corporate Personality" in *New Dictionary of Theology,* 169.

God. Following God and worshipping him qualified the Hebrews to take the land. Those who broke the law like Achan missed it. Even non-Israelites like Rahab shared in the blessing because they followed God. Canaan belonged to God, and only his followers received the blessing of it.

THE CONQUEST OF CANAAN

An understanding of Canaan and its inhabitants helps us understand the strategy and approach to the conquest. Canaan consisted of several city-states. In other words each city had its own king, own government, own territory to control, and its own god or gods. No clear unity of all the cities existed to allow a coalition of several armies to defeat one large invading army. Later, when the strength of the Hebrews became clear, some Canaanite peoples formed alliances but to no avail. The religious setting played an important role as well. The Hebrews were monotheist (the belief in one God); the Canaanites held to polytheism (many gods). Each city worshipped their own god who protected them while demanding their loyalty. This is important to the biblical story because the clash of two armies in essence became the clash between gods. As two children might argue over whose dad is stronger, armies determined the most powerful god on the battlefield. As in Egypt, when God proved his superiority over all Egyptian deities, he revealed that same power in Canaan. A vital issue in the story is the revelation of the one, true God of the universe and all nations—the God who will bless the entire world through his people. This is the central truth of the biblical story.

Joshua's strategy, corresponding to the information above, was to divide and conquer. Joshua determined to cut across the middle of the land and conquer the south first and then the north, one area at a time. Occasionally Joshua encountered alliances. In the middle of Canaan, the Amorite king of Jerusalem formed an alliance with four other Amorite cities (Hebron, Jarmuth, Lachish, and Eglon) to face the Hebrews. Joshua defeated the Amorites with the aid of God who sent a hailstorm killing more Amorites than died in battle. God even made the sun stand still to allow more time. From this battle Joshua and the Israelites moved to the south, defeating the cities there, and then to the north.

JUDGMENT ON CANAAN

One issue that usually troubles twenty-first-century readers concerning the invasion of Canaan is the extensive destruction delivered on those conquered by the Hebrews. God instructed Israel to destroy everyone at Jericho including women and children. On the surface this appears to be a genocide approach, which raises eyebrows today, especially with similar travesties occurring in our world. What explanation could there possibly be?

First, judgment for sin seems to be part of the explanation. When Abraham received his call and the covenant with God, he also learned something about the future. God informed Abraham that a time would come when Abraham's seed would be enslaved in another land and then return to the promised land. "In the fourth generation your descendants will come back here, for the sin of the Amorites has not yet reached its full measure" (Gen. 15:16). Some interpret this passage and the invasion to mean that the sin of the Canaanite people finally reached its full measure, and God used the Hebrews to judge them. Even if that is the case, it still seems harsh for children to be included. However, remember the corporate personality concept. The sin of the parents affected the children.

A second possibility relates to God's wrath and Canaanite barbarism. The peoples of Canaan may not have considered the practice of killing women and children to be such an unusual one. Most likely Canaan and the surrounding lands practiced barbaric activities in their own warfare. They sacrificed humans in religious ceremonies and treated their enemies in the harshest ways. God deals with people in their own situations and eventually leads them to better places and actions. We know God is a God of love by nature but also a God of justice. His judgment, even though always tempered by mercy and compassion, appears more common in the Old Testament part of the story. What seems inappropriate to us may have been normal and acceptable to the people of Canaan and the Hebrews.

Another option concerns the religious purity of the Hebrews. Joshua's last speech warned the Israelites about the Canaanites who remained among them in the land. Since the Hebrews failed to destroy all the Canaanites, several remained among them. The Canaanites practiced fertility cultic worship which included immorality. In addition, their values and way of life differed from what God expected of the Hebrews. God wanted to make sure the Canaanites did not negatively influence his people. Joshua reinforced that idea, "Do not associate with these nations remaining among you. Do not call on the names of their gods or make an oath to them; do not worship them or bow down to them" (Josh. 23:6–7 HCSB). Judges 1 notes that Ephraim, Zebulun, and Asher failed to drive out the Canaanites in their land, and they suffered later because of that failure. Obviously these non-Hebrews presented a risk to the Hebrews spiritually and morally. Had they been annihilated, the risk would have been removed.

However, remember one truth. God's mercy showed up regularly in the story along with his harsh judgment. Those who turned to God survived and were incorporated into the Hebrew family, even non-Israelites. Rahab provided the example for this truth. Later the Gibeonites formed an alliance with the Israelites and lived. God judged sin but accepted those who turned to him.[3]

These options individually may not contain the full answer to the dilemma, but together they help. From all indications the Canaanites sinned in the worst manner possible, and sin according to God required serious judgment. Their time was complete, and the Hebrews conquered them.

---

[3] For a discussion of this issue see Danny Hays, "The Historical Books" in *The Story of Israel: A Biblical Theology* (Downers Grove: InterVarsity Press, 2004), 55–56.

THE DIVISION OF THE LAND

With the conquest completed, the land belonged again to God's people. The allotment of land to each tribe was accomplished by casting of lots. Moses had already promised land to two and one-half tribes on the east side of the Jordan but required them to help conquer the land. Following the conquest the tribes received their land. Joshua specifically gave Caleb Hebron as his inheritance, a well-deserved honor in light of his faithfulness.

Then each tribe settled its allotted land. Judah and Simeon settled in the south. Dan, Ephraim, Benjamin, and part of Manasseh took the middle section of Palestine. Asher, Zebulun, Issachar, and Naphtali acquired land in the north; and Reuben, Gad, and the other half of Manasseh's tribe settled east of the Jordan as promised by Moses. God had a different plan for Levi. The Levites were given cities and the pastures around them in each of the tribal settlements. Six of those Levite cites were designated as cities of refuge. When a Hebrew unwittingly killed another, he could flee to these cities in order to escape an avenging relative of the deceased. The location of these six cities made them accessible to everyone in Palestine and east of the Jordan (Trans Jordan). Israel lived again in the land of Abraham.

THINGS TO CONSIDER

This period of Hebrew history portrays a powerful and faithful God who fulfilled his promises to Abraham and Moses. The people returned to the promised land due to the guidance and strength of God. He began the invasion by giving Jericho to the Israelites without the need for a military attack on the city. This part of the story also laid the groundwork for the stormy existence of the Hebrews in their land. The second battle was lost due to a violation of God's command (Achan), and the invasion ended with the failure to completely rid the land of the Canaanites. This failure provided the negative influence evident in the next part of God's story. Once again it is clear: God remained faithful, but his people were not. God did not give up on them, and his mercy continued to bless them.

STUDY QUESTIONS

1. What does God ask the Hebrews to do in order to remember history, and why is that important?
2. Why is Rahab important to the story?
3. What is corporate identity and responsibility? Why is this concept hard for Westerners?
4. How did the Hebrews conquer Canaan, and what mistakes did they make?

ACT 2

The Period of the Judges

J oshua ended his career by refocusing the Israelites on the covenant with God. First, he delivered a farewell speech to the leaders. In it he encouraged them to be strong and careful to obey all that was written in the Book of the Law. He directed them not to turn to the left or the right of the way of God. Joshua also warned them against associating with the Canaanites who continued to live among the Hebrews. The Canaanite religion and lifestyle endangered the Hebrew religion and way of life under God. Joshua promised that if they allied themselves with the pagan groups still residing in Canaan, God would not give the Hebrews victories. "They will become a snare and a trap for you, a scourge for your sides and thorns in your eyes, until you disappear from this good land the LORD your God has given you" (Josh. 23:13 HCSB). Joshua also warned the leaders about the covenant of God. "If you break the covenant of the Lord your God, which He commanded you, and go and worship other gods, and bow down to them, the Lord's anger will burn against you, and you will quickly disappear from this good land He has given you" (Josh. 23:16). Unfortunately the Israelites did not heed this advice. Eventually their involvement in the ways of the Canaanites caused them to lose the land.

Joshua made his own plans clear to Israel. He assembled all the tribes at Shechem and summoned the leaders. Then Joshua delivered a message from God to the gathering, recounting the history of their deliverance and God's blessings. He called them to renew the covenant, and they all agreed. "We certainly will not abandon the LORD" (Josh. 24:16). Joshua made his choice clear. Whether the Israelites worshipped God, he intended to. "As for me and my family, we will worship the LORD" (Josh. 24:15). He issued the challenge, and the people vowed before Joshua and God to obey the Lord only. But words are not sufficient. Yahweh required action. After Joshua's death the Hebrews entered the most dreadful time of their history because they forgot the promise made to God and Joshua.

THREE HUNDRED YEARS OF DISOBEDIENCE, JUDGMENT, AND DELIVERANCE

The Hebrews conquered and took possession of the new land. Under a system called theocracy, God ruled over his people through judges and priests who carried out his commands. These two groups administered the religious and civil duties. No central capital or unified army existed. God and the covenant (with the Law) provided, or at least should have provided, the glue which held the twelve tribes together as the people of God.

The plan worked poorly; in fact it didn't work at all. The Israelites did not function well under theocracy. The obstinate Israelites constantly rebelled. The end result was a horrible cycle of sin and judgment which lasted for three hundred years. The cycle went as follows: the people sinned usually with idolatry and the immorality associated with it (the gods of the Canaanites), and as judgment God sent an oppressor who conquered, stole from, or harassed the people. When the situation grew unbearable, the people cried out to God for mercy and help. God raised up a judge who led the people into battle against the oppressor, and victory was won. A time of peace and prosperity followed until the sin returned and the cycle repeated itself over and over.

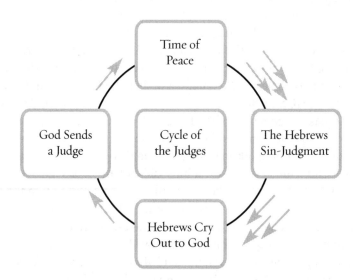

Hebrew sin multiplied when they involved themselves with the Canaanite idols. Many of the original inhabitants of Canaan practiced fertility cults. One of the most popular was Baal worship. The Canaanites worshipped Baal who was god of the sky and rain. His major rivals were Yamm (god of the sea) and Mot (god of death). The Baal myth concerned a deadly battle between Baal and these two gods. If Baal won, a good spring followed with fertile soil for good crops. If Mot triumphed, then death and sterility followed—drought, locusts, or another major disaster. In addition, the myth contains stories of sexual relations between Baal and the female counterpart as well as with animals.[4] As a result sexual immorality became closely connected to the worship of Baal—temple prostitutes, etc. The fact that the Canaanites lived in the midst of the Hebrews increased exposure to this cult. The Hebrews were drawn into idolatry (worshipping other gods) and immorality. When this happened, an oppressor would deliver judgment, and the cycle started over.

THE JUDGES

Many judges presided over parts of Palestine in the three-hundred-year period. The cycle played an important role in each of their stories. In each case the people committed sin, a different oppressor arrived, and the people cried out. God sent them a judge who saved them. The cycle usually concerned a particular locale in Canaan. Judges used various methods to accomplish the task of saving the people. The following are judges listed in the book of Judges: Othniel, Ehud, Deborah and Barak, Gideon, Abimelech, Jair, Tolar, Jephthah, Ibzan, Elan, Abdon, Samson, and Shamgar. Let's look at just a few and see how their stories fit into the larger drama.

EHUD

"The Israelites again did what was evil in the LORD's sight" (Judg. 3:12 HCSB). In this case the Moabites rose up as oppressors, and King Eglon required a tribute to be paid regularly. The Moabites controlled the Israelites for eighteen years, and the oppression was evidently intense. Israel cried out to God, and he raised up a Benjamite named Ehud to deliver them. Ehud fashioned for himself a double-edged sword only eighteen inches long and strapped it to his thigh under his cloak. He delivered the tribute to Eglon and to get a private audience informed Eglon he had a secret. No one can resist a secret; and when the doors were closed, Ehud removed the sword and thrust it into Eglon's rather rotund belly. The text says the king of Moab was so obese that his fat closed in over the handle of the sword so that it was not quickly noticeable that he had been stabbed. Ehud escaped through the window, and the oppressor was dead. When he crossed the Jordan, Ehud sounded the ram's horn and called the Israelite army together. They struck down ten thousand Moabites and won the day and freedom. God provided for them again. The land was peaceful for eighty years.

---

[4] James I. Packer, Merrill C. Tenney, William White, *The Bible Almanac* (Nashville: Thomas Nelson Publishers, 1980), 146–47.

DEBORAH

Deborah served as the only woman judge but not because she sought the job. The Israelites did evil in God's eyes, and an oppressor arrived. Jabin, the king of Canaan, and his commander of the army, Sisera, attacked the Israelites. The oppression grew so harsh that the Israelites called out to God, and he spoke to a prophet and judge named Deborah. She called on a soldier named Barak and told him to deploy his troops and she would lure Sisera to him and ensure the victory. Barak refused to go unless Deborah accompanied him. She agreed but informed the military commander that he would receive none of the honor for the victory; instead it would go to a woman. The battle went well for Israel because "the Lord threw Sisera, all his charioteers, and all his army into confusion with the sword before Barak" (Judg. 4:15). Sisera fled on foot and ended up in the tent of Jael, the wife of a Kenite. She offered hospitality because her family had good relations with King Jabin. However, while Sisera slept, Jael hammered a tent peg through his temple, and of course he died. The stories of the judges seem brutal, but once again it was a barbaric culture and setting. The Israelites enjoyed peace again under Deborah, and she and Jael received the honor for the battle and victory. In the stories of the individual judges, most of them possessed character flaws unbecoming a judge or representative of God. However, Deborah ranks as the most faithful judge of all with the exception of Samuel. Deborah sat in judgment as God's representative for forty years.

GIDEON

Once again Israel sinned, and the Midianites came up from the desert to harass them. Every year when the fields reached harvest time, Midianite armies arrived on camels and confiscated the crop, leaving the Hebrews hungry and in despair. While Gideon hid in a winepress threshing some wheat the Midianites missed, the angel of God enlisted him as the next deliverer. He didn't want the job. God convinced him, and Gideon's first task was to rid his father's house of all idols and worship places that served as the cause for the current judgment. Gideon reluctantly complied. Gideon needed more verification of the power and will of God before taking on the Midianites. "If you will deliver Israel by my hand, as you said, I will put a fleece of wool here on the threshing floor. If dew is only on the fleece, and all the ground dry, I will know that you will deliver Israel by my strength, as you said" (Judg. 6:36–37). God performed this miracle for Gideon. But Gideon wanted more—reverse the miracle leaving the ground wet and the fleece dry. God accomplished that as well. Gideon became God's judge and commander.

When the army congregated, God informed Gideon that he had too many soldiers. Gideon had gathered thirty-two thousand while the Midianite army consisted of 120,000. Do the math. It seemed like Gideon needed more soldiers not fewer. However, God provided a plan to reduce the numbers. Gideon was to ask the men if they were afraid. Those who said yes were relieved. Twenty-two thousand left.

God informed Gideon that his army of ten thousand was still too large. Can you imagine what was going on in Gideon's mind? The plan this time was to take the men for a drink at the river. Those who kneeled down to drink went home. Those who gathered the water in their hands so they could drink while still remaining alert stayed—only three hundred. Now Gideon stood against an army of 120,000 with a mere three hundred men. God does math differently from Gideon.

The battle plan was simple: surround the Midianite camp of 120,000. With three hundred men that seemed impossible. Gideon divided the men into groups of one hundred and sent each group to a different place around the Midianites. Each man took a trumpet, a torch, and an empty jar to hide it in. When Gideon and his men blew their horns, everyone else would follow suit. They would shout, "The sword of the LORD and of Gideon" (Judg. 7:20 HCSB), and then shatter the jars revealing the light of the torches. The goal was to convince the enemy that the Hebrews had surrounded the camp with more than three hundred soldiers. It worked! The Midianites fled in confusion, and Israel won the day. They pursued the enemy until all were dealt with. Gideon refused to rule over the people but instructed them to allow God to rule since he had delivered them. Gideon fulfilled his role as deliverer but later became the source of apostasy for the Hebrews. He accepted gold as spoil from the battle and fashioned an ephod out of it (probably an image of Yahweh).[5] The people started worshipping it, and "it became a snare to Gideon and his family" (Judg. 8:27). No doubt this ephod served as an idol. Forty years of peace followed Gideon's work until the cycle started again.

SAMSON

The cycle repeated as the Israelites did evil in the Lord's sight, and judgment came in the form of the Philistines. Through Manoah and his wife God brought forth the next judge to deliver them. Samson had certain restrictions on him because of a Nazarite vow. He could not drink strong wine, cut his hair, or touch anything unclean. A look at his life indicates he did not keep the vow very well. He saw a young Philistine woman and desired her for his wife even though his parents protested. Samson insisted, and the marriage eventually led to an encounter with the Philistines. When the Spirit of the Lord came upon him, Samson went to Ashkelon and killed thirty Philistine men. Later when his Philistine wife's father disallowed Samson from seeing her and in fact gave her to another man, Samson sought revenge. He caught three hundred foxes and tied their tails together with a torch connecting each knot. He lit the torches and released them into the grain fields of the Philistines. This strange act burned down the grain as well as vineyards and olive groves. When the Philistines asked who perpetrated the disaster, they were told Samson did. The Philistines took out their revenge on the tribe Judah. Judah handed Samson over to the Philistines; but when he arrived at the Philistine camp, the Spirit of the Lord came upon Samson. He broke the ropes binding him and with

---

[5] J. G. G. Norman, "Gideon" in *New Bible Dictionary,* 411.

the fresh jawbone of a donkey killed one thousand Philistines. He judged in Israel for the next twenty years.

Samson fell for a woman named Delilah. The Philistines convinced her to trick Samson into revealing the secret of his strength so he could be overtaken. She tried, but Samson told lies, saying that if he was bound with fresh bowstrings or new ropes he could not break them. In each case he easily freed himself. Finally, he told her the secret: his hair could not be cut. As Samson slept, Delilah cut his hair, allowing the Philistines to subdue him. Samson possessed no strength to resist. They seized him, gouged out his eyes, and put him in prison. Eventually the hair grew back, and Samson prayed to God to allow his revenge. Finally, the opportunity came when the Philistines brought him from prison to the temple for their entertainment. Samson asked a young man to lead him to a place where he could feel the pillars of the temple and lean against them to rest. When he was positioned between the pillars, Samson pressed against them with his renewed strength; and they collapsed, bringing down the temple upon the Philistine capturers. His revenge and the defeat of the Philistines came with one blow.

LESSONS FROM THE JUDGES

Studying the judges, we learn several things. For the most part they were not all that worthy to be leaders, especially men like Samson. Many of them were arrogant, violent, selfish, lustful, and disobedient. However, God still used them to accomplish some specific tasks. They served to deliver the people and judge over them. However, their lack of spiritual leadership resulted in a downward slide, and Israel ended the period looking more like the Canaanites than the people of God. Deborah served as an exception. We learn in this portion of the story that God uses all kinds of people to carry out his work. In spite of the poor character in most judges, God's will was not thwarted. Each of the judges accomplished his or her task under the power of the Spirit of God. He came upon them empowering them to do great and mighty things—the ability to defeat 120,000 with three hundred, the ability to kill one thousand with only the jawbone of a donkey. God's strength allowed this, and the judges served as God's instruments.

We also learn that even though God did deliver the people when they cried out for mercy, it resulted only in a temporary reversal of their sinful ways; and the cycle repeated itself. Perhaps the best phrase to sum up the Period of the Judges is found in Judges 17:6: "In those days there was no king in Israel; everyone did whatever he wanted" (HCSB).That included the neglect of the covenant and the law. This is why this period is generally referred to as the Dark Ages. In the end the Hebrews became like the Canaanites. They thought like them, lived like them, and worshipped like them. The unique people God wanted to create passed from the scene with a few exceptions. Things were so bad that the Hebrews wondered if God was doing anything. However, God was at work and out of this bad situation brought forth the family which would eventually give us the lineage of the Messiah. He was preparing to bring forth David.

RUTH AND BOAZ

The story of Ruth shows how during a bad time in Hebrew history God prepared to bless the Hebrews through a Moabite woman. Moab was a land of fertile fields and enough rain to cultivate them. When a famine struck Canaan, a man named Elimelech along with his wife Naomi and two sons, Mahlon and Chilion, moved from Canaan to Moab to wait out the crisis. While there the sons married Moabite women, Ruth and Orpah. All the men of the family died leaving three widows. Naomi decided to return home and encouraged the daughters-in-law to stay and marry Moabite men. However, Ruth refused, saying she would not leave Naomi. "For wherever you go, I will go, and wherever you live, I will live; your people will be my people, and your God will be my God" (Ruth 1:16 HCSB). Orpah stayed, but Ruth returned to Palestine with Naomi.

In that day two women without husbands fit into the category of most needy. The custom of the day allowed the poor to glean in the fields of the wealthy (meaning some of the harvest was intentionally left for their benefit). Ruth took advantage of this custom and caught the attention of Boaz, the owner of the field and a relative of Naomi's. Another custom called for a brother or nearest relative to take the wife of a man who died. Although not next in line, Boaz inquired of the one who had the right to wed Ruth. Reaching an agreement Boaz married Ruth. This represents an important turn in the biblical story because Ruth and Boaz had a son named Obed who had a son named Jesse who had a son named David. David became the most important king in Hebrew history, and from his line came the final solution to the sin issue—Jesus. Once again the God who promised Abraham that his seed would bless the entire world incorporated a non-Israelite into the formula, first Rahab and now Ruth. Both are listed in the genealogies of Jesus in the Gospels. So out of the darkest time God brought a silver lining. This disobedience of the Israelites did not hinder God's plan.

THINGS TO CONSIDER

The idolatrous practices developed in the Period of the Judges set a pattern that affected the Hebrews for centuries. Would the Hebrews be faithful to God and obey the covenant? Of course not! The story continued to be an up-and-down spiritual battle with the Israelites often turning their back on God and his ways. God maintained patience with them and carried out the plan. The sin problem remained pesky and the grace of God strong. God used all kinds of people to accomplish his task. They were reluctant, rebellious, power hungry, and often immoral people; but God's power proved greater than their weaknesses. God's nature continued to unfold. His Spirit empowered and directed. His patience and compassion repeatedly surfaced when the people cried out. He sent a deliverer. The Period of the Judges revealed an ebb-and-flow pattern of the relationship of the Hebrews with God.

STUDY QUESTIONS

1. What was the cycle of the Judges, and why did it repeat itself?
2. What was the character of the Judges, and how did that affect Israel?
3. How would you compare Deborah, Gideon, and Samson?
4. How is the story of Ruth important to the biblical story of redemption?

EPISODE FIVE

ISRAEL GETS A KING

ACT 1

SAMUEL AND SAUL

The Period of the Judges ended with an adjustment in government for the Hebrews. A period of unification of all the tribes under a king changed the way Israel lived and thought. They became like the nations surrounding them. This new era was ushered in by two last judges who also served as priests.

Israel recognized several offices established by God. As already discussed, judges served as civil servants of God before the people to settle disputes and lead the people. Israel depended on priests to take care of the religious elements of the law—sacrifices, offerings, and worship. These were the people who intervened between God and his people. Of course, the character of the priests affected the efficacy of that role tremendously. Two more offices become clearer in this part of the story. The prophet served as God's spokesman to deliver his message to individuals or the people. More will be said about prophets later. The change of government brought in a king who took over the role of the judge and ruled over the people as God's representative, or at least that was the intent. One man combined three of these offices and acted as the transition to the unified kingdom of Israel. His name was Samuel.

ELI AND SAMUEL

Eli served as judge and priest for Israel in a time when corruption grew daily even within his own family. He exemplified the best and the worst of a man. Eli evidently acted with great integrity and diligence in the roles of judge and priest. He remained faithful to God and obeyed. However, Eli fared poorly as a father. His sons, Phineas and Hophni, acted wickedly in the face of God and the people. They saw the position of priest as one designed to take advantage of the people rather than serve spiritual needs. Because of their sin, they and Eli experienced God's judgment. However, before that occurred, Eli was given one more valuable task from God—to train Samuel.

A faithful Hebrew woman named Hannah reached old age without bearing a son, a great embarrassment for a Jewish woman. In her culture the purpose of a woman was to bear and raise children for her husband. In disgrace Hannah prayed to God for relief with such intensity that Eli assumed she was drunk. Hannah promised God that if she had a son, she would offer him for service to God. She dedicated her baby as a Nazarite even before his birth (1 Sam. 1:11). God answered the prayer, and Samuel was born. At the appointed time Hannah delivered Samuel to Eli in Shiloh. Eli became his guardian, guide, teacher, and mentor. In a sense Eli received a second chance to mold a young boy into a good man. He did a better job this time.

Samuel learned quickly. The biblical story (1 Sam. 2:11, "ministered before the Lord") may indicate that at an early age Samuel served as priest under Eli. He even slept before the ark of the Lord. Perhaps this is why God would speak directly to him as opposed to mediating through Eli. While Eli judged, a word from the Lord or a vision was rare (1 Sam. 3:1). In addition, early on Samuel proved himself to be faithful to God's covenant. God would communicate with Samuel who was committed to the covenant during a time when few were. In addition, Samuel was granted the role of prophet by God and as such became God's spokesperson.

One night as Samuel slept, he heard a voice calling him. Unaware of the source he assumed it was Eli. He went to Eli only to find that he had not called. This happened a second time and then a third. Finally, Eli realized that God was trying to communicate with his young apprentice. He advised Samuel that the next time he heard the voice, he should respond with "Speak, LORD, for your servant is listening" (1 Sam. 3:9). Samuel received the first of many messages from God, and it was a disturbing one. God informed him that Eli's sons were about to receive judgment for their horrible sins, and Eli would also die. Eli insisted on hearing God's message and, although shocked, accepted the verdict. Shortly after, the Philistines attacked Israel, defeating them and taking the ark of the covenant (an indication of deteriorating spiritual condition in Palestine). Phineas and Hophni both died in the battle along with thirty thousand others. At the time Eli was ninety-eight years old and obese. Upon hearing the news of the ark and the demise of his sons, he fell back in his chair and broke his neck. The prophecy fulfilled, Samuel became the next and last judge of Israel. He also served as priest and prophet bridging the gap between the Period of the Judges and the kingdom of Israel.

The ark stood as the symbol of the people of Israel and their God. One would think the Hebrews would have stopped at nothing to recapture it. The biblical story reveals no evidence of that attempt. Israel no longer cared enough to try. God himself returned his ark to the land. In the hands of the pagan Philistines, the ark brought curse not blessing. Israel lost the war, but God exhibited through the ark his ability to handle the enemies alone. The ark arrived in the Philistine city of Ashdod first, and the next morning the idol to Dagon (the Philistine's god) lay on his face in his own temple. The Philistines replaced it only to discover it prone and broken before the ark of the Lord the next day. As God exhibited his sovereignty in Egypt through the plagues, he also reigned over Dagon and all the pagan gods. While Israel could not defeat Dagon's people, God alone defeated the pagan god. Then God afflicted the people of Ashdod with tumors, and they concluded the ark could not remain. "The ark of Israel's God must not stay here with us, because His hand is severe against us and our god Dagon" (1 Sam. 5:7 HCSB). Even the Philistines recognized the power of the God of Israel. They moved the ark to Gath. Then the Lord chastised the people of Gath with tumors, and they moved it to Ekron. Many died or were stricken with tumors. Finally to rid themselves of the suffering, the Philistines returned it to Israel with an offering. Upon seeing it, the Hebrews in Beth-shemesh worshipped and offered sacrifices but made a grave error by looking into the ark. This was probably another sign of their disdain for God's Law. God struck down seventy men for this indiscretion. The ark settled in the house of Abinidab, and his son Eleazer was consecrated to care for it. God's power followed the ark, which of course symbolized the agreement with the people and God's promises as well as his warnings.

THE PEOPLE DEMAND A KING

As noted, Samuel occupied the roles of judge, priest, and prophet before the Israelites. He acted as a circuit judge using Ramah as his home base and traveling to Bethel, Gilgal, and Mizpah, judging all of Israel from those locations. However, when Samuel grew old, he appointed his sons, Joel and Abijah, as judges in Beersheba. Unfortunately, they did not walk in the ways of their father. They cheated people, took bribes, and perverted the justice they were to protect. Obviously, Samuel followed in the ways of Eli as a parent. He could not control his own sons. This theme will repeat itself many times in the story, a person who serves God well but parents poorly.

The Israelites grew weary of this situation and issued an unusual and disturbing request to Samuel: they wanted a king. The elders approached Samuel at Ramah. "Look, you are old, and your sons do not follow your example. Therefore, appoint a king to judge us the same as all the other nations have" (1 Sam. 8:5 HCSB). The desire to be like other nations prompted their request. But this was not Samuel's decision. Israel belonged to God. They were his covenant people even though they didn't act like it. Yet Samuel took the request personally, feeling that it was a direct attack on him. When he spoke to God about it, God encouraged him. God told Samuel that it was not a rejection of him but rather of God. The issue at hand was the rejection of God as king and ruler of his people. In other words, theocracy didn't work well for the Hebrews, and they rejected that form of leadership. This was not a surprise since the track record for Israel was clear. "They are doing the same thing to you that they have done to Me, since the day I brought them out of Egypt until this day, abandoning Me and worshiping other gods" (1 Sam. 8:8 HCSB). So God instructed Samuel to warn them about the normal demands of a king.

Samuel returned to the people and gave them the warning. A king demands his rights. He takes sons and puts them in the military, takes daughters for servants, and taxes the constituency to pay for the army and palace. He takes your best fields and even takes the servants of his people. Samuel warned that eventually they would cry out to God because of the oppression caused by a king, but God would not listen. The people obstinately refused to hear Samuel's argument and demanded a king. In fact, they admitted they wanted a king to lead them into battle against other nations. That would indeed happen. God granted the request and sent Samuel out to anoint a new king and begin the next phase of the story of redemption.

SAUL

If appearance counts, Saul looked the part of the king. "There was no one more impressive among the Israelites than he. He stood a head taller than anyone else" (1 Sam. 9:2). While searching for some wandering donkeys belonging to his father, Saul searched out Samuel for help. Samuel assured Saul the donkeys were found and invited him to a banquet and treated him like royalty. The next day, before he sent him on his way, Samuel anointed Saul with oil; and Saul became the first king of Israel. The Spirit of God took control of Saul and empowered him to serve. Samuel summoned all the people to Mizpah and announced his selection. When the people saw that Saul looked like a king, they shouted, "Long live the king!" (1 Sam. 10:24), and a new era began.

Saul set up his home in Gibeah. Some rejected his leadership, but he said nothing. In fact, Saul never ruled over all the Israelites because some were not ready to be united under one king. He led Israel against the Ammonites and scored a great victory, winning more people over to his side. Samuel called the people together for worship and sacrifices and restated Saul's reign. Samuel continued as priest and prophet, but now the Hebrews had a king who ruled over them as other countries.

Saul's reign began well, but his weak character soon became clear. Theocracy remained as the overarching government of Israel, and the king was to represent God and his Law. Saul struggled with this. Even though he looked the part, Saul's heart was not right for the task. Saul committed three grave sins which eventually cost him his throne. First, Saul usurped the role as priest when that role did not belong to him. He prepared for battle against the Philistines, and Samuel told him to wait until he arrived to offer sacrifices for the men and the battle. Saul waited but grew impatient. Finally in frustration he offered the sacrifices himself, an act reserved only for the priest. "Samuel said to Saul, 'You have been foolish. You have not kept the command which the LORD your God gave you. It was at this time that the LORD would have permanently established your reign over Israel, but now your reign will not endure'" (1 Sam. 13:13–14). God counted this act of sin as a serious breach of the covenant, and it resulted in the loss of Saul's dynasty. After him no others from his family would reign.

The second mistake came in battle with the Philistines. Saul, desperate to defeat these people from the west, issued a rash oath which bound his men to an unwise act. He forced his soldiers to fast until the enemy was defeated. This made sense to Saul, but battle requires energy, and such an oath put Saul's men at risk. Was it not the first task of God's leader to take care of his people? Saul's son, Jonathan, unaware of the oath, ate honey and gained strength for battle. He declared the folly of the oath before the soldiers. Perhaps Saul even lost good men because they grew weak in the battle. This also resulted in an incomplete defeat of the Philistines.

The last and most serious mistake of Saul involved open disobedience against God. This act represented an open break of the covenant with God. Covenant people are to obey first and foremost. How did Saul disobey? As Israel faced the Amalekites, Samuel issued specific directions to Saul. Because of the harshness of the Amalekites toward Israel, Saul was to destroy completely everything and everyone including women, children, animals, and the king. Saul's army struck down the Amalekites and captured King Agag. Although the Israelites destroyed most of the Amalekite possessions and people, under Saul's orders they spared the best sheep and rams and took the king captive. Saul openly disobeyed the word of the Lord. Samuel arrived to investigate; and when he asked Saul about the battle, Saul lied, saying he followed all the directives. Samuel questioned concerning the bleating of the sheep he heard in the background and caught Saul in the lie. The sentence was passed. "Look: to obey is better than sacrifice . . . for rebellion is like the sin of divination, and defiance is like wickedness and idolatry. Because you have rejected the word of the LORD, he has rejected you as king" (1 Sam. 15:22–23). Samuel promised he would never visit Saul again since God rejected him as king, and that promise held true. The Spirit of God left Saul.

STUDY QUESTIONS

1. Who was Eli, and what were his strengths and weaknesses?
2. What happened to the Philistines when they captured the ark?
3. Why did the people want a king, and what did Samuel warn them about?
4. What were the sins of Saul, and what did they cost him?

ACT 2

DAVID THE KING

A NEW KING—DAVID

With Saul's reign ending, God sent Samuel to anoint a new king, even while the old one still sat on the throne. To keep Saul from knowing, Samuel offered a sacrifice of a young cow and invited Jesse. Ruth and Boaz were part of the lineage of David. (Ruth and Boaz had Obed, Obed had Jesse, and Jesse had David.) Samuel consecrated Jesse and his sons for the sacrifice and one by one searched for the next king. The first son looked like a king as Saul had, but God instructed Samuel. "Do not look at his appearance or his stature, because I have rejected him. Man does not see what the LORD sees, for man sees what is visible, but the LORD sees the heart" (1 Sam. 16:7 HCSB). Samuel went through the sons but did not find God's choice. He asked Jesse if there were other sons, and Jesse informed him that his youngest was tending the flocks. Samuel told Jesse to send for him. David "had beautiful eyes and a healthy, handsome appearance," but he was still young. However, God instructed Samuel to anoint him as the next king, and the Spirit of God came upon David. The next king waited to take the crown.

David was a brave and conscientious young man. He tended the sheep and protected them from lions and bears. He also played the harp. Because God's Spirit had departed from Saul, he was distraught; and his servants believed music would sooth him. Saul commanded them to find someone who could play, and one of the young men suggested David, who played the harp as well as being a "warrior, eloquent, handsome and of the LORD" (1 Sam. 16:18 HCSB) was with him. David came to sooth Saul's spirit when it was troubled.

At this time Israel warred against the Philistines. The Philistines boasted one champion fighter named Goliath whose armor probably weighed as much as a boy the age of David. Goliath stood taller by far than the average man of the day. The height of this warrior affects the story. Some Old Testament manuscripts (Masoretic Text) fix the height at "six cubits and a span" or nine feet nine inches while others (LXX Codex) set it at "four cubits and a span" or six feet nine inches.[1] Both heights would put Goliath well above the average height for the day. However, if the shorter height applied, then the Philistine was not much larger than Saul, signifying Saul's unwillingness to trust God and fight while the smaller, younger David trusted God completely. Which one deserved to be king? The story becomes one of comparison between David and Saul to highlight their faith and obedience or lack thereof. Either way Goliath towered over David, and to face the giant required faith and courage on his part.

Goliath challenged the Hebrews to send out their champion to fight and determine the battle. If Goliath won, the Hebrews would serve the Philistines and vice versa. No Israelite dared face Goliath, including David's brothers who served in the army of Saul. For forty days Goliath came forth and issued the challenge, and no Israelite accepted. Early in this encounter David was at home and did not realize the situation. He discovered the crisis when his father sent him back to his brothers with supplies and to check on them. When David heard the challenge, he was appalled that it went unanswered. David offered his services to fight Goliath. Saul discouraged him because of his size and age. But David showed his spiritual character and maturity in his response to Saul. After describing his feats in killing lions and bears, David compared Goliath's fate to the animals. "This uncircumcised Philistine will be like one of them, for he has defiled the armies of the living God. The LORD who rescued me from the paw of the lion and the paw of the bear will rescue me from the hand of this Philistine" (1 Sam. 17:36–37 HCSB). Saul agreed and offered David his armor, which virtually swallowed the boy. David refused and instead selected stones for his sling shot and set out to face the giant. Goliath taunted David with threats, but David remained strong in the Lord. "Today the LORD will hand you over to me" (1 Sam. 17:46). David was correct. Goliath fell when the stone hit him in the head, and David used the Philistine's own sword to cut off his head. Israel won the battle because of the faith and bravery of David, the secretly anointed king. His fame spread quickly, and because of it jealousy grew in Saul.

Eventually Saul turned against David and sought to kill him. Jonathan, Saul's son, became good friends with David and protected him. David remained loyal to Saul even though in God's eyes David was king. He even had an opportunity to kill Saul but did not. The battles with the Philistines did not end, and in one decisive battle Saul and Jonathan died. David grieved over the death of his king and best friend, but the way for David's reign was cleared.

---

[1] For a discussion of Goliath's height, see Carl S. Ehrlich, "Goliath" in *The Anchor Bible Dictionary,* ed. by David Noel Freedman (New York: Doubleday, 1992), 1073.

THE DAVIDIC COVENANT

The Jews referred to David's reign as the Golden Age of Hebrew history. David was the king they dreamed of when they requested one from Samuel. He united all the tribes under one king, and Israel became a great nation. He conquered all the surrounding enemies. Of course most of what David did was through brute force. He captured Jerusalem from the Jebusites and made it the new capital of his kingdom, a key achievement since the city of Jerusalem to this day stands as the most significant city for all Jews. David brought the ark of the covenant to Jerusalem with the intention of building a permanent temple for it. This pleased God, but the temple would be left to David's son to build. When the ark arrived, David danced before it and worshipped with joy. He truly loved God and sought to please him. David worshipped God, wrote psalms, and conquered in God's power. David expanded the kingdom to include all the tribal lands as well as areas surrounding Canaan. He came to represent Israel, and the nations feared him.

David received from God the greatest promise and honor. According to God's plan and promises to Abraham, a solution to the sin problem would eventually come through the Hebrews. David represented the family lineage for that promised solution. God established his covenant with David and promised him the honor. The Abrahamic covenant came close to its fulfillment in David's reign and certainly in David's dynasty. However, David would not build the temple for God. Nathan, the prophet of God, came to David with the message. Nathan explained that even though David would not build the house for the Lord, God would bless David. "The LORD Himself will make a house for you. When your time comes and you rest with your fathers, I will raise up after you your descendant, who will come from your body, and I will establish his kingdom. He will build a house for My name, and I will establish the throne of his kingdom forever. . . . Your house and kingdom will endure before Me forever, and your throne will be established forever" (2 Sam. 7:11–13, 16 HCSB).

God promised that David's dynasty and legacy would last forever. Jesus came from the line of David and established his kingdom which lasts forever. He is the final solution to sin. David was indeed blessed. He was described as being a man after God's own heart. Why? Saul rebelled, but David brought Israel back to Yahweh. He brought the symbol of the covenant back to Israel, and he himself exemplified its significance to the Hebrews by dancing and worshipping upon its arrival. God took center stage again, the place Yahweh deserved among covenant people. Jerusalem became the holy city of worship, and sacrifices became common again.

DAVID'S WEAKNESSES

David was human like the other heroes of the biblical story. He experienced lust and as a result committed some heinous sins. Of course, King David could have any woman in the kingdom for his wife and had already married Michel, Saul's daughter. Yet one night, as David walked on the roof of the palace, he observed a beautiful woman bathing in another building. David desired her and sent for her. Bathsheba was a married woman but did not refuse the king's call. David slept with her that evening, and this immorality led to a pregnancy for Bathsheba. She sent word of her condition to the king.

Bathsheba's husband, Uriah, served in David's army and at that time was on the battlefield facing the Ammonites. David's fear of discovery led him to attempt a cover-up. He sent for Uriah to return in hopes he would sleep with Bathsheba and thereby assume the baby was his own. Uriah, a man of principle, refused to enjoy the comfort of his own home and wife while his men remained in the field. With the plan thwarted Uriah returned to the battle. David sent word to Joab the commander to place Uriah in the fiercest part of the fighting. Uriah died, and David assumed the cover-up was complete. One sin of lust and adultery led David to deceit, abuse of power, and eventually murder. David took Bathsheba to be his wife and evidently forgot about the incident. "However, the LORD considered what David had done to be evil" (2 Sam. 11:27 HCSB).

NATHAN DELIVERED GOD'S JUDGMENT

God did not let David's sin pass. Just as Moses paid for his sin, so would David suffer judgment. God sent his prophet Nathan to deliver a message to David. Nathan did so by telling David a story about two men, one wealthy and one poor. The wealthy man with many flocks entertained a guest. Instead of using one of his own sheep to feed him, he stole the poor man's only lamb, which had become a family pet. David was infuriated over such an injustice and vowed to mete out justice in this case. Nathan replied, "You are the Man!" King David, who could have many women, stole Uriah's wife and had him killed. David realized his sin and confessed it. The judgment was harsh. The baby that Bathsheba carried would not live. Bathsheba gave birth, and the baby died on the seventh day. Once again the judgment seems harsh, but the mercy and grace of God were also involved. God kept his promise and allowed David to remain as king because of his repentance and confession. In addition, David and Bathsheba had another son named Solomon. Solomon would carry on the Davidic line and serve as the next king.

The story of David's sin and the way he dealt with it is an important example for all people. David sinned as all do, and sin carries consequence—death. He repented of the sin and confessed it to God. The result of such repentance is forgiveness. Redemption came to David when he admitted his sin against God and sought healing from God alone.

FAMILY PROBLEMS

David also suffered from the same weakness Eli and Samuel had. David's children were a mess, and David lived with this strife. One of his sons, Amnon, raped one of his daughters, Tamar. Absalom killed Amnon for this transgression. Could things get worse? Yes, Absalom decided to rebel against his father and usurp the throne. He gathered a large number of fighting men and for a while had David on the run. David grieved over this turn of events but had to deal with the revolt. This civil war cost many Israelite lives and eventually Absalom's life. David defeated the rebels. Absalom rode his donkey under an oak tree, and his hair caught in the branches. He was suspended in the air by his hair. Joab thrust three spears into Absalom's heart, and the rebellion ended. David's kingdom was restored.

David lived a life of faith in God but also one filled with sin, grief, and sorrow. He was human, and yet God used this weak and sinful man to accomplish his goals and promised him an eternal throne.

A Man after God's Own Heart?

The story describes David as a man after God's own heart. How can this be said after adultery, deceit, murder, and poor parenting? In fact, were any of Saul's sins worse than those of David? So what is the difference between David and Saul? Saul never received such accolades from God or promises of an eternal kingdom. He lost his kingdom. The clue may be found in David's psalms. When David sinned with Bathsheba, he assumed all was well until Nathan paid him a visit. At that time David confessed his sin and asked for forgiveness. Psalm 51 is the record of that confession. David recognized the covenant relationship with God. He sinned against God, and therefore his only hope of redemption came through God. In the psalm David begged for God's grace and asked that his sin be washed away. He admitted that his sin was against God and he stood guilty before the Lord. David pleaded with God to "create a clean heart" and a "steadfast spirit" within him. "Save me from the guilt of bloodshed, God, the God of my salvation" (Ps. 51:14 HCSB). God alone is the source of redemption as the biblical story clearly indicates.

Psalm 32 records the result of that prayer. "How happy is the one whose transgression is forgiven, whose sin is covered!" (Ps. 32:1 HCSB). David received from God the freedom from guilt and praised God for being his hiding place and deliverer. The difference between David and Saul rested in their hearts. David truly hurt over his sin against God. He cared, and it devastated him. He dealt with it as a covenant person would. He asked for God's forgiveness and grace and recognized God's rightful place in his life. A look at Saul's life reveals little of that contriteness. His arrogance and self-will controlled him; and even when he sinned, he tried to deny it. A person after God's own heart is not sinless. Instead he is a human who sins as all humans sin but hurts and experiences guilt because of it, confesses, asks for forgiveness, and gives God his rightful place. He remembers God. David was that man.

STUDY QUESTIONS

1. What made Samuel such a good judge, prophet, and priest?
2. Why did Saul lose the kingdom?
3. How does God continue the plan of redemption through David?
4. What does the story teach us about sin, repentance, and redemption?

OUTLINE HELP

From the onset of sin God put his plan of redemption into motion. Let's look once again at the outline and see where we are in the biblical story.

THE STORY OF THE BIBLE

Creation	The story begins with God creating the world and human beings.
Crisis	Humans choose to rebel (or sin) against God. Sin brings consequences: pain, suffering, death, and separation from God. All people and all creation are affected.
Covenant	God chooses Abraham and establishes a covenant with him so that he might become the leader of a group of people who will follow God and call other people to follow God. God delights in using his people to bring the rest of the world to himself.
Calling Out	Genesis tells the story of the patriarchs: Abraham, Isaac, Jacob (Israel), and Joseph, who ends up in Egypt. In Egypt the small group of Hebrews grows into a nation and ends up in slavery. God uses Moses to deliver his people through the exodus event.
Conquest	God uses Joshua to help his people take the promised land (Canaan). After the conquest during the Period of Judges, God rules through judges in various parts of the land. This is a dark time for the Hebrews accentuated with sin, idolatry, and oppression.
Kingdom	**God's people acquire a king. Samuel is the link between the judges and the kings. Saul is the first king, followed by David and his son Solomon. God establishes a covenant with David, promising the Messiah will come through his family line and reign forever.**
Kingdom Divided	After Solomon civil war breaks out leading to a division of the kingdom: Israel, the Northern Kingdom; Judah,

	the Southern Kingdom. There are numerous kings, some good but most bad.
Captivity	Israel (Northern Kingdom) is judged for the sin of breaking the covenant when Assyria conquers it in 722 BC and Judah receives a similar judgment later when Babylon conquers it in 586 BC and takes Judah's people into exile.
Coming Home	The people return from Babylonian exile under Zerubbabel, Ezra, and Nehemiah. They rebuild the temple and focus on the law of God.
Christ	About four hundred years later God sends his Son, Jesus the Christ, to save his people from their sins, fulfilling the promise given to Abraham. Jesus is crucified, dies, is raised from the dead, and ascends into heaven to return again later.
Church	Those who accept Jesus become part of the church, the people of God made up of both Jews and Gentiles. God continues to use his people to extend his offer of salvation to a sinful world.
Consummation	God closes history with a final victory over evil. Those who have rejected God will suffer his judgment while those who have received him will live with him in a new heaven and a new earth.

Several important truths surfaced with the kingdom portion of the story. Sin continued to plague the key people, and that fact will not change. In addition, sin carried consequences, and those did not go away even when forgiveness was issued. Theocracy remained the government even when Israel rejected it. When Saul rejected God, then God placed David as king. God's sovereignty rules over his people. In the story of David, we also see that God's story gets messy because he used weak and sinful people as his instruments. Yet God accomplished his goals, and the Abrahamic covenant came closer to fulfillment.

Rebellion, Judgment, and Future Hope

ACT 1

SOLOMON AND THE DEMISE OF THE UNIFIED KINGDOM

D avid grew old and frail. Even before his death a struggle ensued over the kingship. Adonijah exalted himself. However, the prophet Nathan ensured Solomon's coronation as God had promised. God controlled the kingdom's leadership. Before his death David issued final instructions to his son: "Keep your obligation to the LORD your God to walk in His ways and to keep His statutes, commandments, judgments, and testimonies . . . so that you will have success in everything you do and wherever you turn, and so the LORD will carry out His promise that He made to me" (1 Kings 2:3–4 HCSB). Even on his deathbed David thought about obedience to God. The blessings of God depended on a godly lifestyle. Solomon became king.

SOLOMON AND WISDOM

Solomon began his role as king of Israel as a young and inexperienced man. Certainly the role of king seemed daunting. God appeared to Solomon to offer him aid. It was also important that the king of God's covenant people begin with a close relationship to God. At Gibeon through a dream, the Lord presented Solomon a gift opportunity: "Ask. What should I give you?" (1 Kings 3:5 HCSB). Solomon's answer was surprising considering his age. "So give Your servant an obedient heart to judge Your people and to discern between good and evil. For who is able to judge this great people of Yours?" (1 Kings 3:9 HCSB). Solomon asked for the wisdom to reign well over Israel. This request pleased God, and he not only granted it but also bestowed on Solomon all the other things a young man would normally

117

have asked for—riches and honor. Solomon became the wealthiest and most well-known king of Israel. God blessed him as promised.

One event showcased his wisdom as he passed a judgment related to two women and a baby. Two prostitutes had one child each. During the night one of the prostitutes rolled over on her baby and killed it. She switched babies with the other, and as expected, morning brought a dispute. The women appeared before Solomon to hear his verdict. Solomon's solution entailed taking the live baby, cutting it in half, and giving half to each woman. The guilty prostitute readily agreed, but the true mother protested and offered to give up the baby rather than kill it. Solomon had his answer. He counted on the love of the real mother to care for the baby more than her rights. Solomon gave the baby to the mother. Solomon understood human nature. He could lead people because he saw into them and understood. This gift was a greater blessing than the riches and honor he received.

The wisdom Solomon asked for meant something more than what we might consider wisdom. The biblical concept included the understanding and technical skill to accomplish a task, but it carried spiritual significance as well. "Wisdom in the fullest sense belongs to God alone. His wisdom is not only completeness of knowledge pervading every realm of life but also 'consists of his irresistible fulfillment of what he has in mind.'"[1] Solomon requested the ability not only to know what to do but to fulfill God's purpose in it. This gift made for a good start as king. The source of this wisdom was God alone. "The fear of the LORD is the beginning of wisdom" (Ps. 111:10). The practical application of wisdom could be found in the wisdom literature such as Ecclesiastes and Proverbs. Wisdom represented the one thing a king of the covenant people would need to keep the Hebrews close to God.

SOLOMON'S ACCOMPLISHMENTS

With God's help and blessing Solomon continued the golden age of David's reign but with different tools. While David used armies to conquer, Solomon depended on diplomacy and commerce. He built a powerful and wealthy kingdom and established relationships with all those around. Solomon formed alliances and treaties in many cases through marriages to royal daughters of neighboring kings. "He had 700 wives who were princesses and 300 concubines" (1 Kings 11:3 HCSB). With this Solomon opened the doors for the breaking of the Deuteronomic law, which was God's standard for the nation. These foreign wives brought with them their foreign gods. God's law prohibited such. "Make sure there is no man or woman, clan or tribe among you today whose heart turns away from the LORD

---

[1] D. A. Hubbard, "Wisdom," in *New Bible Dictionary,* 1244.

our God to go and worship the gods of those nations" (Deut. 29:18).[2] Solomon imported the problem with marriages.

Solomon was also a gifted builder. He constructed many of the most famous structures in Israel. God promised David that his son would build the temple to house the ark of the covenant. Solomon constructed a magnificent temple following the basic design of the tabernacle in the wilderness. It contained several courts, an altar of burnt offering, lavers, the holy place with the same items found in the tabernacle and the holy of holies where the ark was placed and the presence of God resided among the people. In order to build the temple, Solomon imported cedars and cypress from Tyre. The stones for the structure were cut to the exact size at the quarry so the noise level at the sacred temple site would be kept to a minimum. Solomon drafted thirty thousand laborers along with seventy thousand porters and eighty thousand stonecutters. Thirty-three hundred deputies oversaw the construction and directed the laborers. Upon completion Solomon dedicated the worship center, and it became the standard of comparison for the two temples to follow centuries later.

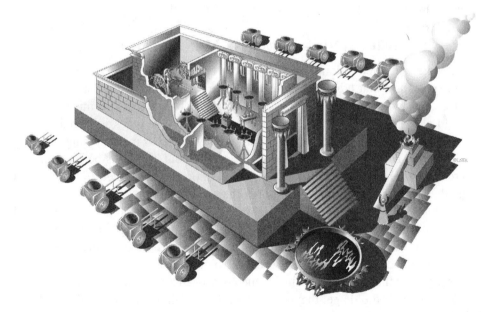

In addition to the temple, Solomon built a massive palace complex, government buildings, and stables. A telling mark of the shift in Solomon's priorities may be seen at this point. "He had spent seven years building [the temple]. It took Solomon thirteen years, however, to complete the construction of the palace" (1 Kings 6:38–

---

[2] Also Deuteronomy 13:6–9: "If your very own brother, or your son or daughter, or the wife you love or your closest friend secretly entices you, saying, 'Let us go and worship other gods' (gods that neither you nor your fathers have known, gods of the peoples around you, whether near or far, from one end of the land to the other), do not yield to him or listen to him. Show him no pity. Do not spare him or shield him. You must certainly put him to death. Your hand must be the first in putting him to death, and then the hands of all the people."

7:1). The palace demanded more of his time and probably was more impressive than the temple. God's promise came true. A king would tax heavily and enslave many of the people to accomplish his tasks. However, in spite of Solomon's apparent priority, he left the indelible mark of his kingship on the land.

Solomon also excelled in other endeavors. For the first time ever Israel controlled a navy in cooperation with Hiram, king of Tyre. The fleet, manned by experienced sailors from Tyre and Solomon's servants, sailed the Mediterranean Sea mostly in trade. Solomon acquired vast amounts of wealth and became known for his riches. He engaged in literary endeavors. He composed three thousand proverbs and 1005 songs (1 Kings 4:32). He studied nature and science and taught about birds, animals, reptiles, and fish. People came from everywhere to hear Solomon teach. In fact, the queen of Sheba heard about Solomon and "his relation to the name of the LORD," and she came to test him with difficult questions (1 Kings 10:1). He answered her questions, and the queen was overwhelmed with his wisdom, palace, and wealth. She praised God and gave Solomon gold, spices, and precious stones. Solomon returned the favor of gifts. Solomon achieved fame in many areas and ruled one of the most significant kingdoms of his time.

SOLOMON'S SIN—THE WISE MAN ACTED UNWISELY

David instructed Solomon clearly before he took over as king. Solomon knew the expectation that God had for him. The key question for any Israelite king or citizen was, will you obey the Lord and thereby be blessed? He promised David he would obey the Deuteronomic law, but unfortunately he quickly veered. "This is written in the law of Moses, so that you will have success in everything" (1 Kings 2:3 HCSB). Deuteronomy and the law clearly laid out by Moses became the standard for Israel and especially her kings. Solomon instead turned to his own way and the ways of those around him rather than follow God.

Solomon's wives exercised the major negative influence on his life. As already noted, they brought to Israel their traditions and pagan religions and influenced the land toward idolatry. The seven hundred wives and three hundred concubines from several countries eventually turned Solomon's heart away from the Lord. They served other gods than Yahweh and convinced Solomon to participate. When Solomon reached old age, they seduced him into following their gods. "Solomon followed Ashtoreth, the goddess of the Sidonians, and Milcom, the detestable idol of the Ammonites. Solomon did what was evil in the LORD's sight, and unlike his father David, he did not completely follow the LORD" (1 Kings 11:5–6 HCSB). Solomon even built worship centers for each of these pagan gods to please his foreign wives. Perhaps a human's greatest fault is to possess a great gift and fail to use it. Solomon, the king who possessed more wisdom than any before or after, failed to use that wisdom and acted foolishly. He broke the first laws of the Ten Commandments, which of course formed the basis of all life under God. He led his people away from Yahweh.

God always punishes rebellion. He informed Solomon that he would lose part of the kingdom as a result of his sin. This would occur when his son, Rehoboam, took over as king. He would lose most of the tribes but would retain Judah and Benjamin. Solomon reigned for forty years over Israel and then was buried with his father. Rehoboam took his place but faced difficulty from the start due to the judgment of God.

A DIVIDED KINGDOM—REHOBOAM AND JEROBOAM OR JUDAH AND ISRAEL

Rehoboam took the throne as the rightful heir of Solomon. However, according to God's judgment on Solomon, another named Jeroboam would break away from Israel, and ten tribes followed him as king of Israel. God encountered Jeroboam to make clear his expectations. "If you obey all I command you, walk in My ways, and do what is right in My sight in order to keep My statutes and My commandments as My servant David did, I will be with you. I will build you a lasting dynasty just as I built for David, and I will give you Israel" (1 Kings 11:38–39 HCSB). This encounter between God's prophet and Jeroboam took place even before Solomon died. Solomon tried to kill Jeroboam, but he escaped to Egypt and remained there until the king's death. Unfortunately the time in Egypt affected Jeroboam much the way it did the Hebrews when they dwelled there. He accepted Egyptian religious practices, which stopped him from meeting God's stated expectations.

The division of the kingdom came shortly after Rehoboam ascended the throne when he faced his first crisis. The people of Israel approached the new king and asked him to ease the harsh yoke of taxes laid on them by Solomon. Some of Rehoboam's advisors agreed he should ease the burden. But he rejected their advice and sought out some younger consultants he had grown up with. They advised him to make the yoke heavier and promised even a harder workload than Solomon required. Rehoboam committed one of the worst errors a king can commit: he refused to listen to his people. As a result the people led by Jeroboam rebelled, and the kingdom divided from that time on. Two kingdoms of Hebrews now existed: Judah to the south led by Solomon's son, Rehoboam, and Israel to the north led by Jeroboam.

Jeroboam ruled the new kingdom to the north consisting of ten tribes (only Judah and Benjamin stayed with Rehoboam). Be careful at this point not to confuse the use of Israel in the story. Up to this point Israel referred to the entire nation with all twelve tribes. At this point the nation is divided with the northern ten tribes being called Israel and the southern two tribes being called Judah. Jeroboam set up Shechem as the new capital. Remember God made clear to Jeroboam that he should live by the statutes and commands of the covenant to ensure prosperity and success. However, Jeroboam left Egypt as a pagan worshipper and never intended to worship Yahweh. In addition, he reasoned that the kingdom of David could rise again and his people might rebel and switch loyalty. After all, the Hebrews were accustomed to worshipping in Jerusalem at the magnificent temple built by Solomon. Jeroboam established a new religious system for the Northern Kingdom of Israel. He set up two new worship centers to rival Jerusalem, one in Dan to the north and the other in Bethel to the south just over the border from Judah. Jeroboam instituted the worship of idols, golden calves. Does this sound familiar? Remember at the foot of Mount Sinai when Moses lingered on the mountain with God, the people grew impatient and pressed Aaron to fashion a golden calf for worship. They reverted back to what they knew in Egypt. Jeroboam brought the same idolatry to the ten tribes. He led the people away from Yahweh. From the beginning the Northern Kingdom focused itself on pagan, idol worship. Jeroboam never exhibited a commitment to the covenant or Yahweh. As we will see, all the kings of the Northern Kingdom were bad in every way; and they all followed in the way of Jeroboam. This eventually brought an early end to Israel and the ten northern tribes.

JUDAH AND ISRAEL COMPARED

Judah and Israel differed immensely from the start; a comparison of the two shows those differences. The united kingdom under Saul, David, and Solomon is usually dated around 1000 BC. The split occurred in 921 BC. The Southern Kingdom of Judah was ruled by one dynasty throughout its existence, the family of David beginning with Rehoboam. The Northern Kingdom of Israel suffered through nine dynasties; a new family line rose regularly and usually by force. Jeroboam received a promise from God that his family would reign as long as he remained faithful to the covenant. That commitment to the covenant never happened, and his family line disappeared from the scene quickly. Judah maintained one capital, Jerusalem, which housed the temple and palace and was considered the most holy city. Israel moved capitals three times: Shechem, Tirzah, and finally Samaria. Even though all the kings of Judah came from David's line, only some walked in the ways of David while others practiced and allowed idolatry and immorality. However, the few good kings kept the people in line with the covenant and the worship of God. This influence slowed the demise of the Southern Kingdom. Judah lasted 350 years. The kings of Israel were all evil. None of them led the people to Yahweh; and as a result the kingdom slid quickly under the presence of gross immorality, social injustice, and idolatry. Israel lasted only two hundred years. Both kingdoms missed God's goals, rejected his plan, and ended in judgment.

THINGS TO CONSIDER

God revealed openly his expectation of his people and their kings. He desired that they be unique and live according to his statutes. When they rejected that life, the justice of God brought judgment: Solomon's sin ended in the division of the land; Rehoboam's sin caused the rebellion; and Jeroboam's sin brought a quick end to Israel. Those who chose to disobey reaped the worst instead of the blessing of God. God is sovereign and in spite of all rebellion and rejection still brings his plan to completion. Even though the path Israel and Judah selected eventually caused them to lose the land, God continued to carry out the plan. God controlled the future, not the kings.

STUDY QUESTIONS

1. What did God grant Solomon to help him rule Israel?
2. What evidence exists to show that Solomon did not lead the people to follow Yahweh?
3. Who were Rehoboam and Jeroboam? What were their mistakes?
4. What were the differences and likenesses of the Northern and Southern Kingdoms?

A NOTE ON THE PROPHETS

God used spokesmen called prophets to attempt to lead the people and their kings back to the Deuteronomic covenant. In the north and the south, these people stood out as some of the most colorful and important in the story. Who were these prophets, and what was their message? The idea of a prophet today brings visions of someone predicting future events. However, the prophets of the Old Testament were much more complex than that. They were unique individuals who came from all walks of life and were used by God to call an obstinate people back to faith. Many times they focused on the king's court but delivered a message for the whole nation. Sometimes their task seemed impossible. Yet they obeyed God.

FORETELLERS OR FORTHTELLERS

Prophets acted as the spokesmen for God to attempt to move the nations from bad to good. God spoke his message of hope, warning, or direction through these men. But was their message mainly forthtelling or foretelling? To foretell is to predict future events and to know what God has planned. Without a doubt many of the prophets were foretellers. Isaiah, Daniel, Ezekiel, and Habakkuk predicted the future for the people. But only about 20 percent of the prophetic material fits into this category of foretelling.

Forthtelling means to speak forth a message from God to the contemporary situation. The other 80 percent of the prophetic material is forthtelling. The prophets acted as preachers of a sort to present a word from the Lord to the Hebrews in their situation.

Some confusion occurs when we try to distinguish foretelling from forthtelling because the prophets blended the distant future events and immediate events into the same picture as they spoke. For example, the first advent of Jesus (his birth) and the second advent (second coming) sometimes get mixed together in the same discussions. This requires careful interpretation on our part. We will see an example of this in the discussion of Isaiah 7. The prophets encouraged, warned, critiqued, and directed God's people much as a preacher today would do. "Thus says the Lord" served as their main sermon starter. Usually this preaching focused on Deuteronomy and the covenant. Everything was judged against that standard, and it became the benchmark for blessing and judgment.

THE MESSAGE

The message of the prophets fits well into a three-point sermon. Almost all the prophets in some way addressed these points.[3] When they spoke to the Hebrews, they proclaimed: (1) You have broken the covenant (Mosaic law), so you must repent! (2) If you do not repent, God will bring judgment. (3) Even in judgment there is a future hope and restoration (new covenant, Messiah, kingdom). These three themes repeat themselves in the prophetic literature. Some of the prophets used all three while others focused on one or two. For instance, the prophet Amos deals mostly with judgment (the only exception being a few verses in Amos 5) while in Isaiah all three themes appear. Included in the message are the ways the people broke the covenant. The prophets detailed the areas of transgression and generally repeated the three categories. These usually appeared in the message as formal legal charges (the Lord has something against you).

What were the charges? First, the prophets charged idolatry, which probably ranked as the worst offence. This broke the first part of the Decalogue which specifically forbade worshipping other gods or making idols. Baal worship rose to become the main area of indiscretion for the Hebrews, dating all the way back to the invasion of Canaan when they allowed the Baal-worshipping Canaanites to remain instead of destroying them. Often the prophets equated this sin with spiritual adultery since the relationship with God was to be exclusive and running after other gods corresponded with committing adultery with another woman. The second charge concerned social injustice. In both Judah and Israel the rich took advantage of the poor, and justice in the courts could be bought for a price. In other words the lower classes had no one to look out for them. The northern prophets leveled this charge frequently at Israel. The last transgression focused on religion itself. Religious formalism reached horrible levels until religion equaled only formality with no heart involvement. The Hebrews believed that if they offered sacrifices and offerings and fulfilled all the religious duties then God would be pleased. The prophets reminded the people that God expected more—their heart, morals, and righteous action. Faith also affected activity so all three of the charges related.

---

[3] These points are identified and explained by Dr. J. Daniel Hays, Professor of Old Testament at Ouachita Baptist University. This discussion on prophets derives primarily from his Old Testament class outlines.

Prophetic Methods

How did the prophets deliver their messages? How does a good communicator or teacher deliver material? Just as a good teacher varies the methods, so did the prophets. Many of them used basic preaching where they simply proclaimed a theme or truth from God to the people. This might include declaration, reproach, threats, or condemnation. Many of the prophets used poetry to convey the message. The poetry focused on strong imagery and figures of speech. Poetry appealed to the emotions, and many of the prophets were highly emotional. Most of the prophets used symbols or object lessons. The visual connected the message powerfully to the audience. All of them used narrative material in the form of story or history. The prophetic message was sometimes complex as were the men and at other times straightforward and plain.

The Prophets

Some of the most significant prophets in the biblical story did not write or leave a written document of their prophecy. There is no biblical book corresponding to their name. For instance, Elijah and Elisha served as powerful prophets to the Northern Kingdom and performed many miracles while delivering the message. But they left no written record of their prophecy. We know of them from the biblical narrative. Many other prophets wrote down their prophecies, or in some cases it may have been written by their students.

Those included in the books of the Bible are the writing prophets. They have been categorized by recipients, dates, kingdoms, and importance or size. Perhaps a look at the categories will help us sort them out. Chronologically the prophets may be listed as follows: Early Prophets, Joel (840?) and Jonah (800); Eighth-Century Prophets, Amos (760), Hosea (750), Isaiah (740–698), Micah (735); Seventh-Century Prophets, Zephaniah (626), Jeremiah (625–585), Nahum (625), Habakkuk (610); Sixth-Century Prophets, Daniel (590), Ezekiel (590), Obadiah (585); Latter Prophets, Haggai (520), Zechariah (520), Malachi (435). Scholars disagree concerning the dates on the list above. Sometimes the prophets are categorized according to their situation and the period in which they prophesied: Hosea and Amos are prophets to Israel (Northern Kingdom) while Isaiah, Micah, Zephaniah, Jeremiah, Nahum, and Habakkuk prophesied to Judah. The exilic prophets are Daniel, Ezekiel, and Obadiah. The postexilic prophets are Haggai, Zechariah, and Malachi. Some list the prophets simply according to biblical order. Many refer to the longest prophetic books as Major Prophets: Isaiah, Jeremiah, Ezekiel, and Daniel. The others are called Minor Prophets. Each prophet spoke for God to his people in a particular situation and need. The themes, issues, and declarations addressed their situation. In that sense the prophets were like the preacher of today who speaks a message from God to a particular congregation in a specific setting with unique needs.

ACT 2

THE DEMISE OF THE NORTHERN KINGDOM

J eroboam, as the first king of the Northern Kingdom of Israel, set the stage for the entire future of the nation. He totally rejected God and the covenant. "Then he made two gold calves" (1 Kings 12:28 HCSB). The kings to follow emulated his life and action. Israel slid quickly into horrible idolatry and immorality. Jeroboam's son picked up where his father left off. "Nadab did what was evil in the LORD's sight and followed the example of his father and the sin he had caused Israel to commit" (1 Kings 15:26 HCSB). Baasha started a new dynasty, but his actions still followed those of Jeroboam. "He did what was evil in the LORD's sight and followed the example of Jeroboam and the sin he had caused Israel to commit" (1 Kings 15:34 HCSB). The die was cast, and each king with each succeeding dynasty followed in the way of Jeroboam—a disastrous situation for the ten tribes.

Each of the kings of Israel sinned and rejected God's way. An outline of the kingdoms and kings can be seen in the chart. Notice the comparisons between the Northern and Southern Kingdoms as already noted.

OMRI AND AHAB

A closer look at some of the more significant kings helps us see the story unfold. The name *Omri* came to be associated with Israel. He reigned forty-four years. He moved the capital to Samaria (last capital until the destruction) which became the central city of the Northern Kingdom just as Jerusalem had become for the south. Nations like Assyria started referring to Israel as the "house of Omri" due to his powerful presence as king. Omri did what was evil in God's eyes and followed after Jeroboam as the kings before him and after. Although Omri probably counted as the more significant king, the name of his son may be more recognizable to many.

Ahab reigned for only half as long as his father, but his personality and actions earned him an infamous place in the biblical story. Ahab married a non-Hebrew woman from Sidon named Jezebel. She worshipped Baal and brought her gods with her. Ahab, influenced by his wife, built a temple for Baal and set up an altar for worship of the idol in Samaria. In addition, he made an Asherah pole which served as a worship center. "Ahab did more to provoke the LORD God of Israel than all the kings of Israel who were before him" (1 Kings 16:33 HCSB). He was a selfish, immature king who seemed to be controlled by an evil and powerful wife. In one instance Ahab wanted to trade one of his vineyards for a vineyard belonging to a man named Naboth. Naboth refused, saying he could not give up family land received in inheritance. Ahab went back to the palace angry and sulking, refusing to eat. Jezebel took care of the problem. She wrote letters in the king's name to officials to set up Naboth for a trial preset with false witnesses and a verdict of stoning. Naboth was stoned to death, and the self-centered Ahab received his vineyard.

ELIJAH, GOD'S PROPHET SENT TO STEM THE TIDE OF EVIL

During Ahab's idolatrous reign God sent a prophet to deliver his message and attempt to turn Israel back to the covenant. Elijah represented the Lord in a powerful and visible way. In order to get the attention of Ahab, Elijah, empowered by God, commanded that there would be no rain or even dew for two years. The famine began, and God cared for his prophet during this time. He lived by the Wadi Cherith where it enters the Jordan, and God provided water for him. Ravens were sent to feed him.

After a while that provision ended, and an angel of the Lord directed Elijah to Zarephath near Sidon where he encountered a widow with her son. She was gathering wood to prepare the last of the food she had for her and her son. Elijah asked her to prepare food for him. She hesitated, explaining the flour and oil she had left represented all that stood between life and death for her house. Elijah told her not to fear. God would care for her by never letting the flour or oil run dry. In her faith the widow obeyed, and the three of them ate. The promised miracle came true. God cared for the widow and her son as God's prophet proclaimed.

Later the widow's son became ill and died. Such a state of affairs is always irreversible, or is it? Elijah took the woman's son and miraculously raised him from the dead. The woman praised him as God's prophet. This story served as a bold contrast between the curse coming upon Ahab's land for rejecting the covenant and God's blessing on Elijah and even a foreigner in Zarephath for obedience and faith. It became a real-life illustration of the blessing/curse warnings in Deuteronomy.

The most famous event in Elijah's life was the encounter on Mount Carmel. Elijah determined that a direct showdown between God and Baal needed to take place in order to convince the Israelites of the truth. Elijah issued a challenge calling on the prophets and priests of Baal to meet him at Mount Carmel; 450 Baal prophets and four hundred prophets of the Asherah pole answered the call. The showdown was set. On the mountain Elijah ordered an altar of burnt offering to be built. Elijah explained the contest to the Israelites. The contest consisted of taking two bulls and cutting them into pieces and placing them on the altar—Elijah preparing one bull and the Baal prophets the other. Then each side would call on their God or gods to send fire from heaven and consume the offerings on the altar. If Baal proved to be greater than God in the contest, then all would worship him; but if Yahweh exhibited his power and strength, then all would turn back to him. The people agreed as did the contestants. Elijah allowed the Baal prophets to go first. Remember the cultural setting: my god is stronger than your god mentality. Here was the ultimate test of that. It was a theological encounter.

The Baal prophets prepared the bull and from morning to noon called on Baal to provide fire. They danced and made noise but to no avail. Elijah mocked them, and they tried even harder to the point of cutting themselves with knives and spears to impress their god. But Baal said nothing: "But there was no sound, no one answered, no one paid attention" (1 Kings 18:29 HCSB). Then Elijah called the people closer and prepared his bull. He took twelve stones representing the twelve tribes and built an altar to the Lord. Elijah ordered the people to dig a trench around the altar and douse the altar with water three times until even the trench was full. That evening God's prophet called on the God of Abraham, Isaac, and Israel to answer so the people would know that he is Yahweh. "Then Yahweh's fire fell and consumed the burnt offering, the wood, the stones, and the dust, and it licked up the water that was in the trench. When all the people saw it, they fell facedown and said, 'Yahweh, He is God! Yahweh, He is God!'" (1 Kings 18:38–39 HCSB). At this Elijah commanded the people to seize the Baal prophets, and the prophet of Yahweh slaughtered them. To Elijah it appeared like this victory would turn Israel toward God. It was indeed a spiritual victory, and Yahweh once again proved he is the only God, the God of Abraham, Isaac, and Jacob—another lesson that Yahweh still cared for his people and that they were wrong to worship other gods.

Jezebel had imported and supported the Baal prophets. They represented her faith and her homeland. When she heard of the slaughter, she issued a grave threat to Elijah. "May the gods punish me and do so severely if I don't make your life like the life of one of them by this time tomorrow!" (1 Kings 19:2 HCSB). Jezebel determined to kill Elijah just as he had killed her prophets. One would expect Elijah to dare her since he had just experienced the power of Yahweh but not so. Elijah fled for his life. He went into the desert, sat down under a broom tree, and prayed

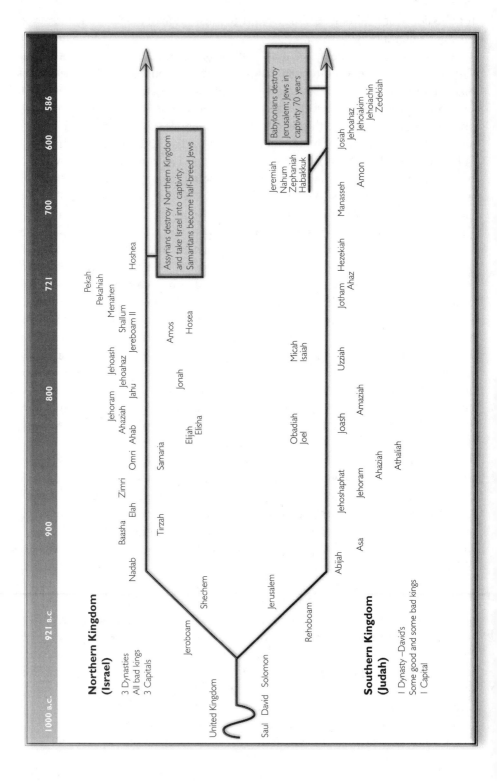

that God would let him die. He couldn't take it anymore. Yahweh spoke to Elijah and cared for him. God fed him, allowed him to sleep, and fed him again. In his exhaustion Elijah needed refreshment and energy to deal with the problem. Finally, God led Elijah to a cave where he spent the night. God encountered Elijah again, asking him why he was in this place. The implication was that Elijah should still be at his task in Israel. Elijah gave God his pity speech. "I have been very zealous for the LORD God of Hosts, but the Israelites have abandoned Your covenant, torn down Your altars, and killed Your prophets with the sword. I alone am left, and they are looking for me to take my life" (1 Kings 19:10 HCSB).

God told Elijah to go out and stand on the mountain. Then God taught Elijah a lesson. First there was a mighty wind that tore even the rocks, but God was not in the wind. Then an earthquake shook the ground, but God was not in the earthquake. Finally, there was a small, soft voice; and when Elijah heard it, he knew it was God. Elijah had seen the awesome power of God on Mount Carmel, and perhaps he thought God always exhibits his power that way. God taught Elijah in this experience that he speaks in different ways; and even when the power is not readily evident, God is still there and acting. God then sent Elijah back to Israel, explaining that seven thousand remained faithful worshippers of Yahweh. He also promised Elijah that Ahab and Jezebel were finished. Elijah was to anoint Jehu as the new king in Israel and Hazael as king in Aram. Jehu's task was to destroy the entire house of Ahab and set up a new dynasty. God also assigned to Elijah the job of anointing his successor, Elisha. Elisha would receive a double portion of power and perform even more miracles than Elijah. In other words, God made clear that Elijah was to get over the pity and return to his assigned work in Israel because God was taking care of business. The prophets served as the spokesmen of God, but God empowered them; and it was his message, plan, and will that they reported. He used prophets but carried on his work of redemption even when they balked or hesitated in their task.

ELISHA

Elijah passed from the scene as miraculously as he had lived his life. God took him up alive in a whirlwind in the presence of Elisha, his replacement. Elijah revealed God's unbelievable power to Israel and became the representative prophet for the Hebrews. However, Elisha by God's decree and empowerment possessed twice the power. He raised a young man from the dead (as Elijah had), caused an ax handle to float, multiplied bread to feed one hundred, and healed an important leper—a powerful man from Syria. Namaan served as general of the army in Syria. Even with his power, he could not escape leprosy. Leprosy plagued the ancient world as a slow death sentence which eventually ate away the body. Those who contracted this bacterial disease needed a miracle. When no help could be found in Syria, a servant informed Namaan about a powerful prophet in Israel. The king encouraged him to make the journey and find the prophet. Namaan approached

Elisha with gifts and a request for a miracle. Elisha instructed the general to go to the Jordan and wash himself seven times in its waters and the leprosy would disappear. Namaan couldn't believe the instruction and balked in anger claiming the rivers in Syria were cleaner. However, his servants reasoned with him saying that if Elisha had instructed him to do some great feat, he would have gladly obeyed. Surely if the directive was simply to wash and be clean, he should try it. Namaan conceded and went to the Jordan. After washing, he was healed and returned with joy to Elisha to present him with presents. Elisha refused the gifts and sent Namaan home.

Elisha delivered the same message his predecessor, Elijah, presented to Israel: turn to the Lord. However, with the exception of the brief victory Elijah had on Mount Carmel, both prophets' words landed on deaf ears. This foreshadows what other prophets (Hosea, Amos) to the Northern Kingdom discovered and many in the south: for the most part the Hebrews did not want to hear God's message and rejected Yahweh, which hastened their destruction. Rejecting the covenant and exercising faithlessness to Yahweh brings judgment. Omri's dynasty ended when Jehu killed the entire family of Ahab.

THE LAST DAYS OF ISRAEL

Around 793 BC Jeroboam II took control of Israel as king; and even as wicked as Israel was, the country entered a long period of affluence and peace, the lull before the coming storm. During this time of prosperity, the rich got richer while the poor struggled. Idolatry flourished even while the people gave token offerings to God. The nation slid toward destruction quickly; but Yahweh, in an exercise of mercy and compassion, sent two last prophets to warn, inform, and call the people to repentance.

AMOS, A MAN FROM JUDAH, PROPHESIES TO ISRAEL (NORTHERN KINGDOM)

God's message to bring Israel back to the covenant relationship came through a prophet from the Southern Kingdom of Judah. Amos lived as a farmer of sycamore trees and a sheepherder. Since Israel enjoyed such affluence at the time, Amos traveled north to do business. God laid a specific and often harsh message on Amos's heart, and he delivered it boldly. Amos began with a prophetic formula: "For three sins . . . even for four" (Amos 1:3). Three represented a full, perfect number; and adding one more meant the sins of Israel had passed that and moved beyond. Now God's judgment was near. Amos's accusations sounded like those levied in a court of law. He accused Israel of syncretism in religion. They gave lip service to the worship of God but mixed with it the worship of Baal and other idols. Syncretistic religion incorporates many beliefs and practices from different systems much like the New Age movement in our world today.

In addition, Amos hit the Israelites hard concerning social injustice. He used bold, biting language when condemning the wealthy women of Israel. "Listen to this message, you cows of Bahsan who are on the hill of Samaria, women who oppress the poor and crush the needy" (Amos 4:1 HCSB). The law made clear that God cared deeply for children, widows, foreigners, and the poor. Several statutes directed the Hebrews on how to take care of them. However, Israel neglected them and sought only to enrich themselves at the expense of those less fortunate. Amos even warned the women that when the destruction came they would be led off by hooks attached to their flesh. God condemned social injustice and called for repentance and a return to the covenant.

Amos used object lessons and stories to convey the message. One of the most well-known today is the plumb-line illustration. A plumb line was used by builders to ensure that a wall was straight up and down rather than leaning. We often use a chalk plumb line to strike a straight line for hanging wallpaper. Amos told the Israelites that God had put his plumb line into their midst and discovered them to be crooked. Israel would fall if they did not straighten up. Obviously the plumb line represented God's law and expectation on the Hebrews. They failed the test.

In harsh terms Amos focused mostly on the judgment to come. However, in Amos 5 he did give some hope. A series of verbs called for action from the Israelites—listen, come back, do good. Amos called them to repent and turn back to God and live. The word *live* was an imperative but served as a promise in the text. Yahweh promised them life if they repented and turned back to him.[4] If they responded positively, then hope was theirs; but if not, destruction. Amos received no positive response at all, as far as history records. The slide toward judgment continued.

HOSEA, THE LAST PROPHET TO ISRAEL

Hosea could be considered the last-chance prophet for Israel. God loved Israel and did not want to judge her. He sent Hosea to pass on that message of love. Hosea's message played out both in his own life and in the words he shared with Israel. He married a woman named Gomer who was repeatedly unfaithful to Hosea. Hosea and Gomer's children reflected the danger of such adulterous activity. Their names were "God scatters," "not loved," and "not my people." Israel was compared to an adulterous wife like Gomer. To go after idols and other gods meant to commit spiritual adultery since the covenant called for absolute fidelity to Yahweh. Finally Gomer left Hosea and was sold as a prostitute to a man who kept her in slavery. God commanded Hosea to buy her back and love her as his wife again. Imagine a spouse committing adultery not once but as a lifestyle and taking him or her back in forgiveness. God used Hosea to exhibit his amazing love for Israel. Hosea's life declared to Israel that no matter what sin they committed or how many times they rejected Yahweh, he still loved them. Hosea's message was one of grace and love.

---

[4] J. A. Motyer, *The Message of Amos* (Leicester, England: InterVarsity Press, 1974), 117.

God wanted Israel to know it was not too late if the people would only turn to him. As with Amos, Hosea received no response.

THE JUDGMENT: ASSYRIA DESTROYS SAMARIA

In 721 BC the Assyrian army led by Sennacherib invaded the Northern Kingdom and conquered Israel. Samaria was destroyed. The Assyrians who worshipped the god of war had gained a deserved reputation of being cruel and harsh captors. As Amos predicted, they took most of the Hebrews into captivity and transported them by attaching hooks into their flesh and leading them out of Israel. Those left were the poor, the weak, the sick, and the old. The Assyrians then imported others to occupy the land. This set the stage for a development the Hebrews learned to despise. Those Jews remaining intermarried with those imported, and the result was a people called Samaritans. Later the Samaritans became among those most hated by good, covenant Hebrews. They considered the Samaritans as Gentiles.

The ten tribes that made up Israel disappeared. God judged them suddenly and completely. Scattered across the Assyrian Empire, they never returned to take over and control their land again. God's promise of destruction as delivered by his prophets was fulfilled. The Northern Kingdom of Israel ceased to exist.

THINGS TO CONSIDER

The Deuteronomic covenant laid the background for all Yahweh desired in his people. In every generation God judged his people according to how they followed the law. The prophets reminded the people of the expectation of Yahweh. Rejection of the covenant meant judgment and removal from the land. Jeroboam, an evil king, sinned first and led the people to follow. The curse promised in Deuteronomy became inevitable unless the people repented. They refused even when God sent prophet after prophet to teach, warn, and call them back. God expected his people to be faithful, moral, and righteous; but they refused. Judgment came.

However, God loves his people regardless of their actions or attitudes. His justice still demands the cost of sin be paid, but he never stops loving. Hosea's message revealed that God constantly calls people to repent and obey. Those who do, find peace and blessing. But sin is a powerful force from generation to generation. However, sin is not more powerful than God's love and provision. God's plan of redemption continued even with the Northern Kingdom destroyed.

STUDY QUESTIONS

1. Who is a prophet, and what message did the prophets speak for God to the Hebrews?
2. How did the ministry of Elijah and Elisha affect Israel, and why were these prophets not more successful?

3. What were Amos's accusations against Israel? Are these sins still a problem today?

4. How does Hosea reveal the love of God in both his life and his message?

ACT 3

THE SOUTHERN KINGDOM SLIDES

R ehoboam listened to bad advice and increased the taxes and hardship of the people. Rebellion led by Jeroboam broke out, splitting the kingdom permanently. Rehoboam began his reign by trying to follow God's covenant but soon followed the way of Solomon in idolatry. From that time the kings of Judah wavered between the covenant and idolatry. God sent prophets to the Southern Kingdom as well. The message remained the same: you have sinned, and judgment is coming; repent and turn to God; but even if judgment comes, there is hope in God. Throughout the history of Judah, these prophets delivered the message with varying degrees of success. However, in the long run the Southern Kingdom did not fare any better than the Northern; the slide just took longer. No doubt the presence of the temple and the prophets lengthened the days of Judah. Leadership may also explain a slower slide to judgment. As stated earlier, the Northern Kingdom had all bad kings who led Israel into idolatry. Judah on the other hand experienced both good (Asa, Jehoshaphat, Hezekiah) and bad kings (Abijah, Jehoram, Ahaziah) and a few in between. Some of the kings of Judah followed God closely and aggressively attempted to lead the people in that way. Others were even worse than the northern kings. The good kings helped slow the downward slide enough to prolong Judah's life as a nation, and the prophets in Judah met with enough success to make a difference and postpone the judgment to come.

GOD SENDS PROPHETS TO JUDAH

JOEL

Although scholars debate as to the time and exact situation, God sent a prophet named Joel to warn Judah of coming judgment (from either Assyria or Babylon) if the covenant continued to be neglected.[5] Joel used an object lesson to depict the horror and danger of the Day of the Lord, the day of God's judgment. He referred to an invasion of locusts that would devastate Judah.[6] Locust swarms were not unheard of in this day and could leave a country barren within days. This resulted in starvation, death, and disease. Joel described the invasion of four different types of locusts, each destroying more fully than the other. "What the devouring locust has left, the swarming locust has eaten; what the swarming locust has left, the young locust has eaten; and what the young locust has left, the destroying locust has eaten" (Joel 1:4 HCSB). Joel called for those who were drunkards to wake up! The Day of the Lord as depicted by Joel would be a day of devastation and destitution.

Joel predicted hope in the midst of harsh warning. Perhaps his most famous prediction concerns one of the most important events in the New Testament—Pentecost. Joel told Judah that a day would come when God would bestow his Spirit on the people and they would prophesy in his name. This is an important prediction since it marked a new way of relating to God. His Spirit would indwell the people instead of residing in the temple. Peter referred to this prophecy at Pentecost. Joel also predicted the destruction of Judah if they persisted in sin and refused to repent, but God's plan of blessing the world would continue even when judgment came and Judah was no more.

ISAIAH (750–698 BC)

God raised up Isaiah to guide some of Judah's kings through a difficult time. He rose to the position of prophet at the close of Uzziah's reign. On the occasion of Uzziah's death, Isaiah received a call from God. In a vision Isaiah found himself in God's throne room seeing God in all his glory. In the presence of God, Isaiah realized his unworthiness and confessed his unclean life and that of Judah. God provided seraphim to touch him with a cleansing hot coal from the altar which removed and atoned for his sin. God then asked an important question. "Who should I send? Who will go for Us?" (Isa. 6:8 HCSB). Isaiah offered himself as God's servant and spokesman. God provided Isaiah with the message of warning, judgment, and future hope for Judah.

Isaiah grew up in the palace environs and was familiar with its protocol and way of life. He served as prophet to the kings, delivering his message to them in hope that they would lead Judah to follow Yahweh. Isaiah continued as prophet through the reigns of Jotham, Ahaz, Hezekiah, and died at the hands of Manasseh. Each of these belonged to the house of David and continued the dynasty God promised. However, not all of these kings represented God well, and so the task of

---

[5] Scholars debate as to the exact date of Joel's prophecy, dating it as early as 847 BC and as late as the late sixth century corresponding to the Babylonian invasion. However, Joel did prophesy to the Southern Kingdom of Judah. A traditional time would be around Isaiah and Micah in late eighth century BC.

[6] There is also debate as to whether the locust invasion refers to an actual event or merely serves as an illustration.

Isaiah with each differed. During this time the Assyrians threatened both Israel and Judah. Israel fell to them in 721 BC. This threat played a large role in the actions of the kings and the message of Isaiah to them. Isaiah called the kings to trust God and not their own military strength or alliances. Judah, as God's nation, would be saved if they remained faithful to Yahweh and obeyed his commands.

During the time of Ahaz (735–715), Assyria moved south against Syria and Israel. These two nations formed an alliance against the invaders and invited Judah to join them. Ahaz refused, and the two kings turned on him. He sought help from Tiglath-Pileser, king of Assyria. Isaiah warned that this was not the best option and offered a sign to Ahaz to confirm the message. Ahaz refused the sign, but Isaiah delivered the message anyway. Isaiah told Ahaz that a child would be born of a virgin and his name would be Immanuel meaning "God with us" (Isa. 7:4–14). Before the child reached his teen years, Assyria would wipe out Syria and Israel. Isaiah encouraged Ahaz to trust God, not a foreign power. Ahaz ignored the advice. In rejecting God, Ahaz turned to evil completely. He adopted idolatry, closed the temple, and even sacrificed children. However, Isaiah's prophecy was fulfilled.

The prophecy concerning the virgin birth has most often been connected to the virgin birth of Jesus. However, there are some interpretive questions to ask concerning this prophecy. "The virgin will conceive, have a son, and name him Immanuel. By the time he learns to reject what is bad and choose what is good, the land of the two kings you dread will be abandoned" (Isa. 7:15–16 HCSB). How would Ahaz have interpreted this sign from the Lord? How did the New Testament writers see it? Herein lies the issue. The language sounds like the baby would be born during the time of Ahaz, and the demise of the Northern Kingdom would shortly follow. We know Israel succumbed to Assyria in 721 BC, so by that time the baby at least would need to be a young boy. However, in the New Testament Matthew referred to this prophecy when speaking of the birth of Jesus to Mary. How can the sign given by Isaiah be fulfilled in the time of Ahaz and in the time of Jesus? As already noted, sometimes the prophets mixed the distant future with the immediate present in their prophecies. That is the case for Isaiah 7. There are cases of double fulfillment of the prophecies. There is a near view and a far view. The immediate fulfillment came in the person of Hezekiah, the son of Ahaz and next king of Judah. The word used for *virgin* can mean either "one who has not experienced sexual relations" or simply "a young woman." In the case of Hezekiah, one of the best kings of Judah, the reference to his mother obviously referred to a young woman. In the case of Jesus' mother, Mary, it meant a virgin who had never had relations with a man. What is important to the story is that Hezekiah and Jesus brought good to Judah as the prophecy stated. In this way, both became Immanuel or "God with us" for the Hebrews. Unfortunately, Ahaz cared little about the immediate or future fulfillment of the prophecy and did what he wanted. Following God was not his priority.

Hezekiah (715–686) took seriously the covenant and Yahweh. He too faced the Assyrian threat but listened to Isaiah. When the new leader of the Assyrians, Sennacherib, sent word to Hezekiah ordering him to form an alliance with Assyria or face destruction, Judah's king sought out the advice of Isaiah. The prophet told him to trust God, who will spread a rumor causing Sennacherib to return home where he will die by the sword. Hezekiah faced a difficult choice: trust God's promise (covenant) or give in to Assyria. He trusted God. An angel of God struck down 185,000 Assyrian soldiers. Sennacherib quickly returned to Nineveh and later, while worshipping in his pagan temple, was struck down with a sword by his own sons. Judah was God's nation, and the promises to Abraham held true. God blessed his people and cursed those who cursed them.

Hezekiah worshipped Yahweh, followed the covenant, and heeded the words of Isaiah the prophet. He ruled as one of the most faithful kings in Judah. He reinstated Moses' laws of worship and called everyone in Judah to observe the Passover. Hezekiah even led the people to take steps to protect the city of Jerusalem in case of siege. He cut a tunnel from the Virgin's Spring outside the city, under the walls and into Jerusalem. The tunnel spanned 1758 feet and was six feet high. The workers cut it through solid stone beginning at each end and meeting in the middle. Such an engineering feat would impress even today. This tunnel led to the Pool of Siloam in the city. In 1880 schoolboys playing hooky from school discovered an inscription telling the story of this tunnel. Hezekiah reigned for twenty-nine years; and Manasseh, his son, took the throne—a turn for the worse for Judah.

Isaiah's prophecy predicted much about the future, both of judgment and hope. Isaiah told both of judgment to come on Judah and of the glorious future with the Messiah. In fact, Isaiah has sometimes been called the Messianic Prophet because of the numerous references to the Messiah. Since the biblical story is about God's redemption, which ultimately took place in Jesus (the Messiah), Isaiah plays an important role. As already discussed, Isaiah predicted the virgin birth of Jesus. He also described the messianic king and kingdom in several places. In Isaiah 9:2–7, the prophet encouraged Judah by contrasting the current darkness with the coming king. "For a child will be born for us, a son will be given to us, and the government will be on His shoulders. He will be named Wonderful Counselor, Mighty God, Eternal Father, Prince of Peace" (Isa. 9:6 HCSB). Here again is an example of the near view of the prophet (Jesus birth) and the far view (his eternal kingdom) in the same prediction. This child or king would reign eternally with justice and righteousness. Chapter 11 paints a beautiful picture of the Messiah's reign. He will execute justice and righteousness, and faithfulness will be his belt. In this kingdom "the wolf will live with the lamb, and the leopard will lie down with the goat. The calf, the young lion, and the fatling will be together, and a child will lead them. . . . No one will harm or destroy on My entire holy mountain, for the land will be full of the knowledge of the LORD as the sea is filled with water" (Isa. 11:6, 9 HCSB).

The Messiah will bring in the perfect society. These are references to the second coming of the Messiah while chapter 7 referred to the first coming.

Isaiah also deals with the work of the Messiah on the cross. Isaiah 53 is sometimes referred to as the Suffering Servant passage because it describes the cross event in Jesus' life where sin was conquered. "We all went astray like sheep; we all have turned to our own way; and the LORD has punished Him for the iniquity of us all. He was oppressed and afflicted, yet He did not open His mouth. Like a lamb led to the slaughter and like a sheep silent before her shearers, He did not open His mouth" (Isa. 53:6–7 HCSB).

The Messiah went to the cross for the sins of the world. Isaiah predicted the final solution to the sin problem. In the last chapters the prophet also described the new heaven and new earth to be established when sin and evil are finally and completely dealt with and all who belong to God are part of that kingdom. The messianic prophet shared God's message of the joy of the future for those faithful to God. His intention was that Judah would be faithful and share in the joy.

God blessed Hezekiah because he was faithful to the covenant and listened to God's messenger. He trusted Yahweh. Covenant remained the main concern from Abraham to Hezekiah. The relationship between God and his people ebbed and flowed. Hezekiah is considered a good king simply because he was faithful to Yahweh. However, his son Manasseh proved to be obstinate and evil. He rejected Yahweh. He did not listen to Isaiah. In fact Manasseh stuffed Isaiah into a hollow log and cut the log in half, killing the prophet in a horrible way. As we will see, Manasseh accelerated the slide to judgment.

MICAH (740 BC)

While Isaiah delivered his message to royalty, Micah prophesied among the common people and defended their cause. Micah, sometimes called the "Democratic Prophet" for his concern over the people on the street, witnessed the social injustice in Judah that corresponded to that in Israel. He warned of the judgment it would bring if left unchanged. He issued warnings to the oppressing judges and leaders in both Israel and Judah. Micah called them back to true religion as opposed to outward religious activity. The theme passage for the prophet was, "He has told you men what is good and what it is the LORD requires of you: Only to act justly, to love faithfulness, and to walk humbly with your God" (Mic. 6:8 HCSB). Micah called for a religion that treated people the way God intended. He predicted a time when Judah would be made desolate if they did not repent. Micah also issued a message of hope, a time when Zion (God's City) would be rebuilt after the destruction and the kingdom extended. God judged the wicked but exhibited loyalty to Jacob and Abraham and the people who lived as they did.

Rejection of God's Way

Even with the efforts of prophets like Isaiah and Micah, the demise of Judah hastened after the death of Hezekiah. Manasseh became perhaps the worst of all the kings of Judah. Unfortunately his reign was the longest in the Southern Kingdom, fifty-five years. He began his treachery by killing Isaiah. He established idolatry as the norm and even sacrificed his own children at pagan altars. The worship in the temple ceased, and over the decades the building fell into decay. Briefly toward the end of his career, Manasseh repented and tried in vain to reverse the degradation of the society; but it was too little too late. Living so long in rejection of the covenant caused the people to forget God and be unaware of his expectations. The king led the people far away from Yahweh. Manasseh's son, Amon, did nothing to improve the depraved situation in Judah. The people, steeped in idolatry and immorality, no longer even knew of the law of God.

JOSIAH (640–609 BC)

Josiah ranked as one of the best kings (judged by his faithfulness to Yahweh and the covenant) of Judah, rivaling Hezekiah. He became king at the age of eight and in steps began reversing the tide of pagan religion in his land. In the eighth year of his reign, he committed himself seriously to follow God. In his twelfth year as king, Josiah started the process of ridding Judah of all pagan temples and worship. The most significant action occurred in his eighteenth year as king when he ordered the cleaning and repair of Solomon's temple, which had fallen deeply into disrepair. This action was essential to bring the people back into covenant relationship with God and to worship him in his temple.

In this work a wonderful discovery was made. Hilkiah, the priest, found a copy of the law. The fact that it was unknown and lost shows the distance between the people and Yahweh. They had forgotten Yahweh completely. When Josiah heard of it, he ordered all the elders to gather in the temple, and he read the law to them. He renewed the covenant in their presence and then had everyone in Judea pledge the same. Josiah like Hezekiah celebrated the Passover again, and faith in God began a slow return. Unfortunately, Josiah died in battle in 609 BC against Neco, king of Egypt. His work to reestablish the covenant, although admirable, was too little too late. Jeremiah, the prophet, composed laments for Josiah, and a singer commemorated his life.

The Last Kings, a Quick Descent

The last five kings of Judah did not follow in the steps of Josiah. Instead they reverted to idolatry and rebelled against God. God sent prophets to warn, but the message fell on deaf ears. The kings and the people were set against following God. As a result the destruction came quickly. Josiah died around 609 BC, and twenty-three years later Judah was no more. God's promise of judgment for the sin of Judah, if they refused to repent, was certain and sure. God took the covenant seriously, but the Hebrews did not.

THINGS TO CONSIDER

The entire story in the Old Testament centers on the covenants established by God with his people. Some of the kings of Judah trusted Yahweh and worshipped him. Others rejected him and led the people to do so. Covenant obedience determined the destiny of Judah. When the reform of Josiah failed to permanently turn the people to Yahweh, judgment came quickly. God remained faithful to his word and continued to exhibit unbelievable grace and patience by sending prophet after prophet to express his love, call for repentance, and warn of consequences. However, as discovered in the creation story, people are endowed with free choice and exercise it reaping the consequences that accompany each choice. Judah and its last kings chose to reject Yahweh.

STUDY QUESTIONS

1. What success did God have with the prophets he sent to Judah?
2. Why were Hezekiah and Josiah good kings?
3. Why were Ahaz and Manasseh bad kings?
4. Why were the prophets and good kings not able to turn Judah toward God?

EPISODE SEVEN

CAPTIVITY AND RETURN

ACT 1

THE JUDGMENT

J udah reached the point of no return, and God prepared the judgment for the sins of idolatry and rejection of the covenant. God's warnings delivered through the prophets were not idle threats. As Assyria became the instrument for judgment against Israel, God employed another powerful pagan kingdom to mete out the judgment for Judah—Babylon.

HABAKKUK, QUESTIONING PROPHET (610–600 BC)

God's choice to use Babylon as the agent of destruction for Judah caused one prophet some consternation. Habakkuk lived and prophesied in the last years of the Southern Kingdom. He watched as Babylon grew and finally defeated Nineveh (Assyrian Empire) in 612. Nebuchadnezzar, king of Babylon, now occupied the place of most feared ruler. His power threatened all the kingdoms in the ancient Near East including Judah. Habakkuk received word from God that the Chaldeans (Babylon) were selected by God to take care of Judah's rebellion. That fact caused Habakkuk to question God. How could God use a nation even more wicked than Judah to punish the Hebrews for their sins? This made no sense to the prophet. He agreed Judah deserved judgment, but so did Babylon. How could this be?

God answered the prophet through a vision. He assured Habakkuk that eventually all evil, including that of Babylon, gets its due judgment. But in this case God chose Babylon to deal with Judah and would deal with the Chaldeans later in another way. Habakkuk ended his prophecy declaring his confidence in a God who would exercise judgment to those who deserved it and bring salvation and strength to those who followed him. Habakkuk exemplified honesty in prayer as he lifted up honest prayers to God out of frustration, and God answered those prayers.

The judgment arrived in Judah in waves. Nebuchadnezzar defeated the Assyrians at Nineveh in 612 BC and then turned his attention to the west. He conquered Judah in 604 BC and at that time exported the best, most intelligent young men back to Babylon to serve in his court. Daniel, Shadrach, Meshach, and Abednego went in that group. Daniel became a prophet in the exile and lived out his life there. Nebuchadnezzar set up Jehoiakim as his vassal to rule in Judah. The second wave came in 597 BC when Jehoiakim rebelled and Nebuchadnezzar invaded to deal with him. The king was exiled to Babylon along with several others including Ezekiel, another prophet of the exile. These captives settled in Babylon along some old, mosquito-infested canals. The last wave descended on Jerusalem in full force. Nebuchadnezzar reacted to Zedekiah's refusal to pay tribute and besieged the city for two years, finally destroying it completely including the temple—the final indication that God's presence no longer dwelt with the nation. Many died; others were deported to Babylon along with the temple treasures. God indeed used the pagan Babylonians to mete out judgment to Judah.

JEREMIAH, WEEPING PROPHET (625–585 BC)

Jeremiah began as God's prophet in the time of the reforming king Josiah, long before the destruction of Jerusalem. He observed Judah in its transition from semi-faithful to depraved and ready for judgment. God commissioned Jeremiah to deliver messages of judgment and hope to the people in their last days as a nation. Jeremiah is sometimes called the weeping prophet because he mourned over the situation in Judah and also because he didn't want the job as prophet. "Oh no, Lord GOD! Look, I don't know how to speak since I am only a youth" (Jer. 1:6 HCSB). In Jeremiah 20, the prophet complained about being a prophet but admitted that when he tried not to proclaim God's message it became like a fire burning in his heart. He couldn't keep it in. Jeremiah acted as a reluctant prophet but one of the most significant as the final days of the Southern Kingdom neared.

The last four kings after Josiah (Jehoahaz, Jehoiakim, Jehoiachin, Zedekiah) turned their backs on the covenant and sent the country into the final slide toward judgment. Jeremiah sought to stem the tide of evil by sending messages to the kings. He also advised the last kings that Judah should submit to Babylon's rule. In 604 he delivered a scroll containing God's word to Jehoiakim detailing God's commands. The king not only ignored it; but as he heard portions of it read, he cut it into pieces and threw them into the fire. The action represented a bold rejection of Yahweh and his prophet. Jehoiakim burned it because he didn't like the political consequences of God's word. Jeremiah responded promptly by dictating the scroll again and issuing a statement to the king. "Therefore, this is what the LORD says concerning Jehoiakim king of Judah: He will have no one to sit on David's throne, and his corpse will be thrown out to be exposed to the heat of the day and the frost of the night. I will punish him" (Jer. 36:30–31). God's word—even when ignored, burned, or rejected—remains God's word and is true regardless of how it is handled. Jehoiakim could not escape God's truth, nor can anyone else.

About the time Jehoiakim burned the scroll, Nebuchadnezzar invaded Judah (604) for the first time, taking several captives back to Babylon. However, he allowed Jehoiakim to stay on as a vassal king. But Jehoiakim wavered between allying Judah with Egypt or Babylon. Jeremiah warned him to submit to Babylon. Nebuchadnezzar invaded again in 597. Jeremiah prophesied to those taken into captivity. The second Babylonian invasion resulted in the transport of several more Hebrews into Babylon including Ezekiel, another prophet. When the captives reached their new home, they were told by false prophets that the exile would be short-lived. These prophets advised them not to settle down but just to wait it out. Jeremiah wrote to the captives with instructions and a prediction. He told them to build houses, plant gardens, take wives for sons, multiply, seek the welfare of the city where you live, pray for the new land, and stop listening to the false prophets who only tell you what you want to hear. Jeremiah assured them the stay would not be short but rather seventy years (two generations). After that the Jews would return. Jeremiah included a message of hope. The captives resided in Babylon as discipline for sin, but God's plan remained intact. "'For I know the plans I have for you'—this is the LORD's declaration—'plans for your welfare, not for disaster, to give you a future and a hope'" (Jer. 29:11 HCSB). God promised a time would come when they would seek him and find him and call to him and he would hear. However, first is the time of discipline and judgment; and in the future God would restore them to Canaan, their homeland.

Jeremiah delivered the same message of judgment and hope to those in Jerusalem. Babylon returned to lay siege on the city in 588 BC, and hope was in short supply. In order to emphasize hope and trust in God, Jeremiah did something unusual. He purchased a piece of land in Judea as a sign that destruction and captivity would not be the end of the Jews in this land. God promised through Jeremiah the people would return and occupy the land again. Jeremiah's family would again inhabit the land he purchased.

A New Covenant

Jeremiah also predicted a covenant change. He served as a transitional prophet to declare that the Mosaic covenant would be replaced. A new covenant would be established unlike that made with Moses. At Sinai God delivered the law to the people. They could see the copy with their eyes and hold it in their hands. An external set of expectations was placed upon God's people. They were to accept it, read it, study it, and live by it. But God's plan of redemption will be fulfilled with a new covenant, Jeremiah explained. This new covenant would be written on the heart of God's people, an internal covenant relationship. "This one will not be like the covenant I made with their ancestors when I took them by the hand to bring them out of the land of Egypt—a covenant they broke. . . . Instead, this is the covenant I will make with the house of Israel. . . . I will place My law within them and write it on their hearts. I will be their God and they will be My people" (Jer. 31:32–33 HCSB).

This prediction looked forward to the coming of Jesus who would establish a personal, internal relationship based on the Spirit. Jesus would place into the heart of the believer his Spirit who would teach, instruct, guide, comfort, and strengthen. God's plan of redemption is Christ's Spirit in the hearts of the people, a final blow to sin.

The people ignored Jeremiah's message, and the destruction of Jerusalem came in 586 BC. Jeremiah described the destruction. Zedekiah, the last king, was only twenty-one years old when the king of Babylon advanced against Jerusalem with his entire army and laid siege. This lasted two years until famine inside the city became so desperate that the warriors fled with Zedekiah. The Chaldeans pursued the Jewish army and slaughtered Zedekiah's sons and commanders before his eyes and deported the king to Babylon. The remaining inhabitants (forty-six hundred in all) of Jerusalem were taken to Babylon; and the city was ransacked and destroyed, including the razing of the temple and the theft of the gold and silver temple articles. With Jerusalem in ruins and the people enslaved, Judah's history as a kingdom ended. The captivity commenced. This historical event declared clearly that God's presence had departed. They were exiles not only physically but spiritually as well. As Adam and Eve were driven from the garden, so were the Hebrews driven from the promised land for sin and rebellion.

After the destruction Jeremiah was treated well by Nebuchadnezzar. Jeremiah moved to Mizpah, where Gedaliah, appointed as governor of Judah by Nebuchadnezzar, resided. The governor was murdered, and the people of Mizpah fled to Egypt. Jeremiah protested, but he was forced to accompany them on the trip. Even in Egypt Jeremiah continued to prophecy concerning the idolatry of the Jews residing there and predicted the conquest of Egypt by Babylon. We know nothing of his death or whether he ever returned to Judah.

EZEKIEL, PROPHET TO THE EXILES (597 BC)

When Nebuchadnezzar invaded Judah the second time, he deported not only the king but also several citizens. Included in that group was a prophet named Ezekiel. While Jeremiah prophesied from Jerusalem during the crisis, Ezekiel prophesied as one of the exiles living in Babylon. He too predicted the destruction of Jerusalem and used unusual object lessons to convey the message of doom to his fellow exiles. In one case he fashioned a model of Jerusalem out of clay and lay down beside it for over a year to symbolize the judgment and siege on the holy city. Each day Ezekiel took a sack lunch to eat while he performed this act. Can you imagine what the Jews walking by must have thought? Surely they noticed the seriousness of the prophet's message because of it.

On another occasion Ezekiel cut off his hair to reenact what would occur in Jerusalem when Nebuchadnezzar finally subdued the city. He used a sharp sword to remove his hair and then dealt with it as the Babylonians would deal with the inhabitants of Jerusalem. He used a sword to chop up one-third of the hair indicating many would die by the sword of the enemy. Another third he cast into the air so the wind could take it away, symbolizing the scattering into captivity. The last third was put to the fire to show that many would die due to the famine and plague brought on by the siege. By this action he proclaimed the seriousness of the judgment about to overtake Jerusalem. The covenant was serious business, and the consequence of neglecting it devastating.

Perhaps the most important theological statement delivered by Ezekiel came through a vision. In the covenant agreement God promised to be with his people and bless them if they obeyed. However, the worst consequence of disobedience was not the destruction of Jerusalem or even the captivity. The greatest judgment involved the separation of the Jews from God. In the wilderness the Lord guided them by night with a pillar of fire and by day with a cloud. When they camped, he dwelt in their midst in the tabernacle. When Solomon's temple was constructed, the holy of holies served as God's dwelling place among the people. What made them God's people and unique among all nations was the presence of the one and only God with them. Because of their sin and rebellion, that presence ceased. In Ezekiel 10, a science-fiction-sounding vision revealed that the glory of God, which dwelled in the holy of holies, was leaving. In the vision the glory of the Lord (represented by a chariot with wheels within wheels) moved away from the threshold of the temple, moved to the eastern gate of the Lord's house, and departed. The message was undeniable. God's throne was on wheels. God would not dwell among a rebellious people but not because he is a vindictive God. The grace and mercy of God delayed a long time as he sent prophet after prophet to sway the Jews back to the covenant. But in the end Judah remained obstinate. God departed from them, making this the worst consequence of the judgment events.

Ezekiel proclaimed hope, matching the pattern of the other prophets. One of his most famous visions graphically depicted hope for Judah. In Ezekiel 37, the prophet recounted an event where the spirit of God transported him to a valley full of bones. Obviously a great battle occurred in the valley, and the remaining broken skeletons populated it. God asked Ezekiel what he saw, and he replied with the obvious. Then God commanded the prophet to prophesy to the bones, and activity commenced. As Ezekiel prophesied, the bones came together forming full skeletons, followed by tendons appearing and then flesh. Dead corpses filled the valley. Then God told Ezekiel to prophesy to the breath that it would enter the dead bodies. The valley, once filled with the carnage of a past war, stirred with life. The message came out of this life drama. "Then He said to me, 'Son of man, these bones are the whole house of Israel. Look how they say: Our bones are dried up, and our hope has perished; we are cut off. Therefore, prophesy and say to them:

This is what the Lord GOD says: I am going to open your graves and bring you up from them, My people, and lead you into the land of Israel'" (Ezek. 37:11–12 HCSB). God promised through Ezekiel that the Jews would return to the promised land and experience life again.

The greatest message of hope coming from Ezekiel's prophecy echoed that of Jeremiah (31:33–34). Ezekiel also prophesied of a new covenant that would be internal and marked by God's Spirit. "I will give you a new heart and put a new spirit in you; I will remove from you your heart of stone and give you a heart of flesh. And I will put my Spirit in you and move you to follow my decrees and be careful to keep my laws. You will live in the land I gave our forefathers; you will be my people, and I will be your God" (Ezek. 36:26–28).

The language of God's promise is covenant language. You will be my people, and I will be your God. However, this covenant differs dramatically from the Mosaic. It is an internal relationship with God's Spirit indwelling the individual. The Spirit moves and directs the believer to follow God's decrees. He creates in his people a new heart and spirit. The presence of God departed from the temple but would return as the Spirit indwelling believers. Both Ezekiel and Jeremiah prepared the way for Jesus, Pentecost, and a new Israel—the church.

THINGS TO CONSIDER

God is a promise keeper. From the beginning he issued promises and kept them, judgment and blessing. God is sovereign. He even used pagan nations to fulfill his goals. Nebuchadnezzar never knew he was God's instrument, but he accomplished exactly what God determined. This practice of God continued into the next act of the story as the sovereign Lord used another king to bring his people back to Canaan. God is also a holy God. Habakkuk declared it in his prophecy. "Your eyes are too pure to look on evil, and You cannot tolerate wrongdoing" (Hab. 1:13 HCSB). God refused to accept and tolerate the sin of any human including his people, Judah. His justice demanded an accounting for this affront to his holiness. He warned, pleaded, and encouraged Judah through the prophets to avoid the judgment by repenting and returning to the covenant, but Judah refused to heed the message. Judgment came in full force in 586 BC. God is a God of compassion and mercy. He promised a return to the land in seventy years. He promised a new covenant marked by his Spirit in the hearts of believers.

STUDY QUESTIONS

1. Why would God use sinful people to judge sinful people?
2. What did the captivity teach the people about God's justice and holiness?
3. What was the worst part of the judgment on Judah?
4. What did Jeremiah and Ezekiel mean by a covenant written on the heart?

ACT 2

THE CAPTIVITY

Most of the people of Judah ended up either dead or in captivity in Babylon as a result of God's judgment. Little remained of the capital city that David conquered and made his capital, which Solomon beautified with a temple and a palace, and tradition established as the center of all civil and religious life of Judah. From the beginning of the exile (604 BC), seventy years passed before the return to begin the process of rebuilding as God promised. In the meantime the Jews made a new life in the home of their captors. Some prophets continued to impact the people. Jeremiah probably went to Egypt with several of the escapees, and some traditions say he may have been killed by his own people. Ezekiel continued to live among the exiles until his death while Daniel lived through the exile until the return.

DANIEL (605–533)

Nebuchadnezzar transported Daniel, along with several other young Jewish men, to Babylon around 604 BC. Daniel—along with Shadrach, Meshach, and Abednego—received training to serve the king's court but desired to remain faithful to Yahweh. That proved difficult, but they held steady. These men and the stories about them became the encouragement for the other Jews in captivity or under oppression to stay true to God and his covenant.

Upon arriving in Babylon, Daniel and his fellow captives resided in the king's palace for the training as court aids. Daniel knew that in a pagan king's house, the food and drink might not be acceptable according to the law of God. Nebuchadnezzar claimed to be a deity, and much of the meat and drink items offered in the pagan temple ended up in the palace for consumption. Daniel and his three friends determined in their hearts not to defile themselves with this food used in pagan worship. Daniel approached the chief official to ask if he, Shadrach, Meshach, and Abednego could eat other things. The official refused, fearing what might happen if these men turned out unhealthy. Daniel then asked the guard for permission to eat only vegetables and drink water for ten days as a test. He agreed, and in ten days the four young Hebrews looked healthier and better than the others. They continued the regimen; and after the training, when they stood before the king, Nebuchadnezzar found them to be best of the bunch. "In every matter of wisdom and understanding that the king consulted them about, he found them 10 times better than all the diviner-priests and mediums in his entire kingdom" (Dan. 1:20 HCSB). Daniel became a close advisor to the king and an interpreter of dreams for him. God used the story of Daniel to reinforce the truth that God blesses those who remain faithful to the covenant. Surely Daniel's example served to encourage Jews suffering oppression for their faith both then and later.

Nebuchadnezzar had a dream that troubled him greatly, and he sought an interpretation. Daniel rose to the occasion while others could not. The dream proved to be a prediction of the future of Babylon and the kingdoms to follow. In the dream Nebuchadnezzar saw a statue made of several different materials. The statue was finally destroyed by a stone which struck it. Daniel first recounted the dream, a feat none of the other advisors could accomplish. The head of the statue was fashioned with gold, the chest and arms of silver, the stomach and thighs of bronze, and the legs of iron. The feet were made of iron mixed with clay, giving the statue a less than stable base. A stone struck the statue in the feet, shattering it so soundly that the wind carried the pieces away like the chaff of grain. The stone became a great mountain. Daniel told Nebuchadnezzar that the golden head represented Babylon. His kingdom would be followed by three other kingdoms represented by the various metals of the statue. The last kingdom represented by the legs would stand until the stone struck the clay-weakened feet. From history we know the following kingdoms to be Babylonian, Persian, Greek, and Roman. The stone came from God, destroyed the Roman kingdom, and established a kingdom that will never be destroyed. The stone was a symbol referring to Jesus who started the Christian movement, which eventually took over the Roman Empire and continues now. As a result of Daniel's work, Nebuchadnezzar recognized Daniel's God. He also appointed his friends as managers of provinces around the kingdom. Daniel remained in the court as an advisor to the king.

Much of Daniel's writing falls into the category of apocalyptic literature. This literature used symbols and visions to convey a message of hope to a people under oppression. Daniel's visions and his life predicted victory for those who are faithful to God. This victory comes through the Messiah who reigns over his people and proves victorious over evil. Daniel predicted both the first coming of Jesus and the second coming. In some cases it is difficult to determine which he speaks of.

Certainly the hope of the Jews and the world rests on the Messiah in all his appearances. Daniel looked forward to the new covenant in his visions.

JEWS AND THE CAPTIVITY

The destruction of Jerusalem and the exile of the Jews to another land under the oppression of another king represented "the boldest possible contradiction of Israel's election and covenant promises."[1] The Hebrews were confused and sought an explanation for the catastrophe. The prophets had offered the answer before the destruction, and during the captivity the Jews began to agree. Israel's failure to obey the covenant and remain faithful to Yahweh brought on this judgment. Therefore, the solution seemed clear: return to the law and to Yahweh. The exilic and especially postexilic Jews focused on the law, and over time a new kind of Judaism developed. The law focus eventually grew into legalism. Because of this emphasis some of the sins that once plagued Israel were avoided. For example, the Jews learned not to involve themselves in idolatry as they did before the fall of Jerusalem.

With no temple, no holy city of Jerusalem, and living in a foreign land, the exiles needed ways of worshipping God. Many believe the synagogue grew up during the exile as a place to worship and study the Torah. If neglecting such things sent the Hebrews into exile, then worship and study of the law must be reemphasized. *Synagogue* simply means "congregation, meeting or gathering of the people." It probably originally referred simply to the gathering of the people in the exile to study the Torah and worship Yahweh. It was probably not until the first century BC or even the first century AD that the word also referred to a building for meeting.

THE PERSIAN EMPIRE RISES

At the end of Daniel's time as prophet, he served under a new kingdom, the Persian Empire. Cyrus the Great arrived on the scene around 559 BC and within ten years became the undisputed king of Media. Isaiah even predicted the arrival of this ruler who would end the exile for the Jews (Isa. 44:28). His kingdom soon entailed all of Persia, the northern part of Mesopotamia, Armenia, and Asia Minor. He turned his attention on Babylon to the south and laid siege to the city in 539 BC. Upon Babylon's defeat, Cyrus the Great incorporated the Babylonian Empire into his own, the kingdom represented by silver in Nebuchadnezzar's statue dream. The Persian Empire practiced different methods for dealing with captives. Cyrus established his rule over them by allowing them to return to their homeland and rebuild the temple. This was common in the ancient near east. By rebuilding the temple of a conquered people, a king declared his divine right to rule over them.

---

[1] D. A. Hagner, "Judaism," in *New Bible Dictionary,* 622.

Returning to their home country also helped keep the conquered people happier under the rule of the Persian king. Cyrus decreed in 538 BC that all the Jews could return to their homeland. The Jews saw this as fulfillment of prophecy. The door opened for God's promise of return to be fulfilled (Ezek. 37; Jer. 29).

THINGS TO CONSIDER

Daniel obviously represented the best scenario of the exile. He remained loyal to the covenant and Yahweh. He presented the model for all the Jews during times of captivity, oppression, and persecution. He also predicted the coming of the Messiah who would establish a new and eternal kingdom. While in captivity the Jews worshipped together, studied the law, and learned some lessons. Idolatry became less attractive to them. Cyrus the Great made it possible for the exiles to return and repopulate the land promised to Abraham. The return would mean much work to rebuild Jerusalem and become the people of God once more.

STUDY QUESTIONS

1. How did Daniel offer an example for other Jews living in exile?
2. What did Daniel predict which gave hope to the Jews?
3. What changes occurred among the Jews while in captivity?
4. Why is Cyrus the Great important to the biblical story?

ACT 3

The Return from Exile
and the Rebuilding of the Temple

With the decree of Cyrus the Great, the first group of exilic Jews made their way back to Jerusalem. The first exiles went into Babylon around 604 BC; and now, as Jeremiah and Ezekiel predicted, they began the return to the land promised Abraham. They will come in three waves being led by people significant to the biblical story. We call this time the Postexilic Period. It includes the rebuilding of the temple and the city of Jerusalem as well as an increased focus on the Law. Several postexilic prophets prophesied, delivering a message from God to the people in this critical time of transition.

The First Exiles Return

Zerubbabel led the first group of exiles back to what was left of Jerusalem in 536 BC. He served as the governor and took on special significance to the prophets such as Zechariah. Returning under the decree of Cyrus, they were even allowed to bear the temple articles taken by Nebuchadnezzar. The gold and silver articles numbered fifty-four hundred and would be placed in the new temple upon completion. The biblical story says that 42,360 returned at this time plus slaves and stock.[2] Many Jews either could not or chose not to return to the promised land. They no doubt followed Jeremiah's advice in Jeremiah 29 and built houses, married off children, planted crops, and made the exilic home a permanent one. Zerubbabel su-

---

[2] There is debate concerning the number of returning Jews to Jerusalem. Ezra's number of 42,360 may refer to the number in the first group returning with Zerubbabel in 536 BC or to the total number to return to Jerusalem in all the groups. He includes Nehemiah's name in the list who didn't return until 445 BC. See Thomas V. Briscoe, *Holman Bible Atlas,* 168–69 for this discussion.

pervised the construction of the temple and served as governor for those returning at this time. Upon arrival many gave a freewill offering to the temple project; and before the work commenced, they worshipped. The foundation was laid, but many of the older returnees seeing its size wept. It would not compare to Solomon's. Many non-Jews surrounding the ruins of Jerusalem opposed the building project and complained to Cyrus. He stopped the work on the temple, fearing another great king would rule over the city. However, under the next Persian king, Darius, the building resumed. Once again the Jews would have seen God's hand in Darius's decree.

This temple project proved to be a daunting one for several reasons. Many of the surrounding people opposed this work and attempted to stop it in several ways. First, they offered to help build, claiming they too wanted to seek and worship God as they always had. Zerubbabel and the other Jewish leaders realized this as deception and probably an attempt to sabotage the work. Since that didn't work, the enemies hired counselors to frustrate the plans and work on the new temple. They sought to convince the Persians to stop it. Cyrus did stop the work.

Other issues hurt the construction progress. Materials were not readily available and certainly not the same kind of materials used for Solomon's temple. As the Jews faced these problems, they tired and questioned why they should worry about the temple when their own houses were still in ruins. They switched focus to personal property instead of God's house. A disappointment also placed a damper on the building. Those older returnees, who had either heard about the glory of Solomon's temple or even saw it, realized that this temple would not match its glory. The resources and workers were not available. As the work slowed to a halt, God sent prophets to reignite the fire for the task. Darius had also reversed the order to stop work on the temple.

HAGGAI (520 BC)

God called a prophet named Haggai, who probably represented the older generation that went into exile and lived through it. As a young man he may have seen Solomon's temple and lamented over its demise. Because of his age, Haggai effectively related to the older generation of returnees. He could understand their disappointment and sadness. As a prophet Haggai had one task: to encourage the Jews to finish God's temple. He argued that even though the houses needed work, the Jews must first focus on God's house. His message sounded like what Jesus would say to followers later in Matthew 6:33: "But seek first the kingdom of God and His righteousness, and all these things will be provided for you" (HCSB).

Something unusual happened. The people actually listened to Haggai and resumed work. Throughout the biblical story most of the prophets met with little success. They were rejected, killed, and ignored; but few saw positive movement in the people because of their message. Haggai presented God's message clearly and effectively.

Zechariah (520 BC)

No doubt Zechariah was the younger of the two prophets sent to prompt temple completion, and his role involved speaking to the younger generation. His first message from God paralleled Haggai's: get busy building God's house. He too met with success, and the people seriously worked to complete the temple. The Jews completed and dedicated the new temple in 516 BC. Jerusalem now looked a little more like home. However, differences existed.

The new temple did not rival Solomon's even though it served to reestablish the sacrificial system and the worship of God. Neglect of the Law and proper worship had sent the Jews into exile. Another difference related to the presence of God. In Solomon's temple God resided among the people in the holy of holies, but God's presence left the temple before its destruction (Ezek. 10). Even with the dedication, God's presence did not return to the temple in the same way. That presence would wait for the Messiah, Jesus, who would be "God with us." The new covenant predicted by Jeremiah and Ezekiel would again establish God's presence with his people as his Spirit dwelled within each of them.

Things to Consider

God fulfilled his promise to return the Jews to Canaan. The returning exiles settled in Jerusalem and began the work on the temple. This project ranked as most important since the rejection of God sent them into exile. When the second temple was completed, the sacrificial system could be reinstituted. The promises of God to bless and bring blessing from Israel seemed possible again. All of these events moved the biblical story closer to its goal. The task of resettling and rebuilding was not yet complete, but God would send others to direct that work. However, during this time the Jews continued to struggle with some of the sins that had sent them into captivity in the first place. Prophets and leaders continued to address those issues as the story continued.

Study Questions

1. What things hindered the Jews from building the temple?
2. Why was it important for the Hebrews to rebuild the temple before anything else?
3. Why does God's presence not inhabit the new temple?
4. How did Haggai and Zechariah help in completing the temple?

ACT 4

Rebuilding Jerusalem

zra led another group to Jerusalem around 457 BC. "Some of the Israelites, priests, Levites, singers, gatekeepers, and temple servants accompanied him to Jerusalem in the seventh year of King Artaxerxes" (Ezra 7:7 HCSB).[3] These people probably helped reestablish temple worship. Ezra helped to reinstate the sacrificial system in Jerusalem as well. Ezra took on an important task of training the people in the Law. He was an impassioned teacher and practitioner of the law. "Because Ezra had determined in his heart to study the law of the LORD, obey it, and teach its statutes and ordinances in Israel" (Ezra 7:10). As Haggai and Zechariah worked to get the temple built, Ezra labored to inform and encourage the people in the ways of God as stated in the Law. After the building of the temple, this task ranked as the number one need in Jerusalem. The people endured seventy years in captivity at the hands of the Babylonians because they broke God's law and rejected the covenant and received judgment for it. The simplest way to avoid a similar judgment in the future involved knowledge of and commitment to God's ways as the priority. Ezra determined to teach them that law and call them to obedience. Ezra's emphasis may have been responsible for moving Judaism into a legalistic direction.

Ezra faced a difficult task. Already many of the returning Jews had taken foreign wives and, as a result, risked pagan influence. Ezra called all the returning exiles together and had them promise to God to send away their foreign wives and children. Ezra 10 even lists those who were guilty of intermarriage with foreign-

---

[3] A chronology of Persian kings might help keep up with the biblical story at this point. According to Thomas Briscoe in *The Holman Bible Atlas,* the kings of Persia important to this section of the story are: Cyrus the Great (559–530 BC), Cambyses II (530–522 BC) (not mentioned in Bible), Darius I (522–486 BC), Xerxes (486–465 BC), Artaxerxes I (465–425 BC), Xerxes II (423 BC) (not mentioned in Bible), Darius II (423–404 BC) (not mentioned in Bible). See chart in Thomas Briscoe, *The Holman Bible Atlas,* 166.

ers. Ezra continued to teach the people the ways of God, hoping they would truly become his people now that they were home in Jerusalem again.

NEHEMIAH (445 BC)

The temple stood in the middle of Jerusalem and served as the religious center of the Jewish people. Houses were built, and the city resumed as an active center of life after a long time in ruin. However, several important projects remained to make Jerusalem the city it needed to be. The most important task concerned the broken and scattered wall of the once great city. In the fortress city of Susa where king Artaxerxes resided, a Jew named Nehemiah served as the king's cupbearer. The cupbearer's job of testing the wine and food of the king for his safety resulted in a close and trusting relationship with the king. However, being in exile, Nehemiah longed for news from Jerusalem concerning resettlement and developments. A group of Jews arrived from Jerusalem, and Nehemiah inquired about the state of the city. The report disturbed him. The Jews were in disgrace and danger because the walls of the city still lay in ruins. The people enjoyed no protection or security. In addition, the rebuilding of Jerusalem corresponded with God's promises to reestablish the Jews in the promised land after the exile. The restoration was incomplete without the wall.

"When I heard these words, I sat down and wept. I mourned for a number of days, fasting and praying before the God of heaven" (Neh. 1:4 HCSB). Nehemiah prayed in his distress and pledged to God that he would return to rebuild the walls if the Lord would move the king to allow it. "Give Your servant success today, and have compassion on him in the presence of this man" (Neh. 1:11). The man Nehemiah referred to was King Artaxerxes. Under Persian rules no one approached the king with a sad face. Nehemiah risked his life to ask the king for permission to go to Jerusalem and rebuild the wall. God answered Nehemiah's prayer, and the meeting went well. In fact, the king not only agreed but sent with Nehemiah letters to the governors guaranteeing a safe journey. In addition, Artaxerxes sent letters to secure building materials for the wall. Nehemiah set out for Jerusalem to rebuild the wall.

Upon arrival Nehemiah waited to inform the people of his purpose. First, he took the time to survey the damage and calculate exactly what needed to be done and what it would require. The story of Nehemiah provides key principles for leadership. Once he knew the scope of the task, Nehemiah organized the people according to gifts and abilities and put them on the wall. Rebuilding Jerusalem's wall displeased many of the non-Jews in the region. Sanballat and Tobiah led the opposition. They mocked the Jews and eventually issued threats. However, Nehemiah's leadership skills met the challenge. While some worked on the wall, Nehemiah stationed others with weapons to protect. The workers continued with a secure feeling.

Perhaps the most significant assurance both Nehemiah and the people had was the power of God in the midst of them. Nehemiah reminded them of this when they became discouraged. God would fight for them. The story says that God frustrated the plans of Sanballat so the work could continue. "The God of heaven is the One who will grant us success" (Neh. 2:20). That became Nehemiah's theme for the task. God did grant success, and the Jews completed the wall in just fifty-two days. That achievement would be remarkable even today; but considering Nehemiah's tools, the opposition he faced, and the daunting task, it could be considered a miraculous achievement. God ensured victory even in the building of Jerusalem's wall. Now the city had a temple, houses and buildings, and a wall to protect it. The return to former status was gaining ground. God kept his promises.

Following the rebuilding of the wall, Nehemiah directed the people to celebrate and worship. He engaged Ezra to read the law publicly to all the people. The people wept when they heard the words of the law. Ezra instructed them not to mourn but rather to rejoice in the Lord for what he had done. They observed the Festival of Booths, looking back to the days the Hebrews lived in the wilderness after being rescued from Egypt. This was followed by a national day of confession. The people confessed their sins before the Lord and vowed before God to obey his laws. The vow included an agreement not to marry outsiders or give wives to them, to keep the Sabbath holy, and to tithe regularly. They dedicated the wall and gave thanks. Jerusalem was resettled, and Jewish life in Palestine resumed.

Nehemiah returned to King Artaxerxes; but while he was away, a priest named Eliashib allowed a foreigner, Tobiah, to have a room in the storehouse of the temple. Nehemiah received permission to return. He cleaned out the rooms and chastised the officials for allowing God's house to be neglected. Other problems required reform as well. Nehemiah chided the people for profaning the Sabbath by selling goods on the special day. The problem of marrying foreigners continued, and Nehemiah reminded them of their covenant commitment. The purity of the priests had declined as well. Nehemiah purified the Levites and reorganized some of their activities. Nehemiah became God's reformer. Why was this needed? The Jews had been back in Jerusalem only a short time, and already they were involved in the same sins of the past with the exception of idolatry. Nehemiah did his best to direct them to Yahweh and the Law.

MALACHI, THE LAST PROPHET (435 BC)

As already noted, the return focused on the Law. It was read, emphasized, and pushed on the people. However, they still struggled with it and in many cases simply ignored it doing as they pleased. God sent one last prophet to point out the most blatant violations of the covenant and correct them. Many of those infractions occurred because of the influence of the surrounding peoples like the Samaritans. Malachi arrived around 435 BC and prophesied God's indictment concerning these sins. He started with the leaders who should have been more faithful. The priesthood suffered with ethical and moral problems. They treated the sacrifices lightly by offering maimed and less than perfect animals. Malachi informed them that this action defiled the Lord's table. By sinning, the priests had caused many to stumble. In addition, they showed partiality to some while ignoring others. God promised through Malachi that these priests would be cursed and their descendents rebuked. The spiritual leaders in Jerusalem needed to improve if the people were to become faithful to the Law again. The priests were responsible to lead, and they were leading poorly. God accused them and judged them for it.

The problem of intermarriage continued to be an issue. The influence of the surrounding peoples had an effect on the Jews. Malachi painted a horrible picture. He accused them of acting treacherously and doing a detestable thing. The men left the wives of their youth, acquired a divorce, and then found younger, prettier wives among those non-Jewish people. Malachi informed them that the Lord's altar was covered with tears because God no longer accepted the offerings. One other sin plagued the Jews. Malachi accused them of robbing God. They refused to pay the tithe that God required and, by doing so, robbed him of his due. Malachi challenged them to test God by giving the tithes and to see if the Lord would not care for their needs in an abundant way. If they refused, God's rebuke would be their reward. As a final warning, Malachi revisited the theme of the Day of the Lord. To continue in the sins would result in being consumed by God in judgment at the end. That day will be a time "when all the arrogant and everyone who commits wickedness will become stubble" (Mal. 4:1 HCSB).

In Malachi's final statement he emphasized God's command to remember the covenant and the importance of living accordingly. "Remember the instruction of Moses My servant, the statutes and ordinances I commanded him at Horeb for all Israel" (Mal. 4:4 HCSB). Malachi ended the prophecy with a prediction of the coming of Elijah to precede the Day of the Lord. "Look, I am going to send you Elijah the prophet before the great and awesome Day of the LORD comes. And he will turn the hearts of fathers to their children and the hearts of children to their fathers. Otherwise, I will come and strike the land with a curse" (Mal. 4:5–6). The Day of the Lord no doubt corresponded with the coming of the Messiah, and John the Baptist represented the Elijah of Malachi's prophesy.

BETWEEN THE TESTAMENTS

The Old Testament portion of the biblical story ended with Malachi around 400 BC, and the New Testament portion began around 4–6 BC with the birth of Jesus. In the intervening four hundred years (Intertestamental Period), the Jews survived the Persians, the Greeks (320 BC), a brief period of independence (142–63 BC), and the Romans who took Palestine in 63 BC. During this time a unique Judaism developed which became the Judaism of Jesus' day. It was characterized by specific groups of people such as Pharisees (strict legalists), Sadducees (Jewish aristocracy who controlled Sanhedrin), scribes (experts in Law), Herodians (supporters of rule of Herods), zealots (extreme Jewish patriots), sinners (common people), and publicans (tax collectors for Rome), and institutions like the Sanhedrin (council of seventy made up of Sadducees and Pharisees), and the synagogue (meeting place away from the temple for worship and study). A strict legalism grew out of this period as many of the leaders and priests realized close adherence to the law was necessary to avoid worse fates than the captivity. At the same time, while suffering under successive occupying forces, the Jewish ideas of the Messiah grew in importance, and the expectation for the Messiah increased. Circumstances became right for the coming of the final solution to the sin problem, Jesus the Messiah.

STUDY QUESTIONS

1. What was the main task of Ezra, and how did he accomplish it?
2. What was Nehemiah's main task, and how did he accomplish it?
3. What was Malachi's main message, and what sins did he condemn?
4. What developments occurred in the Intertestamental Period?

ACT 5

WISDOM: FINDING GOD'S WAY

I n the Old Testament canon several writings focus on the concept of wisdom as the Jews understood that. Most of the information on wisdom appears in the Wisdom Literature (Ecclesiastes, Proverbs, Song of Songs, and Job) and the Psalms. The Jews always connected wisdom to God. "The fear of the LORD is the beginning of wisdom" (Ps. 111:10). The Hebrew writers believed clearly that the wise person recognized God and his place in life. To the contrary, the foolish person rejected God or even lived as if there was no God. The biblical books listed above contain passages that discuss the benefits and dangers of the choice between these two options. The key idea is that life is better with God. To fear the Lord and follow him is the wise choice. The wise person would be the one who takes seriously God and the biblical story of redemption and gives it proper credence and belief. Perhaps a closer look at this Hebrew concept of wisdom is in order.

A DEFINITION OF BIBLICAL WISDOM

In the Old Testament wisdom carried a practical emphasis. It included the art of being successful or accomplishing what is needed. Solomon received wisdom to fulfill the role as king. Its source was always God. It included complete knowledge but also a sense of God's mind or will. It related to the covenant God. Without God the wisdom of the world was doomed to failure.[4] The New Testament also picked up the practical emphasis of wisdom. The wise were those granted wisdom by God. Leaders of the church received it to lead well. It was connected to a relationship with God and represented the ability to see God's reality and the world as God's creation. It included God's way and will. For this reason the cross of Christ

---

[4] D. A. Hubbard, "Wisdom," in *New Bible Dictionary,* 1244.

to the non-Christian appeared foolish, but to the believer it was the way to salvation and hope.

James in his letter compared two kinds of wisdom, worldly wisdom and God's wisdom. The person possessing God's wisdom always exhibits that wisdom in practical ways—good life and deeds done in humility. But worldly wisdom shows itself in selfishness, envy, and boasting. The world values self-advancement and boasting, which always leads to disorder and evil. James contrasted it with God's wisdom. "But the wisdom that comes from heaven is first of all pure; then peace-loving, considerate, submissive, full of mercy and good fruit, impartial and sincere. Peacemakers who sow in peace raise a harvest of righteousness" (James 3:17–18).

James's idea of wisdom is a life controlled by God, who produces in that person proper action. Wisdom begins with and is connected to God. James said, "If any of you lacks wisdom, he should ask God, who gives generously to all without finding fault, and it will be given to him" (James 1:5). God is the source of wisdom in the biblical sense.

PSALMS

The Psalms, written over several centuries by numerous human authors, eventually came together into one collection. Many of the Psalms conveyed the feelings, understandings, and struggles of those who followed God. Often they focus on worship, praise, and dependence. In fact the Hebrews used the Psalms in their worship practices. Not all 150 psalms deal specifically with wisdom, but they offer insight into how those who feared God related to and lived under him. A few of the psalms speak of the choice between wisdom and foolishness directly, presenting the choice and describing the consequences. Psalm 1 contrasts the two ways of life, one with God and one without. Psalm 1 begins with a description of the man who includes God in his life and follows him. "How happy is the man who does not follow the advice of the wicked, or take the path of sinners, or join a group of mockers! Instead, his delight is in the LORD's instruction, and he meditates on it day and night. He is like a tree planted beside streams of water that bears its fruit in season and whose leaf does not wither. Whatever he does prospers" (Ps. 1:1–3 HCSB).

This wise person decided he would not follow the way of rebellion and sin but would instead delight in, meditate on, and follow God's way. The result of this choice stands at the center of the psalmist's message. The wise person experiences a fruitful and vital life. He succeeds in life. Surely no one would reject that kind of life.

To contrast the psalmist speaks of the foolish man who rejects God's way. "The wicked are not like this; instead, they are like chaff that the wind blows away. Therefore the wicked will not survive the judgment, and sinners will not be in the community of the righteous. For the Lord watches over the way of the righteous, but the way of the wicked leads to ruin" (Ps. 1:4–6 HCSB).

Israel and Judah served as the best illustrations of this warning. Because of their wickedness the two kingdoms did not survive but ended in ruin. From the beginning God told Abraham and Moses that to follow his ways resulted in blessing but to reject God ended in curse. Wisdom involved a choice.

ECCLESIASTES

Ecclesiastes offered a different and perhaps more direct approach to wisdom. A so-called teacher wrote this book. The teacher addressed one of the most important questions in the life of an individual. How can one find fulfillment? Ecclesiastes offered several possible answers for this question only to find all but one worthless.

A favorite word in Ecclesiastes is *futile* or *vanity*. The word means "meaningless." The teacher tried wealth to find fulfillment and found it only led to emptiness. He tried relationships, but that too ended in futility. The teacher spent much time in intellectual pursuits (writing, botany, and zoology), but those ended the same way—vanity. He even tried the main Western cultural pursuit—pleasure. But like the other options he found nothing of lasting value. He was powerful and well-known, but these too offered no fulfillment. So where can fulfillment be found? After discussing all the possibilities, the teacher concluded: "Now all has been heard; here is the conclusion of the matter: Fear God and keep his commandments, for this is the whole duty of man. For God will bring every deed into judgment, including every hidden thing, whether it is good or evil" (Eccles. 12:13–14).

The discussion in Ecclesiastes sounds like a man who, having reached old age and having made some poor life choices, remembers or finally figures life out: without God it is worthless, and with him it is life. Maybe the teacher wanted the choice to be clearer for those who followed him.

JOB

The book of Job contains some of the most original poetry found in the Bible.[5] It tells the story of a man named Job and his encounters with his friends and God. Some might see Job as merely a contrived story addressing the problem of evil and suffering—why righteous people suffer. Others see it as the story of a historical figure whose life gives us information on dealing with the problem of evil and suffering. Without evidence to the contrary, we take it as the biblical account of a real man, Job, and his troubles. Not much is known about Job except that he faithfully followed God. The account tells us of his tragic life and how he lived through it. Job is an example of a good person who experienced all the horrible things a person can endure. The story begins with Satan's attempt to prove to God that people serve him only because he gives them good gifts. If the same people lose

---

[5] H. L. Ellison, "Book of Job," in *New Bible Dictionary*, 590.

those good things in life, they will reject God. Here is a wisdom question. Should a person remain faithful to God regardless of circumstance? This question received an answer in Job's situation.

Job possessed many things the world considers important—wealth, a large family, respect from neighbors and family, and health. Satan argued that if he lost these things he would also give up his faith in God. Satan was allowed to test the theory, and bad things happened to a good man named Job. He lost his wealth, his sons and daughters, his servants, and eventually his health. Even Job's wife advised him to curse God and die; but Job considered the way of wisdom, the fear of the Lord, as still the best choice. Several of his friends even doubted his faithfulness to God in the midst of this tragedy. They believed a good person who follows God and obeys his law will be blessed by God. In other words before he lost everything, Job was considered a faithful follower of God because of his possessions and family. Conversely, his friends believed that those who disobey God and sin against him will be punished; they lose all. The friends argued that Job must be a sinner because God was punishing him so severely. According to them the solution required confession and repentance. Job knew that to be untrue.

Job questioned God but did not give up his faith. "But I know my living Redeemer, and He will stand on the dust at last. Even after my skin has been destroyed, yet I will see my God in my flesh" (Job 19:25–26 HCSB). In the end God spoke to Job to ensure him that he is God, and Job as a mere human could not understand all the ways of God. What Job needed was to trust God. In the end trust in God's love, power, and justice carries the believer through. Job agreed. "I know that you can do anything and no plan of Yours can be thwarted. . . . Surely I spoke about things I did not understand, things too wonderful for me to know" (Job 42:2–3). Job confessed his weakness and repented for questioning God. He decided to trust God even in the midst of a horrible circumstance. In the end God restored Job's prosperity with new children, new wealth and health. Job went through tough times and still decided it was wise to follow God.

Many good people suffer in this world. Sin not only affected Adam and Eve, but it tainted and twisted the world and nature. We live in this world affected by sin. Sin brings pain and suffering and eventually death. Many innocent people are touched by it for no particular fault of their own. People die in accidents. Disease strikes many. Like Job these sufferers ask why things happen. The answers may never be known. However, Job's example to Israel was that the wise person trusts God in the midst of distress and suffering. Trusting brings strength and comfort during trouble. God is the best choice in all circumstances. God created the world, sustains it, and remains always the powerful one to trust. The book of Job ended with the sovereign assuring Job and Israel that he is still Yahweh and can be trusted.

Song of Songs

This writing presents some of the most interesting approaches to wisdom we encounter in the Bible. Because of its uniqueness many have struggled with how to interpret its uncomfortable statements. It is the story of a love between two people sometimes described in graphic ways. In the past, scholars attempted to make it less uncomfortable by allegorizing it. Instead of seeing Song of Songs as a love story between a man and a woman they allegorized it to mean the love between Christ and his church or God and Israel. However, even the best interpreter struggles with the language of the text when following those interpretive options.

The point of the Song of Songs is to describe marriage and the love relationship between a man and a woman as husband and wife. It illustrates "the rich wonders of human love" in graphic and bold language.[6] "How beautiful you are, my darling. How very beautiful! Behind your veil, your eyes are doves. Your hair is like a flock of goats streaming down Mount Gilead. Your teeth are like a flock of newly shorn sheep coming up from washing, each one having a twin, and not one missing" (Song 4:1–2 HCSB). The writer described a beautiful woman with great hair, striking eyes, and all her teeth. How would that relate to Jesus and the church? The best option is to take the story at face value. The writer speaks of his lover, and she speaks of him. What could this mean? The wisdom writer wanted to describe a normal, genuine marriage love between two people who love God and live for him. It's about monogamous marriage under the covenant of God. Wisdom deals with all areas of life including marriage. God's desire for marriage is for one woman and one man to love each other deeply. To follow God's ways makes marriage better. By the way, the graphic language reflects how two people who love each other really talk when no one is around. Song of Songs allows us to eavesdrop on the conversation.

Proverbs, the Standard for Wisdom

The book of Proverbs clearly deals with wisdom. It distinguishes between the foolish man and the wise one mostly through a series of two-line poetic sayings. These sayings (written by several authors—Solomon, Agur, Lemuel, and others unknown) are not rules or laws for living but rather models of wisdom. They represent what is generally true or usually true in life. They do not state what is always true. Therefore, the individual proverbs should not be taken as commandments but as direction and guidance. The book of Proverbs has been described as "a guidebook for successful living."[7] Proverbial material was not unique to the Hebrews. Writings like Proverbs survived from Egypt, Mesopotamia, and Greece. However, the Hebrew proverbs differed because of the belief that God is the starting point for

---

[6] D. A. Hubbard, "Song of Solomon" in *New Bible Dictionary,* 1122.
[7] D. A. Hubbard, "Book of Proverbs," in *New Bible Dictionary,* 977.

wisdom. "From beginning to end, Proverbs deals with the practical concerns of an individual who knows God."[8]

Proverbs compares two ways of life by addressing multiple themes and showing how the wise man prospers while the foolish man does not. The first part of the book of Proverbs deals with the positive aspects of wisdom and the negative aspects of foolishness. As in most of the wisdom literature, the writers employ Hebrew poetry to convey the message. This poetry is characterized by parallelism which plays out in various ways. Sometimes a positive statement will be followed by another positive statement saying the same thing but in a different way. At other times a positive will be followed by a negative showing the converse idea. The goal of the poet is to emphasize the truth statement by contrast or repetition.

Beginning in chapter 10, the writers of the Proverbs deal with several themes relating to life showing how the wise and foolish man approaches each. Themes include work, family, friendship, the tongue, language, generosity, and ethics. On the theme of work and industry, Proverbs praises hard work and condemns laziness. "Idle hands make one poor, but diligent hands bring riches" (Prov. 10:4 HCSB). Language and the spoken word get much attention in the Proverbs. Maybe that is because wisdom or foolishness is quickly recognized when a person opens his mouth to speak. "The mouth of righteousness is a fountain of life, but the mouth of the wicked conceals violence" (Prov. 10:11 HCSB). The wise person lives with integrity according to the Proverbs. "Dishonest scales are detestable to the LORD, but an accurate weight is His delight" (Prov. 11:1 HCSB). Virtues like generosity are praised as marks of wisdom. "One person gives freely, yet gains more; another withholds what is right, only to become poor" (Prov. 11:24 HCSB).

To be wise means not only choosing God but also making wise choices in all areas of life. The wise person reflects that wisdom in action and attitude. The wise live uprightly, speak wisely, work hard, and reap the benefits of such living. There are two ways to live life, wisely or foolishly. To live wisely means to choose God's way and live in obedience. By so doing one reaps the benefits of a good life under God. To live foolishly means to reject God's way and live according to one's own rules. The consequence of this decision according to the Proverbs includes poverty, violence, pain, suffering, hatred, and death. The proverbs reflect what is usually true. A hard worker would usually do well in life. However, since that is not always the case, the proverbs only reflect what is generally true.

WISDOM AND GOD'S STORY OF REDEMPTION

God's story is about the redemption of sinners who cannot redeem themselves. Yahweh began with Abraham and through him developed a people, God's own people. Although rebellious they still became the nation through which God provided the salvation to all nations. In line with the wisdom literature, the wise person is the one who takes seriously the story and accepts it as truth. This person

---

[8] David S. Dockery, ed., *Holman Bible Handbook* (Nashville: Holman Bible Publishers, 1992), 351.

grounds his life on these truths and trusts in God. His life is different and better because of it. The foolish according to wisdom teachings rejects the story and decides there is no sin or God or need to believe in him. They live life by their own rules as if there is no God.

Israel was confronted with a choice of two ways to live: believe in the story and the God of the story or reject it. The biblical story indicates that life will be determined by that choice.

THINGS TO CONSIDER

The wisdom literature focuses on the idea of free choice. Adam and Eve possessed the ability to choose God and his way or not. They made the choice, and it affected their lives and ours. All people possess free choice. The wisdom literature calls us to exercise it *wisely*. The biblical concept of wisdom is found in relationship with God. It is life as originally intended. The wise person lives according to God's standards.

STUDY QUESTIONS

1. What is the biblical idea of wisdom, and what is wisdom literature?
2. What does Psalm 1 say about life?
3. What does Ecclesiastes say about fulfillment?
4. What does the book of Proverbs say about life and how to live it?

THINGS TO REMEMBER

The biblical story is God's story of redemption. He promised Abraham a nation through which he would bless the world. That blessing comes in the next episodes of the story. So how far have we come in the story? Where are we now? Let's take one more look at the outline to pinpoint the progress of God's redemptive plan.

THE STORY OF THE BIBLE

Creation   The story begins with God creating the world and human beings.

Crisis   Humans choose to rebel (or sin) against God. Sin brings consequences: pain, suffering, death, and separation from God. All people and all creation are affected.

Covenant   God chooses Abraham and establishes a covenant with him so that he might become the leader of a group of people who will follow God and call other people to follow God. God delights in using his people to bring the rest of the world to himself.

Calling Out	Genesis tells the story of the patriarchs: Abraham, Isaac, Jacob (Israel), and Joseph, who ends up in Egypt. In Egypt the small group of Hebrews grows into a nation and ends up in slavery. God uses Moses to deliver his people through the exodus event.
Conquest	God uses Joshua to help his people take the promised land (Canaan). After the conquest during the Period of Judges, God rules through judges in various parts of the land. This is a dark time for the Hebrews accentuated with sin, idolatry, and oppression.
Kingdom	God's people acquire a king. Samuel is the link between the judges and the kings. Saul is the first king, followed by David and his son Solomon. God establishes a covenant with David, promising the Messiah will come through his family line and reign forever.
Kingdom Divided	After Solomon civil war breaks out leading to a division of the kingdom: Israel, the Northern Kingdom; Judah, the Southern Kingdom. There are numerous kings, some good but most bad.
Captivity	Israel (Northern Kingdom) is judged for the sin of breaking the covenant when Assyria conquers it in 722 BC, and Judah receives a similar judgment later when Babylon conquers it in 586 BC and takes Judah's people into exile.
Coming Home	**The people return from Babylonian exile under Zerubbabel, Ezra, and Nehemiah. They rebuild the temple and focus on the law of God.**
Christ	About four hundred years later God sends his Son, Jesus the Christ, to save his people from their sins, fulfilling the promise given to Abraham. Jesus is crucified, dies, is raised from the dead, and ascends into heaven to return again later.
Church	Those who accept Jesus become part of the church, the people of God made up of both Jews and Gentiles. God continues to use his people to extend his offer of salvation to a sinful world.
Consummation	God closes history with a final victory over evil. Those who have rejected God will suffer his judgment while those who have received him will live with him in a new heaven and a new earth.

UNTO US A CHILD IS BORN

ACT 1

GOD SENDS HIS PROMISED MESSIAH

T he New Testament begins the story of the new covenant by placing extraordinary emphasis on the connection between the covenants of old and the new work God is about to inaugurate. The gospel genealogies strive to show that Jesus is the son of both David and Abraham. What God had been doing from the beginning, and what he foretold through his prophets concerning the fulfillment of his promise to Abraham, was about to happen. God did not begin a new work as much as he was writing the concluding chapter to the story he began when he first created the world. Put differently, the New Testament does not tell a new story; it reveals God's conclusion to the story he has been telling since the beginning.

God sent Jesus in fulfillment of prophetic promise. The timing for Jesus' coming corresponded to a period when God's people were both ripe with anticipation for God to do a new work and stuck in a pattern of worship and devotion that had moved them away from God's original plan. Israel had come to interpret their election as God's people as a matter of position and privilege rather than a matter of purpose and call as God intended. As a consequence they had not become the light to the nations of the world God had called them to be (Isa. 42:6). This confusion of position and purpose was so thorough that it caused them to turn things upside down. In contrast to what God had intended, they became *exclusive* where they should have been inclusive and *inclusive* where they should have been exclusive. Instead of using their unique relationship to God as a vehicle to call the nations to faith in the one and only God of the universe, they used it to *exclude* themselves from the nations. On the other hand, instead of exclusive allegiance to their God, they often gave in to the cultural pressures of the other nations and became *inclusive* of their lifestyles and customs. Although they had returned to the land from their captivity in Babylon, they were in a sense still in exile. They continued to live under the reign and domain of other nations. The bilateral covenant between God and Israel, established through the leadership of Moses, had been irrevocably broken and could not be fixed.

Into this setting Jesus came. In effect, he came to announce that God had not forgotten his covenant promise to Abraham. God's kingdom would dwell among people once again. He would call a new people unto himself who were to be a light to all of his creation (Isa. 42:6; 49:6), a people who would come from all nations and be characterized by the presence of God's Spirit.

THE TIME AND CIRCUMSTANCES OF JESUS' BIRTH

THE GOSPEL STORY ABOUT JESUS' BIRTH

The actual story of Jesus' birth is told only by Matthew and Luke. During the reign of the Roman emperor Augustus, God sent his angel Gabriel to a young virgin in Nazareth called Mary. Gabriel pronounced that God had chosen her to be the bearer of his son. Through a miracle of God's Spirit, she would become pregnant and give birth to a son whose name was to be Jesus. He would be "Son of the Most High" the angel proclaimed, and God would "give to him the throne of his ancestor David." God would give to Jesus the "reign over the house of Jacob forever" and there would be no end to his kingdom (Luke 1:33 NRSV).

Six months earlier one of Mary's relatives, Elizabeth, conceived a son in spite of her old age. This miracle resulted from a promise given to her husband Zechariah by the same messenger angel who visited Mary. Zechariah and Elizabeth would have a son whose name was to be John. He would become the forerunner of God's Messiah, announcing that the kingdom was at hand. This John, best known as John the Baptizer, later baptized Jesus in the river Jordan. John declared himself unworthy to untie the thongs of Jesus' sandals, while Jesus claimed there was no one born of a woman greater than John.

According to Luke's Gospel, Jesus was born at a time when the emperor Augustus decreed a census to count all his subjects. This census required every family to go to the city of their family lineage. This caused Joseph, Mary's husband, to take his pregnant wife to Bethlehem in Judah. In Bethlehem they found no place to stay and had to settle on a field, finding shelter only from a makeshift feeding area for livestock. While there, Mary gave birth to Jesus and laid him in a manger, a livestock feeding trough that functioned as his bed.

As Matthew and Luke tell the story, each with unique details, we learn that angels announced the birth of the Messiah first to the common people of the land,[1] people exemplified by shepherds. These heeded God's announcement and went to

---

[1] Poorer people were called *am ha'arets,* "people of the land," a derogatory title given to them as a group. The Jewish aristocracy and religious parties like the Pharisees viewed the *am ha'arets* with contempt because many were illiterate and unable to observe all details of the Law.

the manger to worship this newborn Savior. Outside Israel, magi[2] recognized that all of the cosmos had been alerted to the event in Judah. Matthew alone tells this story of a group of magi being led to Judah by a star that announced the birth of a king. Arriving in Judah, they visited Herod the king to ask for directions on how to find the newborn king. Upon finding the baby Jesus, they bowed before the manger and offered him gifts of gold, frankincense, and myrrh. Like the shepherds, these foreign magi recognized the significance of this newborn child. Put differently, the announcement of the Savior's birth was recognized by Gentiles and common Jewish people alike; it was missed by the powerful and the religious leaders of Judaism.

Beyond this description of his miraculous birth, the Gospels are silent about Jesus' childhood and early adult life except for two significant events related by Luke. On the eighth day Mary and Joseph brought Jesus to the temple to be circumcised, for name-giving and a thanksgiving sacrifice as was the contemporary custom. While there, two devout worshippers, a Spirit-filled man named Simeon and an eighty-four-year-old prophetess called Anna, recognized the child as God's promised Redeemer of Israel (Luke 2:21–38). What was recognized earlier by shepherds and Gentiles was now apparently visible to all who truly sought God's redemption.

The second event involved Jesus' return to the temple as a twelve-year old. In the temple he became involved in a discussion with teachers of the law, and everyone was amazed at his wisdom and insight. Even before his baptism when his public ministry began, evidence of God's work in Jesus was clear.

JESUS CAME "IN THE FULLNESS OF TIME"

The timing of Jesus' birth was not accidental. The Bible is clear that Jesus came at the exact time God had decided. Many New Testament texts make this clear, but Paul's use of the phrase "fullness of time" (Gal. 4:4; Eph. 1:10 NKJV) to describe the occasion of Jesus' birth captures especially well that the timing was anything but coincidental. Beyond a mere descriptive expression, the phrase indicates that God deliberately chose this particular time in world history to reveal his eternal plan for the nations. The phrase makes void any and all suggestions that Jesus was an extraordinary person that God simply adopted to bring about his purposes. It clarifies in two Greek words (*pleroma chronou,* time's fullness) that the birth, life, and mission of Jesus were willed by God from the beginning.

---

[2] The magi, who nowadays are best known in churches as "the wise men," likely were members of a loosely connected but rather influential and widely respected international group of sages and astronomers. These magi were often prominent individuals, a fact that may have given rise to the later label "holy kings." The Bible says nothing about who they were other than that they came from the east and apparently were involved in astronomy. Neither does the Bible say anything about their number. The suggestion that three magi visited Jesus is a mere guess based on the three gifts.

1. God's Timing and the Historical Situation

On the historical level, "fullness of time" speaks to a point in time that was uniquely suited for the spread of the gospel message. On every level the state of affairs in the world yielded opportunities for the spread of the gospel that were nonexistent both earlier and later. The Hellenization of the world made Greek an almost universal language and allowed an unprecedented level of human communication and interaction. Itinerant philosophers shared their thinking from Rome to Alexandria and from Spain to Jerusalem with no language barrier, and newer Hellenistic philosophies prepared minds for the reception of teachings about a monotheistic God.

Furthermore, the military exploits of Rome resulted in a vast road system and infrastructure that made transportation and the movement of people commonplace. *Pax Romana,* or the Roman Peace, allowed people to enjoy this freedom of movement and to take advantage of newer developments like an emerging postal service. In other words, the world situation enabled followers of Jesus to disperse and the gospel message to have an immediate and somewhat unhindered dispersion to Phoenicia, Cyprus, and Antioch (Acts 11:19). Without hesitation Paul could talk about bringing the gospel to the "ends of the earth" (Acts 13:47), and as he started new churches, he could stay in touch with them through an exchange of mailed letters and repeated personal visits. God's timing for Christ's coming was not accidental.

2. When Did All This Happen?

Pinpointing the exact time for Jesus' birth is not easy. A couple of hints in the biblical text give us some help. We know from other sources that Herod the Great ruled from 37 BC to 4 BC. Since Jesus was born before Herod died, our calendar is at least four years off. Add to this the fact that Herod commanded his soldiers to kill all male babies in Bethlehem two years or younger (Matt. 2:16). This places the birth of Jesus before or around 6 BC.

Quirinius, the governor of Syria mentioned in Luke 2:2, became well-known for a census taken in AD 6 which resulted in a revolt. If this late census corresponds to the census Luke refers to, a discrepancy of eleven to twelve years exists between Luke and other ancient historians like Josephus. This has led some scholars to conclude that Luke confused the dating. However, the fame of a second census in AD 6–7 does not necessarily negate a less known *first* census in 5–6 BC.[3] For example, Luke seems aware of the later census in AD 6 (Acts 5:37), and still he does not hesitate to connect Jesus' birth with Quirinius. At least three scenarios are possible: (1) Luke calls Quirinius governor before he technically had the title.[4] (2) Translating Luke 2:2 to say "the *first* census," is wrong; the Greek word *protos*

---

[3] Notice Luke's deliberate use of "*first* census that happened while Quirinius was governor" (Luke 2:2, author's Italics).

[4] Although some reject this option, it is possible that Quirinius was sent as a special envoy for Augustus at this earlier date. Strictly speaking, the Greek word used for Quirinius here refers to his function as leader or commander rather than to the specific title as governor.

should have been translated "before" like John 15:18. Luke 2:2 would then read, "The census *before* Quirinius became governor in Syria." (3) Augustus ordered a census before the death of Herod the Great in 4 BC, but continuing delays and incompetence by those administrating the census led Augustus to send Quirinius in AD 6 to clean up the mess left by his predecessors.

The problem with our calendar and the date for the birth of Jesus goes back to a monk called Dionysius in AD 525. This dating is off by at least five or six years. Jesus was born in what we now call year 5 or 6 BC.

3. God's Timing and Jesus' Family Lineage

Matthew and Luke, the only two Synoptic Gospels that include Jesus' family line, use it to establish that God's covenants with his people pointed to Jesus from the beginning. Although the Old Testament prophets described what Jesus came to do as "new covenant" (cf. Jer. 31:31), no suggestion appears in either of the testaments that this "new" covenant was disconnected from earlier covenants. In fact, Matthew and Luke are careful to explain Jesus as the fulfillment and climax of God's original plan for his creation.

Matthew carefully shows how Jesus is the son of both David and Abraham, the fathers of the two unilateral covenants God made with Israel. Beginning Jesus' family tree with Abraham allows Matthew to show that Jesus was included in the covenant promise that laid the foundation for Israel's relationship to God (Gen. 12:2–3). God's purpose in using Abraham, and the nation established through his lineage, to bless "all peoples on earth" found its fulfillment in the one being born. The connection to David, the messianic king of Israel's past, likewise affirms Jesus as the one fulfilling God's promise. God promised to establish his kingdom on earth, and the "king" to lead it would come from David's lineage (2 Sam. 7:10–16). Jesus' birth announced that God now would inaugurate the *new* covenant promised long ago by the Old Testament prophets. It was not new in the sense of a radical break with the old but new in that it completed what God had planned from the beginning. God's appointed moment, the "fullness of time," had come! All things would be made "new."

To underscore this understanding even further, Luke continues Jesus' family line back beyond Abraham all the way to God (3:38). Said differently, Luke shows that God's purpose for the world included all peoples of all nations by revealing that Jesus is the "son of Adam." Moreover, he shows that Jesus' birth has significance for all of creation since Jesus' line goes beyond Adam all the way to God; he is the "son of God." According to the New Testament, time and history had since its creation, "in the beginning," been moving toward this point; it was now indeed the "fullness of time."

STUDY QUESTIONS

1. Why do you think the angels announced Jesus' birth to the shepherds rather than the religious leaders in Jerusalem?
2. Why do you think Matthew includes the story of the Gentile magi? What does that event say about Jesus' birth?
3. Why did it matter what was going on in the world at the time of Jesus' birth? Why would no other time in history be equally good for God to send his Son to earth?
4. How does Jesus' genealogy differ in Matthew's and Luke's descriptions? What is the significance of these differences?

ACT 2

INCARNATION AND THE TWO NATURES OF JESUS

J esus' coming to earth was of such magnitude for God's story that it proves necessary to move beyond a mere recounting of the events and comment on the significance of what God did through the incarnation of Jesus. *Incarnation* should not be confused with the similar sounding term, *reincarnation*. *Incarnation* is a term to express what happened when Jesus, who had been with God for all eternity, stepped onto the historical scene as a human being.

It is almost impossible to understand what God did through Christ without some understanding of the incarnation. Moreover, in order to understand who Jesus really is, we must investigate the Gospels' explanation of *how* Jesus was incarnated; that is, we must take a closer look at the virginal conception. The following section, therefore, attempts to give a brief background discussion that is designed to clarify the story that follows.

INCARNATION, GOD'S ENTRY INTO HISTORY AS A HUMAN BEING

More significant than the timing and specific circumstances surrounding Jesus' birth is the theological importance of what God did by sending his Son. Although the following merely will survey a huge issue, it should be noted that it is impossible to overstate the significance of the incarnation. Not only is Jesus God's perfect revelation of himself, but the fact that he stepped into the field of matter, and participated in the history of his own creation, has forever changed human thinking and the pursuit of knowledge.[5]

INCARNATION MAKES THE CHRISTIAN FAITH UNIQUE

The incarnation removes faith from the realm of mythology and places it in the realm of history. In contrast to mythological affirmations, where gods play out various scenarios "in the heavenlies" that have fatalistic consequences for life on earth, incarnation grounds the Christian faith in factual, historical events. God is not out there in the unknown; rather, he chose to step into history and reveal himself in a personal manner. In mythology, talk about god turns into fatalistic assertions; in the Christian faith, talk about God turns into expressions of relationship. In other words, because of the incarnation Christianity is real-life faith. More than merely sending a vision to a prophet, through the incarnation God came to show us how to live.

WE ARE INTERESTED IN HISTORY BECAUSE WE BELIEVE IN THE INCARNATION

Incarnation reminds us of the significance of history as well. True Christian faith cannot be indifferent to historical issues of faith. Christ came and walked among us *in time*; Christians want to know what that meant and means. Different from Gnostic writings, for example, where God merely sends lofty, indefinite, timeless propositions for inner meditation,[6] Christian faith confronts God's actions on the turf of human life and acts and reacts in response to these. Since God's actions are revealed on the field of history, they can be tested and investigated. History is important because God used it as his field to reveal himself. Because he chose to come at a certain time, we seek to know the significance of this. Because he chose to come in a certain place, we are interested in what that place was like.

Because of the incarnation of Christ, Christians cannot be indifferent to historical investigation or to the present situation of the world. The incarnation teaches us that God has not withdrawn himself but desires to engage his creation! He sent his Son into the world to reveal to all humans what life in his kingdom is like. The announcement of God's eager participation in human life through the birth of Jesus on a real field near a real town called Bethlehem gives all people of Christian faith a charge to participate in the real-life situations of this world. The incarnation calls followers of Christ actively to proclaim that God's love is not long-distance love but a present participatory love (Heb. 2:18; 4:15).

---

[5] It was, for example, the Christian view of incarnation that enabled and initiated the pursuit of science as we know it today. For further comments, see Christopher Kaiser, *Creation and the History of Science* (Grand Rapids, Mich.: Eerdmans, 1991), who shows how the Cappadocian fathers developed four principles that enabled science to move along a path of investigation that has led to the present position.

[6] The Gospel of Thomas is an example of Gnostic literature. For a short survey of the major tenets of Gnosticism, see Episode 13, Act 2, "1 John and Gnosticism," pp. 300-301.

THE INCARNATION SHOWS US WHO GOD IS!

At the heart of the Christian doctrine of incarnation lies a statement about the being of Christ. The story of the overshadowing of Mary by the Holy Spirit in order for her to give birth to "the Son of the Most High" shuts down any notion that Jesus was merely a pious person or a prophet that God adopted. Rather, he was 100 percent God and 100 percent man—not just man, not just God, nor 50 percent of each.

The two natures of Christ present difficulty for our finite minds. One way to think about this is to consider everything Jesus said, did, and thought as an expression of who God is or to maintain that everything Jesus said, did, and thought was exactly what God would have said, done, and thought. The problem many Christians face when dealing with the issue of Jesus' divinity is that they talk about Jesus in such a way that there seems to be a complete equation between God the Father and Jesus. Such an explanation of Jesus' divinity makes him equal to God the Father in a way that seems to make heaven empty while Jesus was on the earth. If that were the case, it would be nonsense for the Bible to speak about Jesus praying to God—who was he talking to? To say that Jesus is 100 percent God means that Jesus' being is the same as God's. Everything about Jesus is an exact expression of God, yet Jesus is not the Father.

Opposite the early Christians, who knew Jesus as a human being and therefore struggled with their understanding of his divinity,[7] Christians today struggle with the significance of Jesus' humanity. Living two thousand years after his time on earth, modern Christians find it easier to make him 100 percent God and 0 percent human. Since he is the object of Christian worship and the content of hymns and praise choruses, Jesus' divinity gets most of the focus. However, the truth about Jesus is found in the tension between his divinity and his humanity. That he is 100 percent God means that he is the true Savior, not just one who can point to a saving God. That he is 100 percent human means that he understands humans completely and that he is acquainted with everything we experience as humans.

MARY AND THE BIRTH OF JESUS

The Bible says Mary was a virgin when she conceived Jesus. The issue, therefore, is not as some say "virgin birth," but virginal conception! Scripture emphasizes that Mary conceived because of a supernatural influence of the Holy Spirit

---

[7] "Jesus answered, 'I did tell you, but you do not believe. The miracles I do in my Father's name speak for me, but you do not believe because you are not my sheep. My sheep listen to my voice; I know them, and they follow me. I give them eternal life, and they shall never perish; no one can snatch them out of my hand. My Father, who has given them to me, is greater than all; no one can snatch them out of my Father's hand. I and the Father are one'" (John 10:25–30). "Jesus answered: 'Don't you know me, Philip, even after I have been among you such a long time? Anyone who has seen me has seen the Father. How can you say, "Show us the Father"? Don't you believe that I am in the Father, and that the Father is in me? The words I say to you are not just my own. Rather, it is the Father, living in me, who is doing his work. . . . You heard me say, "I am going away and I am coming back to you." If you loved me, you would be glad that I am going to the Father, for the Father is greater than I'" (John 14:9–10, 28).

without any form of human intercourse. The Son she gave birth to was *willed* by God—not caused by humans.

Much discussion has raged on this subject for several reasons. Enlightenment theologians, working from the accepted presupposition that virgins do not give birth to babies, raised serious objections about the historicity of the accounts describing Jesus' conception. They claimed the Gospel accounts of Jesus' birth were mere fictional tales. Rather than being historical, they considered the stories of the conception and birth of Christ as mythological in the sense that they told a story which captured a truth that could only be expressed through such storytelling. These theologians argued that the Gospel writers never attempted to give a "photographically correct" description of Jesus' incarnation; the Gospels simply told a story that captured God's involvement in Jesus' life from the beginning. Less sympathetic theologians, with the same presuppositions, claimed that the Gospels' account of Jesus' conception was little more than a literary creation designed to give the early Christians a supernatural beginning to the life of their hero. Although many of these points have been argued passionately by astute minds, they fail to persuade.

BIBLICAL REFERENCES TO THE VIRGINAL CONCEPTION

The biblical evidence for the virginal conception seems at first rather scarce. Only Matthew and Luke tell the story, and their stories relate different details. Without even mentioning Jesus' conception or birth, Mark begins his Gospel with Jesus' baptism. John, as is well-known, begins in a completely different way by connecting Jesus' birth to the Jewish and/or Greco-Roman notions of Logos. Paul, whose writings focus on the significance of Jesus' mission, likewise made no direct reference to Jesus' virginal conception. The same can be said of the General Letters. Does this mean that the virginal conception is insignificant for Christian faith? Not at all!

Notice the detail Matthew provides (1:18–25 NRSV):

> Now the birth of Jesus the Messiah took place in this way. When his mother Mary had been engaged to Joseph, but before they lived together, she was found to be with child from the Holy Spirit. Her husband Joseph, being a righteous man and unwilling to expose her to public disgrace, planned to dismiss her quietly. But just when he had resolved to do this, an angel of the Lord appeared to him in a dream and said, "Joseph, son of David, do not be afraid to take Mary as your wife, for the child conceived in her is from the Holy Spirit. She will bear a son, and you are to name him Jesus, for he will save his people from their sins." All this took place to fulfill what had been spoken by the Lord through the prophet: "Look, the virgin shall conceive and bear a son, and they shall name him Emmanuel," which means, "God is with us." When Joseph awoke from sleep, he did as the angel of the

Lord commanded him; he took her as his wife, but had no marital relations with her until she had borne a son; and he named him Jesus.

Luke's description differs in detail but agrees in content (1:26–38 NRSV):

In the sixth month the angel Gabriel was sent by God to a town in Galilee called Nazareth, to a virgin engaged to a man whose name was Joseph, of the house of David. The virgin's name was Mary. And he came to her and said, "Greetings, favored one! The Lord is with you." But she was much perplexed by his words and pondered what sort of greeting this might be. The angel said to her, "Do not be afraid, Mary, for you have found favor with God. And now, you will conceive in your womb and bear a son, and you will name him Jesus. He will be great, and will be called the Son of the Most High, and the Lord God will give to him the throne of his ancestor David. He will reign over the house of Jacob forever, and of his kingdom there will be no end." Mary said to the angel, "How can this be, since I am a virgin?" The angel said to her, "The Holy Spirit will come upon you, and the power of the Most High will overshadow you; therefore the child to be born will be holy; he will be called Son of God. And now, your relative Elizabeth in her old age has also conceived a son; and this is the sixth month for her who was said to be barren. For nothing will be impossible with God." Then Mary said, "Here am I, the servant of the Lord; let it be with me according to your word." Then the angel departed from her.

Other New Testament references that hint at the issue agree with Matthew's and Luke's accounts. Mark 6:3 calls Jesus Mary's son, a highly unusual reference had Joseph been acknowledged as the biological father (cf. Matt. 13:55, carpenter's son; Luke 4:22, Joseph's son). John's reference in 1:13 to God's children being born "not by the will of flesh or the will of man, but by the will of God" is wrapped in the story of the incarnate Logos in such a way that the phrase "not by the will of man but of God" clearly speaks to the "word that became flesh" as well (cf. vv. 10–11, 14). Furthermore, Paul's use of the general Greek term *ginomai* (coming from, originating from), as opposed to the more specific Greek term *gennaō* (to be father of, to give birth to), when he speaks of the coming or the birth of Jesus, does not prove anything by itself, but it does support the stories related by Luke and Matthew (see Rom. 1:3; Phil. 2:7). This last point may be most clearly seen in the contrast between the reference to Jesus' birth in Galatians 4:4 (being born of a woman, *ginomai*) and the birth of Ishmael in Galatians 4:23 (being born according to flesh, *gennaō*). In short, although only Matthew and Luke give full accounts of Mary's virginity at the time of Jesus' conception, the whole body of New Testament literature affirms the same when it touches the issue.

PREEXISTENCE AND HISTORICAL EXISTENCE—WHAT ABOUT JESUS BEFORE HIS BIRTH IN BETHLEHEM?

Although the above references have no value as historical proofs, they do hint at an agreement among the New Testament writers that Jesus' conception was extraordinary. Theologically, the significance of this discussion concerns the nature of Jesus.

God could have chosen to bring Jesus to earth in many other ways. He could, for example, have made a special creation in the same way he created the first Adam; but Matthew's and Luke's Gospel accounts powerfully portray *how* God connected eternity with history. Christ's eternal nature is attested throughout the New Testament and belongs indisputably to the core of Christian theology. Nowhere is this more clearly portrayed than in John's Gospel, which opens with a description of what is normally called Jesus' preexistence. Jesus' preexistence simply refers to the conviction that Jesus always existed, even before his historical birth in Bethlehem.

Given this, it is nearly impossible to imagine a stronger "natural" link between Christ's preexistence and his historical existence than what is described by Matthew and Luke. The virginal conception joins or unites the preexistent (or eternal) nature of Christ with his historical (or temporal) existence in a way that preserves both natures as coexistent. Without the virginal conception, there must have been a point of adoption, a specific historical time or situation where Jesus became "Son of God."[8] The problem with any such notion of adoption is that it ultimately makes Jesus 100 percent man and 0 percent God. Adoption does not change being. This means that the Gospel stories of the virginal conception speak about Jesus' being. He is not just 100 percent *like* God; he is 100 percent God. Or put differently, he is not just 100 percent like God in what he *does*; he is 100 percent like God in who he *is*.

VIRGINAL CONCEPTION AND SINLESSNESS

A number of scholars, especially from the Catholic tradition, have throughout the centuries tried to connect Jesus' sinlessness to his virginal conception. This goes back to Augustine's notion that sin is carried by the male seed.[9] This, however, misreads the biblical material; it makes sin an issue of inheritance and chromosomes. Such a notion runs contrary to Scripture and seems to suggest, at least by inference, that Mary was sinless because she was a virgin.

Rather, the sinlessness of Jesus relates to the virginal conception only in a derived sense. One may say that because Jesus had only one human parent, being born of both Spirit and flesh, he possessed the *possibility* of not sinning. Because he was 100 percent human (born of a woman), he could have sinned; but, because

---

[8] Many things have been suggested to argue this, most prominently Jesus' baptism. Those who claim this say that Jesus became the Son of God at his baptism when God said: "This is My beloved Son" (Matt. 3:17 HCSB).

[9] Some further try to argue that the sexual act is sinful in itself; it follows, therefore, that what comes from it is sinful as well.

he was 100 percent God (born of the Spirit), he also had the option *not* to sin. The first Adam likewise had the option not to sin but chose to follow his own desires and oppose God's will. The second Adam, Jesus, came and restored what the first Adam destroyed (Rom. 5:19). According to the biblical text, Jesus was tempted in all things like us but did not sin (Heb. 4:15).

Christians today should avoid the old Augustinian mistake of making sin a DNA issue tied to the male chromosome. People are not sinful because they are conceived through a sexual act. That Jesus was born of a woman secures that he can relate 100 percent to the human situation. That he was born of God's Spirit secures that the salvation he offers is eternal, from God. For this reason the virginal conception is significant to the story of Jesus.

STUDY QUESTIONS

1. The story of incarnation is an important safeguard against the many twisted Christological ideas common today. Beyond being a miraculous event at the beginning of Jesus' life, how would you explain the significance of the incarnation?
2. How does Jesus' humanity impact your life?
3. How does Jesus' divinity impact your life?
4. Read John 1:1–18 and write down everything it says about Jesus. Reflect on what you find.

EPISODE NINE

THE MINISTRY OF JESUS

ACT 1

Jesus Begins His Ministry

E
xcept for Jesus' miraculous birth and his visit to the temple as a twelve-year-old, the New Testament remains silent about his upbringing. Joseph, who was considered his father, was a carpenter in Nazareth; and most likely Jesus functioned as such until he began his ministry around the age of thirty. Although guesses can be made about his schooling, they remain guesses. The only direct remark the New Testament gives concerning Jesus' intellectual development as a child and young man comes from Luke 2:52, "Jesus increased in wisdom and in years, and in divine and human favor" (NRSV).

THE BAPTISM OF JESUS

All four Gospels place Jesus' baptism at the beginning of his public ministry and connect it to the ministry of John the Baptist. Mark, who spent no time introducing Jesus as coeternal with God (like John) or as conceived by an action of God's Spirit (like Matthew and Luke), places Jesus' baptism at the beginning of his Gospel.

In fulfillment of Isaiah's prophesy (chap. 42) and the promise given to Zechariah and Elizabeth, John the Baptist prepared the way for the coming of God's Messiah. Preaching a message of repentance and calling people to prepare themselves for the coming of the One whose sandals he was not worthy to untie, John baptized large numbers of people who came to hear him in the desert (Mark 1:5; Matt. 3:5; Luke 3:7a). His baptism was a baptism of repentance, but the one he was pointing to would baptize people with God's own Spirit. In John's own words: "I have baptized you with water; but he will baptize you with the Holy Spirit" (Mark 1:8 NRSV). John the Baptist functioned as a bridge between the old and the new covenants: he was the conclusion to the old—a fact to which his dress, lifestyle, and message of doom gave testimony (cf. 2 Kings 1:8); he served the forerunner for the new, proclaiming the outpouring of the Spirit as promised by the prophets.

Jesus came to John at the river Jordan to be baptized. John saw no need to baptize Jesus with the baptism of repentance and at first refused to baptize Jesus. Jesus insisted, however, and John consented. As Jesus came up from the water, "he saw the heavens torn apart and the Spirit descending like a dove on him" (Mark 1:10 NRSV). "And a voice came from heaven, 'You are my Son, whom I love; with you I am well pleased'" (v. 11).

WHY WAS JESUS BAPTIZED?

1. In his baptism Jesus identified with sinful humanity.

To be baptized was Jesus' choice. He did not do so out of necessity or to symbolize his need for spiritual cleansing. John's baptism of repentance made no immediate sense since Jesus had committed no sin requiring repentance. However, according to Matthew 3:15, Jesus wanted to be baptized to "fulfill all righteousness," an expression that pointed to Jesus' desire to identify with humanity. He came to be baptized in response to God's call and in obedience to God's law (Matt. 5:17).

2. Jesus' baptism anointed him for ministry and proclaimed that he was the Messiah.

The voice speaking from heaven when Jesus came out of the water explains who Jesus is: "You are my Son, whom I love; with you I am well pleased" (Mark 1:11). These few words give reference to three well-known sections of Scripture, passages which speak to Jesus' purpose. The words from heaven were Old Testament catchphrases, so to speak. They alerted the listeners to whole stories and sections of Scripture that were central to Israel's faith in God and his promises to his people. This means that when people heard the voice, they were reminded of the greater settings to which the phrases gave reference. Using just a few words, it was possible for God to proclaim his larger purpose in sending Jesus the Christ.

This should not be confusing to modern readers. We know a similar thing today when, for example, a small phrase like "we the people" reminds us of the Constitution; or, "we hold these truths to be self-evident" causes us to think of the Declaration of Independence; or, "the LORD is my shepherd" makes us think of Psalm 23. We do not always need the entire passage recited but can catch the idea with a prompting phrase. That is what happened when the voice from heaven spoke at Jesus' baptism.

"This is my son" refers to Psalm 2:7, a royal psalm first applied to King David.[1] With this brief phrase from a royal psalm,[2] God identified Jesus as sovereign king.

---

[1] "I will tell of the decree of the LORD: He said to me, '*You are my son*; today I have begotten you. Ask of me, and I will make the nations your heritage, and the ends of the earth your possessions'" (Ps. 2:7–8, author's italics, NRSV).

[2] Like "O, say can you see" would do to modern Americans.

Psalm 2 was written as a coronation psalm for the crowning of kings. The reference to "his anointed" (Hebrew: *Messiah*; Greek: *Christ*) in verse 2, speaks to the coronation of a king who is son of David. Other kings of the earth may make their plans (v. 2), but God's anointed will rule the nations (v. 8). His sovereignty will be unbroken (v. 9).

The phrase "whom I love" recalls Genesis 22:2—the account of Abraham's obedient sacrifice to God. God tested Abraham's obedience by asking him to sacrifice his beloved son Isaac.[3] By using this highly recognizable phrase, God identified Jesus as the Son he was willing to sacrifice for the sins of the world. Jesus did not only come to serve as sovereign king; he was to be a king who would give his life as a sacrifice for his people.

The last part of the short statement given at Jesus' baptism points to Isaiah 42:1–9. The clause "with you I am well pleased" reminded the observers of Isaiah's first "Servant Song."[4] In the Old Testament context, this song is the first of four such Servant Songs. It celebrates that God's suffering servant will introduce the new covenant (v. 9) promised by the prophets.[5] He is chosen like Moses (Ps. 106:23) and David (Ps. 89:4) and Israel herself (1 Chron. 16:13; Isa. 41:8). As servant he will fulfill the role of David the king (2 Sam. 3:18). With this reference to the Suffering Servant, who introduces the new covenant and fulfills the role of David, Jesus' ministry is now outlined through a voice from heaven.

The revelatory purpose of Jesus' baptism is evidenced also in the expressed presence of all three persons of the Godhead—God the Father, God the Son, and God the Holy Spirit. Although the New Testament falls short of a formal teaching on the trinitarian character of God, it is understood throughout. The story of Jesus' baptism is one of the important New Testament texts for this doctrine. It shows God the Father speaking, God the Son submitting to baptism, and God the Holy Spirit descending upon the Son.

3. In his baptism Jesus was prepared for ministry.

God inaugurated his Son's public ministry at Jesus' baptism. It was a clarifying event at which God exposed his eternal purposes to everyone as "being fulfilled." God's explicit announcement not only declared his purpose to all those listening; it also gave Jesus a clarity of insight and a new awareness of the saving purpose of his life.

When Luke stated that "Jesus increased in wisdom and in years, and in divine and human favor" (2:52 NRSV), it indicates a development in Jesus' own

---

[3] God said to Abraham, "Take your son, your only son Isaac, *whom you love*, and go to the land of Moriah, and offer him there as a burnt offering on one of the mountains that I shall show you" (NRSV, author's italics).

[4] "Here is my servant, whom I uphold, my chosen, *in whom my soul delights*; I have put my spirit upon him; he will bring forth justice to the nations. He will not cry or lift up his voice, or make it heard in the street; a bruised reed he will not break, and a dimly burning wick he will not quench; he will faithfully bring forth justice. He will not grow faint or be crushed until he has established justice in the earth; and the coastlands wait for his teaching" (Isa. 42:1–4 NRSV, author's emphasis).

[5] "See, the former things have come to pass, and new things I now declare; before they spring forth, I tell you of them" (Isa. 42:9 NRSV).

understanding of his mission and purpose. Although human beings struggle to understand how Jesus, who did not consider equality with God something to be grasped, could empty himself (Phil. 2:6–7), the New Testament is clear that Jesus' willingness to "humble himself" (Phil. 2:8) influenced his knowledge in certain ways. The Gospels clarify this understanding further when they quote Jesus as saying two things that seem contradictory to our finite minds. Jesus' statements that "the Father and I are one" (John 10:30) and that the Father knows what the Son does not know (Matt. 10:36) are not contradictory, however, in light of Luke 2:52 and Philippians 2:6–7. Having emptied himself of his equality with God, Jesus grew in wisdom and stature; his experience of God's declaration at his baptism, therefore, became a defining moment for his own understanding of his person, mission, and purpose.

In the same vein the enabling power of the Spirit who "descended upon him" as he came out of the water should be understood as God's empowering of Jesus' public ministry. Although he was born by the overshadowing of Mary by God's Spirit and although he was aware of his special relationship to God during his growing years (Luke 2:49), the New Testament gives no example of God's special empowerment of Jesus until after his baptism and temptation. The baptism of Jesus, therefore, marks the beginning of his ministry. This also is the reason Mark begins his Gospel with the baptismal event.

THE TEMPTATION OF JESUS

Following the baptism, the Spirit led Jesus into the wilderness. The first three Gospels tell us that he was tempted there for forty days by the devil. Three specific temptations are described, each focused on destroying Jesus' unwavering commitment to God's purpose for his life. Satan's efforts to make Jesus fail his mission used a series of promises and shortcuts that seemed defensible. Giving in to these temptations, however, would have disabled God's plan and taken Jesus in a direction that violated God's call on his life. In that sense Jesus' temptations relate to the temptations all people face.

The first temptation dealt with the issue of identity and perceived need. After forty days of fasting, Jesus was hungry, and the devil reminded him of his significance and his power to fulfill his own needs. "If [since] you are the Son of God, command these stones to become bread" (Matt. 4:3).[6] The point of the temptation is *not* to make Jesus doubt his identity (taking Satan's statement in the negative sense of raising doubt) but rather to dare Jesus to act contrary to God's will (taking Satan's statement in the positive sense of requesting proof). In other words, Satan tried the old trick of appealing to human pride and self-absorption to make Jesus fail. By doing so, he was able to present evil as good. This, of course, is the same

---

[6] The Greek word often translated *if* is probably better translated *since* in this context. The English words *if* and *since* are, of course, related. To say *"if* you are the son" and to say *"since* you are the son" are not opposites. The first negatively questions the situation; the other questions the situation positively through a challenge.

cunning scheme of temptation that humans face again and again. It is often easy to convince people that they are so special that they have the right to do whatever they consider good at any specific moment. At its root it is the sin of self-centeredness, the sin of Adam of Eve.

Satan's ability to make his suggestions seem right was astounding. Turning stones into bread was not inherently wrong; but the timing, situation, and motivation were wrong. Excusing a sin by isolating it from its circumstance is a common human temptation. Misusing a gift from God for personal benefit and calling it good even when it is done for the wrong reasons and in the wrong situation can be tempting. Good gifts from God can be misused and become sinful—food, money, time, sex, speech, etc. Jesus' reply put things straight: "One does not live by bread alone, but by every word that comes from the mouth of God" (Matt. 4:4 NRSV). This response resonates in John 4:34 where Jesus said, "My food . . . is to do the will of the one who sent me and to finish his work." In other words, Jesus teaches that it is better to satisfy the will of God than to feed the immediate desires of the flesh.

The second temptation attacked a different area while using a similar strategy. Satan once again began with a reference to Jesus' identity, but rather than calling for a satisfaction of personal needs, he struck at Jesus' relationship with God. He took Jesus to the pinnacle of the temple and dared Jesus to throw himself down and presume on God's protection. Using direct quotes from Scripture, the devil made testing God sound like an expression of devotion. Jesus, however, immediately recognized the difference between testing and trusting God. He called Satan's bluff by quoting another Scripture ("Do not put the Lord your God to the test," Matt. 4:7) that showed how Satan misused the Scriptures for personal ends.

Again, most people can relate to this temptation. Since the snake in the garden tempted Adam and Eve with a similar snare, humans have excelled in behaving like God was their personal marionette, someone they could command. Making such sin look like Christian devotion is especially abominable; yet this is the temptation that so commonly shows itself in the so-called "prosperity gospel." The bottom line in prosperity teaching is that everything is centered on God's obligation to honor human faith with health and wealth. If humans have enough faith and trust God (or his prosperity evangelists) with their money, God *must* pay them back with health and wealth.

For Jesus' last temptation Satan showed him all the kingdoms of the world and promised to give them to Jesus if he would just move the focus of his worship away from God and unto Satan instead. Again Jesus countered by quoting Scripture reminding the devil that devotion to God could not be divided: "Away with you, Satan! for it is written, 'Worship the Lord your God, and serve only him'" (Matt. 4:10 NRSV). This last temptation was the temptation to reach for one's goals without God. The devil made it look as if Jesus could receive the kingdom without the cross. The scheme looked good, but it was a lie. It suggested that servanthood could be avoided; but, if Jesus had given in to this temptation, he would have become Satan's servant rather than God's.

As with Jesus' two previous temptations, most humans face similar temptation. It is a common lure for most people to believe they are "more free" if they live their life without worshipping God. Reality proves the opposite to be true, however. Once people have become ensnared by Satan's schemes, believing they can live successful lives without worshipping God, they discover how enslaved they have become.

Jesus was the "second Adam" Satan tempted. Opposite the first Adam, however, Jesus withstood every temptation without sinning. The first Adam led all humanity into a rebellion against God; Jesus led all humanity into a restored relationship with God. The story of Jesus' temptation gives us the first clue to how God's Son restored what the first Adam destroyed.

WHAT'S THE DIFFERENCE BETWEEN TEMPTATION, TEST, AND TRIAL?

In the normal use of the English words *temptation, test,* and *trial,* most people sense a clear distinction between the three. The word *temptation* explains situations that try to lure people to act in ways that are clearly sinful or wrong. When people give in to it, their integrity suffers. On a lighter note, people may feel tempted to eat sweets after they have determined to stay away from such. In this scenario the integrity of their determination is on trial. On a heavier note people say they "fall into temptation"; that is, they find themselves in situations that incite them to follow their poorest judgment and give in to their immediate desires. As a result they violate their relationship to God, to their loved ones, and to other people.

The word *test* is different in the normal use of the term. It is an "exam word" of sorts. We can test things or we can test people. In both cases a test checks out what it, or people, are made of. When it comes to personal testing, people can test themselves; or they can be tested by others. Opposite *temptation,* the word *test* usually has a positive connotation (except, maybe, the night before an exam). At least, most people think of tests as something with a positive purpose.

The word *trial* usually relates to difficulties in most people's mind. When someone uses the expression "we are going through trials," they usually mean that they are facing real difficulties—financial, health, relationships, or other issues. *Pain* can almost be used as a synonym for trial in this normal use of the term.

In the original New Testament text, which was written in Koine Greek, one term covers all three ideas—the Greek word *peirasmos*. That is, all three English words are translations of the one word *peirasmos*. It is the particular biblical context where the word is used that determines how we translate it into English. The word *peirasmos* itself does not change between the three different English translations. For example, when Jesus was tempted in the desert by the devil, we call it a *temptation*. We do so because the devil's purpose was to bring Jesus to sin against God.

However, looked at from the other side, we may call it a *test*. We call it a test when God is the active partner. We may say that Jesus was tested by God and proven to be without sin. Even when the devil attacked, Jesus could be trusted not to give in to temptation. He passed the test, so to speak.

Looked at from a third perspective, we may say that Jesus went through difficult *trials*. Jesus' time in the desert with the devil was not an easy period for him. When we focus on the struggle that comes with the testing (or temptation), we call it "going through trials."

Coming to an understanding of the tight connection between these three English terms used to translate one Greek word gives insight into why God allows people to go through difficulties. Getting through a temptation/test/trial successfully gives strength to overcome other temptations/tests/trials. This is exactly what James refers to when he says, "My brothers and sisters, whenever you face trials [*peirasmos* = temptation, test, trial] of any kind, consider it nothing but joy, because you know that the testing of your faith produces endurance; and let endurance have its full effect, so that you may be mature and complete, lacking in nothing" (1:2–4 NRSV).

Let us say we find ourselves in a difficult situation (a financial crisis, for example) where we are tempted to find solutions that completely violate our integrity as Christians. How are we to understand this? The devil wants to use this situation to bring us down; he is *tempting* us. God, on the other hand, uses the situation to *test* us, to strengthen us and check our commitment and maturity. As we ourselves go through this difficult situation, we experience it as a *trial*. If we conquer the temptation successfully, pass the test, we find that the next time we face a similar struggle it is easier to handle. We have learned to tackle it and therefore matured in that area.

An experience like this should not, of course, become an excuse or opportunity to blame God. The Bible states clearly that if we get ourselves into situations where we are overcome by temptation and fall, or give in to it, we have only ourselves to blame (James 1:13–14). God does not test us beyond what we can handle. His purpose is always to strengthen and mature us. The devil, on the other hand, rejoices when he can entice us to act in a way that leads to our own detriment.

All of this makes clear there is a difference between temptation and sin. No one avoids being tempted. Even Jesus was tempted! The difference is between how a person reacts in the face of that temptation, whether they overcome it or are themselves overcome by it. Those who overcome temptation can rejoice because their faith was tested and found strong.

THE CALLING OF THE DISCIPLES

After Jesus returned from his encounter with the devil in the desert, he called twelve disciples to follow him and learn from him. From this point on, these twelve became his most trusted friends and devoted followers. The biblical accounts give us little detail about the specifics surrounding the various calls to follow Jesus. Did the disciples know him from earlier encounters? Did they know him during their childhood years? Had they met during earlier travels he had made between Galilee and Jerusalem (Luke 12:44)? Had they heard rumors about him before he called them? None of this can be known. All the texts say that when Jesus called them to follow him, they dropped what they were doing and followed.

The lists of the disciples' names differ slightly among the Gospels, but the prophetic power of calling precisely twelve cannot be missed. The Gospels' lists of the twelve look like this:

MARK 3:13–19	MATTHEW 10:1–4	LUKE 6:12–16
Simon (Peter)	Simon (Peter)	Simon (Peter)
	His brother Andrew	His brother Andrew
James, son of Zebedee	James, son of Zebedee	James
John (Boanerges, Son of Thunder)	His brother John	John
Andrew[1]		
Philip	Philip	Philip
Bartholomew	Bartholomew	Bartholomew
Matthew	Thomas	Matthew
Thomas	Matthew the tax collector[2]	Thomas
James, son of Alphaeus	James, son of Alphaeus	James, son of Alphaeus
Thaddaeus	Thaddaeus	
Simon the Cananean	Simon the Cananean	Simon the Zealot[3]
		Judas, son of James[4]
Judas Iscariot	Judas Iscariot	Judas Iscariot

[1] Mark prefers to keep the three most prominent disciples together in his list (i.e., Peter, James, John) while Matthew and Luke prefer to keep the brothers, Peter and Andrew, together in their lists.

[2] We might expect Matthew to mention his profession.

[3] *Cananean* is the Aramaic word for *zealot*. Luke translates the Aramaic into Greek.

[4] It seems Thaddaeus (Mark and Matthew) and Judas, son of James (Luke) are the same person. Five of the names in the list are qualified by additional names—e.g., James, son of Zebedee. The name *Judas Iscariot* suggests there was another Judas, Judas son of James. Perhaps Mark and Matthew referred to the other Judas as Thaddaeus because of the stigma associated with Judas. Why Luke did not do so is impossible to know.

WHAT'S THE SIGNIFICANCE OF THE TWELVE DISCIPLES?

By calling twelve disciples, Jesus symbolically announced that God was restoring the twelve tribes of Israel. Jesus' main message was that the kingdom of God had come near. His teaching focused on this message, and the miracles he performed evidenced its truth by revealing the power that belonged to God's kingdom. The calling of *twelve* disciples points to the same! God was in the process of restoring his presence among his people. Like the days of old when God manifested his presence among the twelve tribes of Israel, God now restored it among a new covenant people whose beginnings were found in the twelve. By calling twelve, Jesus announced openly that God was calling Israel back to her purpose. The connection between the twelve disciples and God's eternal purposes was seen most clearly in Jesus' own words: "Jesus said to them, 'Truly I tell you, at the renewal of all things, when the Son of Man is seated on the throne of his glory, you who have followed me will also sit on twelve thrones, judging the twelve tribes of Israel. And everyone who has left houses or brothers or sisters or father or mother or children or fields, for my name's sake, will receive a hundredfold, and will inherit eternal life'" (Matt. 19:28–29 NRSV).

WHAT KIND OF PEOPLE DID JESUS CHOOSE?

Looking at the list of disciples, one is struck by the prominence of average, unschooled people and the complete absence of anyone from recognized Jewish piety or leadership. This was indeed a motley crowd. In God's new and restored Israel, a Roman hireling (Matthew) would work alongside a Jewish freedom fighter (Simon the Zealot). The four fishermen, two sets of brothers, were as different as night and day. Simon was rash and unpolished while Andrew was quiet and cautious; and the Zebedee brothers, John and James, exhibited temper (Luke 9:54) and ambition (Mark 10:37). Philip and Judas, the son of James, seemed rather dense (John 14:8f, 22f) while Bartholomew and Thomas were somewhat skeptical about the whole thing (John 1:46; 20:25). And Judas Iscariot was a traitor who sold Jesus out for thirty pieces of silver (Matt. 26:15).

Jesus' choice of disciples signified how God was in the process of restoring his kingdom and doing it outside the established Jewish religious order. None of the disciples had anything to brag about. The "new twelve tribes" would be fashioned by God himself as he made the wise ignorant and the ignorant wise. Jesus' *twelve* disciples symbolically announced that in God's new covenant kingdom, even unschooled men would speak with the power of his Spirit (Acts 4:13). The only requirement necessary for becoming a part of what Jesus announced was willingness to follow him and trust that he was the one God had sent to redeem his people.

STUDY QUESTIONS

1. In what way does Jesus' baptism reveal the trinitarian character of God?
2. How was it possible for God to outline Jesus' mission through a short statement at Jesus' baptism?
3. The specifics of Jesus' temptations were clearly different from how people normally face temptations. How were they similar?
4. How would you explain the connection between *temptation, test,* and *trial*?

ACT 2

JESUS' MESSAGE AND METHODS

JESUS' MAIN MESSAGE

I f someone asked the question, "What was Jesus' main message?" most people would likely answer "love" or "grace." Jesus told us to love one another, even to love our enemies (Matt. 5:44). Jesus taught that salvation comes by grace rather than by works. Although the last of these statements sounds more like something Paul would later say, both of these elements represent important aspects of Jesus' teaching (e.g., Matt. 22:1–10; Luke 23:43). They are not, however, his main message.

JESUS' MAIN MESSAGE WAS THAT THE KINGDOM OF GOD HAS COME NEAR

The clearest summary of Jesus' message is found in Mark 1:15. Jesus came preaching the good news of God saying: "The time is fulfilled, and the kingdom of God has come near; repent, and believe in the good news" (NRSV). To claim that God's kingdom had come near was such a radically new idea that it ran contrary to the Judaism of the day. Indeed, the statement was so radical that even during the heyday of liberalism, when most scholars considered just about everything in the New Testament nonhistorical and fictional, Mark 1:15 was hailed as the one statement that was so different from the common teaching of Jesus' contemporaries that it had to be Jesus himself who came up with it.

This *is* the centerpiece of Jesus' teaching. The message that God's kingdom has come near sums up everything Jesus said and did. As we shall see, the miracles stand as proof of the nearness of God's kingdom, and Jesus' specific teachings are best understood as application of this overarching message. When Luke reported on Jesus' teaching, beginning with his first synagogue preaching in 4:16, he concluded the section with a summary statement. Jesus said to a crowd that tries to prevent him from leaving, "I must proclaim the good news of the kingdom of God to the other cities also; for I was sent for this purpose" (Luke 4:43 NRSV).

Matthew reported Jesus' message in the same way (4:23). Although he changed the language to "kingdom of heaven," rather than "kingdom of God," he still emphasized Jesus' main message as the presence of God's kingdom. The reason for Matthew's change of language from "kingdom of God" to "kingdom of heaven" involves his reverence for God. Writing primarily to a Jewish audience that was keenly concerned not to take the name of the Lord in vain, Matthew followed Jewish custom and used an alternative term to express the same idea.[7]

When Jesus used the phrase "kingdom of God/heaven," he did not refer to a political area or realm but to the reality of God's renewed presence among people. For Jesus, God's kingdom had nothing to do with Israel's borders; nor did it refer to the restoration of a Davidic kingdom in the geographical and political sense of that term. Rather, Jesus used the phrase to explain that God had stepped into history to make his presence known in order to redeem all his creation from the consequences of the fall. Put differently, in Jesus' teaching the kingdom of God is the sphere where God rules and shows his glory.

In Matthew 12:27–28 Jesus pointed this out clearly: "If I cast out demons by Beelzebul, by whom do your own exorcists cast them out? Therefore they will be your judges. But if it is by the Spirit of God that I cast out demons, then the kingdom of God has come to you." Exorcisms, or the casting out of demons, evidenced the kingdom's nearness. Evil powers were destroyed as they came face-to-face with God's Spirit. Those rejecting Jesus' message remained blinded and outside God's kingdom while those accepting Jesus' message entered into God's kingdom, the sphere where God reveals his ruling glory.

THE KINGDOM OF GOD: A PRESENT REALITY AND AN ANNOUNCEMENT OF THE AGE TO COME

According to Jesus, the kingdom of God is already here. Jesus inaugurated it! The "age to come" has broken into the "present age." God is making his presence felt already now. Yet the kingdom of God is not here in full. Evil still exists. God does not yet fill "all in all" (1 Cor. 15:28). This will only happen at the time of consummation when Christ comes back. We now live between the times. The promised "age to come" has already begun but is not here in full. The "old age" is still here as well. Jesus' announcement of the presence of the kingdom changed the traditional Jewish understanding of God's actions in history (see diagram on p. 200). The Christian view of history, therefore, differs from that of first-century Judaism.

---

[7] There are four exceptions to this change: Matthew 12:28; 19:24; 21:31, 43. Cf. Matthew 6:33.

THE VIEW OF FIRST-CENTURY JUDAISM

According to first-century Judaism, history is divided into two periods. God has promised to restore his kingdom on earth, and when that happens, the present age will come to its end and the "age to come" will begin. Presented graphically, it looks something like this:

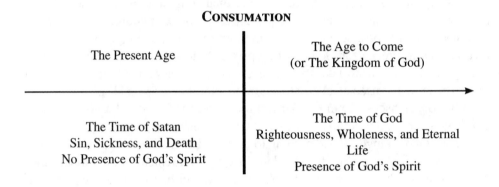

THE CHRISTIAN VIEW

According to the teaching of the New Testament, God has already broken into history through Christ. God has restored his kingdom on earth, and the "age to come" has already begun. God's kingdom has not come in full, however. Evil still roams. The present age will not end until Christ returns to establish his kingdom on earth. Until then God's creation lives between the times. Presented graphically, it looks something like this:

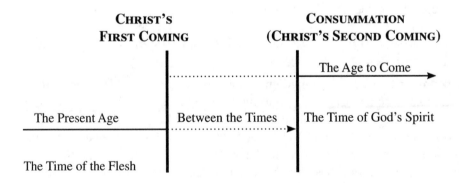

Jesus did not change the Old Testament view (followed by first-century Judaism) that God's kingdom will be restored on earth. God has not given up on history, like much first-century apocalypticism (and much modern apocalypticism) claimed.[8] He does not intend to destroy his creation but rather to restore it or recreate it. It will be a new heaven and a new earth, not the end of the earth and a transportation of the faithful to heaven. Jesus taught that the timing and the process were different from what first-century Judaism believed. God has already begun the final restoration of his creation, Jesus said. His kingdom has come near; his Spirit has been poured out on earth in fulfillment of Old Testament prophecy.

What Christians are awaiting is the complete fulfillment of this—the time when God breaks into history in such a way that the present age, with all its evil and rebellion, comes to an end and the age to come, saturated with God's presence, goodness, and grace, fills all in all. We may call our present experience of God's kingdom "already, not fully." The real thing has come already, but its fullness still awaits.

WHO WILL ENTER THE KINGDOM OF GOD?

The Gospel accounts give clear indication that Jesus explained how God desires for all people to accept his invitation to enter the kingdom. In his parable about the wedding feast (Matt. 22:1–10), the invitation to participate went out to all—first to all the obvious guests and then to everyone, even ones deemed least likely to be invited ("invite anyone you find . . . good and bad," vv. 9–10). The king told his attendants to broadcast his invitation so widely that his wedding hall would be full. No one was beyond his invitation. Yet, when the king came to greet his guests, he spotted one without a wedding garment and concluded that this person had entered the party without first accepting the king's invitation. The parable concluded that the invitation had gone out to all, but not everyone would accept and therefore be chosen as guests. The parable contained a message for everyone: God's invitation goes to all, but there are prerequisites for entering God's kingdom.

1. To enter God's kingdom, you must repent (Mark 1:15).

The summary statement of Jesus' teaching in Mark 1:15 places repentance, people's conscious awareness of their need for divine forgiveness, at the forefront of the requirements given for entering God's kingdom. This call to repentance ran through all of Jesus' teaching. Jesus called for a heartfelt change of attitude and mind that would bring a thoroughgoing recognition that any attempt to enter God's kingdom apart from his invitation through Christ would fail. Jesus' purpose in making the kingdom's presence visible among people was to reveal God's desire for fellowship with his creation. This clarity of God's desire called people of humility to a repentance that made a restoration of their fellowship with God possible. Jesus opened the door so that humanity's self-promoting rebellion against God, which had excluded them from God's presence, now could be forgiven through human

---

[8] Apocalypticism has to do with visions and preaching about the end-times. For more on apocalypticism see pp. 315–17.

repentance. The humble person who repented would enter God's kingdom; the proud, who refused to repent, remained outside the kingdom.

2. Entrance into God's kingdom requires a trusting childlike faith (Matt. 18:3–5).

Jesus' likened the kind of faith called forth by genuine repentance to the trusting faith found among children. In Matthew 18:3, Jesus explained the result of repentance as becoming like a child who is not afraid of humbling himself or who has no pride that stands in the way of a trusting relationship. Jesus sought to remove the idea of faith in God from a mere cognitive assent to the Law of God with all its specific regulations and restore it to its original understanding as a trusting relationship. To enter God's kingdom, Jesus taught, is to enter into a trust-based relationship with God.

3. God's kingdom calls for obedience to God's will (Matt. 7:21–23).

The trusting relationship Jesus called for played itself out as obedience. In Jesus' teaching, obedience was not to be understood in legal or even military terms. It was not primarily about following laws, commands, or instructions but rather about acting in trust. There is a difference between how a child is obedient to a parent he or she trusts and how a law-abiding citizen keeps a certain law. When a loving parent asks a child to do a certain thing, the child obeys without considering the parent's request as law or command. The same holds true in a strong marriage or a good friendship. Only when a distrust of motives (or an uncertainty about the wisdom of the parent or the friend in a given matter) enters the picture does the situation and the nature of the request/command change. When there is complete trust in the one requesting or commanding, obedience becomes a matter of natural response. That was why Jesus could say, "If you love me, you will obey what I command" (John 14:15). It is in this way that obedience is a prerequisite for entrance into God's kingdom.

THE METHOD OF JESUS' TEACHING

JESUS TAUGHT IN PARABLES

A parable is a story that illustrates a moral or spiritual truth from a well-known situation or story. Jesus picked up on situations people would recognize immediately, like the parable of the sower where the picture of a farmer sowing his fields was instantly recognizable to his listeners. He could also use a well-known story, anecdote, or accepted idea like the parable of the rich man and Lazarus where he used an accepted notion about the fate of the righteous and the unrighteous to teach that some people would not believe even if someone came back from the dead (Luke 16:31). Whether Jesus used a situation or a story as the background for a parable, his use of parables gave his listeners, many of whom were uneducated and unlearned, a way of understanding that would have been difficult to attain through any other teaching method. Furthermore, teaching through parables enabled Jesus to correct popular ideas about God without getting into detailed arguments. Like narratives or illustrations in general, the story itself can carry deep truths that are unrelated to the particulars of the story told.

Many of Jesus' parables are called kingdom parables. They are so called because they begin with the phrase: "The kingdom of God is like . . ." Kingdom parables do not differ in character from the other parables of Jesus. He used them to illustrate and describe what he meant when he spoke about the kingdom of God.

A NOTE ON THE INTERPRETATION OF PARABLES

AS A RULE, JESUS' PARABLES HAVE ONE MAJOR POINT

The interpretation of the parables has proven to be an issue for many theologians and pastors throughout church history. Rich as they are in detail, parables seem to evoke an enormous creativity among interpreters. Allegorical approaches to interpretation made scholars of old ascribe incredible significance to details of a parable that had no other purpose than to enable the storytelling. In the parable of the good Samaritan, for example, various interpreters from Christian history have tried to give meaning to the road the man walked along, the ambushing he experienced, and so forth. In the prodigal son parable, some have tried to find representation for the partying friends he found when he left his father, the pigs from whose trough he ate, the robe he was given when he came back, etcetera.

The influential bishop Augustine of Hippo (ca. AD 400) suggested one of the most intriguing allegories of this kind. Explaining the parable of the good Samaritan, Augustine saw the man who was beaten as representative of Adam. This man (Adam) was going from Jerusalem to Jericho, representing mankind's fall from the state of original bliss[9] to his painful situation of mortality.[10] The robbers who attacked the man were the devil and his demons; they stripped him of his clothes, an act representing the stripping of Adam's immortality. That they left the man as half dead meant that humanity is spiritually half dead because of sin and half alive because of the knowledge of God. The priest who walked by the wounded man without helping represented the Law while the Levite represented the prophets. The good Samaritan was Christ himself; his binding of the wounds signified sin's limitation. The oil poured on the man's wounds referred to the comfort found in hope while the wine represented exhortation to spirited work. The Samaritan's donkey carrying the man to the inn signified the body of Christ, whereas the inn itself was the church. The two denarii used to pay the innkeeper represented the two commandments of love. The innkeeper was the apostle Paul, and the return of the good Samaritan to check on the wounded and repay whatever else he might owe the innkeeper was a reference to the resurrection of Christ.

---

[9] Jerusalem, representing the city of heavenly peace.

[10] Jericho, representing the moon because the word for *moon* in Hebrew has the same root as the word *Jericho*; moon signifies mortality.

Intriguing as this interpretation may be, it is clearly nothing more than a conjured imaginative explanation. Nothing in the text gives any indication of any of the things Augustine suggested, and he could have chosen to make every element in the story represent something entirely different. He made the parable illustrate something he wanted to say rather than letting the parable say what Jesus intended for it to say (and what those who heard him say it understood).

Such fanciful allegorical interpretation was forcefully and convincingly rejected by the scholar Adolf Jülicher. The main claim of his two-volume work on parables, that parables are simple moral stories with only one point, was an important corrective to what we have just described. In his eagerness to state his case forcefully, however, he went beyond the evidence of his findings. Rather than saying that all parables have only one point, it will be more correct to affirm that they have one *major* point.

Some parables can be shown to have two or three points or two subpoints to the one major point. The best way to determine whether a parable has more than one point is to look for more than one major character in the parable. Look at these examples:[11]

Possible two-point parables. The parable about the wise and the foolish builders (Luke 6:47–49) places equal emphasis on the wise and the foolish builder. The interpretation of this parable should therefore contain both a negative and a positive conclusion. Two points can be made. Still, the one *major* point is the superiority of the wise man to the foolish man.

In the parable of the rich fool (Luke 12:16–21), both the rich farmer and God himself act as main characters. The parable says something about both of them. It will not be an overinterpretation to say that Jesus is saying something about the foolishness of the thinking of the rich man *and* something about the character of God. Again two points are made. Still, the one *major* point is the foolishness of not recognizing God's involvement in life's affairs.

Possible three-point parables. Probably the best example of a three-point parable is the prodigal son (Luke 15:11–32). Clearly each of the three main characters—the father, the younger son, and the older son—receive special attention.

The equation of the father with God seems obvious and speaks to his character as loving, forgiving, and patient as he waits for those who have gone astray. The emphasis on the straying son, the errors of his ways, and especially his repentance and return, receive so much focus in the parable that no one could miss the enormity of the restoration that followed his repentance. The older son likewise seems to be more than just a peripheral figure. The sustained emphasis on his rejection of the father's goodness, and his consequent absence at the banquet given by the father to celebrate the younger brother's conversion and return, seems too elaborate to dismiss as nonsignificant to the point of the parable (which is the case with the fattened calf, the robe, the gold ring, etc.). In short, Jesus seems to make three points here—one about God, one about the importance of repentance and coming back to God, and one about the danger of self-righteousness. Still, the one *major* point is the character of God who eagerly waits for those who have gone

---

[11] For more examples and further discussion of this, see Craig L. Blomberg, *Interpreting the Parables* (Downers Grove, Ill.: InterVarsity Press, 1990).

astray to find their way back to him, and who are saddened when those belonging to him will not rejoice with him when it happens.

The parable of the talents (Luke 19:12–27) represents another possible three-point parable. Again, it emphasizes three characters. The first is the master who asks ten of his servants each to administrate a portion of his wealth while he is away to be appointed king. The two good servants who had done well with what they had been entrusted represent the other character. The master entrusts them with even more when he returns. Although they had not done equally well with what they had been entrusted, the point is still that they both did well. The two should not be distinguished in the interpretation of the parable. The third character is the bad servant who did nothing with what the master had entrusted him. Nothing good will come his way, the parables show. We hear nothing about the response of seven of the servants. Those mentioned are simply representatives of two types of responses and attitudes. The parable emphasizes three distinct characters; and the interpretation, therefore, should move beyond a simple one-point conclusion. Still, the one *major* point is that those who are faithful with what God has given them will be blessed with even more. The king values the faithfulness of his servants!

Going beyond these three points, to make a point out of the size of the various earnings or their consequent rewards, moves outside the intention of the parable. Neither should anything be made of the final remarks of the king about his enemies. All of that is a simple part of the parabolic story. The overarching rule for parable interpretation is that it has one *major* point; only when a parable has more than one major character can further points possibly be made. Moving beyond that will turn the interpretation of parables into little more than personal allegorical guesswork.

CHART OF GOSPEL PARABLES

PARABLES	MATTHEW	MARK	LUKE
Salt	5:13		
Light under a bowl	5:14–16	4:21–23	8:16–17; 11:33–36
Houses on rock and on sand	7:24–27		6:47–49
New cloth on an old garment	9:16	2:21	5:36
New wine in old wineskins	9:17	2:22	5:37–39
Sower and soils	13:1–23	4:1–20	8:4–15
Weeds in the field	13:24–30, 36–43		
Mustard seed	13:31–32	4:30–32	13:18–19
Yeast	13:33		13:20–21
Hidden treasure	13:44		
Pearl of great value	13:45–46		

PARABLES	MATTHEW	MARK	LUKE
Dragnet	13:47–50		
Master of a household	13:52		
Lost sheep	18:12–14		15:1–7
Unforgiving servant	18:23–35		
Workers in the vineyard	20:1–16		
Two sons	21:28–31		
Wicked tenants	21:33–41	12:1–9	20:9–16
Wedding feast	22:1–14		
Fig tree as herald of summer	24:32–33	13:28–29	21:29–31
Faithful servant	24:45–51		12:42–48
Ten maidens	25:1–13		
Talents and servants (minas)	25:14–30		19:11–27
Sheep and goats	25:31–46		
Seedtime to harvest		4:26–29	
Creditor and the debtors			7:41–43
Good Samaritan			10:25–37
Friend at midnight			11:5–8
Rich fool			12:13–21
Watchfulness		13:35–37	12:35–40
Fig tree without figs			13:6–9
Places of honor at the wedding feast			14:7–14
Great feast			14:15–24
Counting the cost			14:28–33
Lost coin			15:8–10
Prodigal son			15:11–32
Unjust servant			16:1–8
Rich man and Lazarus			16:19–31
The master and his servant			17:7–10
Unjust judge			18:1–8
The Pharisee and the tax collector			18:9–14

JESUS TAUGHT THROUGH PREACHING

Although the Gospel of Mark records little of Jesus' preaching, it is clear from the collected accounts of the other Gospels that one of Jesus' primary teaching methods was preaching. The largest and most distinct collection of Jesus' sermonic material appears in Matthew 5–7, the Sermon on the Mount. One of the major traits of this material is Jesus' use of the Old Testament and his reinterpretation of its meaning in light of the presence of God's kingdom.

The Sermon on the Mount opens with the Beatitudes, a series of statements promising blessing to those who belong to the kingdom: "Blessed are the poor in spirit, for theirs is the kingdom of heaven" (Matt. 5:3). Taken together one may say the Beatitudes describe Jesus himself, but more importantly they define the aspirations and the attitudes of those who will enter the kingdom. The promises given are not attached to actions people may do, or positions they may hold, but to the attitudes and convictions of the heart that move the will of listeners to look beyond themselves to see what God is doing through Jesus Christ. Where Jewish leaders had focused on law, legalism, and position as expressions of their relationship to God, Jesus taught that the internal attitude of the heart was the true measuring stick of a person's relationship to God. Internal attitudes would lead to genuine and nonhypocritical actions whereas external actions contradict internal attitudes and thus are little more than expressions of hypocrisy. In many ways, therefore, Jesus' words seemed to militate against the powerful, the influential, and the religious leaders of the day—people whose position and actions were considered definitive of God's will. However, Jesus' teaching did not aim to stereotype or classify groups but to inspire and instruct individuals.

With this new focus on the quality of people's relationship with God, the Sermon on the Mount moves to a discussion of how this new understanding influences a person's understanding of the Law. Jesus did not abolish the Law but affirmed it by focusing on its fulfillment (Matt. 5:17). Rather than approaching God's commands from a legalistic perspective (obeying the letter of the Law), he reads it relationally (focusing on the intention of the commandments).

For example, a legalistic reading of the commandment on manslaughter points to the words "do not kill." A relational reading of this Mosaic commandment, on the other hand, asks what would make a person desire to kill. The answer to this will move focus to the intention of the commandment and the issues of the heart. Jesus therefore says, "Do not get angry."[12] This same focus on the underlying attitudes of the heart surfaces also in other issues Jesus dealt with in this sermon. In his teaching on adultery, for example, Jesus insists the matter cannot be reduced to a verbatim reading of Moses' words, "You shall not commit adultery;" rather,

---

[12] "You have heard that it was said to those of ancient times, 'You shall not murder'; and 'whoever murders shall be liable to judgment.' But I say to you that if you are angry with a brother or sister, you will be liable to judgment; and if you insult a brother or sister, you will be liable to the council; and if you say, 'You fool,' you will be liable to the hell of fire" (Matt. 5:21–22 NRSV).

focus must remain on the cause, "Do not look at a woman with lust."[13] That is, an attitude of heart precedes the action. According to Jesus, God looks beyond the action to the sincerity of the commitment in the believer.

No one listening to Jesus quoting Moses and saying, *"You have heard it said, but I say,"* could have escaped the question of authority. By what authority was Jesus able to change what to them were the plain words of Moses? The conclusion from Jesus' preaching seemed inescapable: the Mosaic covenant, built around the Law given at Sinai, was being transformed before their eyes. The new covenant as promised by Jeremiah (31:33ff) and Ezekiel (36:26ff) was breaking through. Jesus' preaching pointed to it; the authority with which he spoke clarified it; the miracles he performed evidenced it. The kingdom of God had come near; and those poor in Spirit, as defined by the Beatitudes, could see it. The rich and proud leaders of Judaism who opposed it could not.

JESUS TAUGHT BY USING QUESTIONS

Much can be said about the use of questions as a teaching method. It will suffice at this point simply to notice that by using this method Jesus was able to let both his disciples and his opponents draw inescapable conclusions about him. Rather than arguing, debating, and postulating, Jesus' use of questions allowed him to say things about himself and his mission that might have been impossible to say in any other way.

For example, through questions Jesus asked, Peter concluded that Jesus was "the Messiah, the Son of the living God" (Matt. 16:13–17; Mark 8:27–29; Luke 9:18–20 NRSV). When opponents tried to trap Jesus with their questions, he countered their questions with his own, using the opportunity to teach them about their relationship to God. Their answer to his questions then became the answer to their own questions. For example, they asked him whether they should pay taxes to Caesar. He asked them to show him a coin and then to tell him whose face was on the coin. Their answer was "Caesar's." Jesus replied, "Give to Caesar what is Caesar's, and to God what is God's" (Matt. 22:15–22; Mark 12:13–17; Luke 20:20–26). The conclusion was unspoken but impossible to miss. Rather than being concerned about their financial situation, and their relationship to the Roman emperor, they should be concerned with their relationship to God. As the Roman coins bore the image of Caesar, their hearts should bear the image of God. The real question was not whether they had to return to Caesar what bore Caesar's image but whether they were returning to God what bore God's image.

Jesus used questions repeatedly. Look at the following: Mark 8:27–32; 8:19–20; 10:38; Matthew 17:25; 21:31; Luke 10:36; 22:35. See also Mark 3:1–4; 11:27–33; Matthew 12:11–12; Luke 7:39–42.

---

[13] "You have heard that it was said, 'You shall not commit adultery.' But I say to you that everyone who looks at a woman with lust has already committed adultery with her in his heart" (Matt. 5:27–28).

STUDY QUESTIONS

1. What was Jesus' main message, and how did it differ from the message of other teachers in first-century Judaism?
2. What is allegorical interpretation, and why is it problematic?
3. When can a parable be said to make more than one point?
4. What is the difference between the legalism taught by the Pharisees and the focus of Jesus' message?

ACT 3

Jesus' Miracles and Ministry

Jesus' Miracles Revealed
the Presence of God's Kingdom

The main purpose of Jesus' miracles was teaching. They served as teaching tools and functioned as an affirmation that Jesus spoke the truth. The best illustration of this may be found in Matthew 11:2–6 (par. Luke 7:18–22) where John the Baptist, confused by his prison sentence and the events that had unfolded, sent his disciples to ask Jesus, "Are you the one who is to come, or are we to wait for another?" (NRSV). Jesus' answer evidences that he saw his miracles as proof that God's kingdom truly had come near. "Go and tell John what you hear and see: the blind receive their sight, the lame walk, the lepers are cleansed, the deaf hear, the dead are raised, and the poor have good news brought to them. And blessed is anyone who takes no offense at me" (NSRV). The most common miracles performed by Jesus were the exorcisms of demons; that evil spirits were driven out by the Spirit of God was nothing short of direct verification that God's kingdom indeed had come near.[14]

Miracles Are Supernatural

We do not call ordinary things that happen repeatedly and obviously miracles. That we wake up every morning may be a miracle in one sense, but that is not what we think about when we say miracle. When we say *miracle,* we usually refer to the unexpected and unexplainable, that which is supernatural. By *supernatural*

---

[14] "But if it is by the Spirit of God that I cast out demons, then the kingdom of God has come to you" (Matt. 12:28).

we mean that which goes beyond the mere natural, that which breaks the normal understanding of the "laws of nature"—in other words, that which requires an intervention from God!

1. A specific timing of an event can prove to be miraculous and thereby show God's hand.

Sometimes the mere timing of an event can be so incredible that although the occurrence itself is not out of the ordinary, its timing makes it anything but "natural." This, for example, was the case with several of the plagues that haunted Egypt before the Exodus. Huge swarms of locusts, as an example, are not unnatural, but the timing and the prophetic foretelling of it made it so.

Enlightenment Worldview
God does not interfere
with natural laws.

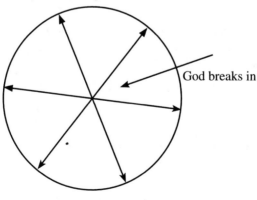

Action and Reaction

Cause and Effect

A closed continuum

No outside power

The World

Christian Worldview
God can break in and do a miracle
by overwriting natural laws.

God breaks in

The World

2. A miracle breaks the law(s) of nature and thus defies a natural explanation.

Since the enlightenment, the common Western worldview has had no room for miracles. By definition, everything must be explained by the principle of cause and effect, action and reaction. According to enlightenment thought, we live in a closed continuum, or universe, with no influence from the outside. With this presupposition, miraculous events do not exist and turn by definition into "things we cannot yet explain." There is no need for God and no room for God—except, maybe, as a necessary psychological phenomenon needed to avoid moral chaos. But for the "real world" a natural explanation exists for everything, even if humans do not know it yet.

Contrary to this enlightenment worldview, which has greatly impacted both academic theology and practical church life and teaching, the Christian worldview allows God to break in and act in spite of the laws of nature. It is because of this openness that true miracles, inexplicable to the natural order, are possible.

JESUS' MIRACLES INCLUDED ALL ASPECTS OF LIFE

As mentioned earlier, Jesus' miracles served primarily as teaching tools. Jesus never performed miracles simply to wow his audience. His aim was to prove that his teaching about the kingdom was true and to point to God's unique presence in his life. The subtle but important distinction between Jesus' miracles and the miracles of the disciples is that Jesus was able to command the demons; he himself possessed the power to cause a miracle to happen. The disciples and the church, on the other hand, could only request that God would act through them. We may say that Jesus, having the power of God, spoke as God whereas his followers acted as servants who had no personal possession of power to work miracles. They could perform such only when Jesus empowered them to do so.[15]

Because Jesus' miracles were teaching tools about God's renewed presence, they covered the whole spectrum of human experience—the created world, the human struggle with disease and illness, the power of evil in the world, and the power of death.

1. Jesus performed nature miracles, proving his power over creation.

NATURE MIRACLES	MATTHEW	MARK	LUKE	JOHN
Calming the storm	8:23–27	4:35–41	8:22–25	
Feeding the 5,000	14:13–21	6:30–44	9:10–17	6:1–14
Walking on the water	14:22–33	6:45–51		6:16–21
Feeding the 4,000	15:32–38	8:1–9		

---

[15] See, for example, Mark 9:17–18: "Someone from the crowd answered him, 'Teacher, I brought you my son; he has a spirit that makes him unable to speak; and whenever it seizes him, it dashes him down; and he foams and grinds his teeth and becomes rigid; and I asked your disciples to cast it out, but they could not do so'" (NRSV).

NATURE MIRACLES	MATTHEW	MARK	LUKE	JOHN
Coin in the fish's mouth	17:24–27			
Fig tree withered	21:18–22	11:12–14, 20–25		
Miraculous catch of fish			5:1–11	
Turning water into wine				2:1–11
Another catch of fish				21:1–11

2. Jesus healed sickness and disease, demonstrating his power to set people free.

HEALING MIRACLES	MATTHEW	MARK	LUKE	JOHN
Healing a leper	8:2–4	1:40–42	5:12–14	
Healing the centurion's servant	8:5–13		7:1–10	
Healing Peter's mother-in-law	8:14–15	1:29–31		4:38–39
Healing a paralyzed man	9:2–8	2:3–12	5:18–26	
Healing a woman with a hemorrhage	9:20–22	5:25–34	8:43–48	
Healing a man with a withered hand	12:10–13	3:1–5	6:6–10	
Healing of two blind men	9:27–31			
Healing a Canaanite daughter	15:21–28	7:24–30		
Healing blind Bartimaeus	20:29–34	10:46–52	18:35–43	
Healing a blind man at Bethsaida		8:22–26		
Healing a deaf and mute man		7:32–37		
Healing a crippled woman			13:11–13	
Healing a man with dropsy			14:1–4	

HEALING MIRACLES	MATTHEW	MARK	LUKE	JOHN
Healing ten lepers		17:11–19		
Healing Malchus's ear		22:50–51		
Healing Capernaum official's son				4:46–54
Healing sick at pool of Bethesda				5:1–15
Healing a man blind from birth				9:1–41

3. Jesus exorcised demons, announcing his power over evil.

EXORCISM MIRACLES	MATTHEW	MARK	LUKE	JOHN
Many demon possessed	8:16–17	1:32–34	4:40–41	
The Gerasene demoniac	8:28–34	5:1–20	8:26–39	
A possessed man	9:32–34		11:14–15	
A blind, mute, and possessed man	12:22–23			
The epileptic boy	17:14–21	9:14–29	9:38–43	
A possessed man		1:23–26	4:33–35	

4. Jesus raised people from the dead, proclaiming the end to the most powerful consequence of human sin.

JESUS RAISING THE DEAD	MATTHEW	MARK	LUKE	JOHN
Widow's son			7:11–17	
Jairus's daughter	9:18–19, 23–25	5:22–24, 35–43	8:41–42, 49–56	
Lazarus raised				11:1–44

Jesus' Ministry Included
the Weak and the Powerless

Jesus came to preach the gospel to the poor. Like the prophets of old, he emphasized God's special concern for the poor, the downtrodden, and the powerless. As Luke portrayed Jesus' ministry, he not only resounded the prophetic charge against Israel, that they had forgotten to be concerned about the poor; he spelled out specifically that he had come to proclaim good news to the poor and to set the oppressed free.[16]

Jesus Shows Special Concern for Those Who Live In Poverty

Jesus picked up the Old Testament prophetic message that social injustice was an abomination to God; God had a special love for those whose only strength was found in him.[17] This was such a big theme in Jesus' ministry that to investigate it goes beyond the scope of this survey. A couple of examples will suffice. Compare, for example, the large gifts given by wealthy people to the temple treasury to the few coins given by a poor woman; Jesus concluded that she gave the greater gift (Mark 12:41–44). Similarly, in Luke's version of the Sermon on the Mount, the so-called Sermon on the Plain, Jesus proclaimed a blessing on the poor, not the "poor in the spirit" like in the Beatitudes found in Matthew (Luke 6:20). Teaching on hospitality and humility during a banquet at the house of a prominent Pharisee, Jesus spoke to the issue directly: "He said also to the one who had invited him, 'When you give a luncheon or a dinner, do not invite your friends or your brothers or your relatives or rich neighbors, in case they may invite you in return, and you would be repaid. But when you give a banquet, invite the poor, the crippled, the lame, and the blind. And you will be blessed, because they cannot repay you, for you will be repaid at the resurrection of the righteous'" (Luke 14:12–14).

In Luke's Gospel, this event is followed directly by the parable of the great banquet where the host (God) invites the crippled, the poor, the blind, and the lame. At a later event, when a rich ruler came to Jesus to ask about righteousness, Jesus told him that he would have a treasure in heaven if he sold all he had and distributed it to the poor (Luke 18:22).

Jesus Associated with the Sick, with Those of Questionable Repute, and with the Socially Unacceptable

Jesus' association with social outcasts was another difference between Jesus and other rabbis which spelled out the special character of God's kingdom. People with leprosy, demon possession, and other illnesses were considered outside of God's

---

[16] "When he came to Nazareth, where he had been brought up, he went to the synagogue on the sabbath day, as was his custom. He stood up to read, and the scroll of the prophet Isaiah was given to him. He unrolled the scroll and found the place where it was written: 'The Spirit of the Lord is upon me, because he has anointed me to bring good news to the poor. He has sent me to proclaim release to the captives and recovery of sight to the blind, to let the oppressed go free, to proclaim the year of the Lord's favor'" (Luke 4:16–18 NRSV). See also Luke 7:22.

[17] See also Galatians 2:10 where Paul expresses the same understanding.

blessing. As a result, they became isolated from society and from the worship of God. According to Jesus' teaching and ministry, such an understanding ran contrary to God's will. God possessed a special love for the poor and the downtrodden, and his kingdom included such people; in fact, it especially included such people.

Contrary to the traditional teachings of first-century Judaism, Jesus not only spoke to the "untouchable"; he touched them, healed them, and brought the presence of God's kingdom to them. Beyond those who were physically ill or demon possessed, Jesus reached out to those whose lifestyle exemplified unrighteousness. Thieves, robbers, prostitutes—people whose moral character left much to be desired—met in Jesus someone who received them with transforming love. Rather than rejection they found acceptance, and this reception into the kingdom resulted in their conversion and a change of lifestyle that brought forth genuine kingdom righteousness. The same held true for sinners, tax collectors, and Gentiles. Where Judaism disassociated itself from such, Jesus sought fellowship.

The merging of life and teaching in Jesus' ministry brought the quality of God's renewed presence to the forefront. Rather than calling for legalism, the exact keeping of the words of the Law, Jesus called for conversion and transformation, a loving relationship with God, and a humility before God, who gladly would receive all who desire his transforming power.

STUDY QUESTIONS

1. How would you define a miracle?
2. On what basis do some people reject the existence of real miracles?
3. What was the main purpose of Jesus' miracles?
4. Why do you think Jesus' ministry showed special concern for the poor and needy?

EPISODE TEN

"A PROPHET MUST
DIE IN JERUSALEM"

ACT 1

JESUS' ENTRY INTO JERUSALEM

J esus' message about the presence of God's kingdom proved too great a challenge for the Jewish leadership to accept. Having taught throughout Israel, Jesus gained a large following and was perceived by various religious factions and leaders as a threat to their authority. Although, according to Luke, Jesus' death happened in keeping with God's plan (Acts 2:23), it came as the culmination of a determined effort on behalf of the Jewish leaders. Many discussions with Pharisees and scribes had led to this point. The hollow legalism of their teaching fell short when faced with Jesus' relational interpretation of the Old Testament. Moreover, many of the direct charges from Jesus' teaching about the hypocritical nature of the worship performed by the establishment of first-century Judaism had revealed the barrenness of their relationship with God. Even the power of his miracles pronounced judgment upon priests and scribes who could not produce such evidence of God's presence (John 3:2). Beyond this, Jesus inflamed their anger even further through controversial events like the cleansing of the temple. In the minds of the Jewish leaders, Jesus from Nazareth posed a threat that needed to be dealt with in the severest way possible.

THE PASSION WEEK

The most significant portion of the gospel story deals with the last week of Jesus' life. Referencing Jesus' suffering during the last days of his life, the Christian church calls this week Passion Week.

Passion Week begins as Jesus approaches Jerusalem for a Passover celebration. In the Gospel account, Jesus' move toward Jerusalem for his final Passover began much earlier during a conversation with his disciples in a place as far away as Caesarea Philippi. Having always been careful not to let people call him Son of God or Messiah (because he did not want predetermined ideas about what a Messiah should be or do to determine his ministry), he now asked his disciples directly who people took him to be.

Peter answered that most people saw him as a prophet. When he asked the disciples who they thought he was, Peter answered: "You are the Christ [Messiah], the Son of the living God." This confession began the clear pronouncements of Jesus as the true Messiah. After this event every event described in the Gospels points to the significance of this confession. The nature of Jesus' identity was no longer hidden but could be spoken of freely, even if for a while only among the disciples (Matt. 16:20; Mark 8:20). In both Matthew's and Mark's Gospels, Jesus responds to this statement by teaching his disciples about his coming death.

Following Jesus' prediction of his death, the gospel narrative is now focused on the Jerusalem event. In the Gospel of Mark, Jesus' journey to Jerusalem and the climactic events that occurred when he arrived, take up about half the text. Immediately following the prediction of Jesus' death, Mark's Gospel gives a description of an event, usually called the Mount of Transfiguration, where God confirmed Jesus as his Son and called for the disciples' obedience to Jesus. Although they confessed Jesus as the Messiah, the disciples clearly had not understood what Jesus tried to tell about the nature of his Messiahship. This became clear when they began to discuss who among them would get the most prominent seats in the new government Jesus would establish (Mark 10:35–45). For the readers of the Gospel, however, the significance of what was about to happen was coming into focus. Even blind people would begin to see (Mark 10:46–52).

THE TRIUMPHAL ENTRY INTO JERUSALEM

Passion Week begins the Sunday before the Jewish Passover. What has now become known in churches as Palm Sunday is a remembrance of the event that initiated Passion Week. Described in all four Gospels,[1] the event is best understood on the background of the messianic enthusiasm that had captured the people's imagination and their hope for an overthrow of the occupying Roman power. In spite of Jesus' persistent teaching that his kingdom was not of this earth, and his careful avoidance of titles that gave indication of political ambition, the popular conviction that the Messiah would restore the nation of Israel to its earlier political prominence remained largely unchanged. Even Jesus' faithful followers found it difficult to understand his new teaching and its implications. The high level of anticipation among vast numbers of Jews that God's Messiah would set them free in the political sense of that term thrust Jesus into a scenario where the people were trying to crown him as a political Messiah to be enthroned in Jerusalem. In the minds of the Jewish population, Jesus had proven he was the Messiah, which they interpreted to mean he would restore the Davidic reign of Israel.

---

[1] Matthew 21:1–11; Mark 11:1–11; Luke 19:28–40; John 12:12–19.

The specific elements of the triumphal entry indicate that the whole event should be understood as an eschatological event—that is, it evidenced that end-time prophecies were being fulfilled and God was engaging history in the way he had foretold. Jesus' descent from the Mount of Olives placed the whole account in an eschatological framework that anticipated God's day of reckoning with the nations. The connection to Zechariah's prophecy in 14:1, 3–4a (NRSV) ("See, a day is coming for the LORD. . . . Then the LORD will go forth and fight against those nations as when he fights on a day of battle. On that day his feet shall stand on the Mount of Olives, which lies before Jerusalem on the east") leaves little doubt that the event yielded significance that went far beyond the mere coincidental culmination of human longing.

Beyond the reaction of the enthusiastic crowd, which misunderstood the extent of what Jesus was doing, Jesus himself intended to signify a last-day kind of action by God. God was indeed sending his promised Messiah King to Jerusalem, as Zechariah had promised. Jesus' actions as described in Mark 11:1–7 (and parallel passages) fit exactly Zechariah 9:9, "Rejoice greatly, O daughter Zion! Shout aloud, O daughter Jerusalem! Lo, your king comes to you; triumphant and victorious is he, humble and riding on a donkey, on a colt, the foal of a donkey" (NRSV). Jesus set up his entry into Jerusalem in such a way that no one could doubt that he came as the promised King of Israel[2]—not as an earthly political king, as they expected, but as the King promised by God.

The anticipation bolstered by this event, which in the mind of the people functioned as a de facto announcement of the coming of the "age to come," knew no limits. The hosanna shouts of the people were chanted prayers meaning "save now." Liturgical use of the phrase in Jewish worship services had turned it into a shout of acclamation for Yahweh similar to "hallelujah." It was commonly shouted by pilgrims as they approached Jerusalem, and it could even be used to greet a great rabbi; but the fervor and the excitement of this event, which included the paving of the road with coats and palm branches, gave these shouts an even stronger focus. This elevated significance of the phrase becomes even more obvious by the addition of the interpretative follow-up quote from Psalm 118:26. The point is made when "Blessed is he who comes in the name of the Lord!" is defined even further by the sentence, "Blessed is the coming kingdom of our father David" (Mark 11:9–10). Put differently, according to the crowd, the salvation proclaimed by the hosanna shout resided in the one who comes in the name of the Lord, and his coming announces the coming of the promised kingdom. What Jesus had preached and brought witness to through his miracles, the coming of God's kingdom, was now moving toward its full exposure on the Jerusalem scene.

---

[2] See also Zephaniah 3:14–16.

THE CLEANSING OF THE TEMPLE

The day after the triumphal entry, Jesus entered the temple area and caused a tremendous disturbance to the daily routine. As with the triumphal entry, all four Gospels describe this event in some detail, albeit that John's chronology differs from the others.[3] Many commentators hold that this event was the last straw for the Sadducees and the Pharisees, and the temple cleansing became the direct cause for their final decision to have Jesus killed.

To understand the event, a little bit of background proves necessary. More than being a city with a temple, Jerusalem was a temple with a city growing up around it. The significance of the building and the entire temple area cannot be exaggerated and may be difficult for people today to grasp fully. Solomon built the original temple, which the Babylonians destroyed in 586 BC. However, when Cyrus of Persia allowed the Jews to return to Jerusalem beginning in 538 BC, Zerubbabel rebuilt the temple. This temple did not reflect the glory of Solomon's temple, so in 20 BC, to gain favor with the Jews, King Herod the Great began a grand-scale restoration that was still in progress at the time of Jesus. The temple was a grand complex of courts and colonnades; and the temple building itself, which only high-ranking priests could enter, represented only a smaller section of it, albeit the most important part.

Most sacrifices happened outside the building where the altar of burnt offering also stood.[4] Along the walls of the outer court, a huge enclosed plaza open for everyone, ran a roofed colonnade. In this colonnade money changers had their booths and did their business. They were not, as some might think, in the temple building or even in one of the outside courts closer to the temple.

The money changers and animal traders were there to aid the sacrificial system. When pilgrims came to Jerusalem to worship and sacrifice, they did not have to bring the animals from their home or buy them from vendors outside the temple. The selling of animals was, in this sense, helpful and somewhat biblical. The same held true for currency. Pilgrims from Galilee and even foreign countries needed to exchange their money into the standard currency used in the temple. With hundreds of thousands of pilgrims coming to Jerusalem during the Passover festival, business boomed; and the whole place was buzzing with commerce.

In this environment, where commerce and the business of religion had taken priority over true worship and sincere dedication to God, Jesus let his rage be felt. With prophetic force he turned over tables and stopped the machinery of the temple system while charging that they had transformed God's house from a house of prayer into a den of robbers. In line with his former confrontations with the leaders of Judaism, when Jesus had accused them of turning what should have been an inward heartfelt devotion to God into an external exhibit of religious duty, Jesus now applied this message to the center for Jewish worship.

---

[3] Matthew 21:12–17; Mark 11:15–18; Luke 19:45–48; John 2:13–22. Scholars give various explanations for this change. See commentaries on John for further discussion of the issue of John's chronology.

[4] Most study Bibles and some regular Bibles have helpful sketches of the temple layout.

The major significance of the temple cleansing was to show that the old expression of Judaism had been so corrupted that it had to be replaced. The way into the presence of God did not go through money changers, priests, and animal sacrifices. Relationship and obedience was what mattered, not mere external expressions of religion.[5]

In the Gospel accounts this focus becomes extraordinarily clear. Mark's Gospel wraps the cleansing of the temple in the story of the withered fig tree. On his way to the temple, Jesus saw a fig tree; he was hungry, but when he reached for fruit he found nothing but leaves on the tree. Because of that he cursed the tree. Then Mark gives the account of the temple cleansing. Later, as Jesus left the temple area, his disciples noticed that the fig tree had withered to its roots. To any original reader of Mark, the withering of the fruitless fig tree was symbolic of what just happened to the fruitless expression of Judaism in the temple.

Matthew removes the fig tree account and ties the temple cleansing to the triumphal entry account. This did not alter the significance of the event, but it did make the portrayal of the cleansing look more like a theophany, a manifestation of God. The One entering the temple was none other than God's Messiah. The crowd of ordinary people recognized that, but the Jerusalem leaders and the religious machinery did not. In Luke's Gospel, Jesus wept over the city because its people did not realize "their time of visitation from God." The emphasis in Luke is not so much on the hustle and bustle of the temple activity as it is on the lack of prayer that disabled their ability to see and understand what God was doing.

When Solomon finished building the temple and had dedicated it to the Lord, God accepted it by filling it with his presence (1 Kings 8:10–11). When the people return from the exile and rebuild the temple, the filling of God's presence is noticeably absent from the accounts of the temple dedication. When Christ, as the expression of God's presence, entered the temple, he came with a fury that rejected and overturned the expressions of worship he found. Second-temple Judaism had come up bankrupt; God was doing a new thing, and Jesus' revelation of God's new work spelled doom upon those who opposed it.

The Tuesday of Passion Week was a day of controversy and teaching.[6] The decision to kill Jesus had been made, and confrontations abounded. The Gospels record how various parties among the Jewish leaders teamed up to question Jesus and try to trap him with political and theological conundrums. The chief priests and the elders questioned Jesus' authority (Matt. 21:23). The Pharisees and the Herodians tried to trap him with a question designed to make him issue a political statement that would have been wrong regardless of his answer (Matt. 22:15, 17). The Sadducees confronted Jesus with a theological scenario, the answer to which would make him give a statement that ran contrary to common knowledge about God (Matt. 22:23–28). Finally, some experts in the Law brought a legal

---

[5] Cf. 1 Samuel 15:22: "And Samuel said, 'Has the Lord as great delight in burnt offerings and sacrifices, as in obedience to the voice of the Lord? Surely, to obey is better than sacrifice, and to heed than the fat of rams.'"
[6] See Matthew 21:23–24:51; Mark 11:27–13:37; Luke 20:1–21:36.

question to which an unwise answer would put all Jesus' teaching in jeopardy (Matt. 22:35–36).

The confrontation grew even sharper by Jesus' own teaching on that day. His answers exposed his questioners as charlatans (Matt. 21:27) and as less than competent experts (Matt. 22:45). Jesus responded with parables that placed tax collectors and prostitutes as more likely recipients of God's kingdom than the Pharisees and compared his opponents to evil tenants who killed their landlord's son. In a teaching given directly to the crowd and his disciples, he called the Jewish leaders hypocrites and blind guides for the people. The confrontation was razor sharp, and the stage was set for the events that were to take place during the last part of the week.

STUDY QUESTIONS

1. What were the expectations of the general population when they gave Jesus a "royal" entry into Jerusalem on the first Sunday of Passion Week? Why did they greet him this way?
2. Where in the temple area did Jesus overturn the tables of the money changers? Find a map of the temple area and locate it.
3. What story surrounds the temple cleansing in Mark's Gospel? How does this story influence the reading of the temple cleansing?
4. What did Jesus do during Tuesday of Passion Week?

ACT 2

JESUS' LAST SUPPER AND HIS CRUCIFIXION

THE LAST SUPPER AND THE LORD'S SUPPER

The Gospels record nothing about the events of Wednesday. Possibly this was simply a day of rest.[7] For the events on Thursday, the Gospels make their focus the evening supper, Jesus' last Passover celebration with his disciples. Celebrating this traditional banquet meal, Jesus reinterpreted several of its major elements by connecting them to the soon-to-follow events of his own suffering and death on the cross. The meal originally intended as a meal of thanksgiving and remembrance for what God did during the exodus from Egypt now became a meal of thanksgiving and remembrance for the new covenant salvation that became a reality through Jesus' work on the cross.[8]

THE LAST SUPPER

The six elements of the traditional Jewish Passover meal:

1. The Passover Lamb
   The lamb reminded the people of the protection given by the blood of the lamb as the angel of death passed over their doors, entering only the homes lacking the protective blood smeared on their doorposts.

---

[7] This discussion of the events of the various days of Passion Week does not aim to engage the debate about the exact chronology of the week or to list the possibilities of other scenarios including the comparison between the Synoptic Gospels and John. For a couple of biblical references suggesting the difficulty in establishing a chronology, compare Mark 14:1 and John 12:1.

[8] The Jewish meal gave thanks and remembered how God, before he led them out of captivity and into freedom, sent plagues on the Egyptian people and *passed over* the households of his own people because they had slaughtered a lamb and smeared its blood on their doorposts.

2. Unleavened Bread

   Unleavened bread reminded people of their quick departure from captivity. They did not have time to bake bread but had to be ready to move at God's command without being held up by the mundane things of life.

3. Bowl of Salt Water

   Salt water reminded people of the tears and sorrow of captivity. When struggles and hardships came their way in the land of freedom, they should not forget the daily sorrow and pain they knew in captivity.

4. Bitter Herbs

   The bitter taste reminded people of the bitterness of slavery. As time passed and people forgot the harshness of slavery under masters other than Yahweh, the taste of bitter herbs contrasted the sweetness of God's goodness. They were now free and no longer slaves.

5. Fruit Puree

   This reminded the people of the clay used to make bricks during their slavery. Slavery was real; it was not a mere concept but a harsh reality of forced labor without rewards they should not forget.

6. Four Cups of Red Wine Mixed with Water

   The wine reminded the people of God's promises. The Exodus event was the proof that God spoke the truth. His covenant promises could be trusted. Exodus 6:6–7 spells it out: "Therefore, say to the Israelites: 'I am the LORD, and I will bring you out from under the yoke of the Egyptians. I will free you from being slaves to them, and I will redeem you with an outstretched arm and with mighty acts of judgment. I will take you as my own people, and I will be your God. Then you will know that I am the LORD your God, who brought you out from under the yoke of the Egyptians.'"

Jesus' reinterpretation of this meal was profound. The new interpretation did not contrast the old as much as it fulfilled it. What began as Jesus' last supper with his disciples (celebrating how God's great deeds in the past pointed to what was to come) turned at the end of the meal into the Lord's Supper. It became an event that celebrated that the promise of a new future God gave in the historical event of the Exodus now had been fulfilled. The Exodus was a historical type, or pointer, to what God was doing on the spiritual level for all of his creation—every tribe and every nation.

The parallels between the Passover meal and what we call the Lord's Supper are evident:

PASSOVER MEAL	LORD'S SUPPER
God remembered his covenant with Abraham.	Jesus brings the Abraham covenant to its fulfillment by establishing the promised new covenant in his blood.
Slavery in Egypt.	Slavery in sin.
Deliverance from Egypt.	Forgiveness from sin (Matt. 26:28).
Blood of the Passover lamb.	Blood of Jesus is the blood of the true "Passover lamb." The application of his blood makes the angel of death pass over people's sin.
The individual elements of the Passover meal are interpreted and explained.	The individual elements of the Lord's Supper meal are interpreted and explained.
A call for future celebration.	A call for future celebration.

THE LORD'S SUPPER

Jesus' reinterpretation of the Passover meal can be summarized into four sayings that explain the meaning of the Lord's Supper.

1. When taking the bread and breaking it, Jesus said, "This is my body" (Matt. 26:28). This obviously does not mean he equated his body with the bread. The disciples no doubt understood him to say that the bread he held in his hand represented his body. And, when he broke it, it illustrated what would happen to his body. It would be broken as well. Interpreting the action of breaking the bread, Jesus therefore pointed to himself and his suffering on the cross and the events preceding it. In other words, where the unleavened bread of the Passover reminded the people of their quick departure from Egypt, it was the broken bread that had significance for Jesus' interpretation. In contrast to the Passover meal, the celebration of the Lord's Supper does not emphasize the unleavened character of the bread but the brokenness.

2. Jesus' second interpretive word was, "This is my blood of the covenant, which is poured out for many for the forgiveness of sins" (Matt. 26:28). Again, Jesus' use of the phrase "this is" should not be misunderstood to mean that he equated his blood with the wine—or vice versa. Rather, holding the wine that reminded Passover celebrants of the saving power of the blood of the lamb, Jesus reinterpreted its significance and said that it now

should represent *his* blood which would be poured out. In the celebration of the Lord's Supper, the "blood of the covenant" has reference to the saving power of Jesus' blood, and the pouring and drinking of the wine illustrates that Jesus' sacrificial death brings about the new covenant promised by God.

3. Jesus' third saying, "I will not again drink of this fruit of the vine until that day when I drink it anew with you in my Father's kingdom" (Matt. 26:29; Mark 14:25; Luke 22:16), reinterpreted the significance of the elements of the meal as much as it announced that the whole meal had eschatological significance—that is, it celebrates God's promise for the future. In line with his earlier teaching (e.g., John 14), Jesus said that the meal, as the Lord's Supper, was a reminder of the coming messianic banquet. Rather than simply pointing to a future of freedom from political oppression, as the Passover meal did, the Lord's Supper was to give a foretaste of the messianic meal that all of God's people will participate in at Jesus' return.

4. Reinterpreting the divine command to celebrate the Passover meal yearly (Exod. 12:2–3; Num. 9:1–2; Deut. 16:1) and use it to remind the following generations about what God had done (Deut. 6:20–23), Jesus said, "Do this in remembrance of me" (Luke 22:19). Similar to the old covenant, the celebration of the New covenant was designed to remind Jesus' disciples, and all the following generations of believers, of what Jesus did for their salvation. Paul understood the significance of this when in a letter to the church in Corinth he wrote: "I received from the Lord what I also passed on to you, the Lord Jesus, on the night he was betrayed took bread" (1 Cor. 11:23–26). The Lord's Supper, a Passover meal reinterpreted into a fulfillment celebration, is to be observed by followers of Jesus until his return (1 Cor. 11:26). The new symbolism of this meal neither contradicted the old, nor did it correct it. It simply proclaimed its fulfillment! It was the same story; God had just added the chapter that showed the full meaning of all earlier chapters.

During the meal Jesus exposed Judas as the one who would betray him to the Jewish authorities who had been waiting for a chance to capture him when he was not surrounded by crowds of people. Judas left Jesus and the other disciples and went to the chief priests to inform them of Jesus' plans for the remainder of the night. Jesus and the rest of the disciples stayed and finished the meal. When the meal was over, they concluded it the traditional way by singing a hymn. After the hymn they returned to the Mount of Olives and entered the garden of Gethsemane.

GETHSEMANE, BETRAYAL, ARREST, AND TRIALS

Coming to Gethsemane, Jesus felt overwhelmed at the prospects of what he knew would take place within the next twenty-four hours. He asked his three closest disciples—Peter, John, and James—to accompany him farther into the garden. Here Jesus revealed his distress and concern to them and asked them to stay behind as he went a bit farther to pray alone.

Being alone, Jesus, overcome with agony, prayed fervently for God to find some method to accomplish his purpose other than the one Jesus faced already. Jesus' anguish did not stem from fear of death and physical pain as much as from a struggle with his knowledge that God's wrath against sin would soon fall on him with full strength. Jesus' cry on the cross, "My God, my God, why have you forsaken me," (Matt. 27:46) reveals the depths of Jesus' concern. For the one who had enjoyed the full presence of God since his conception, no greater pain could be imagined than its absence. With no help from his disciples, who slept while he prayed, Jesus conquered his anguish and surrendered his situation to the Father's will.

When Judas appeared with a large group of armed people,[9] he identified Jesus with a kiss. A kiss served as a common greeting expressing warmth and welcome among friends and family, or it was an expression of honor to a highly esteemed Rabbi by a beloved disciple. Judas' kiss was, therefore, especially appalling and functioned as an expression of utmost hypocrisy that would have horrified Matthew's early readers.[10] Facing Judas and the armed soldiers, Jesus surrendered himself while questioning why they chose this place for his capture when they could have arrested him anytime they wanted in the temple. Reminding the soldiers that he was not at their mercy, since they were merely a part of God's plan designed to fulfill what prophets had said long ago (Matt. 26:56), Jesus followed them to the house of the high priest.

At the house of the high priest, Jesus faced a quickly called illegal trial. Preliminary hearings commenced before Annas, the former high priest[11] and father-in-law of the present high priest, Caiaphas (John 18:12–14, 19–23). While these hearings were going on, Peter and John made their way into the courtyard of the high priest's mansion to observe the event. While there, a girl recognized Peter as one of Jesus' disciples. Peter, however, afraid of the consequences of his relationship with Jesus, denied three times that he even knew him. The scenario fit exactly what Jesus had predicted during the Passover meal in the upper room earlier that evening.

Jesus remained inside Annas's house until about three the next morning, approximately the time the cock would crow in Jerusalem in April. It was now Friday

---

[9] John's use of the word *detachment* (18:3) need not refer to a Roman military presence. It could simply refer to a Jewish unit from the temple guard. The Gospels' emphasis on the armed crowd seems to focus on the excessive force they represented. Their only task was to capture twelve peasants.

[10] Cf. Proverbs 27:6, "Wounds from a friend can be trusted, but an enemy multiplies kisses."

[11] Annas was high priest from AD 6 to 15 when he was deposed by the Romans.

morning. Before the night had passed, Jesus would have faced Annas, Caiaphas, and the Jewish council, called the Sanhedrin. The Jewish council tried to find credible witnesses to speak against Jesus, but when they failed, they asked him directly if he was the Son of God. When Jesus answered in the affirmative, they gave him the death sentence for blasphemy. This decision was reached early in the morning (Matt. 27:1; Mark 15:1; Luke 22:66–71).

A NOTE ON THE LEGALITY OF THE SANHEDRIN'S TRIAL OF JESUS

The Jewish trial was illegal in every way:

1. According to Jewish trial procedures described in Mishnah Sanhedrin 4:1, a trial involving a capital case must begin during the daytime.[12] Jesus' trial began during the night. The illegality of this timing was further precipitated by the meeting in the high priest's mansion. Mishnah Sanhedrin 11:2 calls for trials to be held in the hewn-stone chamber which was inside the temple gate, a place distinct from the high priest palace. Luke's reference (22:66) to their change of location in the morning probably indicates that the gates were closed for any meetings to be held during the night.

2. Mishnah Sanhedrin also required that the verdict in a capital trial had to be delayed by at least one day. An acquittal could be given the same day, but a guilty verdict had to be delayed overnight.[13]

3. Trials should not be held on the eve of Sabbaths and festival days. This rule tied to the former rule about delaying a guilty verdict to the following day. If someone were found guilty the day before a Sabbath or a festival day, the final decision should be postponed to the following day.[14]

4. According to Old Testament Law (Lev. 24:15), blasphemers were guilty of a capital crime, and the penalty was death by stoning. To provide some legal protection, the rabbis had given rather strict definitions of what constituted "blasphemous." "He who blasphemes is liable only when he will have fully pronounced the divine name" (*m.Sanh* 7:5). Nothing Jesus said during the trial fulfilled this definition.

5. Many other procedural errors, like, for example, that an accused could not be convicted on the basis of his own testimony alone, could be mentioned. However, the debate about whether all rabbinic rules of law were fully uti-

---

[12] "In capital cases they try the case by day and complete it by day" (*m.Sanh* 4:1). Jacob Neusner, trans., *The Mishnah: A New Translation* (New Haven: Yale University Press, 1988), 590.

[13] "In capital cases they come to a final decision for acquittal on the same day, but on the following day for conviction" (*m.Sanh* 4:1). "If they found him innocent, they sent him away. If not, they postponed judging him till the next day" (*m.Sanh* 5:5).

[14] "The sole difference between the festival and the Sabbath is in the preparation of food alone" (*m.Besa* 5:2). Cf. Josephus who cites the decree of Caesar affirming that "they [the Jews] be not obliged to go before any judge on the Sabbath day, nor on the day of the preparation to it, after the ninth hour" (*Ant.* 16 §163). See further Philo *Migr. Abr.* 16 §91, and the Dead Sea Scrolls, CD 10.18.

lized at the time of Jesus is beyond the interest of this brief survey. Suffice it to say that the Mishnaic code referenced here reaches back before AD 70.[15]

Since Israel was under Roman rule, the Sanhedrin did not have the authority to kill Jesus without Roman consent. For that reason they took Jesus to the Roman governor, Pilate. When Pilate heard Jesus was a Galilean, he sent him to be tried by Herod Antipas, who was in Jerusalem for the Passover celebration.[16] Herod listened to the accusations of the Jewish leaders, after which he mocked, ridiculed, and questioned Jesus. Without deciding on his fate, Herod sent Jesus back to Pilate.

When Jesus stood before Pilate for a second hearing, Pilate became convinced of Jesus' innocence (Luke 23:15–16) and decided to flog him publicly before releasing him. The Jewish leaders, however, successfully aroused the crowd to call for Jesus' crucifixion. In an attempt to please the crowd and still save Jesus, Pilate suggested that they could choose between the release of Jesus and a notorious killer named Barrabbas. His plan backfired when the crowd called for the release of Barrabbas. Pilate finally gave in to the demands of the crowd and handed Jesus over to the soldiers for crucifixion. The soldiers further mistreated Jesus, beating and ridiculing him, and dressing him in a purple robe while pressing a crown of thorns on his head to symbolize a defeated king.

THE CRUCIFIXION AND DEATH OF JESUS

After the mockery by the soldiers, Jesus was taken outside the city to a hill called Golgotha for crucifixion. Due to Jesus' complete exhaustion caused by his flogging and beating, the soldiers forced a bystander named Simon, an African from Cyrene, to carry the cross. Upon arrival, they offered Jesus wine mixed with myrrh to ease the pain. Jesus, however, refused and was subsequently crucified between two criminals.

Crucifixion was one of the cruelest methods of execution ever known. Although the Persians probably invented it, the Romans adapted crucifixion as the ultimate punishment for slaves and political rebels from the provinces. The law prohibited the crucifixion of Roman citizens. The normal procedure called for public flogging after which the accused was nailed to a pole. Different crosses were devised, some shaped like an X, but the most common pattern took the shape of a T.

As the arms of the crucified were stretched out to each side and nailed to the crossbeam, the weight of the body pulling down made breathing difficult. With the feet nailed to the vertical beam, breathing became possible only as the crucified pushed his body upward placing all the weight on the nail that pierced the feet or

---

[15] For a fuller discussion and a good overview of Jesus' trial, see Joel B. Green, Scot McKnight, and I. Howard Marshall, eds. *Dictionary of Jesus and the Gospels* (Downers Grove, Ill.: InterVarsity Press, 1992), s.v. "Trial of Jesus" by Bruce Corley.

[16] Herod Antipas was son of Herod the Great. He was tetrarch in Galilee. A tetrarch was a ruler of a fourth of a region.

the heels. The nails fastening the hands were driven through the wrist since the tissue in the middle of the hands could not handle the weight of the body.

Since no vital body parts were damaged, death was extremely slow. A crucified person could survive several days before exhaustion took away strength to raise the body for breathing and death occurred due to suffocation. If needed, soldiers could speed up the death process by breaking the legs of the victim which made it almost impossible to breathe. In the case of Jesus, whose legs they did not crush, the speediness of his death was due to the massive blood loss and circulatory failure caused by his severe flogging, what medical literature calls hypovolemic shock.[17]

According to the Gospels, Jesus was crucified at nine in the morning on Friday and died later that afternoon. He hung on the cross about six hours before he died (Mark 15:34). During this time several miraculous events occurred that affirmed his claim to be the Son of God. Beyond these miraculous events the Gospels detail seven words or statements uttered by Jesus while he was hanging on the cross.

During the first three hours on the cross, from nine in the morning until noon, the gospel story focuses on the crucifixion itself and the people involved. The last three hours highlight the divine involvement in this event and the significance of Jesus' death for God's plan for his creation. According to the accounts in the Gospels, the sun darkened around noon and remained dark until Jesus' death. As we will discuss below, the Gospel record of the cross event reveals two areas of theological significance—what it did for humankind and what it did to God.

According to the Gospel record, Jesus spoke seven sentences while on the cross. These seven sentences are not found in any one Gospel and can therefore not be systematized into a specific and deliberate message intended either by Jesus or those recording the words. Three are recorded only in Luke, another three only by John, and one by both Matthew and Mark. Whether these words are quotes or summaries of longer statements cannot be known. Nor is it possible to discern whether the seven sentences give an exhaustive list of what Jesus spoke on the cross or if they simply function as examples of the kind of things he said. Together, though, these sentences express the message he had preached. He spoke forgiveness to those crucifying him (Luke 23:34) and salvation to one of those crucified with him (Luke 23:43). John records Jesus' concern for his mother now that he would not be with her anymore (19:26) and his own physical need to drink when dehydration set in (19:28). The depth of Jesus' spiritual agony when the darkness of sin's power overwhelmed him is expressed by the words "my God, my God, why have you forsaken me" (Matt. 27:46; Mark 15:34). Since Scripture consistently portrays Jesus as being one with God, this crushing experience of God's absence can only be understood as the moment where Jesus experienced the full force of the power of darkness and evil—the moment when God dealt with the price for the sins of

---

[17] For more on Jesus' death from a medical perspective, see William D. Edwards, Wesley Gabel, and Floyd E. Hosmer, "On the Physical Death of Jesus Christ," *JAMA* 255, no. 11 (21 March 1986).

humanity.[18] The atonement affected at this moment took care both of God's anger against sin and the redemption of human guilt. Immediately after this, Jesus stated that his mission had been accomplished.[19]

Beyond the words spoken on the cross, extraordinary things happened that likewise spoke to the ultimate significance of the cross event. The sun darkened at noon and remained dark until three in the afternoon, the time of Jesus' death according to the Gospels' record. At the point of his death, the curtain in the temple that separated the room called the holy of holies, where the ark of the covenant was kept and where God's special presence supposedly resided, was torn. The tearing of one's clothes was a common expression of severe desolation and sorrow. The tearing of the curtain to the entrance to the holy of holies symbolized God's pain. Gentiles who stood as spectators to Jesus' death now became convinced that he was the Son of God (Mark 15:39); and even some members from the Sanhedrin, the council responsible for his death sentence, now stepped forward to affirm their conviction of what God was doing through Christ. One of them, Joseph of Arimathea, asked for Jesus' body and buried him in a tomb he owned.

THE THEOLOGICAL SIGNIFICANCE OF THE CROSS

Each Gospel tells the story of Jesus' death in a slightly different way. No real disagreement exists between them, but each has its own theological distinctives—emphases that point out what they saw as the most significant elements of God's work:

1. Mark
   a. Jesus' death was a payment for sin; he gave his life as a ransom for many (10:45; 14:22–25).
   b. The disciples did not really get it. Mark highlights their failure and misunderstanding. They deny, betray, and flee.
   c. The cross makes a clear proclamation that Jesus is the Son of God (15:39).

2. Matthew
   a. Jewish leaders have a high profile. Matthew highlights their responsibility in Jesus' death (26:3, 57; 27:25).
   b. Scripture is fulfilled. What happened on the cross is in accordance with Old Testament Scripture (26:14–25, 50; 27:3–10).
   c. Crucifixion itself and the people's reaction are narrated in some detail. The event and how it happened is significant in Matthew (27:39–44, 51–53).

3. Luke
   a. Jesus' suffering and time of passion is a time of intense demonic activity. Jesus struggles not against human opposition but against evil forces (Luke 22:3, 31, 53b).

---

[18] As some claim, it is possible that Jesus quoted all of Psalm 22 and that the Gospels express that by this simple reference to his words. It is just as likely, however, that Jesus simply quoted this one line from Psalm 22 reminding everyone of the whole psalm. (See discussion on Jesus' baptism above.)

[19] In John's Gospel Jesus says, "It is finished" (19:30); in Luke's, "Into your hands I commend my spirit" (23:46).

   b. Jesus' innocence is highlighted (23:2, 4, 6–16, 34, 43, 47).

   c. Jesus is the prophet/martyr who trusts God and fearlessly proclaims God's justice in face of rejection and execution.

4. John
   a. Jesus remains totally in charge. He is not merely a victim of evil men's schemes.
   b. Jesus' death becomes an act of self-revelation (13–17).
   c. Jesus triumphs over cosmic powers of darkness.

From an even broader perspective, Jesus' death is theologically significant exactly because it is both the centerpiece and the framework of the universal story told by the Bible. In broad outlines the biblical story goes like this:

1. Peace and tranquility reigns (Gen. 1–2).
2. Trouble in paradise destroys the tranquility and peace (Gen. 3–11).
3. God is on a save-and-rescue mission to bring things back to peace and tranquility (Gen. 12–John; Matthew–Revelation).
4. Tranquility and peace will be restored (eternity, end of Revelation).

The cross fits into this outline as the centerpiece that gives meaning to the rest of the story. The heart of the biblical story is the cross of Christ. The cross retells the biblical story from the center. Instead of a simple linear, historical account of how God has interacted with his people and all of his creation, the cross explains this story from its midpoint yielding significance to all previous *and* to all subsequent human experience of God and reality. In summary fashion:

1. The cross explains the human need. People are characterized by a level of sin and self-centeredness which turns all personal endeavors toward restitution into mere self-promotion. Their unavoidable predicament, and the inescapable penalty for this reality, is death.
2. The cross outlines God's problem. The relationship he desires with his creation, due to his abundant love, is repudiated by his holiness which cannot disregard sin.
3. The cross reveals God's solution. God's love provides what his holiness requires. What humans have destroyed, God himself restores. God takes the penalty for human sin and self-promotion upon himself through the death of his only son. By removing the hindrance for fellowship between God and humans, people receive the opportunity to accept his forgiveness.
4. The cross compels human response. As God proves his limitless love, people must respond to receive it and experience God's forgiveness.

STUDY QUESTIONS

1. How does Jesus reinterpret the Jewish Passover in light of the new covenant?

2. Modern courts have specific procedures that must be followed so that a case is not thrown out. What rules were violated when Jesus was tried? Why should the Jewish court have found him innocent?
3. Who invented crucifixion as a means for capital punishment, and who became famous for its use? What causes death when people are crucified?
4. What happened when Jesus died? What were the physical or natural manifestations?

THE GRAVE COULD NOT HOLD HIM

ACT 1

Jesus' Burial and Resurrection

J esus died on Friday afternoon at three,[1] the day we call Good Friday. Since his death occurred on a Friday, the day of preparation for the Sabbath, the Jews wanted his body taken down and buried before sunset. No bodies should hang on a cross during the Sabbath. Soldiers broke the legs of those hanging next to Jesus to speed up the process of dying;[2] but, since Jesus apparently had already died, they did not break his legs. Instead they pierced his side with a spear to ensure he truly was dead before they took him down (John 19:31–37).

Late Friday afternoon, Joseph of Arimathea, a prominent member of the Jewish Council, asked Pilate for the body of Jesus. After checking with the centurion to see that Jesus was dead, Pilate allowed Joseph to have the body. According to the Gospels, Joseph took down the body, wrapped it in linen cloth, placed it in a tomb cut out of the rock, and rolled a large stone in front of the opening of the tomb. John 19:39 further adds that a fellow council member named Nicodemus helped Joseph and brought the spices needed to embalm the body.[3]

After the Sabbath, early Sunday morning, three women went to the grave to anoint or further embalm Jesus' body. As they approached the tomb, they discussed how to get the stone that blocked the entrance rolled away. Great was their surprise when they saw that the stone was already pushed aside. Entering the tomb, they did not see the body of Jesus but found instead another man dressed in a white

---

[1] The day began at six in the morning. When Jesus died at the ninth hour, it was three in the afternoon (Matt. 27:46, 50; Mark 15:34, 37; Luke 23:44–46).

[2] See discussion on the crucifixion in episode 11, Act 2.

[3] For more on Nicodemus, see John 3:1–20.

robe.[4] This white-robed man informed them that Jesus had risen from the dead as he had foretold he would. The man requested that the women go back to Peter and the other apostles with instructions to meet Jesus in Galilee.

If Jesus was placed in the grave shortly before six on Friday evening, and the women came early Sunday morning, there was only thirty hours between the time of burial (Mark 15:47; Matt. 27:61) and the discovery of the empty tomb. The common notion that Jesus was in the grave for three days is not correct. Rather, as the Bible also states, Jesus would rise again on the *third* day. The confusion between three days and the third day probably rests in a different way of counting. To our modern minds, "three days" is something different from "on the third day," but this was a distinction not made in first-century Jewish thinking.[5] As the New Testament counted days, Sunday was Jesus' third day in the grave, Friday was the first. Jesus rose from the dead on Sunday—the third day!

DISCUSSION ABOUT THE HISTORICITY
OF THE RESURRECTION

The heart of the resurrection message is that Jesus is God! Everything Jesus said and did during his ministry on earth is validated through the resurrection. The resurrection authenticates Jesus' miracles as acts of God. The resurrection validates his message as a message from God. The resurrection proclaims that Jesus did not die as an imposter and a rebel but as the Son of God. Since dead men do not rise, the resurrection is *the* evidence of God's work through Jesus. The historicity of the resurrection, therefore, becomes the test point for the truth value of all Christian claims. Christianity stands or falls with the historicity of the resurrection. If the resurrection did not happen as a true historical event, Christian "faith is futile" (1 Cor. 15:17), and Christian people are "to be pitied above all" (1 Cor. 15:19).

OBJECTIONS TO THE HISTORICITY OF THE RESURRECTION

The objections to the historicity of Jesus' resurrection have been manifold. Militating against one of the primary beliefs of the enlightenment, that all miracles must have a natural explanation, the resurrection by definition could not happen. There was no room for it in the modern worldview. Ernest Troelsch's claim

---

[4] Mark 16:5 calls him a man. Matthew recounts that an earthquake attended the appearance of an angel in white clothing who descended to remove the stone as the women arrived (28:2–3). Also in Matthew, Jesus himself appeared to the women before they returned to the disciples (28:9–10). In Luke's Gospel the stone was rolled away when the women arrived, and as they wondered how that happened, two angels appeared before them to remind them of Jesus' pronouncement of his resurrection before his death. John's Gospel only mentions Mary Magdalene and reports that she ran back to Peter as soon as she noticed that the stone was rolled away. Although different in recorded details, all the Gospels tell the story of the women being the first to visit the grave on Sunday morning. When they arrived, they found the stone rolled away, and the tomb was empty.

[5] Cf. Matthew 27:62–64a: "The next day, that is, after the day of Preparation, the chief priests and the Pharisees gathered before Pilate and said, 'Sir, we remember what that impostor said while he was still alive, "After *three* days I will rise again." Therefore command the tomb to be made secure until the *third* day'" (NRSV, author's emphasis).

that past experiences do not differ essentially from the present[6] has to a greater or smaller degree been followed by most scholars of the modern era. According to Troelsch, the means "by which criticism becomes possible at all is the use of analogy. The analogy to what happens before our eyes and to what happens in us is the key to our criticism."[7] In other words, if an event cannot be shown to be analogous to normal experience, then by definition it cannot be called a historical event. Since the resurrection defies comparison to so-called normal and repeatable human experience, modernity rejected it as a historical event.

To overcome this difficulty, some biblical scholars of the modern era who could not reject the resurrection, because of Paul's claims in 1 Corinthians 15 et al., reinterpreted the resurrection stories as mythical—that is, they were stories that spoke about the deep reality that Jesus continued to live in the hearts of his followers. Truth, they said, is not found in the historicity of these accounts but in the deeper meaning these resurrection stories reveal. What matters is not that Jesus literally came back from being bodily dead to being bodily alive but that the Jesus who was killed became alive in a life-changing way in the hearts of those who believed in him. Because of this reality, these existentialist theologians claimed, a present-day believer has the exact same experience of the resurrected Jesus as the early believers who knew the historical Jesus. They too merely experienced the resurrection of Christ in their hearts.

Although the preaching in many evangelical pulpits from Sunday to Sunday concludes with an altar call that invites people to have a life-changing heart experience of Jesus, the interpretations outlined above clearly do not do justice to the biblical accounts of the resurrection. The unique and sovereign feature of the Christian religion is that even its metaphysical claims are anchored in history. That's what Paul meant when he said that unless the resurrection was a true event happening in history, the Christian faith is to no avail and Christians are to be pitied more than anyone else (1 Cor. 15:17–19).

Critics who have proposed objections to Jesus' resurrection, or critics who have worked to explain how and why Jesus' resurrection could not have happened as a historical event, can be found in every historical period of the Common Era. The following list of objections is a mere representation of an almost uncountable number of finer points.[8] They represent in summary fashion the big arguments:

1. Jesus fell into in a coma; he merely appeared to be dead.
   As with all objections, arguments for this claim vary; but the bottom line of all arguments in this direction is that Jesus was not truly dead. His resurrection was really resuscitation.

---

[6] Ernst Troeltsch, "Über historische und dogmatische Methode in der Theologie," in Gesammelte Schriften, zweiter band, *Zur religiösen Lage, Religionsphilosophie und Ethik,* ed. Ernst Troestsch (Berlin: Scientia Verlag Aalen, 1962), 729–53.

[7] Ibid., 722. Author's translation.

[8] For a full discussion of the historical issues involved in a discussion on the resurrection, see N. T. Wright, *The Resurrection of the Son of God* (Minneapolis: Fortress, 2003).

2. Wrong tomb or no tomb?

    Jesus may not have been buried at all; or, if he was, his disciples did not
    know the location of the tomb and went to the wrong one. As was often the
    case with peasant criminals, it is likely that Jesus never had a tomb. The
    disciples simply found an empty tomb and claimed it was Jesus'. Another
    theory suggests that someone did take Jesus' body and put it in a tomb the
    disciples did not know about. When they looked for him, they discovered
    an empty tomb, thought it was Jesus', and invented the empty tomb story.

3. Theft.

    Jesus' tomb was indeed empty but not because he actually rose from the
    dead. Rather, someone stole his body.

4. Hallucinations.

    Jesus' disciples experienced hallucinations due to mass hysteria or some
    similar kind of psychological phenomenon. They never actually saw an
    empty tomb.

5. Mythological parallels.

    Fashioned after rather common contemporary myths about dying and ris-
    ing gods, Jesus' disciples invented a resurrection story of "their god."

6. Unreliable records.

    According to the New Testament, Jesus did rise from the dead. But the
    New Testament records of Jesus' words and deeds are historically unreli-
    able and cannot be trusted for historical research.

These six objections touch on a sufficient number of the issues raised by those
rejecting Jesus' resurrection as a historical event to merit a response. The responses
that follow are not intended to exhaust all aspects of each question but aim to show
that these objections are less than persuasive. The responses are not biblical arguments in the sense that they simply rely on the trustworthiness of the Scriptures
these objections reject. Rather, these responses attempt a logical and historical
reasoning that renders the above objections unlikely.

EVIDENCE FOR THE HISTORICITY OF THE RESURRECTION

1. Jesus really died.

Anyone reading the accounts of the trials and crucifixion of Jesus will be im-
pressed by the brutality of Jesus' treatment. Edwards, Gabel, and Hosmer give a
good medical evaluation of Jesus' treatment and conclude that no human being
could survive what he went through.[9]

The brutal beatings included a series of lashes by a whip made from leather
strips into which were tied small, sharp metal pieces designed to rip the human
flesh. The six hours of hanging on the cross fastened by nails through the wrists

---

[9] Edwards, Gabel, Hosmer, "On the Physical Death of Jesus," William D. Edwards, Wesley Gabel, and Floyd E.
Hosmer, "On the Physical Death of Jesus Christ," *JAMA* 255, no. 11 (21 March 1986).

and the heels brought further exhaustion and dehydration resulting in hypovolemic shock. To ensure Jesus' death, soldiers thrust a spear through his side. Although this may not have pierced his heart, it would have punctured enough organs to cause mortal damage to an already severely injured body.

Add to this the partial embalming in connection with Jesus' burial and the wrapping of his body, including his head, in grave clothes. This last treatment no doubt obstructed his ability to breathe. The claim that Jesus was not dead, but merely in a state of shock or in a coma, seems extremely unlikely. A rejection of the resurrection on the grounds of this argument, therefore, is at best far-fetched.

2. Jesus was buried in a tomb.

The claim that Jesus never was buried in a tomb or that the disciples went to the wrong tomb likewise seems unreasonable. It is almost impossible to imagine that the disciples would invent a story about a tomb belonging to a prominent member of the Sanhedrin that sentenced Jesus to death unless it was true. To further include Nicodemus, who also was a Sanhedrin member, in the story makes it even more unlikely that the story was made up. If the disciples desired to concoct a story about an empty tomb, they would not have used the names of prominent members of the Jewish council who could easily disprove its facticity. And, indeed, had it not been so, Joseph and Nicodemus most likely would have exposed the disciples' story as false.

Furthermore, the timing of Jesus' burial late on the day of preparation made the story suspect in itself. It simply does not sound like an invented story. Had it been invented, or had the story simply been developed later as the stories about Jesus were told and retold, it is almost impossible to imagine that no other burial tradition would have been developed alongside it. Since this did not happen and this is the only burial tradition we have of Jesus, it seems most reasonable to conclude that what we have is a description of what actually happened.

Add to this that the story places women as the first witnesses to the empty tomb. This may not seem important in our time and society, but in first-century Judaism women could not serve as witnesses because their testimony was considered inherently suspect. If, therefore, the disciples had fabricated the story of the empty tomb, it is highly improbable that they would place women as primary witnesses. When the Gospels place women as witnesses at the crucifixion, at the burial site, and at the empty tomb, the only logical conclusion is that the Gospel writers merely reported what happened (Mark 15:40–41, 47; 16:1–6). Were these stories fabricated, the disciples would have placed prominent trustworthy men in these positions.

3. Jesus' tomb was empty.

Was the tomb empty because someone stole the body? If so, did the disciples themselves steal it, or was it the Jewish leaders? Both these suggestions are highly unlikely! It could not happen because guards were protecting the tomb. The soldiers possibly could have been bought off or been removed in some other way. Rather, suggestions of theft prove unlikely due to the historical situation and the evidence that follows the resurrection account.

First, it is unlikely that the disciples stole the body since we have no indication that they really expected the resurrection. In fact, when they first heard about it, they doubted it. Even after Jesus reportedly had appeared to Peter and several other apostles, some continued to doubt the resurrection. After Jesus' death the disciples were distraught, and there is no indication they were looking forward to Jesus' resurrecting from the dead.

Moreover, it is an indisputable fact that after Jesus' death his followers were under extreme pressure, being both tortured and killed for their faith. That in itself, of course, is not exceptional. Martyrdom, risking one's life for the faith, has a pedigree that reaches far back in history. However, although it is understandable that some are ready to die for what they *believe to be true* (that's the essence of martyrdom), it is completely irrational, even unthinkable, that someone would be willing to die for what they *know to be false*. If the disciples had stolen the body themselves, and therefore knew the resurrection stories were fabricated, it is unimaginable that they would die for such a story. This fact alone makes it incomprehensible that the disciples stole Jesus' body from the grave.

Could it then have been the Jewish leaders who had the body removed to make sure the disciples did not steal it? Not likely! First, the earliest Jewish explanation *presupposes* the empty tomb. This is never really questioned. The Jewish leaders were working overtime to try to disprove that the disappearance of Jesus' body was due to his resurrection from the dead. Given this scenario, it would have been easy to kill all rumors about Jesus' resurrection by simply producing the body. As Christian preachers proclaimed the resurrection of Christ, the only thing the Jewish leaders needed to do was to present the body of the dead Jesus. If they had stolen it, they could have settled the case once and for all. Since that never happened, the claim that they stole the body loses credibility.

4. The disciples did not hallucinate.

Hallucination occurs when expectations become so strong that individuals cease to distinguish between their hopes and reality. As already mentioned, nothing indicates that the disciples had any anticipation of Jesus' resurrection. Theologically, their expectations regarding resurrection tied to the general resurrection of all people at the end of the age. They did not expect anyone to be resurrected before then.

Hallucinations could also happen as a result of mass hysteria. If all the disciples had come together and created an ecstatic atmosphere that aroused their faith's imagination, an argument for hallucination could have been attempted. However, all evidence points in the opposite direction. The recorded postresurrection appearances of Jesus happened in a variety of places, at various times, and to various groups of different sizes (cf. 1 Cor. 15:5–8). None of this provides a basis for the claim of hallucination.

5. The resurrection was not a new variation on the story of the dying and rising of gods.

Mythological parallels in ancient stories about the dying and rising of gods are so different from the resurrection story of Jesus that any claim of parallelism seems utterly stretched. Most of these mythological stories tie to fertility cults and have to do with a cyclical understanding of history and the harvest calendar. Mythological gods rise in the spring, are in their prime during the summer and early fall (the harvest season), only to die during the winter in order to rise again next spring. Furthermore, these stories are so laden with mythological detail that almost no similarity exists between them and the story of Jesus. The claim that Jesus' resurrection parallels mythological stories fails to convince. It leaves no credible argument.

6. Further evidence for the historicity of Jesus' resurrection exist.

The objections to the historicity of Jesus' resurrection are driven by philosophical presuppositions that disallow the possibility of a resurrection even before any historical investigation has begun. When Jesus' resurrection is studied without such presupposition, massive amounts of historical detail point to the resurrection as a verifiable event in history.

Beyond the above, several additional points can be made in favor of the historicity of Jesus' resurrection. Although not conclusive in themselves, they complement the arguments given above:

  a. The message of Christianity spread rapidly.
  b. The disciples were transformed from frightened, discouraged people[10] into bold witnesses.
  c. Paul's conversion from prosecutor to preacher assumes the resurrection (Acts 9).
  d. The disciples began observing the first day of the week (Sunday) as the day of worship rather than the Sabbath (Saturday).
  e. Neither the Jews nor the Romans ever produced evidence to contradict the resurrection.
  f. The church has existed and continued growth for almost two thousand years.

STUDY QUESTIONS

1. What were the names of the two men from the Jewish council who buried Jesus?
2. What was the problem in having women be the first witnesses to the resurrection? Does this, then, strengthen or weaken the story of the empty tomb? How?
3. In your mind, what is the strongest argument against the historicity of the resurrection?
4. How would you answer this objection?

---

[10] Mark 14:50, 66–72; John 20:19.

ACT 2

JESUS' POSTRESURRECTION APPEARANCES AND ASCENSION

POSTRESURRECTION EXPERIENCES WITH JESUS

According to Acts 1:3, Jesus appeared to his disciples repeatedly during a forty-day period after his resurrection. These appearances varied in both character and location, but in each case those he appeared to were left with no doubt: the Jesus they had seen die was no longer dead but alive and living among them. They could see him, talk to him, and touch him. He was not a ghost, a spirit, or a vision but one who had come back from the dead in bodily form.

Although the biblical texts do not maintain the resurrection body of Jesus had the same physical properties as the body that was crucified, similarities abound. In terms of differences, the resurrected Jesus could, for example, appear in the midst of a gathering in spite of the door being closed (John 20:19, 26) and disappear again without using the exit (Luke 24:31). Although such events may suggest the resurrection appearances were mere visions and/or extraordinary psychological experiences of the disciples, the biblical texts vehemently reject such notions. According to Luke 24:36–43, for example, Jesus rebuked his disciples when they considered him a ghost at one of these appearances. To eliminate all doubt that he was a mere spirit, the resurrected Jesus invited the disciples to touch his body and to see and feel his scars. To eliminate any question that may have remained, Jesus asked for something to eat, and he ate it in their presence (24:42f).

PLACE/ PEOPLE	MATTHEW	MARK	LUKE	JOHN	ACTS/PAUL
Women leaving the tomb area	28:9–10				
Mary Magdalene at the tomb		16:9–10		20:14–17	
Two disciples on road to Emmaus		16:12–13	24:13–31		
Peter			24:34		1 Cor. 15:5
Ten disciples in the upper room			24:36–49[1]	20:19–23	
Eleven disciples in the upper room		16:14		20:26–31	1 Cor. 15:5
Seven disciples fishing				21:1–23	
The disciples on a Galilee mountain	28:16–20	16:15–18			
More than 500[2]					1 Cor. 15:6
James and then all the apostles[3]					1 Cor. 15:7
The ascension of Jesus		16:19	24:50–51		Acts 1:7–9
Paul					Acts 9:3–6

[1] Luke used the term "twelve" in a technical sense here that does not reflect on the absence of Judas. "The Twelve" simply became a term referring to the group of disciples.
[2] This may be a reference to the appearing at the giving of the Great Commission in Matthew 28. Other suggestions have included Pentecost (Acts 2:1f) although the text does not indicate an appearance of the resurrected Lord at Pentecost.
[3] Paul seems here to refer to two different events that are not recorded in the Gospels. "Then all the apostles" could, of course, refer to one of the meetings in the upper room described in John 20.

Paul, in his discussion of the resurrection, made a distinction between the physical body and the spiritual body. The former decays; the latter does not. Still, both are bodies; and neither Paul nor the Gospel writers make any distinction in terms of personhood between the crucified Jesus and the resurrected Jesus. The same Jesus who was crucified and buried was now alive and with his disciples once again.

A total of eight postresurrection appearances are recorded in the Gospels; one is mentioned in the book of Acts, and two are referred to by Paul.

THE GREAT COMMISSION

Of all the postresurrection appearances, the appearance described in Matthew 28:16–20 is the most important for the later church.[11] During that meeting with his disciples, the resurrected Jesus outlined his purpose for their ministry and for the church soon to be established. Modern churches generally call the charge Jesus gave his disciples at this event the Great Commission.[12]

Because the most common English translations have placed an imperative form of the word *go* in front of the charge ("Go therefore"), the word *go* has often received the most attention and been taken to be the imperative and the true charge of the commission. However, in the original language, Matthew's only imperative is "make disciples." This imperative is then modified, or explained, by three participles that give content to the charge. Make disciples by going, baptizing, and teaching.

A translation that takes the syntax of the original text seriously will read something like this: "Make disciples [or, "You all must make disciples"—the imperative is plural, referring to the group] of all nations by going, by baptizing them into the name of the Father, of the Son and of the Holy Spirit, and by teaching them to obey everything that I have commanded you [all]." The emphasis, in other words, is on disciple making, on making people from all nations committed followers of Jesus. To accomplish this, Christians must go to the nations, they must baptize them into a relationship with the God who has revealed himself through Christ and who empowers those who follow him by his Spirit, and they must teach them to obey what Jesus has commanded. Only that fulfills Jesus' commission. Any effort focusing on one of the participles (going, baptizing, or teaching), rather than on the imperative verb "make disciples," misses the point of Matthew 28:16–20. Only *together* do the three participles define what Jesus meant by the command to make disciples.

The Great Commission contains *one* imperative and *one* promise. The power to fulfill the commandment rises from the promise that follows. Jesus said, "Make disciples, and you can make sure that I will be with you until the end of the age." For the disciples to carry out the command, they need the enabling power that flows from Jesus' presence. The command finds its reason and its strength within the promise. In this way Matthew 28 runs completely parallel to Acts 1:8: "You will receive power when the Holy Spirit comes on you; and you will be my witnesses in Jerusalem, in all Judea and Samaria, and to the ends of the earth."

---

[11] "Therefore go and make disciples of all nations, baptizing them in the name of the Father and of the Son and of the Holy Spirit, and teaching them to obey everything I have commanded you. And surely I am with you always, to the very end of the age" (Matt. 28:19–20).

[12] The English-speaking world uses the phrase "Great Commission." Other languages like German, for example, call it "The Mission Commandment."

JESUS' ASCENSION INTO HEAVEN

Forty days after his resurrection, and after several meetings with various groups of his disciples, Jesus was lifted up before the disciples' eyes, ascending into the sky before being covered by a cloud (Acts 1:9). As the disciples remained standing, gazing into the sky, aghast at what they had just seen, two angels appeared before them and told them that Jesus would return the same way he was taken away. In the meantime they should get on with the commission Jesus had given them.

It is important not to miss the theological point of the ascension. It is not included simply to give a conclusion to Jesus' life that parallels the story of Elijah (2 Kings 2:11). Rather, Jesus' ascension was a necessary part of God's plan. The New Testament texts consistently emphasize that Jesus would leave in order to send his Spirit. The presence of the earthly person of Jesus was to be replaced by the Spirit of Jesus. As a human being, Jesus' presence was limited by time and space; the presence of Jesus' Spirit, on the other hand, would be without such limits. Put differently, when Jesus walked on the earth, he was either in Jerusalem or in Galilee; he could not be in both places at the same time. After sending his Spirit, he would inhabit every place his followers would go. Jesus had spelled this out to his disciples earlier in his ministry when he said: "It is for your good that I am going away. Unless I go away, the Counselor[13] will not come to you; but if I go, I will send him to you" (John 16:7).

The ascension, therefore, must be understood in light of Acts 1:8 (see above). He ascended to heaven in order to send his Spirit to empower his disciples and enable their ministry. What this means is that genuine Christian ministry would have been impossible without Jesus' ascension. According to Acts, Christians have no ministry without the Spirit of Jesus. This is also why they were to wait for ten days until the Spirit came before they could begin their ministry. The ministry of the disciples (and the church) was not their own; they were to continue *Jesus'* ministry. They would be filled with *his* Spirit, which would enable them to do *his* ministry. Their character, their thinking, their attitude, their speech, their work, and their fellowship would be characterized by Jesus' Spirit, not their own. This would be true in Jerusalem, in Judea and Samaria, and anywhere they went.

WHO IS JESUS CHRIST?

As the church continued to follow the Great Commission, spreading the message of the Gospel and helping new people become dedicated followers of Jesus, the question of Jesus' identity naturally arose. This, of course, is not a new question. The question of Jesus' identity has haunted people since the manger in Bethlehem. The disciples, and all those following Jesus, saw God's work through him and

---

[13] The word translated *counselor* in most English translations refers in this context clearly to the Spirit. However, since our word *counselor* has a different sense from the Greek word it translates, it may be better to translate it by the English word *spokesperson*. Other translations suggest *helper* and *comforter*, both of which capture an aspect of the Spirit's work; but *spokesperson* may best capture the notion that the Spirit speaks on behalf of Jesus. The Greek word used here was used in other places as a legal term referring to an *advocate*.

knew him to be God's only Son. The Pharisees, and all those who opposed him, refused to recognize his message and his work as coming from God. This tension has not changed since then; there are some who know him to be God's only Son and others who think of him as anything but that. The question of who Jesus is continues to face people today.

C. S. Lewis put the issue in perspective and cut through much of the confusion that so often surfaces in such discussions. He makes the choice everyone faces crystal clear:

> I am trying here to prevent anyone from saying the really foolish thing that people often say about Him: "I'm ready to accept Jesus as a great moral teacher, but I don't accept His claim to be God." That is the one thing we must not say. A man who was merely a man and said the sort of things Jesus said would not be a great moral teacher. He would either be a lunatic—on a level with the man who says he is a poached egg—or else he would be the Devil of Hell. You must make your choice. Either this man was, and is, the Son of God: or else a madman or something worse. You can shut Him up for a fool, you can spit at Him and kill Him as a demon; or you can fall at His feet and call Him Lord and God. But let us not come with any patronizing nonsense about His being a great human teacher. He has not left that open to us. He did not intend to.[14]

Lewis's argument is sharp and clear. The claims of Christ must be either true or false. If they are false, Jesus would either have known that they were false, which makes him a liar, or he believed his own claims to be true although they were false, which makes him a lunatic.

On the other hand, if the claims of Christ are true, he must be Lord and God. His claims were simply so strong that no lesser title will do. If Jesus is Lord and God, every person must respond. Only one of two responses is possible; one can either respond with commitment and obedience, or one can respond with indifference and lack of commitment. The latter would in effect be the same as denying the truthfulness of Christ's claims.

Sketched out, C. S. Lewis's argument looks like the diagram on the following page.

---

[14] C. S. Lewis, *Mere Christianity* (1943, 1945, 1952; repr., New York: Simon and Schuster, 1996), 56.

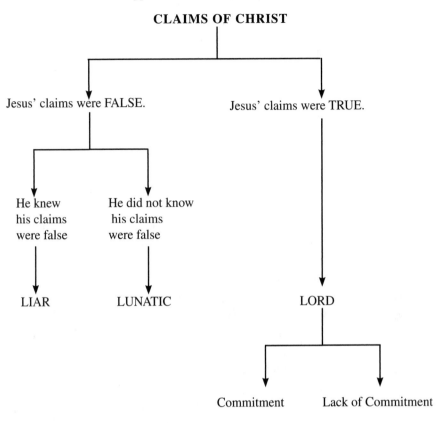

CLAIMS OF CHRIST

Jesus' claims were FALSE.

Jesus' claims were TRUE.

He knew his claims were false

He did not know his claims were false

LIAR

LUNATIC

LORD

Commitment   Lack of Commitment

STUDY QUESTIONS

1. After Jesus' resurrection he showed himself to different groups of disciples. What is the significance of the variety of these appearances?
2. How do the biblical texts emphasize that the resurrection appearances were more than visions and that the resurrected Jesus was more than a spirit?
3. What is the commandment in the Great Commission, and how is this command explained further?
4. Why was Jesus' ascension necessary? How did it affect the disciples' ministry?

THE STORY OF THE BIBLE

Creation   The story begins with God creating the world and human beings.

Crisis   Humans choose to rebel (or sin) against God. Sin brings consequences: pain, suffering, death, and separation from God. All people and all creation are affected.

Covenant	God chooses Abraham and establishes a covenant with him so that he might become the leader of a group of people who will follow God and call other people to follow God. God delights in using his people to bring the rest of the world to himself.
Calling Out	Genesis tells the story of the patriarchs: Abraham, Isaac, Jacob (Israel), and Joseph, who ends up in Egypt. In Egypt the small group of Hebrews grows into a nation and ends up in slavery. God uses Moses to deliver his people through the exodus event.
Conquest	God uses Joshua to help his people take the promised land (Canaan). After the conquest during the Period of Judges, God rules through judges in various parts of the land. This is a dark time for the Hebrews accentuated with sin, idolatry, and oppression.
Kingdom	God's people acquire a king. Samuel is the link between the judges and the kings. Saul is the first king, followed by David and his son Solomon. God establishes a covenant with David, promising the Messiah will come through his family line and reign forever.
Kingdom Divided	After Solomon civil war breaks out leading to a division of the kingdom: Israel, the Northern Kingdom; Judah, the Southern Kingdom. There are numerous kings, some good but most bad.
Captivity	Israel (Northern Kingdom) is judged for the sin of breaking the covenant when Assyria conquers it in 722 BC, and Judah receives a similar judgment later when Babylon conquers it in 586 BC and takes Judah's people into exile.
Coming Home	The people return from Babylonian exile under Zerubbabel, Ezra, and Nehemiah. They rebuild the temple and focus on the law of God.
Christ	**About four hundred years later God sends his Son, Jesus the Christ, to save his people from their sins, fulfilling the promise given to Abraham. Jesus is crucified, dies, is raised from the dead, and ascends into heaven to return again later.**
Church	Those who accept Jesus become part of the church, the people of God made up of both Jews and Gentiles. God

| | continues to use his people to extend his offer of salvation to a sinful world. |
| Consummation | God closes history with a final victory over evil. Those who have rejected God will suffer his judgment while those who have received him will live with him in a new heaven and a new earth. |

THIS GOSPEL SHALL BE FOR ALL PEOPLE

ACT 1

A Sound as of a Rushing Wind

Although the Acts of the Apostles, popularly called the book of Acts, or simply Acts, seems to begin a new section of the New Testament, its function is to provide a continuation of the gospel story. At first glance two different stories seem to be told; the Gospels tell the story about Jesus, and the book of Acts tells the story about the early church. However, properly understood, these stories cannot be separated. The whole point of the book of Acts is to show that the church continues the story of Jesus.

Overlapping the end of the Gospel story, Luke's second volume sets the stage for phase two of the Jesus story. Jesus, who came to earth as God's incarnate Son through the virgin Mary, who spent his life on earth teaching (through words and miracles) that God's kingdom had come near, and who broke the stronghold of sin and rebellion against God through his death and resurrection, was now ready to pour out his Spirit in order to guide and empower his followers to continue the ministry he had begun. As Luke opens the book of Acts, he goes out of his way to show that the ministry of the early church related directly to the ministry of Jesus.

The disciples were not religiously motivated political radicals who used their newfound convictions to build a front against Rome. Nor were they yet another group of hopeful and pious Jews eagerly awaiting a cataclysmic end to the earth. They were not even extraordinarily well-trained disciples of a controversial Jewish rabbi who simply wanted to further his teachings. The work of the apostles went far beyond a mere conviction of mind and the retelling of former experiences with their rabbi. Rather, according to Luke's description, these disciples did not operate in their own strength, and they were not guided by their own desires and understanding. This was why they could not begin their ministry immediately after Jesus' ascension but had to wait for a filling of God's Spirit that would enable them to speak God's words and do God's deeds. Luke's point was to show that there was no essential difference between the words and work of the earthly Jesus and the words and work of the resurrected Christ now present through his Spirit in his disciples.

ACTS AND PENTECOST

From the beginning God had guided his people by his Spirit and through his prophets. Under the old covenant God had declared his Law on tablets of stones mediated through Moses. When Israel discarded God's Law and directives, prophets filled with God's Spirit were able to hear his word and would try to call the people back to God's Law.[1] Under the new covenant, promised by these prophets (Jer. 31:33f; Ezek. 36:26f; Joel 2:28f), God would write his Law on human hearts, guiding and convicting them directly with his Spirit. In effect, he would turn everyone into prophets. As Luke shows in Acts 2, it was the fulfillment of this new covenant promise that happened to the followers of Jesus on the day of Pentecost.

Ten days after the ascension, the Holy Spirit came and empowered *each* of the disciples for ministry.[2] Before that day they were frightened disciples hiding from public view. All their training, memories, and experience proved insufficient in light of the task before them. When the Spirit of Jesus came upon each of them, however, they were empowered to continue Jesus' ministry with his words, his character, and his power. Like Jesus they would preach the presence of God's kingdom, demonstrate its presence through miracles, and bring people of all races and social levels into a new relationship with God.

Through the outpouring of the Spirit at Pentecost, Jesus instituted the church that he constituted earlier. Therefore, in a real sense, the day of Pentecost became the church's birthday. The necessity of the Spirit's enabling power for Christian ministry came to full force in Paul's letter to the Romans. Here Paul boldly declared that it was the presence of Jesus' Spirit in a person's life that proved whether this person was a Christian or not. Paul said, "Anyone who does not have the Spirit of Christ does not belong to him" (Rom. 8:9 NRSV). According to Paul, Christian life and ministry are not possible without Christ's Spirit.

The Jews celebrated Pentecost as a yearly festival connected with both the harvest and the covenant. As a harvest festival, it was a thanksgiving celebration for God's providence. As a celebration of the covenant, it functioned as a renewal ceremony for the giving of the Law at Sinai. Pentecost's origin in the Exodus account (23:16)[3] gave the outpouring of God's Spirit in Acts 2 an immediate context

---

[1] Most of the prophets used Deuteronomy, recalling the blessings and curses outlined there. Some, like the priest Ezekiel, primarily used Leviticus.

[2] The text is unusually strong in its emphasis that the Spirit came upon *each of them,* not just on the group. This clearly was a point Luke did not want his readers to miss!

[3] "You shall observe the festival of harvest, of the first fruits of your labor, of what you sow in the field. You shall observe the festival of ingathering at the end of the year, when you gather in from the field the fruit of your labor" (NRSV). (Cf. Exod. 34:22; Lev. 23:15–21; Num. 28:26.) Pentecost was one of three major feasts in the Jewish calendar.

of presence, provision, and historical purpose (Deut. 16:9–12).[4] God's people had come to Jerusalem from far away to celebrate their deliverance from captivity and God's dwelling among them (Deut. 16:11). As God's people gathered to celebrate and commemorate the giving of the Old covenant, God fulfilled the promise of a covenant he had given through his prophets. The fresh outpouring of God's Spirit upon the disciples represented more than an extraordinary phenomenon happening to a few people in a corner of Jerusalem. It was evidence that God was establishing his new covenant by making his presence directly available to all who would accept what he had done through his son Jesus Christ.

When the day of Pentecost arrived, a group of disciples numbering about 120 assembled in a house. Suddenly they heard a sound as of a mighty wind, a sound that reminded those who heard it of Old Testament theophanies (1 Kings 19:11–12; 2 Kings 2:11) and of the law-giving at Sinai (19:16–19). The sound proved to be nothing less than the promised outpouring of God's Spirit "upon all flesh."

The evidence of the Spirit's outpouring was immediate. From being frightened people hiding in a house behind closed doors, the believers now spoke with conviction to huge crowds in the streets of Jerusalem. Their transformation, and their empowered insight into God's purpose, came with such power that more than three thousand people were converted and baptized after the apostle Peter's sermon. In this sermon Peter explained how everything that happened to Jesus happened according to God's plan and for God's purpose. He continued to explain how the transformation of the Christian believers evidenced that God now had poured out his Spirit upon all flesh as he had promised he would do in the last days (Joel 2:28f). What God had promised would happen in the last days was now happening before their eyes.

ACTS AND THE SPREAD OF THE GOSPEL

To understand how the book of Acts explains the deeds of the resurrected Jesus (the work of his Spirit in the Christians), it proves helpful to consider possible outlines of the book. One option is to look at Acts from the perspective of the church's geographical expansion. Luke gives his outline away in Acts 1:8, "You will be my witnesses in Jerusalem, and in all Judea and Samaria, and to the ends of the earth." The first seven chapters of Acts describe the work of the Spirit in Jerusalem and Judea. Chapters 8 through 12 tell the story of how this work moved beyond the borders of Judea. Finally, the last sixteen chapters bring God's kingdom to the ends of the earth.

Another significant way of reading Acts is to focus on major personalities. The first twelve chapters of Acts document the work of Peter and the beginnings of the

---

4 "You shall count seven weeks; begin to count the seven weeks from the time the sickle is first put to the standing grain. Then you shall keep the festival of weeks to the LORD your God, contributing a freewill offering in proportion to the blessing that you have received from the LORD your God. Rejoice before the LORD your God—you and your sons and your daughters, your male and female slaves, the Levites resident in your towns, as well as the strangers, the orphans, and the widows who are among you—at the place that the LORD your God will choose as a dwelling for his name. Remember that you were a slave in Egypt, and diligently observe these statutes."

church in Israel; the last sixteen chapters chronicle Paul's work and the expansion of the church into the Gentile nations. From this perspective it becomes important to notice the incredible finesse of Luke's portrayal. In many ways Peter and Paul mirror Jesus' work as described in Luke's Gospel. Luke put his narrative together in such a way that his Gospel account of Jesus' ministry parallels his account of the ministry of the Spirit-empowered church in Acts. The place and the details obviously change, but the story remains the same. What Jesus does in the Gospel of Luke, Peter and Paul repeat in Acts. Furthermore, what Peter does in the first half of Acts, Paul repeats in the second half of Acts.

MIRACLES BY PETER IN ACTS	MIRACLES BY PAUL IN ACTS
Many signs and wonders (2:43)	Many signs and wonders (14:3)
Healing of a lame man (3:1ff)	Healing of a lame man (14:7ff)
Rebuke of Ananias and Saphira (5:1ff)	Rebuke of Elymas suddenly blinded (13:8ff)
Shaking of a building by prayer (4:31)	Shaking of a building by praise (16:25ff)
Healing by the shadow of Peter (5:15)	Healing by the handkerchiefs of Paul (19:12)
Sudden healing of a paralytic at Lydda (9:33ff)	Sudden healing of dysentery (28:7ff)
Resuscitation of Tabitha (9:36ff)	Resuscitation of Eutychus (20:9ff)
Removal of chains in prison (12:5ff)	Removal of chains in prison (16:25ff)

MIRACLES OF JESUS IN LUKE	MIRACLES OF PAUL IN ACTS
Casting out demons (4:33–37, 41; 8:26–39; 11:20). Cf. Acts 10:38.	Casting out demons (16:16–18)
Healing of a lame man (5:17–26)	Healing of a lame man (14:8–14)
Healing of many sick (4:40; 6:17–19)	Healing of many sick (28:9)
Curing of fever, causing the sick to stream in and be healed (4:38–40)	Curing of fever, causing the sick to stream in and be healed (28:7–10)
Raising of dead (7:11–17; 8:40–42, 49–56)	Raising of dead (20:9–12)
Affirming that the person is not really dead (8:52)	Affirming that the person is not really dead (20:10)
Physically imparted healing power (5:17; 6:19; 8:46)	Physically imparted healing power (19:6, 11–12)
Those healed by Jesus gratefully supply the necessities of life to their healer (8:2–3).	Those healed by Paul gratefully supply the necessities of life to their healer (28:10).

Although several scholars rightly point out that interpreters should show caution when drawing conclusions from these comparisons, one should not overlook their significance for the understanding of the biblical story. The book of Acts is not primarily concerned with the personalities leading the spread of the gospel to the Gentile world but with the Spirit who continues to expand his work to the ends of the world. What began in Israel through the work of Christ now spreads to the whole world through the work of Christ's Spirit.

Luke's interest in the spread of the gospel surfaces also in his repeated summary statements on its progress. He gives five such summary statements in Acts:

1. Acts 6:7: "The word of God continued to spread; the number of the disciples increased greatly in Jerusalem, and a great many of the priests became obedient to the faith" (NRSV).
2. Acts 9:31: "Meanwhile the church throughout Judea, Galilee, and Samaria had peace and was built up. Living in the fear of the Lord and in the comfort of the Holy Spirit, it increased in numbers" (NRSV).
3. Acts 12:24: "But the word of God continued to advance and gain adherents" (NRSV).
4. Acts 16:5: "So the churches were strengthened in the faith and increased in numbers daily" (NSRV).
5. Acts 19:20: "So the word of the Lord grew mightily and prevailed" (NRSV).

From this it becomes clear that Acts also can be read as a simple progress report:

1:1–6:7	The expansion of the earliest church in Jerusalem—the apostles pray, preach, and suffer.
6:8–9:31	The first geographical expansion caused by the stoning of Stephen—conversion of Paul.
9:32–12:24	The first expansion to the God-fearing Gentiles—conversion of Cornelius.
12:25–16:5	The first geographical expansion into the Gentile world—Paul's first journey and the Jerusalem Council.
16:6—19:20	Westward expansion into Europe—Paul's second and third journeys.
19:21–28:31	The gospel reaches Rome—conclusion of Acts.

The Spirit guided the church's progress from Jerusalem to Rome and beyond. From its earliest beginnings, the church has relied on the power and guidance of the Spirit to handle new challenges—pressures from internal struggles as the gospel brought together people who traditionally would not have fellowship with one another (Acts 6) and persecution from outside sources as zealous Jews were determined to stop the ongoing expansion of the Christian message (Acts 7).

READING ACTS AS HISTORY AND THEOLOGY

Reading Acts is not necessarily a straightforward matter. As shown above, Acts recounts the historical expansion of the early church, but Luke moves beyond the mere recording of history and desires to show how the operation of the Spirit in the early church reveals a pattern for the Spirit's work. Put differently, Luke is not satisfied with giving a history lesson; he aims to show that the story told in Acts has normative value for the church. It is a paradigm for how the Spirit operates.

This principle of analogy falls into place as one story is understood in the light of a former story. One example of this is Luke 13:33 where Luke's citation of Jesus' words ("I must go on my way today and tomorrow and the day following; for it cannot be that a prophet should perish away from Jerusalem" [ESV]) indicates that Jesus' death in Jerusalem was patterned after former episodes that were considered parallel. In this way earlier historical events occasioned by God became teaching moments that could be used as imperative instruction for the New Testament church.

Luke made use of this approach to history writing, also called typology, when he reported on Jesus in his Gospel and on the apostles in his book of Acts. Because the New Testament events gained theological significance from analogous events in the past (Old Testament), the significance of the present events (New Testament) must in similar fashion give meaning to future events (the continued life of the church). In other words, the ministry patterns of Jesus and of the apostles were consequential for the church's future ministry patterns, not just for the historic moment at which it happened (Luke 6:40).

This is seen most vividly in Luke 4:18–19, where the program for Jesus' ministry (and Luke's Gospel) is laid out as an introduction to the ministry that followed Jesus' baptism. Similarly, Acts 1:8 gives the blueprint both to Luke's account of the beginning of the Christian church *and* to the program for its continuation. In other words, Luke did not mention Jesus' speech in the Nazareth synagogue for the sake of historical recounting; he noted it because it outlined Jesus' ministry pattern. The same holds true for Acts 1:8. This text is not included simply as a historical reference to something the resurrected Jesus said but as a description of how the Spirit works and what he empowers believers to do.

This tension between history and theology makes reading the book of Acts challenging. Which of the events, for example, are merely descriptive of how the early Christians acted then, and which of the events are significant for a genuine understanding of the Christian life and faith? How do modern Christians understand it when the early disciples cast lots to determine who God had chosen to replace Judas as an apostle (Acts 1:21–26)? Is this a mere historical event, or does it have pattern value for how the church should choose its leaders through all time? The same questions could, and should, be asked concerning many situations in Acts.

The best way to sort this out is to ask whether an event or an approach is repeated. Does the New Testament, for example, give repeated examples of the use of lots when leaders are chosen? The answer to that is clearly no! The account in Acts 1 is, in fact, our only example. The same can be said about the day of Pentecost described in Acts 2. The disciples were gathered in a house waiting for the Spirit to come before they could begin their ministry "in the Spirit." Is this event ever repeated? Again the answer is no! The rest of Acts (and all the letters that follow) takes the Pentecost event for granted. The Spirit had now come, and his empowering presence would hereafter come to people at the moment of their conversion (Acts 2:38). In fact, the absence of the Spirit became evidence that genuine conversion had not yet happened.[5]

Other events, however, as when the disciples gathered for prayer to ask for God's miraculous involvement in their lives, are recorded over and over again. The same holds true for the request that the Spirit would continue to empower the believers.[6] Luke recorded such events to show how the Spirit works and how the Christian church should operate throughout time.[7] To do justice to the book of Acts, modern readers must struggle with the tension between simple descriptions of historical events (what happened) and Luke's theological emphasis on how the Spirit works through the church. Put differently, we can neither reduce the book of Acts to a simple recording of historical events, nor can we claim that every historical detail should be repeated by the modern church.

As will become obvious in the next episode, the ongoing work of the apostles depends completely upon the Spirit's enabling presence. It is because the Spirit continued to grant his presence that the good news about God's kingdom overcame all hindrances and continued to spread to the ends of the earth (28:31). It moved from Jerusalem to the nations of the Gentiles, for "they will listen" (28:28).

---

[5] This was the situation in chapters 8 and 19 of Acts. In Acts 8:13 it looks as if Simeon had come to true faith without receiving the Spirit, which only came in verse 16. However, as the situation shows, Simeon had not truly converted. The statement in verse 16 that "the Holy Spirit had not yet come" had to do with the early connection between the apostles from the first church in Jerusalem and the expanding church. The church began in Jerusalem and spread from there to Samaria and the ends of the earth (Acts 1:8). In chapter 19, some from Ephesus had been baptized with the baptism of John the Baptist and had therefore not received the Spirit. When Paul later arrived in Ephesus, he found some believers who had heard some preaching about Jesus but who had not become true Christians. He therefore baptized them again with a Christian baptism and made sure they had received the Spirit. For, as Paul said in Romans 8:9, "Anyone who does not have the Spirit of Christ, does not belong to Christ." It is not a matter of waiting for a repeat of the Pentecost event.

[6] Cf., for example, Ephesus 5:18 where Paul reminds his readers to continue to be filled by the Spirit. The grammatical form of the Greek word translated "be filled" in this context refers to a continuing or a repeated filling.

[7] For more specific guidelines on this, see J. Scott Duvall and J. Daniel Hays, *Grasping God's Word,* 2d ed. (Grand Rapids: Zondervan, 2005).

STUDY QUESTIONS

1. What was the significance of the Old Testament celebration of Pentecost? In what way does the New Testament event of Pentecost parallel the Old Testament celebration?
2. What is the significance of Acts 1:8 for the reading of the whole book?
3. How many summary statements are there in Acts, and how are they important for the understanding of the book of Acts?
4. How would you decide whether an event described in the book of Acts is purely descriptive of a historical event or whether it should be understood to have instructive value for the modern church?

ACT 2

THE CHURCH IN JERUSALEM
AND THE EARLY SPREAD OF THE GOSPEL

T he story of the resurrected Jesus as told in the book of Acts begins with the ascension of Jesus. Ten days after this event, the Holy Spirit, which Jesus promised to send to his disciples after his departure, came with transforming force. One hundred and twenty disciples were gathered in a house in Jerusalem during the Jewish celebration of Pentecost when the Spirit of Jesus filled each of them with a new experience of God's presence. According to Acts, this caused them to begin immediately to preach the gospel in the streets of Jerusalem, a proclamation that resulted in scores of people coming to faith and being baptized into the name of Jesus Christ. The Christian church was born!

After the birth of the church, witnessing continued; and new people were added to the group of Christians daily. The group grew by the thousands[8] and mostly met in homes encouraging one another and sharing the Lord's Supper.[9] This new group of Christians, although a diverse and somewhat scattered group, experienced themselves as *one* community. They were people of the new covenant, filled with God's Spirit, and living out the prophetic call given repeatedly by the Old Testament prophets. The old prophetical charge to Israel, that God's people had turned their worship into ritualistic formality with little concern for a genuine heartfelt relationship with God, *and* that they no longer cared about the poor, was heeded by the early Christians. These new Christian converts, empowered by the Spirit, created a new community where the worship was Spirit-filled and characterized by a thoroughgoing devotion that included all aspects of life (2:42–44). Their newfound

---

[8] Notice the incredible growth: Acts 2:41, 47; 4:4; 9:9, 31; 11:21, 24, 26; 14:1; 16:5; 17:4.

[9] There is no evidence that the whole church ever met together at once in one facility. Massive as it was in terms of numbers, no single facility could hold them all. Rather, the church developed into smaller communities held together by the teaching of the apostles and the direct inspiration of the Spirit.

devotion to God included a keen awareness of God's concern for the poor, and they began to share everything they had to the point of selling their possessions and distributing the proceeds to those in need (2:45–46).

As the massive numbers of new converts continued to join the new movement, the Christian church naturally included people from all walks of life and from a vast diversity of backgrounds and languages. Soon practical issues of the church's structure and order began to emerge. While some of the new converts were generous and giving, enjoying tremendous respect (4:36–37), others were selfish and could best be characterized as scheming hypocrites (5:1–10). The fellowship meals and the distribution of food to the needy began to face issues based in preconversion social structures (6:1). This created pressures from within that threatened to destroy the new community. To deal with this the apostles selected a group of deacons[10] who were to care for the practical issues of the church so the apostles themselves could continue their work of prayer, studies, and teaching.

Pressures grew from the outside as well. Peter and John, the apostolic leaders of the new movement, faced the Sanhedrin and were beaten, jailed, and told to stop teaching about Jesus (5:17–42). When the teaching did not stop and the number of Christians continued to increase, the Jewish leaders stepped up the persecution of the Christians, making an example of one of the deacons named Stephen by stoning him to death (7:57–60). The person leading the charge against the Christians and overseeing the stoning of Stephen was a Pharisee named Saul, or Paul.[11]

THE CONVERSION AND CALL OF PAUL (ACTS 9)

After the stoning of Stephen, the Christians scattered throughout the region, especially Syria. The large group of Christians fleeing to Antioch[12] formed a church and began to lead Gentiles to faith in Christ. This caught the attention of the Jerusalem church who subsequently sent a representative to Antioch to check out what was happening (11:19–22). The movement of the Christians to Syria did not escape the attention of Saul either. A leader among the Pharisees, and a violently avid opponent of the Christians, Saul decided to go to Damascus to hunt down the Christians and stop the spread of the movement there (9:1–2).

On the road to Damascus, Paul encountered a blinding light that forced him to the ground, and he heard the voice of the resurrected Jesus accusing him of persecuting the church. When Paul rose to continue, he remained blinded and followed the orders given by Jesus. He went to Damascus where he found Ananias, a Christian leader who prayed for Paul. As the Spirit filled Paul, he regained his

---

[10] *Deacon* is a Greek word that means "servant."

[11] Saul was his Hebrew name; Paul, his Roman name. It is not correct as some have claimed that Saul changed his name to Paul after his conversion. Rather, as a Jew holding Roman citizenship, he was given both names: *Saul* expressed his Hebraic heritage, and he used it as his official name in his zeal to gain significance as a Jewish leader; *Paul* was his given name as a Roman citizen born in Tarsus and the name he used during his childhood years in Greco-Roman schools (Cf. Acts 13:9 NRSV: "Saul, also known as Paul").

[12] Antioch in Syria was the third largest city in the world at the time and a good hiding place for someone wanting to escape persecution from zealous Pharisees.

sight, and Ananias subsequently baptized him. Saul the persecutor became Paul the preacher. By a direct call from the resurrected Jesus, Paul became the apostle to the Gentiles.[13]

According to Acts, Paul wasted no time. He began immediately to preach that Jesus was the Son of God with the same zeal he earlier applied to his persecution of the Christians. Both Christians and Jews were confused—the Christians because they were concerned he was merely pretending; the Jews because the power of his preaching in their synagogue convinced large numbers that Paul's new message was true. Barnabas, a trusted Christian from the church in Jerusalem, convinced the Christians in Damascus of the genuineness of Paul's conversion. The Jews now began a plot to kill Paul. Paul escaped Damascus by the help of the Christian church who helped him back to Tarsus via Caesarea. After the conversion of Paul, the church enjoyed a period of peace and continued growth (9:31).

The conversion experience of Paul, and his call to become an apostle to the Gentile world, literally changed the course of world history. Indisputably, no single person, except for Jesus himself, has had a greater transformative impact on world history than this man from Tarsus. His zeal and his message of salvation by grace through faith in Jesus Christ changed the way people thought from Jerusalem to Rome. Paul's message enabled people from all nations, all backgrounds, and all traditions to come to know the God of Abraham, Isaac, and Jacob through his Son Jesus Christ. The impact of this message proves immeasurable. It called all Christians to participate in suffering, and it led to a new concern for social care, new systems of mercy, and new studies in healing. World history was changed; Paul's message of eternal salvation for all who will believe what God had done through Christ brought a transformation of human thinking that changed everything.[14]

Who was this man God used in such a significant way? Many books describe Paul's life and ministry, and the scope of this book allows only an outline of his life. Paul was born in Tarsus in the province of Cilicia (22:3). He enjoyed Roman citizenship (22:25–29; 23:27), a privilege and a birthright resulting from the status of Tarsus as the capital of Cilicia.[15] His Jewish parents traced their ancestry back to the tribe of Benjamin (Rom. 11:1; Phil. 3:4). We know of only one sibling, a sister (Acts 23:16).

---

[13] In Paul's mind there was never any consideration that his encounter with the resurrected Jesus was anything less than a postresurrection appearance. This was more than a mere vision, and it compared directly to former resurrection appearances as experienced by the other disciples. His call and his authority as an apostle were directly based on this meeting with the risen Lord. When opponents questioned his apostolic authority, he reminded them that he was called directly by the risen Jesus (Gal. 1:1, 11–12).

[14] See also discussion on the incarnation in episode 8, act 2.

[15] Pompey made Tarsus the capital of Cilicia in 66 BC. Mark Antony later gave the city freedom, immunity, and citizenship—a privilege that was affirmed by Augustus. Tarsus was known as a center for culture, education, and philosophy. The Jewish colony there is said to have been established by Antiochus IV Epiphanes around 171 BC.

Growing up with Jewish parents in a Hellenistic environment like the one in Tarsus made Paul fluent in both Greek and Hebrew and well versed in the writings and philosophies of both cultures. The major part of his education, however, probably happened in Jerusalem under one of the most well-known and highly respected rabbis, a man called Gamaliel (22:3). Studying under Gamaliel meant that Paul studied to become a rabbi himself.[16]

Dating the birth of Paul is no easy matter. The strongest evidence for a specific timing appears on an inscription found in Delphi, in Greece, which places Gallio as Proconsul in Achaia in AD 51 and 52. Connecting this time with Paul's stay in Corinth (Acts 18:12–16) and counting backwards gives Paul a birth date somewhere around AD 10.

A chronology of Paul's life looks something like this:

Roman Birthright in the Diaspora
    Born in Tarsus of Cilicia (Acts 22:3)   AD 10
    Schooled in Greco-Roman thought (Acts 17:18, 28)
    Privileged by Roman Citizenship (Acts 21:39)

Jewish Upbringing in Jerusalem
    Rabbinic Education under Gamaliel (Acts 22:3; 26:4)
    A strict Pharisee of Benjamin's tribe (Rom. 11:1; Phil. 3:5)
    Persecutor of the church (Acts 7:58; Gal. 1:14–24)

Conversion at Damascus
    Stoning of Stephen (Acts 7:58–8:3)   AD 34
    Heavenly Vision on Damascus Road (Acts 9; 22; 26)
    Baptism by Ananias (Acts 9:18)
    Retreat to Arabia and Damascus Preaching (Gal. 1:17; Acts 922, 27)

Silent Years in Syria and Cilicia
    Flees Jews for Tarsus (Acts 9:30)
    Ten Unknown Years (2 Cor. 12:2; Gal. 1:21)   AD 37–46
    Recalled to Antioch by Barnabas (Acts 11:25; 12:25)

Gentile Mission in the Eastern Provinces
    The episodes in Acts can be grouped into three tours which commence and terminate at the church in Antioch.

---

[16] Rabbis were required to be married. If Paul had already finished his studies by the time of his trip to Damascus and was a recognized teacher of the Law in his own right, thereby having the authority to lead a persecution of Christians, he must have been married. However, if Paul had not yet finished his studies, traveling to Damascus under the mandate of other rabbis (Acts 26:10), it is possible that he had received an exemption from marriage until he had finished his Torah studies. If the latter is the case, the traditional reading of 1 Corinthians 7:8 ("To the unmarried and the widows I say that it is well for them to remain unmarried as I am") is correct. Paul was never married, and he compares his situation to the unmarried. If the former is the case, Paul had been married, and he compares his situation as a widower to the widows.

The First Missionary Tour (Acts 12:25–15:35)
    Paul might have written Galatians here before the
    Jerusalem conference (Acts 14:28; 15:1–2).
    Voyage to the Island of Cyprus   AD 46
    In the Province of Galatia
    The Jerusalem Conference (Acts 15)   AD 48–49
The Second Missionary Tour (Acts 15:36–18:22)
    In the Province of Macedonia   AD 50
    In the Province of Achaia
    Gallio proconsul in AD 51 July (Acts 18:11–
    12). 1 & 2 Thessalonians written from Corinth.
    18-month stay in Corinth ends in AD 52.
Third Missionary Tour (Acts 18:23–21:16)
    Two/three–year Ephesian Ministry   AD 53–55
            1 Corinthians written from Ephesus
            (Galatians may also have been written
            here).
    Journey to Jerusalem with Offering   AD 57
            2 Corinthians and Romans written in
            Greece.

Captivity and Death in Rome
    Arrest in Jerusalem (Acts 21:27)
    Two-year Imprisonment at Caesarea (Acts 24:27)   AD 57–59
    Voyage and Shipwreck (Acts 27:1–28:14)
    The Roman Imprisonments
        Two-year House Arrest in Rome (Acts 28:30)   AD 60–62
            Prison epistles written from Rome.
        Release and subsequent work
            Pastoral Epistles (1 Timothy and Titus)
        Second Imprisonment
            2 Timothy
        Martyrdom   AD 66–67

CHRISTIANITY MOVES BEYOND JERUSALEM (ACTS 10–11)

PHILIP AND SAMARIA

As outlined in Acts 1:8, the gospel quickly moved beyond Jerusalem. After the stoning of Stephen, Acts tells of a revival in Samaria due to the preaching of the evangelist called Philip, one of the seven deacons elected in Jerusalem. When the church in Jerusalem heard what was happening, they sent Peter and John to Samaria. As they prayed for those turning to Christ, the Spirit came upon the

Samaritan believers distinguishing them as true followers of Christ on par with the believers in Jerusalem.

Philip then miraculously met with an official from the Ethiopian court on his way back to Ethiopia from Jerusalem. Engaging in a conversation with the Ethiopian who was reading from the book of Isaiah, Philip explained the good news. Upon hearing it, the Ethiopian official believed in Philip's message and asked to be baptized. Philip baptized him, and the gospel now made its way to Ethiopia, carried by a black Gentile eunuch.[17] Philip then returned to Caesarea (Acts 8:40).

PETER AND THE GOSPEL'S PROGRESS TO THE GENTILES

Chapter 10 of Acts shows how the gospel moved into the Gentile Greco-Roman world. Peter, still somewhat caught in his first-century Jewish mind-set (believing Jews should maintain separatism from Gentiles) had a vision in which God instructed him to eat from a table filled with unclean animals. When he refused, God rebuked him and said that he should not call unclean what God declared to be clean. As Luke tells the story, Peter's vision resulted from the prayers of a Roman centurion, Cornelius, who was a God-fearing Gentile. God answered Cornelius's prayer and told him to send for Peter. When they arrived at the place where Peter was staying, Peter understood the meaning of his vision. He followed the men to Cornelius' house where he preached the gospel to this group of Gentiles.

While he was preaching, the Spirit of God fell upon the group. This forced Peter to conclude that since God had included these Gentiles into his kingdom, Peter had no choice but to include them into the church. Upon this realization he baptized them, recognizing that with God there is no partiality. When Peter returned to Jerusalem, some of the Judaic Christians criticized him for his actions. However, he explained how God had given "them the same gift that he gave us when we believed in the Lord Jesus Christ" (11:17 NRSV), and his testimony convinced the Jerusalem church. They concluded that God had given "even to the Gentiles the repentance that leads to life" (11:18).

THE CHURCH IN ANTIOCH

As mentioned above, Christians fled Jerusalem; and large numbers settled in Antioch Syria for safe haven in the big city. Upon arriving in Antioch, some shared the message about Jesus to Gentiles. When these Gentiles accepted the preaching of the Christians as truth from God, many became believers and joined the fellowship of the Christians. This was truly revolutionary. When news reached the Jerusalem church, they dispatched Barnabas, one of their most trusted members,

---

[17] Much of Ethiopia was Semitic and thus had close language ties to Hebrew. The Ethiopian might have been a so-called "God fearer," a non-Jew attracted to the monotheism of the Jewish faith. If so, he would have been in Jerusalem to worship. When Luke mentions that he was a eunuch (8:27), it may have been to underscore the radical character of the gospel message. The Law prevented a eunuch from becoming a proselyte Jew and thus effectively kept him outside the kingdom of God. The gospel, however, made no such restriction and included him as a full member of God's new people. What mattered was that he had faith in Jesus as the Son of God who came to fulfill God's plan for the salvation of his creation.

to check out the situation in Antioch. He reported back that God performed a great work in the city.

Needing help as the Antiochean church continued to grow, Barnabas went to Tarsus in search of Paul. Christians in Damascus had helped Paul escape to Tarsus after his conversion (9:30) because angry Jewish leaders sought to kill him. Nothing is recorded about him from these years, and scholars are not sure of Paul's activities during this time of about ten years (Gal. 1:21–23).[18] Most likely Paul used these years to study and pray, unlearning some of his former education and relearning what Scripture was teaching about God's work through Christ. Second Corinthians 12:2–4 may refer to some of his experiences during that time.

Paul returned to Antioch with Barnabas. Together they taught the church for a year, and many new Christians were added daily. The group grew strong and became recognized in Antioch as something other than a mere sect or version of the Jewish religion. According to Acts 11:26, "It was in Antioch that the disciples were first called 'Christians'" (NRSV).

In Jerusalem, things grew worse. Not only did they suffer a famine,[19] but King Herod killed and imprisoned many of the disciples. The situation in Jerusalem was dire, and even more people fled. Meanwhile in Antioch the number of disciples who followed the teachings of Jesus continued to grow (12:24), and the church decided to send out Barnabas and Paul as missionaries. After a season of prayer, Paul and Barnabas, accompanied by Barnabas's nephew, a young man from Jerusalem named John Mark, embarked on their first missionary journey.

STUDY QUESTIONS

1. What are some of the ways in which the early church heeded the message of the Old Testament prophets?
2. Paul was also called Saul. Why two names?
3. What helps us get a firm historical dating for Paul's life?
4. What was especially important about Peter's visit to Cornelius' house? What did that mean for the later expansion of the church?

---

[18] Traditionally this period in Paul's life is referred to as the Silent Years.

[19] The reference in Acts 11:29f to the famine relief efforts by the Antiochean church in favor of the church in Jerusalem speaks to the close interconnection between the two. Antioch was more than a mere offshoot of the Jerusalem church; it was the international arm of the Christian movement. The famine prophesied by Agabus (11:28) is described by Josephus as happening during the reign of Claudius in AD 46.

ACT 3

PAUL'S FIRST AND
SECOND MISSIONARY JOURNEYS

PAUL'S FIRST MISSIONARY TRIP INTO THE EASTERN PROVINCES
(ACTS 12:25–15:35)

Setting out to spread the gospel further into the Gentile world, Barnabas, Paul, and Mark traveled eastward into the general region of Asia Minor called Galatia. Following a well-known pattern from Old Testament times where God spoke to his people first and through them to the Gentiles, Paul and his company visited the Jewish synagogues first before they turned to the Gentiles (13:46–47).

Leaving Antioch the three men sailed to Cyprus, Barnabas's birthplace. On Cyprus the three missionaries were asked to preach to the island's proconsul, Sergius Paulus. Hearing their word and seeing the power of God's Spirit, who instantly blinded a magician trying to oppose God's work, Sergius Paulus became a Christian believer. As Paul and Barnabas left Cyprus for Perga on the southern coast of Asia Minor, John Mark left them to return home. The text gives no indication as to why Mark left, but it was a contentious move that later split Paul and Barnabas. From Perga they traveled further inland to Antioch in Pisidia. Here they visited the synagogue on the Sabbath, where, after the reading of the Law when worshippers were asked to comment, Paul stood up and explained the gospel. Those listening in the synagogue became intrigued and wanted to hear more. The following Sabbath great crowds gathered to hear more, but some became jealous of Paul and Barnabas and turned the crowd against them.

Paul and Barnabas therefore turned to the Gentiles who gladly received them and their message. This success continued, and the Word spread to the whole region. However, those opposing Paul and Barnabas convinced prominent citizens to drive them out of their region.

Leaving Antioch in Pisidia, they walked about ninety miles southeast to Iconium, a strongly Hellenized city located on a plateau of 3,370 feet elevation. Here they found little success for the message and had to flee to avoid a stoning. They fled to Lystra and Derbe and the countryside surrounding these towns. In Lystra Paul healed a man paralyzed since birth. The people took that to be a sign that the gods had come down so they called Barnabas Zeus and Paul Hermes since he served as the main spokesman.

Rather than accepting such adulation, Paul and Barnabas attempted to explain the gospel. Again their opponents successfully aroused the crowd against them, and this time they did not get out in time. Paul was stoned, dragged out of the city, and left for dead. Fortunately Paul survived, and those who had come to faith through his preaching came to his rescue. The next day he and Barnabas left for Derbe. Derbe received them well, and many people came to faith. When they had finished their ministry in Derbe, they returned by the same route they had come (except for Cyprus) strengthening the churches they had started and establishing a leadership of elders in each of them (14:22–23).

Coming back to Antioch, they remained with the church for a while encouraging them and reporting how God had opened a door for the gospel among Gentiles. While there, converts from the Jerusalem church came to Antioch teaching that salvation through Christ required circumcision to be effective. This teaching enraged Paul and Barnabas who consequently brought a group from the church in Antioch to Jerusalem to resolve the issue.

THE APOSTOLIC COUNCIL IN JERUSALEM (ACTS 15)

The apostolic council in Jerusalem, reported in Acts 15, easily ranks as one of the most important meetings of the early church. The outcome of this meeting enabled the continued spread of the Christian gospel in the Gentile world. It is probably not exaggerated to claim that, if the conclusions of this meeting had been the opposite of what they were, the Christian movement would have become little less than just another first-century Jewish sect. However, God's Spirit ruled the conversation, and the council decided not to burden the Gentile Christians with the Law of the old covenant (15:28–29).

How did they reach that conclusion? Paul and Barnabas arrived in Jerusalem reporting, in a fashion similar to Peter's earlier explanation of the events in Cornelius's house, how God's Spirit had fallen upon the Gentiles of Asia Minor. "God, who knows the human heart, testified to them by giving them the Holy Spirit, just as he did to us; and in cleansing their hearts by faith he has made no distinction between them and us," they argued (15:8–9 NRSV). After further reporting on the evidence of God's work among the Gentiles and further argumentations from Scripture, the Jerusalem church decided to send Paul and Barnabas, along with some of the members from Jerusalem, back to visit the Gentile churches. They were to bear a letter stating that the only requirements from the Law to be placed on the Gentile churches were "that you abstain from what has been sacrificed to idols and from blood and from what is strangled and from fornication" (15:29 NRSV).

The letter brought much joy to the church in Antioch. It seemed that a major issue with the potential to split or even destroy the young church had been solved. The church in Antioch enjoyed the ministry of the visiting prophets from the Jerusalem church, Judas and Silas, for a good while. When they left, they were sent off in peace (15:33). [20] The foundation was laid, and the hindrances for a renewed mission effort among the Gentiles were removed. Paul and Barnabas were now getting ready to leave on a second missionary journey.

PAUL'S SECOND MISSIONARY JOURNEY (ACTS 15:36–18:22)

The second voyage to spread the gospel reached beyond Asia Minor into Europe. A serious issue arose, however, at the outset of the trip. Barnabas wanted to bring his nephew, John Mark, who had left them at the beginning of the first journey, but Paul did not trust John Mark to come along this time. This disagreement resulted in a separation between the two missionaries. As a result Barnabas took Mark and went back to Cyprus, while Paul chose a traveling companion named Silas.[21] Silas was the prophet from Jerusalem who had come to Antioch to deliver the letter from the apostolic council.

Paul and Silas began their trip revisiting the churches in Asia Minor that Paul and Barnabas had started during their first trip three or four years earlier. Going through Cilicia, they came to Derbe and Lystra, where a young man named Timothy joined them. Timothy, one of the converts from Paul's first visit, had now gained a good reputation among the churches in Lystra and Iconium. Having a Jewish mother and a Greek father, Timothy had grown up in a Hellenistic environment with a strong knowledge of Jewish Scriptures.

Although Paul had fought hard, and would continue to fight, to convince everyone that the new covenant people of God did not need to be circumcised, he still allowed Timothy to be circumcised. Paul wanted to avoid problems with Jewish believers when they went to the synagogues to explain the gospel.[22] Going from church to church, the three missionaries encouraged and strengthened the churches as they delivered the letter explaining the decision made by the Jerusalem Council.

---

[20] Most likely, only Judas left since Silas shortly thereafter went with Paul on his second missionary journey.

[21] Silas was also called Silvanus (2 Cor. 1:19; 1 Thess. 1:1; 2 Thess. 1:1; 1 Pet. 5:12).

[22] Technically Timothy was Jewish because his mother was Jewish, but because his father was Greek, he had not been circumcised as a child.

Paul's job as a leather worker took him from city to city where he could find employment.[23] Undoubtedly, Paul and his coworkers spent time seeking God's guidance about where to go, but such prayers were not disconnected from practical issues. From studies in the first-century migrant patterns of skilled workers like Paul, it seems that Paul's travels corresponded to the location of leather worker guilds.

A change of direction came in Troas, a harboring town on the coast of the Aegean Sea, when Paul saw a vision of a man from Macedonia calling him to come and share the gospel. Paul and his coworkers now entered Europe for the first time. Landing in Neapolis, they continued to Philippi, a Roman settlement and a leading city in Macedonia. Their stay in Philippi brought both victories and struggles. A strong church was founded, but it came at a price that included flogging, severe beatings, and imprisonment.[24] After God miraculously freed Paul and Silas from a prison in Philippi, they went to Lydia's house to encourage the congregation of Christians. Lydia was a well-to-do freedwoman (former slave) from Thyatira who worked with textiles. She was a God fearer when Paul first met her and had become their first convert in Philippi. In Philippi, as in most other places, these infant churches met in the house of one of their most prominent church leaders.

Paul and his companions left Lydia's house to travel to Thessalonica, Macedonia's largest port city at the time. As was his pattern, Paul first went to the synagogue, the place where faith was most likely to be found. Here for three Sabbaths he preached and argued that Jesus was the Messiah. This led to the conversion of a large number of people, which, beyond the traditional Jewish population, included many God-fearing Greeks and a number of "prominent women." The specific mentioning of prominent women was significant because of the influence they yielded in the Macedonian culture. According to inscriptions found in the area, wealthy Macedonian women had gained a strong reputation for their influence in both social and civic affairs. Now, as patrons of the church, these upper-class women enjoyed an even higher status than they had in society in general, and the new church benefited from the "approval" their participation gave it.

It did not take long, however, until jealous religious opponents of Paul and Silas succeeded in stirring up a crowd of uneducated ruffians against them. They experienced persecution everywhere they preached the gospel, but in Thessalonica persecution came upon them with such force that for safety the believers sent Paul and his companions off to Berea by night. In Berea Paul's team faced less opposition, and in the synagogue the Jews were more eager to search the Scriptures. This resulted in a large number of them becoming Christians. The church in Berea, which according to Acts 17:12 included Jews, Greek women, and men of high

---

[23] Paul is often called a tent maker. This is not as accurate as the term *leather worker*. Tent-making was a big part of a leather worker's task but not the only part. Paul was a craftsman working with leather and producing any leather product requested.

[24] From the letters Paul wrote to his churches, it seems that he treasured his relationship with the Christians in Philippi more than most.

standing, became so strong that Paul left Timothy and Silas there to strengthen the church even more while he moved on to Athens.

In Athens Paul met with a sophisticated culture and a complicated mix of philosophy and religion. He quickly noticed the exorbitant number of altars in the city, one for every imaginable god and situation—even one for an unknown god, just in case. Paul picked up on this when he met with the famed council at Areopagus, a group of philosophers who enjoyed their role as something like a judicial council on religious and philosophical questions.[25]

Attempting a clever defense for the Christian faith, Paul noted that he knew the God that was unknown to them. Making use of Stoic philosophical terminology and quoting the Greek poet Epimenides, Paul gained a hearing and received an invitation to come back for further conversation. However, only a few became believers, and Scripture gives no report of a lasting church in Athens. Whether this result was because his rationalistic and apologetic approach to evangelism failed proves difficult to determine. Some suggest that such was the case. They base their argument on Paul's statement to the church in Corinth where he said he had decided he would know of nothing except Christ crucified—a message that would be foolishness to the wise but bring salvation to those who believed (1 Cor. 1:20–25).

Paul came to Corinth directly from Athens. If Athens was the academic capital of Greece, Corinth took center stage for politics and commerce. The capital city of the province of Achaea, Corinth had been Athens' archrival in the struggle for prominence, a battle it had won long before Paul got there. As a key port city, it earned the reputation as *the* center for trade and commerce.

Paul arrived in Corinth at the height of its prominence. In 46 BC, Caesar decided to rebuild Corinth, and Augustus later made it the capital of Achaea and appointed a governor. A hustling and bustling city attracting trade from both east and west, Corinth was the natural home of trade guilds. When people of the same trade came to a city, instead of competing against one another, they moved into the same area of town, if not the same house, and formed guilds to share the work. Since people in these guilds share life in such a close way, their fellowships often became religious and ritualistic, worshipping a patron god and eating sacrificial meals together.

It was here Paul met Pricilla and Aquila, Italian Jews who had been forced to leave Rome due to Claudius's decree that all Jews be expelled from Rome. Because of the religious character of many guilds, practicing Jews, who refused to participate in such, found fellowship with one another instead. There is a good chance this was what started Paul's relationship with Aquila and Pricilla. Paul moved in, and they worked together in the leather trade.

---

[25] Areopagus refers both to the council and to the hill where they traditionally assembled (a place located below the Acropolis and above the Agora marketplace. It is known today by its Latin name, Mars Hill). At the time of Paul, it is likely that the Areopagus met in the so-called *Stoa Bacilicos,* an area of the *Agora,* or marketplace, where Paul naturally would have focused his ministry.

When Timothy and Silas joined Paul in Corinth, they found him witnessing primarily among Jews; but as this group continued to oppose him, he moved to a house next to the synagogue belonging to a God-fearing Gentile who had come to faith in Christ. From here he launched a ministry that kept him in Corinth for eighteen months (Acts 18:11).[26] During this time, a strong but trouble-filled church came into existence.[27]

Accompanied by Pricilla and Aquila, Paul left Corinth to return to Antioch. They traveled via Ephesus where he left Pricilla and Aquila. With a promise to come back soon, Paul left Ephesus after only a short stay to go up to Jerusalem to speak to the church. From there he went down to Antioch.[28]

STUDY QUESTIONS

1. To which region did Paul's first journey go? Who accompanied him?
2. What was the significance of the apostolic meeting described in Acts 15?
3. What happened as Paul and Barnabas were ready to go on their second journey?
4. Where and how did Paul most likely meet Priscilla and Aquilla?

---

[26] There is a good chance that Paul's extended stay in Corinth also became the beginning of his letter-writing ministry. He was concerned about the persecution of the young Christians in Macedonia, especially Thessalonica. Reports had told him of their struggles and of some of their theological questions. These were answered in his two letters to the Thessalonian church which were written around AD 51. It is possible that Paul's letter to the Galatian churches is earlier. Paul may have written Galatians as a response to reports that Judaizing Christians had visited the churches he started on his first journey. They preached a gospel that opposed Paul's emphasis on grace requiring Christians to keep the Law of Moses.

[27] The Corinthian correspondence, of which only two letters are still in existence and included in the New Testament, suggests a strained relationship between Paul and the Corinthian church. This correspondence, which may have included four letters from Paul, occurred during Paul's third journey and most probably during his prolonged stay in Ephesus. He may even have visited Corinth a couple of times (one visit is rather certain, 2 Cor. 2:1) during this stay. Fortunately, as 2 Corinthians (which may be Paul's fourth letter to the Corinthian church) indicates, Paul and the Corinthians resolved their differences.

[28] When Acts consistently says that people go down from Jerusalem to Antioch, although Antioch is north of Jerusalem, it is due to Jerusalem's exalted status as the place for the temple. No matter the starting point, people always go *up to* Jerusalem. No matter the destination, people always go *down from* Jerusalem. It has nothing to do with direction and nothing to do with Jerusalem being located on a mount. It is strictly an expression of reverence.

ACT 4

PAUL'S THIRD MISSIONARY JOURNEY, HIS ARREST AND FINAL DAYS

PAUL'S THIRD MISSIONARY JOURNEY (ACTS 18:22–21:16)

A LONG MINISTRY IN EPHESUS

From what we know, Paul did not spend much time in Antioch between the second and the third missionary journeys. After strengthening the new Christians in the city, he returned to Ephesus through the region of Galatia. In Ephesus he found some people who had become believers through the preaching of a powerful orator from Alexandria named Apollos. Apollos had heard someone preach the gospel and had become convinced that Jesus was God's promised Messiah; but he had not heard of, or been filled with, the Holy Spirit. When Pricilla and Aquila heard him preach in Ephesus, they pulled him aside and explained "the Way of God to him more accurately" (18:25 Phillips).

The twelve believers Paul met when he came to Ephesus had become convinced by Apollos's preaching, but they did not know about the Holy Spirit. They had been baptized only by the baptism of John (19:3), a Jewish baptism for repentance that was preparation for Jesus' coming. After Paul discovered their mere assent to the message about Christ, rather than becoming true Christians filled by Christ's Spirit, he prayed for their reception of the Spirit and baptized them into Jesus Christ.

Ephesus stood as the most important city in the Roman province of Asia and held significant political influence in the Roman Empire. A proud city, it also served as religious headquarters for the famed temple of Artemis, which was considered one of the seven wonders of the ancient world. Commercially, it likewise exercised enormous influence. Paul undoubtedly recognized its strategic significance for the spread of the gospel and made it his dwelling place for the next two to three years.

He began his ministry in typical fashion by first visiting the synagogues. He continued this pattern for three months, after which he chose to move to the lecture hall of Tyrannus. This hall may have been owned by one of the guilds, but it is also possible that a philosopher named Tyrannus used it for his own lectures in the morning and rented it to Paul for the afternoon (or the other way around).[29] Philosophical lectures were common in Ephesus, and since Tyrannus' hall was a public place, it would enable all interested people to attend so that in the course of two years "all the residents of Asia, both Jews and Greeks, heard the word of the Lord" (19:10 NRSV).

After a while Paul's teaching, and the miracles God did through him, influenced public behavior, and it hurt the business of those who were profiting from the sale of religious artifacts in the city. They rioted against Paul, and although Acts records that Paul himself avoided direct involvement in the riot, he left Ephesus rather quickly, asking Timothy to remain as pastor of the church.

Paul's stay in Ephesus was fruitful in many regards. Beyond the city itself, the gospel spread to important towns in the surrounding area and throughout the Lycus Valley. Acts does not report any imprisonment in Ephesus, but it seems from Paul's Corinthian correspondence (see footnote 1) that he might have been imprisoned there and written his letters to the Corinthian church from this prison. It is also possible that he wrote his letter to the churches in Galatia from this prison.

THE COLLECTION FOR THE CHURCH IN JERUSALEM

Leaving Ephesus, Paul went to Troas (2 Cor. 2:12), and from there he sailed back to Macedonia to strengthen the churches there. In Macedonia he met Titus returning from Corinth, and he reported that Paul's letters had corrected the situation and the church had decided to discipline the offenders and be reconciled to Paul. This occasioned Paul's last letter to the Corinthians, where he wrote:

> For even when we came into Macedonia, our bodies had no rest, but we were afflicted in every way—disputes without and fears within. But God, who consoles the downcast, consoled us by the arrival of Titus, and not only by his coming, but also by the consolation with which he was consoled about you, as he told us of your longing, your mourning, your zeal for me, so that I rejoiced still more. For even if I made you sorry with my letter, I do not regret it (though I did regret it, for I see that I grieved you with

---

[29] Some ancient manuscripts claim that Paul taught there daily from 11:00 AM to 4:00 PM. That seems likely since this would somewhat coincide with the hottest time of the day, the time for the siesta.

that letter, though only briefly). Now I rejoice, not because you were grieved, but because your grief led to repentance; for you felt a godly grief, so that you were not harmed in any way by us. For godly grief produces a repentance that leads to salvation and brings no regret, but worldly grief produces death. For see what earnestness this godly grief has produced in you, what eagerness to clear yourselves, what indignation, what alarm, what longing, what zeal, what punishment! At every point you have proved yourselves guiltless in the matter. So although I wrote to you, it was not on account of the one who did the wrong, nor on account of the one who was wronged, but in order that your zeal for us might be made known to you before God. In this we find comfort. In addition to our own consolation, we rejoiced still more at the joy of Titus, because his mind has been set at rest by all of you (2 Cor. 7:5–13 NRSV).

Having sent this letter to prepare for his visit, Paul left Macedonia for Corinth where he stayed for three months.[30] From Corinth he planned to sail to Antioch in Syria, but when he discovered a plot against him, he decided to return through Macedonia. This would be the safer option since any ship going to Syria at that time of the year would have included a number of Jewish passengers trying to reach Jerusalem in time for Passover. Such a journey would make Paul an easy target for assassination.

At some point during the time of Paul's third journey, he recognized the need to bridge the growing gap between the expanding Gentile church and the Jewish church in Jerusalem. He wanted to show the unity that existed between all Christian churches whether they were purely Jewish, purely Gentile, or a mixture of the two.

The letter written by the Jerusalem church to be read in all Gentile churches stated that they were to "remember the poor." What better way to express unity across all borders and barriers than to do a collection among all Gentile churches for the poor in the Jerusalem church. Paul expressed this vision in his letters to the Romans: "At present, however, I am going to Jerusalem in a ministry to the saints; for Macedonia and Achaia have been pleased to share their resources with the poor among the saints at Jerusalem. They were pleased to do this, and indeed they owe it to them; for if the Gentiles have come to share in their spiritual blessings, they ought also to be of service to them in material things" (Rom. 15:25–27).

Coming back through Macedonia, Paul held a meeting with members from various churches in Troas. After a week of preaching and fellowship, Paul continued to Miletus where he met with the elders from the Ephesian church before he sailed off, hoping to be in Jerusalem in time for Pentecost. This turned out to be

---

[30] Paul probably wrote his letter to the Christians in Rome during this time in order to introduce himself. Rome was *the* major city Paul had still not visited.

a sad and emotional meeting since Paul predicted that it would be the last time he would see them (Acts 20:37–38).

CAPTIVITY, IMPRISONMENT, AND DEATH IN ROME
(ACTS 21:17–28:31)

Paul landed in Tyre, a port north of Caesarea. Here he stayed with the Christian disciples for about a week before going to Jerusalem. During this time the believers continued to discourage Paul from going to Jerusalem. Paul persisted, however, and stopped in Caesarea to visit with Philip, who lived there with his family. While in Caesarea, Agabus, the prophet who earlier foretold the famine in Jerusalem, prophesied that if Paul continued to Jerusalem, he would be captured and handed over to the Roman authorities. Undeterred, Paul set out for Jerusalem, responding to Agabus's prophecy with assurance that he was ready to give his life for Jesus Christ if need be.

PAUL'S ARREST IN JERUSALEM

Arriving in Jerusalem, Paul met with James and the church elders to report all that God had done throughout the Gentile world. Again Paul was warned that his message that circumcision was of no avail had enraged thousands of Jewish believers who stood ready to kill him. To ease the conflict, the Jerusalem church leaders advised Paul to undergo a public and visible purification ritual in the attempt to preempt false accusations. This proved to have little or no effect. As soon as Jews from Asia recognized Paul in the temple area, they stirred up the crowd charging that he had brought non-Jews into the temple. This caused an uproar in the whole town, and only because of the intervention of soldiers did Paul avoid being lynched on the spot.

The soldiers brought Paul to the Roman authorities who, after checking his identity, allowed him to address the upset crowd. When Paul used this opportunity to give his testimony and preach the gospel, the crowd responded by calling for his death. However, as a Roman citizen the authorities could not punish him without a Roman trial. Wanting to determine the Jewish charge against Paul, the Roman tribune called the Sanhedrin asking them to confront Paul in his presence. Nothing came of this meeting except a reaffirmation by the Jews to have Paul killed.

PAUL'S IMPRISONMENT AT CAESAREA

The plan to kill Paul came to the attention of the tribune who, in order to avoid further trouble, sent him to Felix, the Roman governor stationed in Caesarea. As Paul stood before Felix to defend himself, he again used the situation to give his testimony and to share the gospel. He did so with such force that Felix on several occasions brought Paul back from his prison cell to discuss the matter further. This went on for two years until Felix retired and was replaced by Festus.

As a favor to the Jews, Felix left Paul in prison. The chief priest tried to make the most of this by requesting Festus to grant them a favor by returning Paul to Jerusalem for trial. Standing before Festus, Paul requested that he be heard by the emperor rather than by a court in Jerusalem. Festus had no choice but to grant Paul his wish, and he made plans to send Paul to Rome.

Before shipping off Paul, Festus met with King Agrippa to talk about Paul. The conversation raised Agrippa's interest, and he asked that Paul be brought before him. As Paul stood before Agrippa, he unashamedly told the king what God had done, how he had met the resurrected Jesus, and how multitudes of Gentiles had found faith in Jesus Christ. His story moved Agrippa to the point where he responded, "Are you so quickly persuading me to become a Christian?" Paul replied, "Whether quickly or not, I pray to God that not only you but also all who are listening to me today might become such as I am—except for these chains" (26:28–29 NRSV).

After the encounter, Agrippa concluded that Paul had done nothing wrong and could be set free had he not appealed to the emperor. Why then did Paul make such an appeal? It is impossible to know fully Paul's reasoning on this matter. It could be that Paul made his appeal to Caesar to avoid an ambush in Jerusalem, but it is just as likely he envisioned a situation where he in Rome would have a special opportunity to explain the gospel before Caesar himself. If Caesar came to faith, the gospel would almost surely reach to the ends of the earth.

PAUL'S TRAVEL TO ROME AND HIS ROMAN IMPRISONMENT

Paul's voyage to Rome was an eventful one. Setting out from Caesarea, he sailed on board a smaller coasting boat from a town close to Troas. A coasting boat remains close to the coastline at all times. They disembarked on the Lysian coast in the town of Myra. From here they boarded a cargo ship bound for Italy, but difficult winds forced them to dock on the south side of the island of Crete. By this time October had rolled around, and the fall and winter weather made sailing difficult and dangerous. Paul therefore suggested they stay where they were for the winter. The centurion guarding Paul and the captain of the ship thought it better to move on, however, and winter in Phoenix on the far west side of Crete.

This decision proved fatal for both the ship and the cargo. The wind soon picked up and forced the sailors to empty the vessel of its cargo to stay afloat. Soon they simply drifted as a storm pounded the ship before it finally ran aground and was splintered a short distance from the island of Malta.

Everybody on board reached Malta safely and found the local population extraordinarily kind and helpful. At one time, as Paul was gathering firewood, he was bitten by a viper. Those watching it thought he would surely die and took it to be punishment from God, but when he remained unaffected, they concluded that he was a god. This provided Paul an opportunity to preach the gospel on Malta and to heal the sick.

When spring came, they boarded a ship and sailed to Italy. In the port of Puteoli, they found some Christians who invited them to stay for a week after which they went on to Rome. Arriving in Rome, they were greeted by Christians who had heard Paul was coming. Still not charged properly as a Roman citizen, Paul was allowed to stay on his own with soldiers guarding him day and night. This continued for two years.[31]

Only three days after his arrival in Rome, Paul called together the Jewish leaders to explain his situation to them. Since they had not received a letter or message from Jerusalem speaking evil against Paul, they invited him to tell them more. They returned in large numbers to hear what he had to say. His preaching caused some disagreement among those listening, but nothing is told of any violence.

The book of Acts concludes with Paul's conversation with those who came to hear his teaching. He taught that God had sent his salvation to the Gentiles, for "they will listen" (28:28), and he "welcomed all who came to him, proclaiming the kingdom of God and teaching about the Lord Jesus Christ with all boldness and without hindrance" (28:30–31 NRSV). The gospel had reached Rome and was now being proclaimed without hindrance.

Acts, however, ends before Paul's beheading under Nero in AD 66 or 67.[32] To learn more about the last years of Paul's life, we look to Paul's letters and to some literature outside the biblical material. Romans 15:28 states that Paul desired to visit Rome on his way to Spain after he had delivered the gift from the Gentile churches to Jerusalem. Whether he accomplished this is not certain, but it is possible. Clement, who was bishop in Rome at the end of the first century (about thirty years after Paul's death), affirmed in his letter to the Corinthians that Paul reached Spain after his release from house arrest. If so, Paul was in Spain when Rome burned in July AD 64. It is not likely, however, that Paul traveled as far as Britain, as some legends claim. At least, no serious evidence exists for such a claim.

From Paul's Pastoral Letters,[33] it is clear that after his release Paul revisited the churches in the east. He left Titus in Crete to take care of the church there (Titus 1:5). From there he traveled to Miletus south of Ephesus, where he left Trophimus sick (2 Tim. 4:20). En route to Macedonia, he stopped in Ephesus to visit Timothy (1 Tim. 1:3). Sailing from Troas, he left his coat, books (scrolls),[34] and parchments

---

[31] During his two years of house arrest, Paul wrote his letters to the Ephesians, Colossians, and Philippians. These are sometimes called his Prison Letters. They are primarily letters of encouragement that also include some doctrinal discussions.

[32] As a Roman citizen Paul could not, like many other Christian martyrs, be crucified or die by other protracted, torturous methods.

[33] Paul's letter to Titus and his two letters to Timothy.

[34] These probably were copies of various sections of the Old Testament. It is unlikely that Paul carried the whole Septuagint or any scrolls from Greek philosophers.

(notes, letters, and personal documents)[35] with a believer named Carpus (2 Tim. 4:13). After Troas, he arrived in Nicopolis on the Adriatic Sea where he spent the winter waiting for Titus (Titus 3:15).

When Paul returned to Rome, he was imprisoned and placed in the Mamertine prison, a cold, dark, and wet rock cell below ground. The precise charge against him is uncertain, but he may have been charged with arson relating to the burning of Rome. At any rate, by this time Rome had outlawed Christianity. It was now considered a new religion and was no longer protected as a sect under Judaism. It was, therefore, dangerous to associate with Paul, and most Christians deserted him (2 Tim. 4:16), including some of his closest coworkers (2 Tim. 1:15; 4:10). Only Luke remained with him, and Paul asked Timothy and Mark to come as well (2 Tim. 4:11).

Paul likely endured two hearings before Nero. At the first trial he pleaded his own case and that of the gospel, which he still hoped to bring to all the Gentiles. He apparently succeeded at this first defense (2 Tim. 4:17). Scripture gives no information concerning the second defense, but since Nero died in AD 68, and all evidence points to Paul's being martyred under Nero. His death most likely occurred in early spring AD 66 or 67. The last known ministry of Paul was his second letter to Timothy. He probably wrote this shortly before his decapitation. In it he writes his own epitaph (4:6–8): "As for me, I am already being poured out as a libation, and the time of my departure has come. I have fought the good fight, I have finished the race, I have kept the faith. From now on there is reserved for me the crown of righteousness, which the Lord, the righteous judge, will give me on that day, and not only to me but also to all who have longed for his appearing" (NRSV).

GETTING A GRIP ON THE SEQUENCE OF ACTS (MEMORIZATION HELP)

1. Preparation for Pentecost
2. Pentecost: The Coming of the Spirit
3. The Holy Spirit Works through the Apostles
4. The Gospel Spreads in Spite of Obstacles
5. Threats to the Church
6. Stephen, the First Martyr
7. Philip the Evangelist
8. The Conversion of Paul
9. The Ministry of Peter beyond Jerusalem
10. Christianity Comes to Antioch
11. Paul's First Missionary Journey
12. Debate over the Acceptance of the Gentiles—Jerusalem Council

---

[35] This would include blank note sheets, draft copies of his own letters, etc. Likely this was bound in a codex format, somewhat like a modern book. See E. Randolph Richards, *Paul and First Century Letter Writing* (Downers Grove, Ill.: InterVarsity Press, 2004), chapter 14.

13. Paul's Second Missionary Trip
14. Paul's Third Missionary Trip
15. Paul's Witness in Jerusalem
16. Paul's Witness in Caesarea
17. Paul's Journey to Rome
18. Paul's Witness in Rome

STUDY QUESTIONS

1. How long did Paul stay in Ephesus, and where did he primarily preach the gospel in that city?
2. A significant part of Paul's third journey was to do a collection for the Jerusalem church. Why do you think Paul made such a collection?
3. What happened when Paul came to Jerusalem? And to Caesarea?
4. What happened when Paul came to Rome? Where did he go before his final imprisonment and death?

CHURCH GROWTH AND CHURCH STRUGGLES

ACT 1

CHURCH STRUGGLES
AND THE EXAMPLES FROM
1 CORINTHIANS

T he letters of the New Testament run parallel to the story line explained
in the previous episode. As such they tell the same story from a different
perspective, or rather, they add content to the issues that surfaced when the
Christian gospel was preached and churches were started throughout the Roman
Empire.

Two groups of letters are generally recognized in the New Testament, Paul's letters and the general letters. Ten of Paul's letters were written to churches and three
to pastors. They all deal with specific issues relating to the challenges confronting
each of the churches or pastors Paul addressed. In other words, Paul's comments
directly concern issues faced by individual local churches and are therefore somewhat specific to these particular local situations. However, it would be wrong to
conclude from this that issues faced by one church are unrelated to those faced by
another church. Broadly speaking, Paul's letters address situations, conflicts, and
challenges that may face all churches everywhere at any time. Although details
vary, all churches faced with the challenge of ministry, preaching, teaching, evangelism, numerical growth, personality conflicts, external hostility, etc., recognize
the value and relevance of Paul's letters for their own particular situation.

Paul himself recognized the commonality of most issues facing churches. He
encouraged churches to exchange his letters with other churches (Col. 4:16),[1] and

---

[1] "After this letter has been read to you, see that it is also read in the church of the Laodiceans and that you in turn read the letter from Laodicea." Cf. also 2 Peter 3:15, "As our dear brother Paul also wrote you with the wisdom that God gave him."

letters like the Ephesian letter probably represent letters specifically designed to circulate between churches. In fact, churches almost immediately began to exchange the letters they received from Paul and other apostles. Full collections of Paul's letters circulated quickly throughout the churches.[2]

The general epistles share the same universal appeal. Although they tend to be more general in their treatment of topics and issues, as the name indicates, the real reason for the name "general epistles" is that they are named by their authors rather than their recipients, for example, the letter of James or the first letter of Peter. As in Paul's letters, the specific issues of the time determine the content of the general letters. Yet all the letters of the New Testament have a personal, spiritual, social, cultural, philosophical, and organizational character that relate to issues faced by all churches in all times.

In this way, the letters tell the story of the highs and lows, the joys and sorrows, the successes and failures of the church. Without a direct story line, they tell the story of God's interaction with his people in a way that expands and deepens the understanding of the historical sketch given by Luke in the book of Acts.

Various Church Issues: Problems and Solutions

As God's story unfolded in the life of the early believers, solutions corresponding to God's purpose had to be found. Paul's first letter to the Corinthian church provides a good example of the kinds of problems faced by the early churches and the solutions given.

Factions in the Church

The Corinthian church suffered through problems arising from fast growth among people of different backgrounds (1 Cor. 3–4). As various itinerant preachers visited churches, some Christians began to claim special allegiance to certain preachers of their personal liking. Rather than focusing on their missionary task and their Christian growth, they focused on human leaders. This created confusion and factions in the church that stole its energy and made Christ's body dysfunctional.

Paul's theological response was to remind the church that they were God's temple and to destroy the temple of God was serious business that eventually would lead to God's destruction of them. Rather than allowing preference for a specific leader to create dissension, the church members should consider how God used each of these leaders for different purposes in the building of the church, God's temple. As the master builder, Paul had laid the foundation that subsequent leaders built upon. This foundation was Jesus Christ, and no one should attempt to alter it. The foundation was indisputably solid, but God would reveal the quality of the building raised on top of this foundation as either weak or strong. Each person

---

[2] Cf. Edgar J. Goodspeed, *An Introduction to the New Testament* (Chicago: University Press, 1937), 211. "Every Christian document shows acquaintance with Paul's letters—the Revelation, Hebrews, 1 Clement, 1 Peter, the letters of Ignatius and Polycarp, the Gospel of John. This is, in fact, the key to the later literature of the New Testament; it is all written in the presence of the collected Pauline letters."

building on the foundation should, therefore, be careful of what he was building. Paul's aim was to encourage the church to look at the strength of the church rather than at individual leaders and personalities. The quality of their work was revealed in the strength of what they built in the church.

IMMORALITY IN THE CHURCH

A constant problem in a large city of trade with a transient population like Corinth was promiscuous sexual behavior. An extraordinary example of this had occurred in the church, and their lack of ability to deal with it revealed a serious lack of maturity on the part of the believers (1 Cor. 5). They should have known that immoral behavior defiles the body and exemplifies the absence, rather than the presence, of Christ. Rather than being proud of their freedom in Christ, which they interpreted to mean total permissiveness, they should have judged the man who acted in this way and excluded him from the church. Since God had already judged his actions as evil, they should too. Immorality occurs outside Christ's body; the Christians were not to be judges of that, but within the body such evil should not be allowed. It is like yeast in dough, Paul argued; even a little of it will soon saturate the whole.

The confusion among the Christians in Corinth rose from their acceptance of the culturally common understanding of separation between spirit and matter. They had grown up learning from popular philosophers of the day that all matter, or material substance, was evil while spirit, or spiritual substance, was good. Applied to human beings, this meant the body was of no real significance and could be treated as one pleased. What mattered was the soul, or the spirit. As long as a person did not violate the soul, this person's standing before God remained unchanged. This common Greco-Roman thinking, dating back to Plato, ran contrary to biblical thinking. According to biblical revelation, God did not create human beings as divisible, or as consisting of separable parts. A person is one unity, and their body is not separable from other aspects of their lives. Consequently, how people treat their bodies matters to God. Paul called them to make sure they did not allow a different way of thinking to sneak into the church. Mature Christians should help younger Christians realize the danger in following worldly philosophy.

MARRIAGE AND FAITH, BELIEVERS AND UNBELIEVERS

Chapter 7 takes up the issue of marital relationships. Beginning with the sexual aspect of marriage, Paul affirmed that each partner in a marriage belongs to the other and therefore should consider his/her own body as belonging to the other. This helped the married Christian avoid the temptation of immorality, which God abhors, because it violated his intentions for human relationships. Married people should, therefore, care for each other's sexual needs while the unmarried and the widowed should marry if they cannot withstand the temptation to immorality. Paul stated his argument directly and based it on a clear theological principle.

The same held true as Paul presented a Christian theological solution to the nonsexual aspect of the marital relationship. Since the physical and the spiritual were intertwined in the fellowship that existed between a husband and a wife, it followed that both spouses must be Christians and filled with God's Spirit. Christians were to adhere to certain guidelines when seeking marriage. Believers should never marry nonbelievers since they could not have genuine spiritual fellowship. For, as Paul argued, there can be no fellowship between light and darkness, and no agreement between God's temple and idols (2 Cor. 6:14–16).

When an unbeliever who was already married became a believer, another theological principle came into play. In such a case the believer should remain with the unbeliever since the unbeliever was sanctified (made holy in the eyes of God) by the believer. It was not that the unbeliever was saved by association, but in such a mixed marriage the children benefited from the believing parent.[3] The children should, therefore, not be an excuse for divorce. In order to follow God's design for the marriage, Christians should not cause or seek the divorce but rather attempt to lead the non-Christian spouse to faith in Christ. Should, however, the non-Christian spouse desire the divorce, the Christian was free and would become like an unmarried person.[4]

STRONG AND WEAK CHRISTIANS

The eighth chapter in Paul's letter to the Corinthians moves the discussion to the question of how Christian freedom relates to discipleship. How were stronger and more mature Christians to relate to fellow Christians whose faith may be weaker and not as mature? Are believers free to do anything as long as they do not violate the teaching of the gospel? Paul takes up the particular and, for the Corinthians, pertinent issue of meat offered to idols. Were Christians free to eat that? The plain and unqualified answer was yes! Idols are not real, said Paul, and Jesus had clearly taught that "it is not what goes into the mouth that defiles a person, but it is what comes out of the mouth that defiles" (Matt. 15:11 NRSV).

However, the Corinthians faced a more complex issue. Meat offered to idols through pagan rituals was often sold and eaten at fellowships and ritual meals that were considered a part of the worship of a certain idol. This connection to pagan worship made the meat itself appear to have spiritual qualities granted by the idol. The problem arose not because believers were tempted to participate in the sacrificial meals and fellowships or because no other meat was available but because this meat often sold at a cheaper price in the marketplace. Stronger believers knew that

---

[3] Paul may at this point also be considering the social reality that in the Roman world the father usually retained custody of the children in the case of a divorce. If the father was the nonbeliever, this would leave the children without Christian influence.

[4] The issue of whether Paul's remarks mean that a believer is allowed to remarry is contended among scholars. Paul's use of the term "not bound" does seem to give reference to Jewish divorce documents which told the woman that she was free to remarry any man. However, 1 Corinthians 7 never touches the issue of a second marriage for a believer. Paul simply argues that if a nonbeliever desires a divorce, the believer is free to accept it for the sake of peace (1 Cor. 7:15). Paul does not state it is wrong to remarry under this circumstance; he simply does not speak to the issue.

meat remained unchanged by rituals, and they did not become unclean by buying and eating it. They knew they could eat the meat without getting involved in the worship of the idol. Weaker believers, however, were confused by the actions of these believers. They thought that since these other believers ate the meat, they probably also participated in the worship. In other words, they concluded that since some believers ate the meat offered to idols, it might be possible to serve Christ without giving up their old pagan, non-Christian, lifestyle. It did not have to be an either/or.

This was, of course, a wrong conclusion. Paul's theological solution to this was to remind everyone that it was the responsibility of the stronger to take care of the weaker. If an action of the stronger Christian, even when it was in line with Christian teaching, could lead a weaker Christian astray, it should be avoided. No one possessed the privilege of exercising their rights if it meant that the faith of other believers was shaken and discouraged rather than strengthened and encouraged. Believers were instead to abstain to make sure no one misunderstood and fell away from the faith.

WORSHIP AND WOMEN

After Paul in chapter 10 had warned the Corinthians about getting involved in pagan worship, he turned to address the issue of abuse of freedom in Christian worship services. The issue in chapter 11 is tightly woven to specific cultural expectations of place and time and can be difficult for modern readers to understand. The issue concerned proper head coverings for Christian worship.

Because believers came from various social levels and backgrounds and fellowshipped in the same church, social and cultural issues repeatedly came to the fore. In the ancient world a woman's hair served as an object of lust for men, and decent women therefore covered their hair, if not their heads. Failing to cover one's hair provoked lust and signaled a lifestyle highly inappropriate for Christians. While poorer women lived with this reality, upper-class women, who could afford elaborate hairstyles, refused to cover their hair as they took pride in parading their fashion.

Paul's direct theological response followed the line of thinking outlined above in the discussion of strong and weak Christians. The specific arguments obviously differed, but the undergirding theological principle remained the same. Since failing to cover one's hair could easily bring confusion and misunderstanding, leading some to conclude that it signaled adherence to a lifestyle unacceptable to followers of Jesus, Paul advised that all women should wear a hair covering when they spoke in church.

To strengthen his argument, Paul even suggested that the hair itself was a kind of head covering. Using the ancient debate method called *reductio ad absurdum* (reduction into the absurd), Paul argued that if a woman refused to cover her hair she might as well remove the natural head covering as well, the hair itself, by shaving it off. That, of course, would be absurd, unthinkable, and even disgrace-ful for any woman at that time. Paul's argument was made; the Christian churches should not allow women to speak in church without a head covering (11:13–16). To do so would send the wrong message.

SPIRITUAL GIFTS AND PERSONAL PROMINENCE IN THE CHURCH

Chapter 12 deals with the problems associated with spiritual gifting. When God's Spirit gifted the believers for ministry, these gifts differed in character and kind in order to equip the church to minister in a variety of ways and at a plurality of levels. Since the reception of a spiritual gift was unrelated to spiritual maturity, sinful human nature often took pride in these gifts. Some gifts gave the recipi-ent more public exposure than others—gifts of prophecy, speaking, and healing. Other gifts, like the gift of speaking in tongues, seemed to yield stronger evidence of the possession of spiritual power than, for example, the gift of helps. For this reason, believers who received gifts that seemed more spiritual or supernatural began to claim spiritual superiority over believers whose gifting seemed more natural or normal.

Again Paul responded theologically, showing that God's concern related to the whole community as the body of Christ. A gift was given to an individual for the common good of the church (12:7). No individual glory should be gained from any gift; God was not playing favorites. The believers should not think of them-selves as individual believers as much as members of a body. In a human body the eye cannot say to the ear that it is not needed. Nor can a foot tell a hand that it is more important. All parts work together. The church works the same way, Paul ar-gued. Every believer is baptized into one body by the same *one* Spirit. And God's Spirit simply distributes his gifts as he chooses (12:11).

DOCTRINAL TEACHING ON THE RESURRECTION OF CHRIST AND OF THE BELIEVER

Doctrinal issues surfaced as well, and Paul hit on these throughout his letters—sometimes at length and sometimes briefly. Chapter 15 gives a long discussion on the doctrine of the resurrection. In Paul's thinking, the resurrection provides the basis for all Christian teaching about any subject. Indeed, without it everything else falls. Therefore, at the end of his first letter to the Corinthians, Paul sum-marized the topics he covered throughout the letter with a lengthy exposition on the doctrine of the resurrection. Apparently, some in Corinth had claimed that the resurrection was less than essential to the Christian faith, and they suggested that not even Christ had risen from the dead (15:12).

To explain what happens when Christians are raised, Paul used an illustration they could understand. He compared the burial of the body and its resurrection to the planting of a seed (15:35–44). When a seed is put into the ground, it dies, Paul explained, and when it has died, a new plant comes up. The new plant is not the same as the seed that was sown. It is not the same seed that comes back up again. The two are not unrelated, of course, but they are not the same. There are different kinds of seeds, and these different kinds of seeds produce different kinds of plants.

So it is with the resurrection body, Paul taught. What you bury is mortal, weak, and perishable. What comes up at the resurrection is immortal, powerful, and imperishable. What dies is physical; what is raised is spiritual. Death will, in other words, not have the final say. As new life springs from the seed when it dies in the form of a new plant, new life will be granted to mortal bodies at the time of resurrection. God's eternal kingdom will not be inherited by flesh and blood, which is perishable and mortal, but by those who are to be raised imperishable and immortal. Those who claimed, therefore, that resurrection of the dead did not occur had not understood God's promise that the physical, perishable, and mortal would be swallowed up by death. To reject the resurrection was to give death the final victory. As it was, however, the reality of Christ's resurrection proved that death had lost its victory. Believers should not be confused. Their eternal inheritance was secure; they would be raised to eternal life and given spiritual and immortal bodies.

STUDY QUESTIONS

1. Paul wrote to specific churches dealing with the specific issues they faced. In what way do Paul's letters address issues in modern churches?
2. What is Paul's theological argument when he talks about overcoming factions in the church?
3. How did the Platonic view of body and soul differ from the biblical view of body and soul?
4. What is Paul's basic argument when he speaks about "strong" and "weak" Christians?

ACT 2

CHURCH STRUGGLES AND CHRISTIAN THINKING

SOCIAL AND CULTURAL ISSUES

As Paul started (and dealt with) churches in areas that ranged from small country towns in Asia Minor to large thriving cities in Europe, social issues of almost every kind came to the fore. Moreover, local groups of Christian believers included within themselves people who traditionally would have been socially estranged from one another. As the gospel was overcoming cultural barriers of all kinds, preconversion attitudes began to raise their heads among the new believers. The churches were gatherings of people from extremely diverse backgrounds. When people, who under normal circumstances would never even talk to one another, suddenly found themselves seated around the same table, or praying for one another in the same group, social and cultural issues automatically became a part of the church's conversation.

The New Testament letters deal with many of these social and cultural issues. Paul's solutions usually followed a theological method based on an imperative/indicative structure. What this means is that Paul reminded his readers of who God is, or what God had done (the indicative, or the reality), and then concluded from that what the believers therefore should do as a consequence (the imperative, or the command). In other words, Paul's argumentation follows a "since God has done this, you must do this" pattern. Ephesians offers an example of this when Paul argued that God has torn down the wall that divides; therefore, do not have any division among you (Eph. 2:14f).

One of the clear lines of social division in the Roman Empire was the division between slaves and slave owners. Although slaves sometimes held rather prominent positions in a household, and consequently in the society, they remained the property of their owners. Rather clear guidelines governed this relationship and determined the etiquette, or the protocol, for their behavior toward each other. Now when a slave and his owner both became believers, and therefore Christian brothers, a multitude of questions arose. Did the social distinction remain? Since they were now brothers, was the owner supposed to set the slave free? If the slave was the more mature Christian of the two, how would that affect his relationship to his owner? If Christ had truly made them one, should the slave still take orders from his owner?

One letter from Paul dealt with this issue almost exclusively—the letter to Philemon. Philemon was a Christian slave owner, led to faith by Paul, whose slave, Onesimus, ran away. A runaway slave could be punished any way the owner saw fit. Onesimus visited Paul in prison, and Paul led him to faith in Christ. After discipling Onesimus, and benefiting from his help, Paul sent the runaway slave back to Philemon with a letter. In this letter Paul reminded Philemon how he obtained eternal life through his conversion and how Onesimus now, through his own conversion had received the same gift of eternal life. So, as Paul explained to Philemon, although you may have lost him for a short while, you have now gained him back for eternity (v. 15). Therefore, rather than punishing Onesimus for running away, you should receive him back with joy and treat him, not as a slave but as a brother (v. 16). Better still, Paul asked Philemon to receive Onesimus as a special brother, one who is Paul's partner (v. 17).

The teaching of Paul's letter on this matter went far beyond the teaching of various thinkers and philosophers of the day. While contemporary conventions of letter writing and etiquette prevented Paul from asking Philemon to free Onesimus as a slave, this was probably what he meant when he said to Philemon, "I am writing to you, knowing that you will do even more than I say" (v. 21 NRSV). In a sense his argument ran like this. You owe your life to Jesus Christ who has graced you with eternal life. This same Jesus who called you has also called Onesimus and given him eternal life. Paul's argument is clear. Because of what God has done for you, Philemon, you owe it to God to treat Onesimus like a brother and make him a free man.

Onesimus, on the other hand, should not forget his responsibilities as a brother either. When Paul taught about the responses of slaves to their new situation as believers, he told them to remain in the condition or status they were in when they became believers (1 Cor. 7:21–24). It was significant that they evidenced God's presence and remained useful for God's kingdom regardless of their situation. They could be useful for God whether slaves or free. Slaves called by Christ are "free in the Lord," and free people called by Christ are "slaves of Christ" (see 1 Cor. 7:22).

PERSONAL ISSUES

Beyond issues relating to the congregational life of the church, and questions arising from cultural and social structures, difficulties of a more personal character abounded as well. Many of the problems facing the early churches resulted from personality conflicts. It goes beyond the purpose of this book to deal with each of these individually, but Paul references them throughout his writings.

Personality conflicts were found on all levels. Paul confronted immature Christians who, because of their eloquence, considered themselves wiser than Paul and able to "outperform" him spiritually (1 Cor. 2:1–6, 12–16). Individuals groping for power attempted to divide the church, and the response the church gave these often evidenced that most members were infant Christians rather than spiritually mature (1 Cor. 3:1–3). Other preachers who opposed Paul seemed to trace his itinerary to undermine his preaching. After Paul left a new church he had just started, or one he had revisited, these opponents showed up trying to undo everything he had taught and done (Gal. 1:6f). Beyond these kinds of personal attacks on Paul, individual church members, even in his favorite church in Philippi, fought among one another (Phil. 2:3–5). The many personality conflicts burdened Paul. In a summary statement on his sufferings for Christ, he listed false brothers and sisters along with his anxiety for the churches in the same breath as he mentioned beatings, shipwrecks, and hunger (2 Cor. 11:25–28). The story of conflict and strife between Christian believers who placed themselves before the gospel of Christ unfortunately became a part of the story of God's work among his churches.

PHILOSOPHICAL AND RELIGIOUS ISSUES

Many of the New Testament letters deal with false teaching. When it came to the question of a religious smorgasbord, the ancient world did not differ much from the modern. Then, like today, people were bombarded by disparate philosophies including religious ideologies and worldviews. Pluralism in its religious and philosophical expression ruled the day.[5] The Christian faith was merely one of the dishes on the table. This made many people spiritually open (as it does today), but it also made it easy for many people, even people who had become Christian believers, to get confused and entangled with several religions at the same time.

Beyond the obvious problem of "truth," one of the results of such a piecing together of various teachings is that the story, the so-called meta-narrative, disappears. There is no longer any overarching cohesive story that holds it all together.

---

[5] There is a difference between social pluralism (plurality of races, social customs, and cultures), and philosophical and religious pluralism, which promotes the idea that every person creates his or her own truth by piecing together tidbits from a plurality of philosophies and religions. Social pluralism represents a positive reality which, to avoid confusion, probably is better labeled as social diversity. Although many individual churches opposed such diversity during certain times in history, the character of historic Christianity has made the church the greatest promoter of social diversity. The first church, from its earliest beginnings, bore strong testimony to God's power to reconcile disparate social and ethnic groups. Philosophical and religious pluralism, on the other hand, is a negative ideology that rejects the notion of ultimate truth and the biblical claim that there is but one God—the one who has made himself known through Christ alone.

Each event becomes utterly unique with no real relationship to other events. The Christian story, God's story, the story being told in the Bible (and explained in this book) aims to give structure to all of life and its decisions. For a Christian who faces a new situation, or a dilemma, there should be no confusion. The grand narrative of the Bible should give guidance to all of life's decisions. Beyond specific teachings on specific topics, God's grand story gives direction where specific words of direction seem absent. This is called a "worldview." The biblical story is the story of how God views the world. Those who align their thinking with the perspective of this grand narrative will have a biblical worldview—a worldview that is often different from commonly accepted worldview(s) generated by popular culture.[6]

In a real sense, knowing God's story will create a moral grid in the human mind that will ultimately guide all decisions. Throwing that story out will do nothing but make room for another story—another story where personal benefit and pleasure is confused with goodness, where selfishness is confused with love, and where local answers are confused with universal truth.

THE COLOSSIAN HERESY

Paul dealt with issues of pluralism in his letter to the Colossians. Some people from Colossae wanted to combine their own personal philosophies, or the dominant spirituality of their culture, with the Christian message. To this Paul replied that Christ is sufficient and no additives are needed.

A look at certain characteristics of the methods used by these opponents may prove helpful in understanding the issues:

1. Eloquence can make any argument believable. The use of well-formulated arguments, using culturally accepted norms or ideas as a point of reference, can make even false statements seem plausible (2:4). Even philosophical ideas contrary to the Christian faith can become persuasive (2:8). True or false, eloquent people can muster an argument for anything. Paul told the Colossian church not to be intrigued by the attractiveness of sheer eloquence.

2. Claiming to have special knowledge and access to unusual insight obtained through private visions attracts listeners. Paul reminded his readers that God gave his full revelation for everyone to know and check out. No one possesses special privilege and access to knowledge that goes beyond what God has revealed through Christ and Scripture. Claims of special visions, or direct revelations from God that cannot be known by all believers, are therefore false (2:18). Those who claim such

---

[6] One modern example of this suffices as an illustration. Most business-savvy literature will teach that priority always should be given to people and situations that will give a person the greatest chance for personal promotion. Personal success seems to demand good time management, and good time management means to prioritize spending time with people who can help one's career. Put succinctly, this is the worldview promoted by a survival-of-the-fittest philosophy. The biblical story stands in contrast to this. The Bible presents a story about how God calls his people to consider those who have nothing to give and who can help no one's career. It is a story about trusting God against all odds and giving time to the least of his. It may even be called a philosophy for the survival of the weakest. The strongest emphasis seems to be on grace, mercy, and love.

may appear to have wisdom, but they are nothing more than self-promoters claiming a self-imposed piety (2:23).

3. Claims of special knowledge and unusual insight usually come attached to declarations of extraordinary mystical experiences. The intrigue of apparently a special access to the divine, and a special experience of extraordinary spiritual character, easily leads people who are hungry for a stronger and more direct experience of God astray. To counter such claims, Paul reminded the Colossians that all Spirit-filled Christians have equal access to God. God does not mediate exclusive knowledge to some believers by angels or visions that is unattainable for other believers (2:18).

4. Often those who puff themselves up as people with divine insight going beyond what God has revealed through Christ and his word will lay new burdens, including strict rules and regulations, upon their followers. It may sound and look different from being placed back under old covenant legalism, but it is not. Keeping rules imposed by men does not set people free to serve Christ; it makes them slaves of those who established the rules (2:16–17, 21–23).

Paul was keenly aware of the temptation believers faced with this. Desiring to know God better, and longing for stronger experiences of his presence, predators and pocket philosophers often found easy targets among well-meaning Christians. The antidote against such was to heed Paul's constant warning that Christ was sufficient, and all that God wanted to reveal was revealed in him. No additives were needed.

1 John and Gnosticism

John, writing to a group of churches, dealt with a new teaching that was just beginning to creep into Christian assemblies. Some, who earlier associated with Christian churches, now subscribed to a heresy that in its full-blown form would be called Gnosticism. Gnosticism took different forms, but common to all was the teaching that reality consisted of two entities, spirit and matter. Spirit was good; matter was evil. Applied to Christ, this teaching rejected both the incarnation and the suffering of the cross.

The Gnostics allowed no connection between spirit and matter; since Christ was good, he had to be pure spirit with no true relationship to matter. As a pure spirit, Christ came to earth and took a dwelling in the body of a person called Jesus from Nazareth. It was not that Christ became man, or that Jesus was God, but that Christ simply used Jesus' body as a shell. In other words, God did not send his Son to become a part of this world as fully man. Nor did he take part in its suffering since the Christ Spirit could have no connection with matter. Christ did not die on the cross for the sins of mankind since, according to Gnosticism, spirit cannot die. The only thing dying on the cross was the body of the man Jesus who was different from Christ.

For Gnostics, Christ's spirit came to earth to give human beings knowledge, or *gnosis,* the Greek word from which the label *Gnosticism* derived. Salvation, therefore, became a matter of special knowledge, not of redemption from sin. Put succinctly, salvation was the escape from the body through special knowledge.

Gnosticism presented a danger to the Christian movement because of its immediate appeal. Gnostic evangelists used much of the Christian language, and by making appeal to well-known and accepted Platonic ideas in the Greco-Roman society, they presented a message that allowed Christians to remain in their preconversion convictions and lifestyles while gaining the special knowledge needed for eternal salvation. Being a Christian meant that Christ, by the special knowledge he imparted through Gnostic teachers, set people free from the bondage of the body.

Beyond negating Christ's atoning sacrifice, this separation of matter and spirit, body and soul, led to the distortion of Christian morals. Since matter exercised no influence on spirit, Christians were free to use their bodies as they pleased. Contrary to the teaching of Scripture, ethical living was of no consequence for salvation. The body could be used or misused in any possible way. Some became licentious, surrendering to sexual immorality, etc., while others became ascetics, depriving the body of even basic needs like food and water.

This naturally led to asocial behavior as well. There was no need to show love toward fellow believers or anyone else. Those possessing saving *gnosis* could be proud and feel superior. They were an exclusive group who had no need to show love toward others. Opposite the clear teaching of Scripture, that genuine knowledge of God and genuine love for God express themselves in obedience, the Gnostics claimed to have fellowship with God through their knowledge.

John answered all this by repeatedly emphasizing the character of genuine Christian faith. In terms of *doctrine,* to be Christian a person must believe that Jesus is the Christ (2:22) and that Christ came in the flesh (4:2–3). Unless Christ himself became flesh, he could not atone for the sins of humankind. In terms of *ethics* and *morality,* to be a Christian a person must see a clear connection between obedience and faith. The only way people can be certain they know God, John said, is if they obey his commandment (2:3–6; 5:3). If someone does not obey and still claims to have fellowship with God, he is a liar (1:6–10). The Christian faith, therefore, also has a *social* dimension. No one can be a Christian believer without love. Love for other people is the manifestation of genuine faith (3:24; 4:7–21). Those who hate, or those who do not care about their fellowman, bear evidence that they are not believers, regardless of their words (2:9, 11).

STUDY QUESTIONS

1. What does "indicative/imperative structure" mean in connection with Paul's letters?
2. What was Paul's argument in his letter to Philemon when he sent Onesimus back?

3. How would you explain the word *worldview*? How would you illustrate how the biblical worldview differs from another worldview?

4. What do you see as the biggest problem with Gnostic-type expressions of Christianity? Do you see any such expressions today?

ACT 3

CHURCH STRUGGLES AND ISSUES OF FAITH

THE BOOK OF HEBREWS AND THE OLD COVENANT

Philosophical and religious attacks on the Christian faith came not only from Gentile sources but from Jewish sources as well. As the distinction between first-century Judaism and Christian believers became more and more evident, Jewish congregations increased the pressure on those converting to the Christian faith. Jewish converts to the new covenant faith of the Christians were excluded from their families and fired from their jobs in the Jewish communities. As a rule, Christians no longer met with Jews in their synagogues, and the mounting intellectual attacks from Jewish groups forced Christian believers to deepen their understanding of the difference between the covenant of Law and the covenant of grace.

Jewish converts to Christianity found themselves more and more isolated, and the pressure to recant their confession of Christ and return to the synagogues grew exponentially. As Jews living in a Gentile world, many of them had felt like outsiders in the larger society all their lives. They had grown accustomed to being scorned, blamed, and asked to leave certain areas of the Roman Empire. In those situations, however, they had found solace within their families and the Jewish community in general. Now, as Christians, this "safety net" had been taken away. Still scorned by the Gentiles who continued to consider them Jewish, they now faced a Jewish community that considered them worse than Gentiles. Their only support came from the small and often struggling group of Christian friends who met in a home or small apartment.

The author of Hebrews wrote into this kind of situation. Hebrews is as much a sermon as a letter. It is a document meant to be read in struggling Christian congregations where Jewish converts needed to be encouraged in their commitment, strengthened in their argument, and guided in their decisions. The point made by the writer of Hebrews was that the new covenant of grace was superior to the old covenant of the Law. It encouraged believers not to revert to Judaism and not to be confused by old covenant arguments.

Attractive as turning back to Judaism may seem on both the personal and the religious level, the Christian faith is superior in every way, Hebrews argued. Christian faith was not something new but rather the appearance of the reality God had intended from the beginning. The experience of the Christians was nothing less than the fulfilled promise of the old covenant prophets.

On this basis the author of Hebrews argued for the superiority of the covenant of grace over the covenant of the Law in every area.

1. Jesus is clearly superior to the angels since God never called any of the angels his Son (1:4–5). In fact, the angels exist as servants of Christian believers (1:14).
2. Jesus is superior to Moses. Moses was faithful as a servant *in* the house of God whereas Jesus as God's Son was faithful *over* the house of God (3:3–6).
3. Jesus guaranteed a superior covenant. If perfection was attainable under the Levitical priesthood of the old covenant, arising from the order of Aaron, there would have been no need for the promise of a new priest arising from the order of Melchizedek.[7] Jesus was that promised priest since he had not become a priest through the legal requirements of physical descent as the Levitical priests had (7:11–22). Furthermore, whereas other priests were prevented from continuing their service by their own death, Jesus' priesthood would be eternal (7:23–25).
4. As a high priest, Jesus exercised a superior ministry; and since the sacrifice he brought was faultless, he had become a superior mediator of a superior covenant. If the first covenant had been equally faultless, there would have been no need for a second covenant (8:6–7).[8]
5. Throughout the Old Testament, giants of faith had experienced suffering and remained faithful. For that they had been commended, but they had not received what was promised. God had now provided something superior for new covenant believers whose suffering is rewarded by their reception of God's promise (11:39–40). The direct access to God, longed for by old covenant saints, was now made available to new covenant believers.

---

[7] Cf. Psalm 110:4, "The LORD has sworn and will not change his mind, 'You are a priest forever according to the order of Melchizedek'" (NRSV).

[8] The reference to the second covenant points back to Jeremiah's promise in 31:31–34.

Since the new covenant was superior in every way, Christians should have no attraction to the old covenant. The old led to bondage under Law, while the new led to freedom under Christ! On this note, the message of Hebrews still speaks to the pitfalls of a Christian faith that sounds and feels more like a covenant of law than a covenant of grace. Even today some Christian believers desire to spell out the specifics of what they consider a "Christian lifestyle" to such an extent that they reduce the Christian faith to a list of do's and don'ts. Hebrews speaks with strong force against the attraction of going back into old covenant faith.

Spiritual Issues—Faith and Works

The question of the relationship between faith and works stood at the forefront of the discussion and tension within the early church. It related almost directly to the issues dividing Judaism and Christianity. The Law clearly required certain works or deeds from God's people, but how did this relate to the Christian understanding of grace? If the sacrificial system had been nullified by Christ's death on the cross, what influence did that have on the greater question of obedience to God's Law?

Doctrinal issues about Christ aside, a Christian believer's works of faith were by some early Christians confused with Judaism's works of the Law. This confusion was solved at the doctrinal level during the apostolic meeting described in Acts 15, but it continued to cause division between the Christians. The contention was kept alive by so-called Judaizers,[9] who traveled as itinerant preachers proclaiming adherence to Mosaic Law as a part of the Christian message and by Gentile preachers influenced by the Platonic notion of separation between spirit and matter. Pressure and counterpressure forged the debate. Arguments grew sharper or more polemic, and new formulations fostered misunderstandings with which the postapostolic church continued to struggle.

Although modern scholars continue to debate the issue, with some claiming that James and Matthew wrote against Paul while Luke tried to bridge the divide, it seems rather evident from the New Testament that Paul and James came to an agreement on the matter (see Acts 15). The seeming discrepancy between Paul's underscoring of God's grace as the avenue for salvation and James' emphasis on obedience and works as the evidence of faith does not lead to the conclusion that the New Testament teaches two different doctrines of salvation. It does not even mean that Paul and James differed in their understanding of spirituality and the Christian faith. They simply wrote to two different audiences emphasizing two different aspects of salvation.

Understanding James's reference to works of faith as something different from works of Law makes the claim that James was a Judaizer who focused on undermining Paul's message of salvation by grace alone unwarranted. Actually James's

---

[9] Many of these Judaizers had ties to Pharisees who had become convinced that Jesus was the promised Messiah but who also understood Christ's work as a mere extension of the Mosaic covenant.

language corresponds well to the language Paul used to frame his introductory letter to the Romans. Paul both opened and concluded that letter by the phrase "obedience of faith." Opening the letter, he explained his own mission as one to "bring about the obedience of faith among all the Gentiles" (1:5 NRSV). Concluding the letter, he reminded the Romans that the eternal God, through the Old Testament prophetic literature, had commanded that his revelation be brought to the Gentiles "to bring about the obedience of faith" (16:26). Neither James nor Paul imagined a separation of faith and works. That developed much later in the history of the church.

The apparent conflict between James and Paul came from their different use of the same Old Testament text. Referring to the same event in Abraham's life, namely the sacrificing of his son Isaac (Gen. 22), James concluded that Abraham, since he brought Isaac to the altar, not only believed God but acted on that faith. His action evidenced his faith and made him righteous (Gen. 15:6). Therefore, James concluded, "A person is justified by works and not by faith alone" (James 2:24 NRSV). Paul concluded what seemed to be the exact opposite. Since the Law did not come until four hundred years later, the covenant given to Abraham had to be a covenant of faith. Abraham was not saved by keeping the Law but by his faith in God. Therefore, Paul concluded, "We know that a person is justified not by the works of the law but through faith in Jesus Christ. And we have come to believe in Christ Jesus, so that we might be justified by faith in Christ, and not by doing the works of the law, because no one will be justified by the works of the law" (Gal. 2:16 NRSV).

Notice James does not suggest justification by law, nor does Paul speak of faith without works. As with everything else, context determines meaning! Paul spoke to a situation in which the new believers in Galatia were being told by Judaizers that without being circumcised according to the Law of Moses, their faith in Christ was in vain. To combat this, Paul argued that the only requirement for salvation was faith in Christ.

James dealt with a different situation. He addressed a group who had decided that works of faith and works of the law were the same thing. Since they were saved by grace and not by law, faith did not need to prove itself in the life of a believer. Mental assent was sufficient. This, James argued, is false. Genuine faith will always express itself in real and visible actions of obedience. If there are no works of faith, there likely will be no faith. Paul would agree! Put succinctly, Paul spoke to the preconversion experience about prerequisites for salvation; James spoke to the postconversion experience about evidence for the genuineness of faith.

ORGANIZATIONAL AND LEADERSHIP ISSUES

Starting new churches and helping them stay focused on their purpose as effective agents for God's kingdom necessitated an organizational structure that aided such a goal. In spite of inner strife and external persecution, the Christian churches continued to expand and strong leadership was mandated to avoid chaos. Several of Paul's letters dealt with structural issues,[10] but his last letters, the Pastoral Letters, along with the fourth chapter of his letter to the Ephesians, paid special attention to the issue of church leadership.

Paul's first and most obvious teaching on this matter stated that God builds his church on the basis of spiritual endowment, not on human strength and social prominence. The reference to leadership and structure in Ephesians 4:11–13 reads like this: "[God] gave some to be apostles, some to be prophets, some to be evangelists, and some to be pastors and teachers, to prepare God's people for works of service, so that the body of Christ may be built up until we all reach unity in the faith and in the knowledge of the Son of God and become mature, attaining to the whole measure of the fullness of Christ."

According to this, a person's position in the leadership structure of the church depended on his or her particular spiritual gifting. Since God did not consider a person's position, the point of gifting was never prominence but usefulness. All leadership positions were equally significant, and the individuals filling them were only there to make use of the specific gift of grace they had received from God.

The function of leadership became clear in Paul's description of purpose. Leaders—whether apostles, prophets, evangelists, pastors, teachers, or anything else—should not consider their position a reward from God but a tool for the church. God had empowered them for the purpose of preparing the church for ministry. They were to guide and encourage the church to grow into a mature Christian faith which would enable its members to find unity of faith through a deepening knowledge of Christ. The goal for the church was to attain the whole measure of the fullness of Christ. Put differently, the task of a leader in a Christian church was to lead the individual church member to become like Christ—or more precisely, the church as a whole to become Christ's body. Empowered by Christ's Spirit and led by people especially gifted by this Spirit, the church was to grow into a portrayal of Christ himself.

Such lofty goals naturally limited the number of candidates for leadership positions. Human nature, being what it is, could easily stand in the way of someone's gifting and thus remove them as candidates for leadership in God's church. When Paul, therefore, listed the qualities needed for leadership, he focused almost exclusively on moral qualities that expressed spiritual maturity.

It is more than interesting that Paul's lists of leadership qualifications, given primarily in his first letter to Timothy chapter 3 (cf. Titus 2), contain no reference to special spiritual gifting—no word about gifting to heal, intercede, prophesy, speak in tongues, etc.[11] It is as if Paul thought that the necessity of specific gifting for a particular leadership position was too obvious even to mention. That someone needed to be gifted went without saying, but gifting alone was insufficient for a Christian leadership position. Not all who had the right gifts were qualified

---

[10] Cf. Romans 8 and 1 Corinthians 12.
[11] The exception may be the phrase "able to teach" (1 Tim. 3:2).

to lead. To be able to lead the church to become Christ's body on earth, a leader needed to exemplify a maturity worthy of imitation. A Christian leader, therefore, could not be a new convert (3:6) since a new convert could not possibly have matured sufficiently in Christ to lead his church. Consequently, such a person would likely misunderstand his position as a Christian leader and consider it a privilege of prominence rather than a task of purpose.

The qualifications for church leadership that spell out necessary spiritual maturity fall into three categories:

Moral Qualifications (1 Tim. 3:1–7; Titus 1:5–9)
√   Above reproach (3:2; 1:6)
√   Temperate—must be self-controlled (3:2; 1:8)
√   Sensible (3:2; 1:8)
√   Dignified—has to do with appearance (3:3)
√   Not given to drinking (3:3; 1:7)
√   Not violent, but gentle—engaged in spiritual warfare, not physical violence (3:3; 1:7)
√   Not quarrelsome (3:3; 1:7)
√   Not a lover of money (3:3; 1:7)
√   Not arrogant/overbearing/self-willed (1:7)
√   Lover of goodness

Home-Life Qualifications (1 Tim. 3:1–7; Titus 1:5–9)
√   Husband of one wife (3:1; 1:6)[12]
√   Hospitable (3:2; 1:8)
√   Manage own household well (3:4; 1:6)

Spiritual Qualifications (1 Tim. 3:1–7; Titus 1:5–9)
√   A good teacher (3:2)
√   Not a new convert (3:6)
√   Good reputation among "outsiders" (3:7)
√   Just/upright (1:8; cf. 1 Thess. 2:10)
√   Devout/holy (1:8; cf. 1 Thess. 2:10)
√   Have a firm grasp of the Word (1:9)
√   Be able to encourage and refute others (1:9)

CULTURAL ISSUES

Jesus was not a Baptist, a Methodist, or any other type of Christian from the United States or Western Europe. Being a Christian is a transcultural experience.

---

[12] This is a difficult phrase to unwrap. It could mean one of several things: (1) It could mean that leaders should be male, yet the New Testament gives a number of examples of female leadership. (2) It could mean that leaders should be married, yet the New Testament offers a number of examples of unmarried leaders—Paul likely was one of them (see discussion above). (3) It could mean that leaders should be nonpolygamists and nonadulterers; they were to be faithful spouses whose lifestyles reflected God's singular faithfulness toward his people.

It transforms the lifestyle of believers who then in turn may influence the culture they live in. Christianity does not belong to a specific culture. Christianity lives and breathes from the presence of God's Spirit and may express itself in many different ways.

The problem with the Judaizers was that they wanted everyone to become Jews before they could become Christians. The story of the New Testament militates against such an understanding. When issues surfaced in the churches, convictions were evaluated in light of God's Word, not in light of cultural norms. The Christian churches of the New Testament strove to have unity in Christ while, at the same time, resisting uniformity of culture. As is well-known, not many churches were, or became, like the church in Jerusalem.

STUDY QUESTIONS

1. Hebrews deals with the danger of falling back into the old covenant of law. How can that question be applied to issues facing today's churches?
2. How do you understand the difference between Paul's emphasis on grace and James' emphasis on works?
3. What is the purpose of spiritual gifts?
4. How would you explain the connection between spiritual gifts and spiritual maturity? How does this relate to Christian leaders?

THE STORY OF THE BIBLE

Creation	The story begins with God creating the world and human beings.
Crisis	Humans choose to rebel (or sin) against God. Sin brings consequences: pain, suffering, death, and separation from God. All people and all creation are affected.
Covenant	God chooses Abraham and establishes a covenant with him so that he might become the leader of a group of people who will follow God and call other people to follow God. God delights in using his people to bring the rest of the world to himself.
Calling Out	Genesis tells the story of the patriarchs: Abraham, Isaac, Jacob (Israel), and Joseph, who ends up in Egypt. In Egypt the small group of Hebrews grows into a nation and ends up in slavery. God uses Moses to deliver his people through the exodus event.
Conquest	God uses Joshua to help his people take the promised land (Canaan). After the conquest during the Period of Judges,

	God rules through judges in various parts of the land. This is a dark time for the Hebrews accentuated with sin, idolatry, and oppression.
Kingdom	God's people acquire a king. Samuel is the link between the judges and the kings. Saul is the first king, followed by David and his son Solomon. God establishes a covenant with David, promising the Messiah will come through his family line and reign forever.
Kingdom Divided	After Solomon civil war breaks out leading to a division of the kingdom: Israel, the Northern Kingdom; Judah, the Southern Kingdom. There are numerous kings, some good but most bad.
Captivity	Israel (Northern Kingdom) is judged for the sin of breaking the covenant when Assyria conquers it in 722 BC, and Judah receives a similar judgment later when Babylon conquers it in 586 BC and takes Judah's people into exile.
Coming Home	The people return from Babylonian exile under Zerubbabel, Ezra, and Nehemiah. They rebuild the temple and focus on the law of God.
Christ	About four hundred years later God sends his Son, Jesus the Christ, to save his people from their sins, fulfilling the promise given to Abraham. Jesus is crucified, dies, is raised from the dead, and ascends into heaven to return again later.
Church	**Those who accept Jesus become part of the church, the people of God made up of both Jews and Gentiles. God continues to use his people to extend his offer of salvation to a sinful world.**
Consummation	God closes history with a final victory over evil. Those who have rejected God will suffer his judgment while those who have received him will live with him in a new heaven and a new earth.

EPISODE FOURTEEN

LOOKING FOR A CITY

ACT 1

GOD'S FUTURE FOR HIS PEOPLE

THE BOOK OF REVELATION

God's story does not end with the events of the early church. Rather, it is an ongoing story, a story with a final conclusion still to come. Old Testament prophets looked forward to a new era where God's reign would be restored on earth. Jesus proclaimed that God's kingdom had already come near although not in full. Paul announced that the day would come soon when every knee would bow and every tongue would confess that Jesus is the Lord, the Son of God. Although God's kingdom already proved its presence among people, a time would come when Christ would fill all in all (Col. 1:15). History and the human experience of reality were to be radically altered when God would reestablish his full rule and presence on earth. The story was to come full circle. The blissful situation of the garden of Eden before the fall would again become the experience of faithful believers.

The final book of the Bible, Revelation, or the Apocalypse, describes this Christian vision of God's future for his people. The book of Revelation was written to give encouragement to suffering Christians. It was a vision from God to John the apostle that described how those who were faithful to the call of the gospel would come to experience a new heavenly reality on earth. In this way Revelation was a prophetic book. Beyond calling for commitment in the present, it foretold what God had planned for the future.

The Book of Revelation, A Vision Written Down

1. Revelation was written to give hope.

In the nineties of the first century, during the reign of the Roman emperor Domitian, the apostle John was exiled to one of the rocky volcanic islands of the Aegean Sea called Patmos. As a punishment for preaching the Christian message in Ephesus, Roman officials placed John on this island located some fifty miles southwest of Ephesus en route between Ephesus and Rome. Roman governors often used banishment to semi-isolated islands as a form of punishment, and the small Aegean islands off the coast of Asia seem to have been preferred by the Romans. Banishment was an alternative to execution or enslavement. John's age may be the reason he received this type of punishment.

Worship that blurred the line between the divine and the human, which was a common feature in the ancient world, could still be found in some areas during the first century. Rome itself considered allegiance to the Imperial Cult a simple matter of courtesy or a symbol of loyalty. Greek and Asian regions of the empire, however, took a more serious approach to worship; and full temples were built for the emperors. Although a number of the emperors themselves considered this deification a mere sign of reverence, some of them expected to be worshipped as gods. One of these was Domitian. Paranoid and ruthless, Domitian demanded that everyone call him *kyrios* (lord) and that they consider him worthy of genuine worship. Although he was one of the most hated emperors, refusal to worship his image in places like Ephesus equaled an act of rebellion, or even treason, against the empire.

From historical sources, it does not appear that Domitian singled out Jews and Christians for special punishment, but their refusal to call him by the name that the Jews reserved for God, and which for Christians represented a confession of faith in Christ, made them natural victims of his wrath. Actually, since the time of Nero, the persecution of Christians had only escalated. Differentiating even further, the situation of the Asian Christians was considerably grimmer than that of the influential Jewish population. According to Josephus, the large Jewish population of Ephesus had long enjoyed special privileges.[1] One of these was an unofficial exemption from emperor worship, which had followed as a consequence of their allowance to celebrate their own religion.[2]

Wealthy Jews, who enjoyed these special privileges in Ephesus, were embarrassed by the insurgence a few years earlier in Palestine that had resulted in the Roman destruction of the temple. As a result, they sought to exclude themselves

---

[1] Josephus, *Ant* 14.226–27. "Alexander, the son of Theodorus, the ambassador of Hyrcanus, the son of Alexander the high priest and ethnarch of the Jews, appeared before me, to show that his countrymen could not go into their armies, because they are not allowed to bear arms, or to travel on the Sabbath days, nor there to procure themselves those sorts of food which they have been used to eat from the times of their forefathers—I do, therefore, grant them a freedom from going into the army, as the former prefects have done, and permit them to use the customs of their forefathers, in assembling together for sacred and religious purposes, as their law requires, and for collecting oblations necessary for sacrifices; and my will is, that you write this to the several cities under your jurisdiction."

[2] Cf. Josephus, *Ant* 14.262ff.

from any association with groups that could be considered insurgent. Synagogues all over Asia, therefore, expelled Jewish Christians (Rev. 2:9; 3:7–9), who consequently came to be thought of as vile and atheistic dissenters who opposed the unity of the empire.

Revelation is the story of how God had not forgotten these faithful believers, who suffered incredible maltreatment and horrifying punishment at the hand of the Romans. In the face of unceasing persecution and torture, Christians were beginning to ask for God's visible hand of victory. Their martyrdom was in its essence an oxymoron. According to God's promise those who were faithful and stood firm in their obedience to God's word would be blessed and have a long life on earth. However, those recanting their Christian faith had a long life on earth. Christians who were faithful to God became martyrs, and their lives were cut short; they were cut short exactly (and only) because they were faithful and obedient.

The purpose of Revelation was to proclaim that God would vindicate himself and give final victory to faithful believers. It may look bad now, the book of Revelation said, but things will change; those who overcome in the present will come to reign with Christ when he returns.

2. Revelation was written using apocalyptic language.

John wrote down his God-given vision using a style called apocalyptic language. Foreign to the modern reader, apocalyptic language makes heavy use of extreme symbolism. The story is told and truth is conveyed through the use of symbolic word pictures. To those who are on the inside, those who understand the written symbols, it all makes sense. To those who are unfamiliar with the situation described, and the symbols used to describe it, the meaning of the text remains difficult to penetrate.

One of the best modern analogies to this may be political cartoons. They likewise tell a story (using graphic symbols) that only makes sense to those who know what goes on. When it is current and everyone recognizes the symbols or images used to sketch the political commentary, it speaks powerfully to its readers. When, however, a political cartoon gets dated and those seeing it do not recognize the images used, it becomes difficult to understand.

A modern but dated political cartoon could read something like this if it was written rather than drawn:

> Behold, I saw a large bear sitting on the top of a hill with both claws reaching to strike an eagle descending from above. Below it, behind it, and all around it were smaller bears gazing upon the large bear as she was fighting the giant bird. The reach of her arms was like the rays of the moon, far and extended. Her claws were sharp like the blades of mighty swords. Her eyes, dark and gloomy, spewed fire and spelled doom upon everyone who was caught by her gaze. Above her I saw a giant eagle with wings that reached from the east to the west.

With a gleam from his eyes that was sharper than the noonday sun,
the white-headed bird dispelled all the darkness engulfing the bear.
Soaring outside the reach of the vicious claws, he moved the wind be-
neath his wings with a force that caused the smaller bears to stumble.
It was a fight that wrapped around the universe, and . . .

Now, for someone who does not understand the picture, the description above
is little more than a fight between two animals. To others, who also do not understand the picture but who desperately want to find symbolic value in the picture,
all kinds of scenarios can be made up. Interpretations can be given that speak to
the distinctions between birds and bears, others that talk about soaring as opposed
to reaching or about the white head of the bird as a opposed to the brown head of
the bear. Others again may want to give psychological interpretations of sorts. The
possibilities will be endless.

To those who understand the picture and the situation into which it was given,
however, it is rather straightforward. The eagle represents the USA and the bear,
the USSR. The eagle is the common symbol for America, and the bear is the common symbol for Russia. All the written picture says is that the USA and the USSR
are (were) involved in a conflict and that some of the smaller countries that used to
be led by Russia are (were) stumbling and falling away from Russia's domain.

For such a picture to make any sense, it has to be drawn at a certain time in a
certain situation. Other times and other situations would have required different
pictures. Not many young people today, for example, would understand the picture
just given; and, given the present political situation in the world, it would make
little sense even to draw such a picture.

Apocalyptic language works in a similar fashion. The language should not be
pressed in detail. As in the story above, the details only help to paint the picture. Every detail does not contain a hidden message. When, therefore, the early
believers read John's description of his vision, they immediately recognized the
symbolism, saw the broad lines of the story, and understood the message. Modern
Christians, reading the same text, have the disadvantage of being so far removed in
both time and circumstance that the symbolic nature of the language has become
difficult to penetrate. Serious studies can open up some of the text, but modern
readers should recognize the difficulties apocalyptic language presents and focus
on the main point without getting sidetracked by the intriguing interpretive possibilities of the details.

Apocalyptic language is cataclysmic. That is, it involves heaven and earth in
gigantic events that alter the course of history and the universe. It has an enormous
breadth of scope and can in one broad sweep include all of history from its primor-
dial beginnings to its final end. Although apocalyptic language occurs commonly
outside the biblical literature, there is a distinction between biblical and nonbiblical apocalypticism. Biblical apocalypticism is theocentric, which means that God
is at the center and in charge of all that happens. Nonbiblical apocalypticism pres-

ents a cataclysmic and cosmic fight between good and evil where the outcome hangs in the balance.

Also, nonbiblical apocalypticism usually works from the presupposition that matter (the world and everything in it) is evil, whereas the biblical texts consider matter as created by God and, therefore, essentially good. Apocalyptic texts from the Bible have not given up on the present world. Not everything is evil; how people live makes a difference. Ethics is important; people's lifestyles and decisions have eternal significance. In the biblical Scriptures there is always hope for the world. As a contrast, nonbiblical apocalyptic texts typically have given up on the present and are simply awaiting the world's destruction. Where nonbiblical apocalypticism is satisfied asking the philosophical and unanswerable question, "Where does evil come from?" biblical apocalypticism asks the question, "How have we sinned?" Biblical texts, even in their apocalyptic sections, always work from the assumption of God's kingship.

THE BOOK OF REVELATION IS A VISION WRITTEN TO BRING HOPE

1. A new heaven and a new earth fulfill a vision of hope.

Describing the story of God's future for his people, John looked forward to a new heaven and a new earth. His vision was a vision of hope. God had not given up on his creation. Following the language of Isaiah,[3] rather than that of the parallel apocalyptic writing of his day, he talked about how God would renew his creation. The old earth would pass away, but a new earth would come to be. The same would hold true about heaven. God would even change his own dwelling when the time comes for him to make all things new.

The significance of this language should not be missed. Rather than declaring eternal doom on his creation, God promised a change that would bring his creation to the point of its original intent. The whole earth will be changed into a new "garden of Eden" where God walks and talks to his creation and where the presence of his goodness will saturate reality in such a way that all things will be made new (21:5).

The dysfunctional relationship between God and human beings that has plagued history since the fall will be changed as well. God will again dwell with humans in a perfect relationship (21:1–4). The "already but not fully" experience of God's kingdom that Christians have known since the coming of Jesus, and more broadly since the day of Pentecost, will be replaced by a full and complete experience of God's presence. Believers, who now see dimly, will be brought back into the full light of God's presence.

---

[3] "Behold, I will create new heavens and a new earth. The former things will not be remembered, nor will they come to mind" (Isa. 65:17). "As the new heavens and the new earth that I make will endure before me, declares the LORD, so will your name and descendants endure" (Isa. 66:22).

2. Evil will be punished and the faithful vindicated.

According to John's vision of the future of God's story, God will not destroy his own creation but rather the evil forces that led them astray.[4] These evil forces, led by their chief master and strategist, Satan himself, will face God's crushing judgment and eternal punishment. The faithful believers, who at the time of Revelation were facing the excruciating horrors of relentless punishment, should not lose heart. Their suffering is temporary, and they should go through it knowing that it is not the end.

The evil one and all his helpers will not get the last word. They will be punished, and their punishment is not temporary but eternal. While it might have looked to faithful and suffering Christians as if evil spirits and evil people had the upper hand (since unstoppable punishment rained down upon them), the day would soon come when Satan himself, along with all those he had gathered to help his cause, would face God's eternal wrath: "And the devil who had deceived them was thrown into the lake of fire and sulfur, where the beast and the false prophet were, and they will be tormented day and night forever and ever" (20:10 NRSV). Moreover, God's wrath and punishment of forces opposing him would not end with human and spiritual powers but be complete in its destruction of every opposing force; even death and Hades will be thrown into the lake of fire (20:16).[5]

The promise was unmistakably clear. The devastating situation that faithful believers experienced at the moment would be turned upside down. In the end, those who had held out and stayed faithful through their suffering would come to reign with God.[6]

STUDY QUESTIONS

1. John wrote Revelation from the island of Patmos. Why was he there?
2. Why was it a problem for Christians to call the emperor "lord"?
3. Why is Revelation so difficult to read for modern Christians?
4. What was the central promise of Revelation to the early Christians?

---

[4] The book of Revelation does not speak about a rapture where some people are taken away while the rest of God's creation is destroyed. The idea of a rapture comes from 1 Thessalonians 4:17.

[5] The Greek word *Hades* translates the Hebrew word *Sheol* which merely names the place of the dead. This should not be confused with *Gehenna* which is the word used for what most people traditionally think of as hell.

[6] Revelation 5:10; 20:4, 6; 22:5 (cf. Dan. 7:18).

ACT 2

GOD BRINGS HIS STORY TO ITS CLIMACTIC END

THE SECOND COMING OF CHRIST

More than simply sharing a vision of hope that points to God's final vindication of his people, the book of Revelation tells the story of God's conclusion to the drama of history. As God's story nears its final point of fulfillment, historical events will unfold according to God's planned order. Beyond merely declaring a simple end to history's flow, Revelation seems to outline a flow of final events that read like a final crescendo to the story that began in Genesis. The promise announced by the Gospels and the book of Acts, that Jesus Christ will come back to gather his faithful unto himself, is reemphasized and detailed by Revelation.

Since, however, Revelation makes use of apocalyptic language, which is packed with symbolism, the text appears less than straightforward to modern readers. Discussions about how Revelation is to be understood abound, and explanations of how various images and symbols are to be interpreted flourish. Serious Bible-believing Christians, including strong evangelical scholars, argue diverse, even disparate, viewpoints. The natural human infatuation with the possibility of knowing God's plans for future events has led to an exorbitant amount of literature on the subject of the end-times. Still, at least among scholars, patterns of interpretation seem to develop along the lines of four (or maybe five[7]) different perspectives.

Common to all Christian believers is the anticipation of Christ's return to earth.[8] The Gospels, Acts, and the letters of Paul refer to Jesus' second coming as a point of hope and comfort for Christians. This holds true also of Revelation, but Revelation's detailing of the event further places Christ's return in the context of judgment. Jesus comes back to announce the beginning of the end, a time of judgment that will be joyful for believers and painful for unbelievers. Although the specifics of how and when this judgment occurs are interpreted differently among scholars, all Christians agree that the second coming of Christ points to the end of our world as we know it today.

Most of the significant discussion centers on the understanding of the millennium, or the thousand-year reign of Christ, described in Revelation 20:1–6:

> And I saw an angel coming down out of heaven, having the key to the Abyss and holding in his hand a great chain. He seized the dragon, that ancient serpent, who is the devil, or Satan, and bound him for a thousand years. He threw him into the Abyss, and locked and sealed it over him, to keep him from deceiving the nations anymore until the thousand years were ended. After that, he must be set free for a short time. I saw thrones on which were seated those who had been given authority to judge. And I saw the souls of those who had been beheaded because of their testimony for Jesus and because of the word of God. They had not worshiped the beast or his image and had not received his mark on their foreheads or their hands. They came to life and reigned with Christ a thousand years. (The rest of the dead did not come to life until the thousand years were ended.) This is the first resurrection. Blessed and holy are those who have part in the first resurrection. The second death has no power over them, but they will be priests of God and of Christ and will reign with him for a thousand years.

Scholars generally debate four different views that are labeled according to how Christ's return relates to the millennium: postmillennialism, amillennialism, historic premillennialism, and dispensationalism (or dispensational premillennialism). Each view brings God's story to its end in a slightly different way.

---

[7] A view called the Preterist View falls outside of the present discussion. The Preterist View has more to do with a specific view of the book of Revelation than it does Christ's second coming. Preterists hold to a strict historical interpretation of Revelation. Everything in Revelation pertains to the first- or second-century Christians and has no prophetic value for the future.

[8] The biblical teaching is so clear on this point that all scholars of the biblical text affirm it as an integral part of the Christian faith. Those who reject a second coming of Christ do so on a different basis; they are guided by presuppositions that disregard the biblical text.

POSTMILLENNIALISM

Guided by strong presuppositions, the postmillennial view was especially strong in the nineteenth century prior to the two world wars. Postmillennialists hold that Christ's second coming will occur after (post) the thousand years. The thousand-year reign is, in other words, going on at the moment as the kingdom of God is being extended through the preaching of the gospel throughout the world. The world is in the process of becoming Christianized; and when the total number has come in, Christ will return to proclaim victory. Postmillennialism is a highly optimistic view building on the belief that righteousness and peace are on the increase in the world.

This view was common during the heydays of the enlightenment when the majority of scholars from every discipline, and most people in general, had become convinced that complete world peace was within reach and that illiteracy and poverty were soon to be eliminated. Many, if not most, saw the enlightenment and the progress it produced in so many areas of human life as evidence of *the* blessing that would solve the morass haunting humanity throughout history. Christians during this period found it easy and natural to interpret the positive aspects of the enlightenment as evidence of the extension of God's kingdom in the world.

Then, in 1914, came the First World War. This marred the optimistic view held by many philosophers and theologians, and when only twenty years later the Second World War broke out, this optimism pretty much disappeared and along with it the postmillennial view of history.

In the view of postmillennialists, the final chapters of God's story would run something like this: the millennium will not be essentially different from the present age although sin will be significantly on the decrease due to the rapid expansion of the Christian message. The present age will gradually, but surely, give way to the millennial age as every day is getting better. Christ will come back at the end of the thousand years, which does not refer to a literal one thousand years. Great awakenings, as seen during the revivals of Wesley, Whitefield, and Edwards will further advance the gospel and accomplish God's purpose prior to Christ's return.

Christ's return will be visible for all people and be followed by a general resurrection of both the righteous and the unrighteous before the judgment of all people. Those who do not know Christ will be judged according to their works, and those who are Christian believers will be judged according to their attitude and level of commitment to Christ. The believers will be saved from condemnation and eternal punishment and will enjoy God's eternal presence and blessings. The degrees of rewards granted believers in the eternal state will be calculated on the basis of their faithfulness during their natural or earthly life.

AMILLENNIALISM

In contrast to postmillennialism, the amillennialist view remains a common view among scholars and Christians in general. Its pedigree sports a list of prominent proponents reaching back to early church fathers like Clement of Alexandria and Augustine, and it includes prominent church theologians from almost every period of church history. Many of the largest Christian denominations hold to a version of amillennialism; for example, it is the official position of the Roman Catholic Church, the position held by Reformed churches in general, and the understanding of many Lutherans, Presbyterians, and Baptists. Although amillennialists disagree on some of the specifics details, the general understanding of amillennialism is as follows:

Amillennialists differ radically from postmillennialists in their view of the present age, but their outline of the events of the last days of history, or the time of Christ's return, differs little. Majoring on the apocalyptic character of Revelation, they understand all numbers to have a symbolic value that points to a greater reality than the literal meaning of the terms. As the amillennial name indicates, amillennialists reject a literal thousand-year reign of Christ. Rather, they see *thousand* as a symbol of perfection that refers to a period of time that is "perfect" in the eyes of God. One thousand, they say, is ten to the third power (10^3). Since the number ten signifies perfection and since anything lifted to the third power establishes it even further, amillennialists claim the terminology of one thousand years simply is Revelation's way of saying that God's timing is perfect.

Christ will return at the end of this age at the time God has already determined (Matt. 24:36). Different from postmillennialism, however, amillennialists do not hold to an overly optimistic view of history. They see the period of the church's presence on the earth as a time when good and evil struggle against each other or exist intertwined like a field that grows both wheat and weeds (Matt. 13:24–30). Evil may even get the upper hand until harvest time, the time of Christ's return, when everything is sifted and the weeds are burned (Matt. 13:36–43).

Amillennialists do not see Jesus' second coming as imminent in the immediate sense of that term. Several events clearly outlined in Scripture must occur before his coming. First, the gospel must be preached to all nations, and the calling of the Gentiles must reach its full number (Matt. 24:14; Mark 13:10; Rom. 11:25). Second, Israel must come to faith in Jesus as God's Messiah. This may not refer to the nation of Israel as a whole but rather to a certain number of Jews determined by God (Rom. 11:26). Third, Christians must face a period of great tribulation that will sweep the earth and cause a huge apostasy from the faith. Although the biblical references to this may point historically to the destruction of Jerusalem in AD 70, these texts also speak prophetically about the last days (Matt. 24:9–12, 21–24; Mark 13:9–22; Luke 21:22–24). Fourth, the Antichrist must be revealed. Notwithstanding that historical figures, who persecuted the church during the first century, have been referred to as antichrists by biblical authors, *the* final and true Antichrist will come as an eschatological person before the return of Christ. Fifth, wars, false prophets, miracles inspired by Satan himself, and signs in the heavens will precede Christ's coming. All these things must occur during the present age of the church *before* Christ will return.

Like the postmillennialists, amillennialists understand the return of Christ and the time of judgment as one big event. When Christ returns, he will come personally and physically in an event that will be visible to all. Resurrection of both believers and unbelievers will happen at the same time (Dan. 12:2; John 5:28–29; Acts 24:15; Rev. 20:13–15).

The purpose of the resurrection is judgment. Both the resurrection and the judgment will be general in the sense that it will assign each person to his or her eternal destiny. Believers will be raised to eternal bliss and unbelievers to eternal punishment. Christ himself will be the judge, and he will judge on the basis of the revelation or light received by each individual. Believers will be judged on the basis of their relationship with Christ (John 3:18, 36; 5:24) whereas nonbelievers will be judged on the basis of their works (Matt. 12:36; 25:35–40; 1 Cor. 4:5). Believers, therefore, will be rewarded according to the level of their faithfulness (Luke 19:12–19; 1 Cor. 3:10–15), while nonbelievers will experience varying degrees of suffering (Luke 12:47–48).

In summary, according to amillennialism, God's story will come to an immediate end in God's perfect time. Until then, as Christian believers have experienced it since the beginning, the goodness of God's grace will continue to be interrupted by Satan's evil schemes in an ongoing struggle. Suffering will not escape the Christians; but when Christ returns, he will judge all people. Those who have been faithful believers will find complete forgiveness from their sin and be rewarded by God's eternal blessings.

HISTORIC PREMILLENNIALISM

The biggest distinction between historic premillennialism and amillennialism is that historic premillennialism sees Christ's return and the final judgment as a two-stage event. Jesus' second coming will occur before (pre) the thousand-year period, and the final judgment will occur at the end of that period. Although historic premillennialists can agree with amillennialists that "thousand" probably should not be taken literally, they do see this time period as a distinct period that follows the return of Christ. According to historic premillennialism, the thousand-year reign will be a time when Christ establishes his kingdom on earth.

Historic premillennialism also agrees with amillennialism that no sharp distinction should be made between Israel and the church. God's story concludes with a description of how suffering believers are vindicated and eternally rewarded without making a distinction between Jews and Gentiles. According to historic premillennialism, God does not have a special plan of salvation for Israel. Since, for example, the New Testament clearly applies Isaiah 53 to the church, it is impossible to claim that Old Testament prophecies, originally spoken to the nation of Israel, must be literally fulfilled. Historic premillennialists argue that the New

Testament is replete with references to how Old Testament prophecies are fulfilled by the church which has become the "spiritual Israel" (Rom. 2:28–29; 4:11, 16; 9:26–26; Gal. 3:7, 29). To historic premillennialists, this does not mean that God has forgotten his old covenant people, just that they, too, must come to faith in Christ and be included in the church.

Historic premillennialists take the flow of the final chapters of Revelation to be descriptive of the flow of the end-time events. According to Revelation 19:6–10, the return of Christ will be like a wedding banquet where Christ is united with his bride, the church. Such a celebration grows out of the first resurrection which will occur immediately upon Jesus' second coming and include all believers from all ages of history (20:4–5). Also at this event Christ will conquer his enemies, throw the Antichrist and the false prophets into a lake of fire (19:20), and cast Satan in a bottomless pit where he will be bound for a thousand-year period (20:2–3).

The time leading up to the return of Christ will be a time of tribulation. Historic premillennialism follows the teaching of the early church that Christians will not escape the time of tribulation. They will be caught up with Christ only as he returns to establish his kingdom on earth. This millennial kingdom does not differ in essence from the kingdom already established in heaven from where Christ already rules, seated at the right hand of the Father (Phil. 2:5–10). Rather, it is to be the culmination of the kingdom that was *already established* at Christ's first coming but which is *not* to be *fully established* until his second coming (1 Cor. 15:24; 1 Tim. 6:15; cf. Acts 2:34–35) and finally consummated at the end of the thousand years after the destruction of death, the final enemy (1 Cor. 15:23–26).

Since Satan is bound during the millennium, there will be no external source for spiritual deceit or rebellion against Christ. The millennium, therefore, will be a time of great peace and righteousness. God's kingdom promises will be fulfilled. Under the perfect reign of Christ and his faithful believers (2 Tim. 2:12; Rev. 5:10; 20:6), creation will be liberated (Rom. 8:18–23), the curse on nature and humanity will be removed (Isa. 11:6–9; 35:5–6), and the earth will bear fruit as before the fall (Amos 9:13).

At the end of the thousand-year reign, Satan will be loosed for a little while during which time he will lead a final rebellion against God's kingdom, gathering the people from all corners of the earth who failed to come to genuine faith during the millennium (20:7–9). This rebellion ends when Satan is thrown into the lake of fire where he will be tormented for all eternity (20:10). Following Christ's crushing of this final rebellion, the second resurrection will bring all nonbelievers before the white throne judgment of God (20:11–15). These will be judged on the basis of their work, and if their names are not found in the book of life, they will face the second death and be thrown into the lake of fire with Satan, the Antichrist, the false prophets, death, and Hades. After the destruction of all evil and of death, the final state of God's kingdom, the new heaven and the new earth, will be the reality.

DISPENSATIONALISM OR DISPENSATIONAL PREMILLENNIALISM

More of a modern approach developed as late as the nineteenth century. Dispensationalism became popularized in America through the Scofield Reference Bible whose marginal comments guided millions of users. [9] Dispensationalism agrees with historic premillennialism that Christ's return occurs before the millennium. It differs from historic premillennialism, however, on some rather significant points, which, for the most part, find their roots in dispensationalism's insistence on a literal fulfillment of Old Testament prophecies upon national Israel. Since many of the Old Testament prophecies remain unfulfilled in terms of national Israel, dispensationalists claim that God, to be true to his word, must fulfill his promises to Israel. This fulfillment will happen during the thousand-year reign when Christ returns to rebuild the temple on the temple mount in Jerusalem and to reinstitute the temple worship.

This insistence on the literal fulfillment of Old Testament prophecy has led dispensationalists to claim a God-ordained distinction between Israel and the church that results in two different plans of salvation—one for the church and one for Israel.[10] According to dispensationalism, the present age, or dispensation, is called the church age. The church age exists for the church to spread the gospel to the Gentile world. The church dispensation will come to an end at the time of the rapture, which according to dispensationalists means that all Christian believers will be lifted up and taken away from the earth (1 Thess. 4:17). When Christ comes back for his church at the time of this rapture, his coming introduces a time of severe tribulation that will last for seven years (Dan. 9:24–27). The tribulation that ensues after the Christian believers are removed from the earth is designed to judge the unbelieving Gentiles (Isa. 26:21; Jer. 25:32–33; 2 Thess. 2:12) and discipline disobedient Israel (Jer. 30:7; Ezek. 20:37; Dan. 12:1; Zech. 13:8–9). The dispensationalist argument for the pretribulation rapture of the church springs from the conviction that God has no need for the church on the earth during this period of judgment and discipline.

After the period of tribulation, Christ will return again with the saints that were raptured before the tribulation. Upon this third coming, both Old Testament and New Testament believers who have died will be resurrected to inherit the kingdom (Rev. 20:4). Nonbelieving Jews and Gentiles who are alive at this return will be judged. The Jews will be judged on the basis of their faithfulness as stewards of God's Word (Matt. 25:14–30) and their willingness to receive Christ at his return (Matt. 25:1–13). The Gentiles will be judged on the basis of their treatment of the Jews (Joel 3:2; Matt. 25:40). Jews receiving a positive judgment will come to reign

---

[9] Dispensationalism claims history is divided into seven dispensations or ages. These are named the dispensation of: (1) Innocence, Genesis 1–3 (Adam and Eve); (2) Conscience, Genesis 4–8 (Adam to Noah); (3) Human Government, Genesis 8–11 (Noah to Abraham); (4) Promise, Genesis 11–Exodus 18 (Abraham to Moses); (5) Law, Exodus 18–Acts 1 (Moses to the cross); (6) Church, Acts 2–Revelation 19 (Pentecost to millennium); (7) Millennium, Revelation 20 (millennial kingdom).

[10] The attempt here is not to give a full description of dispensational premillennialism but rather to point to the places where it differs most clearly from historic dispensationalism.

in the millennial kingdom (Matt. 25:21), while a positive response for the Gentiles gives them inheritance in the kingdom along with other believers (Matt. 25:34).

During the millennium Christ is to rule as king from Jerusalem seated on the throne of David. All God's covenants to Israel will be fulfilled including the new covenant with its promise of forgiveness. Christ will call Jews from all the nations to gather in Jerusalem where they will be converted to faith in Christ and restored to the promised land under the rule of Jesus, the Messiah. It will be a time of peace, comfort, and joy without poverty and illness. When the millennium ends, the white throne judgment will introduce the eternal state where the faithful believers will come to enjoy God's eternal blessing on a new earth while the nonbelievers will face God's eternal damnation.

CONCLUDING GOD'S STORY

Although the apocalyptic language of Revelation proves difficult for both scholars and general Bible readers, disagreements about finer details should not cloud the clear picture. The big lines are clear. When God draws his story to its conclusion, he brings it full circle. His ultimate destiny for his creation remains an earthly one. Parallel to the experience of human beings, who will be given a new body for the eternal life after their resurrection, the physical world itself will receive a new earth for its new redeemed existence. Christians are not looking forward to the end of the world but to the end of the world as we know it. The bondage to this fallen age will be lifted and the whole creation will share in the bodily resurrection (Rom. 8:18–23).

This new eternal state will not make human beings equal to God. He will continue to be God, and human beings will continue to be creatures. One may say that it is because humans will remain creatures of God even in the eternal state that the earth God created as the scene for his created order will continue to be needed in eternity. The "new heaven and the new earth" correspond to the resurrection of the body. Even in the eternal state, where the redeemed believers dwell in God's full presence, the distinction between God and his creation will not be obscured.

At the time of the eternal state, God's story will have run its course and reached its fulfillment. The perishable will have been replaced by the imperishable. God will dwell eternally among people as their God; "they will be his people, and God himself will be with them" (21:3). This covenant promise given first to Abraham, and repeated throughout the history of God's dealings with his people, has now come to its complete and eternal fulfillment.

The center of the new earth will be the Holy City, the New Jerusalem. In the center of the city stands the temple, the throne of God. This temple will be without a veil because no veil will be necessary to hide God's face. God's "servants will worship him; they will see his face, and his name will be on their foreheads" (21:3–4 NRSV). The goal of redemption has been met; people will be able to see God's face. No one has ever seen God's face, but it was the mission of Christ, who is close to the Father's heart, to make God known (John 1:18). The new earth, inhabited by people who came to know God through Christ's mission, will be the arena where God reveals his full glory and allows people to gaze upon his face.

The curse from the rebellion started by Adam and Eve in the garden will have been lifted. John's vision of God's future for his people brings God's story to a conclusion where a new redeemed society lives on a new earth where all evil has been destroyed and where God again will dwell in the midst of his people. Indeed, they shall not only know him as he is; they shall see him face-to-face.

STUDY QUESTIONS

1. What major point in the events of the end-times do all Christians agree upon?
2. What does the word *millennium* refer to?
3. According to premillennialism, who will be judged at the white throne judgment?
4. What will happen to the earth when eternity begins?

THE STORY OF THE BIBLE

Creation	The story begins with God creating the world and human beings.
Crisis	Humans choose to rebel (or sin) against God. Sin brings consequences: pain, suffering, death, and separation from God. All people and all creation are affected.
Covenant	God chooses Abraham and establishes a covenant with him so that he might become the leader of a group of people who will follow God and call other people to follow God. God delights in using his people to bring the rest of the world to himself.
Calling Out	Genesis tells the story of the patriarchs: Abraham, Isaac, Jacob (Israel), and Joseph, who ends up in Egypt. In Egypt the small group of Hebrews grows into a nation and ends up in slavery. God uses Moses to deliver his people through the exodus event.
Conquest	God uses Joshua to help his people take the promised land (Canaan). After the conquest during the Period of Judges, God rules through judges in various parts of the land. This is a dark time for the Hebrews accentuated with sin, idolatry, and oppression.
Kingdom	God's people acquire a king. Samuel is the link between the judges and the kings. Saul is the first king, followed by

	David and his son Solomon. God establishes a covenant with David, promising the Messiah will come through his family line and reign forever.
Kingdom Divided	After Solomon civil war breaks out leading to a division of the kingdom: Israel, the Northern Kingdom; Judah, the Southern Kingdom. There are numerous kings, some good but most bad.
Captivity	Israel (Northern Kingdom) is judged for the sin of breaking the covenant when Assyria conquers it in 722 BC, and Judah receives a similar judgment later when Babylon conquers it in 586 BC and takes Judah's people into exile.
Coming Home	The people return from Babylonian exile under Zerubbabel, Ezra, and Nehemiah. They rebuild the temple and focus on the law of God.
Christ	About four hundred years later God sends his Son, Jesus the Christ, to save his people from their sins, fulfilling the promise given to Abraham. Jesus is crucified, dies, is raised from the dead, and ascends into heaven to return again later.
Church	Those who accept Jesus become part of the church, the people of God made up of both Jews and Gentiles. God continues to use his people to extend his offer of salvation to a sinful world.
Consummation	**God closes history with a final victory over evil. Those who have rejected God will suffer his judgment while those who have received him will live with him in a new heaven and a new earth.**

LAST THOUGHTS:
THE MEANING OF THE STORY
IN THE 21ST CENTURY

WORLDVIEW

Worldview speaks of how a person sees the world and interprets it in life. Everyone has a worldview which determines how they live. A worldview consists of a set of beliefs that guide actions and choices. Personal stories are part of a worldview. They provide some of the tools by which humans make sense of life. The story of God's creation, redemption, and consummation of all things provides a framework to view the world. But the biblical story claims to be more than just one of the stories; it is *the big story* that functions as the interpretive framework for all other stories including personal stories. The story this book retells and explains is the meta-narrative that connects all of life's smaller stories and gives them meaning.[1]

As the story of all stories, this narrative forms the basis of the Christian worldview. All personal stories in a Christian's life are interpreted in light of God's story. All decisions Christians make should be shaped by God's story. As with all worldviews, the meta-narrative shapes the way people think and the way they answer the basic questions of life. Because it finds its origin in God's revelation of himself, it often yields different answers from other worldviews. The following chart lists the basic life questions and compares the answers generated by various worldviews.[2]

---

[1] For further discussion of how the meta-narrative of the Bible affects all other stories, see Kevin Vanhoozer, "Introduction: Hermeneutics, Text, and Biblical Theology" in *A Guide to Old Testament Theological Exegesis,* ed. Willem A. VanGemeren (Grand Rapids: Zondervan Publishing House, 1997), 36

[2] Used by permission of Scott Duvall.

Basic Worldview Questions	Modern Answer	Postmodern Answer	The Biblical Worldview
Where are we?	We are in a world of resources that can be known by science and controlled by technology.	We are in a world of our own making (virtual reality).	We are in a world created and sustained by God.
Who are we?	We are autonomous. We are in control, and we are confident.	We are like people with multiple personality disorder. We are not an autonomous self; we are many selves.	We are human beings created in the image of God for the purpose of loving God and other human beings.
What's wrong?	Anything that threatens progress and questions of control of our own destiny.	Any grand system of truth (including scientific naturalism or the biblical worldview).	We have chosen to rebel against our Creator. Our sin prevents us from having a relationship with God.
What's the remedy?	We must devise our own remedy. We must save ourselves.	We must get rid of any story or program that claims to have the answer for every person.	God has come to our rescue in Jesus Christ whose life, death, and resurrection provide a way for us to relate once again to God.

With every life question comes a corresponding answer based on the view one has of reality and truth. The modern worldview focuses on man's ability and technology. In a sense it sees a man-made world with man-made solutions to problems. The postmodern worldview rejects the modern concept and understands the world in less universal terms. Individuals and groups make their own world, and their own personal stories become their interpretive framework. This results in relativism and an individual focus. Postmoderns reject the notion of a meta-narrative that gives structure and meaning to all experiences.

This book has dealt with God's story which, as the explanation of all reality, yields answers to all the big questions of life. Where are we? We live in a world created and sustained by God. God is the reason for all things. Who are we? We are human beings created in the image of God for the purpose of relationship with God and others. What's wrong in the world? As the biblical story explains, sin entered the world through humans and affected negatively everything including humans' relationship to God. What's the remedy? God orchestrated a plan of redemption through Jesus Christ, his Son. Jesus provides the way to life through his own life, death, and resurrection. All of life centers on this story of redemption. The creating and redeeming God who loves his creation and desires only what is best for it becomes the foundation for all life.

All decisions and actions in life can and should find guidance from this story. If God is Creator, humans should live and act as created beings and not as their own gods. If Jesus is the only way to find true life, the best choice is to trust in him. The biblical story speaks of gaining life from death through the redemption provided by Jesus on the cross. Without it, all people are separated from God.

TRANSFORMATION OF WAY OF LIFE

The story not only affects the way a person thinks; it impacts action as well. A person who accepts God's story as true lives a certain way! That is because participation in God's story alters human behavior. In the Old Testament, wisdom literature provided guidance for this change of lifestyle; the New Testament explains it as life with Christ. A person who accepts Jesus becomes a new creature; the old has passed away, and all things have become new (2 Cor. 5:17). A Christian offers himself to God as a sacrifice and is transformed because of it (Rom. 12:1–2). The focus of a Christian is to live for God. "And whatever you do, in word or in deed, do everything in the name of the Lord Jesus, giving thanks to God the Father through Him" (Col. 3:17 HCSB).

God's story transforms the person who surrenders his/her life to Christ. That person puts off the old way of life, which grew out of other worldviews, and acts differently. A good beginning description of the life of a Christian can be found in Ephesians 4:25–5:2.

> Since you put away lying, speak the truth, each one to his neighbor, because we are members of one another. Be angry and do not sin. Don't let the sun go down on your anger, and don't give the Devil an opportunity. The thief must no longer steal. Instead, he must do honest work with his own hands, so that he has something to share with anyone in need. No rotten talk should come from your mouth, but only what is good for the building up of someone in need, in order to give grace to those who hear. And don't grieve God's Holy Spirit, who sealed you for the day of redemption. All bitterness, anger and wrath, insult and slander must be removed from you, along with all wickedness. And be kind and compassionate to one another, forgiving one another, just as God also forgave you in Christ.

Therefore, be imitators of God, as dearly loved children. And walk in love, as the Messiah also loved us and gave Himself for us, a sacrificial and fragrant offering to God (HCSB).

INDEX

BIBLICAL AND THEOLOGICAL TOPICS

amillennialism, 321–23

apocalyptic, 15, 152, 315–17, 319, 322, 326

Apocrypha, 13, 18

ark of the covenant, 17, 77, 89, 104, 110, 119, 233

ascension, 7, 12, 246–247, 249, 257–258, 265

Baal, 4, 94–95, 125, 128–29, 132

Babylonian captivity, 147–49, 151, 153, 158, 162, 173–74

baptism, 8, 68, 175, 182, 189–92, 262, 268, 278

canon, 13, 16–18, 163

corporate personality, 87–89, 91

covenant, 43–45, 47–48, 73–75, 93, 110, 147–48, 150, 173–74, 177, 227–28, 303–05, creation, 1, 11, 16, 23–29

cross, 7, 68, 76, 78, 140, 225, 229, 231–34, 242

crucifixion, 231–33, 242–43

Day of Atonement, 77

disciples, 195–97

dispensationalism, 320, 325–26

dominion, 25–27, 30

evolution, 28–29

Former Prophets, 12–13

Gethsemane, 7, 229

Gnosticism, 300–01

Gospels, 14–16, 18

Great Commission, 248

Heilsgeschichte, 68

Historical Books, 12, 14

historical premillennialism, 323-24

Hyksos, 61–62

idolatry, 4, 6, 94–95, 107, 120, 122, 125, 127, 132, 136, 138, 141, 148, 153, 160

image of God, 25–26, 29, 35, 208, 330

incarnation, 179–81, 300

inspiration, 16, 18

intertestamental period, 161–62

Israel, Northern Kingdom, 121–22, 127–35

Judah, Southern Kingdom, 121–22, 136–42

Judaism, 44, 73, 153, 158, 161, 175, 198–201, 208, 216, 219, 222–23, 243, 284, 303–05

Judges, 93–100

kingdom of God, 198–203, 208, 283, 321

Last Supper, 225–28

Latter Prophets, 12, 126

law, 73–78

Lord's Supper, 226–28, 265

Messiah, 6, 87, 99, 125, 139–40, 152–53, 157, 161–62, 174, 189, 190–91, 208, 220–21, 223, 275, 326

Minor Prophets, 126

Miracles, 68–69, 210–14, 260

missionary journey, 8, 17, 272, 274, 278

Passion Week, 219–20, 223

Passover, 6–7, 66, 68–69, 86, 139, 141, 219, 220, 222, 225, 227–28, 231,

Pentecost, 7–8, 36, 137, 150, 258–59, 263, 281, 317

Pharisee, 8, 162, 215, 219, 222–24, 250, 266

postmillennialism, 321–23

priest, 77–78, 94, 103

prophet, 103, 124–26

propitiation, 77–78

publican, 162

resurrection, 7–8, 11–12, 204, 240–47, 294–95, 321, 323–24, 326

Revelation, 313–18

sacrifice, 75–78, 191, 301

Sadducee, 162, 222–223

Sanhedrin, 7, 16, 162, 230–31, 233, 243, 266, 281

second coming, 124, 140, 152, 319–22, 324

Septuagint, LXX, 13, 17, 109

synagogue, 153, 199, 272, 274–75, 279, 303, 315

tabernacle, 3, 5, 77–78, 119, 149

temple, 119, 155–57

temptation, 31–32, 194–95, 291, 300; *of Jesus*, 192–94

Ten Commandments, 3, 73, 120

theodicy, 34

Torah, 12, 17, 153

trial of Jesus, 229–30

virgin birth, 138–39, 181

Vulgate, 12

Wisdom, 163–69

Writings, 12-13, 16–18, 45, 163, 167, 180, 182

BIBLE PLACES AND PEOPLES

Aaron, 65, 67, 72, 74, 78, 80–81, 122, 304

Abraham, 1–3, 43–49

Achan, 88–89

Ai, 90

Amos, 125–26, 132–34

Arabian desert, 80-81

Assyria, 134, 138–39

Babylon, 145–48, 151–53

Bethel, 46, 52, 105, 122

Bethlehem, 174, 176, 180, 184, 249

burning bush, 2, 64–65, 73, 76

Caesarea, 220, 267, 270, 281–82

Caleb, 79–80, 92

Canaan, 45–46, 90–92

Cyrus, 153–56, 222

Dan, person: 56, 93; place: 122

Daniel, 146, 151–54

David, 108–13

Deborah, 3, 95–96, 98

Egypt, 47, 54–56, 61–70

Eli, 103–05, 111

Elijah, 126, 128–32, 161, 249

Elizabeth, 5, 174, 183, 189

Elisha, 126, 131–32

Esau, 51, 53

Ezekiel, 5, 12, 124, 126, 146–50, 155, 157, 208

Ezra, 158–60

Gideon, 3, 95–97

Goliath, 109

Habakkuk, 124, 126, 145–46, 150

Hagar, 47

Haggai, 126, 156, 158

heaven, 2, 7, 9, 52, 72, 129, 140, 190–91, 199, 201, 215, 249, 316–17, 324

hell, 318

Hezekiah, 136–41

Hosea, 126, 132–34

Isaac, 48–52

Isaiah, 137–40

Ishmael, 47–48, 50, 183

Jacob, 51–55

Jeremiah, 146–148, 151

Jericho, 85, 87–88, 90, 203

Jeroboam, 4, 121–22, 127, 132, 136

Jerusalem, 110, 158–62, 219–24

Joel, 5, 126, 136–37

John, 197, 229, 269, 300–01

Jordan, 45–46, 85–86, 92, 95, 128, 132, 174, 190

Joseph, OT, 54–56

Joseph, NT, 174–75, 183, 189

Joshua, 72, 79, 85

Josiah, 16–17, 141, 146

Kadesh Barnea, 79–80

Luke, 18, 284

Malachi, 12, 126, 160–61,
Mark, 18, 271–72, 274
Mary, 138, 174–75, 181–84
Matthew, 197
Moses, 61–66
Mount Carmel, 129, 131, 132
Nathan, 110–111, 117
Nebuchadnezzar, 145–48, 151–53, 155
Nehemiah, 159–60
Omri, 127–28
Paul, 266–69, 272–85
Persia, 153, 222
Peter, 229, 259–60, 266, 269–70
Pharaoh, 55, 61–63, 65–66
Philip, 269–70, 281
Rebekah, 50–52
Red Sea, Reed Sea, 67–69, 80, 86
Rehoboam, 4, 121–22, 136

Rome, 9, 18, 162, 176, 257, 261, 267, 276,
    281–84, 314
Ruth, 99, 108
Samaria, 122, 127–28, 133–34, 248, 249, 259,
    269–70
Samson, 3, 95, 97–98
Samuel, 96, 103–07, 108, 110–11
Saul, OT: 106–10, 112, 122; NT: 266–67
Silas, 274–77
Sinai, 63, 71, 73–76, 78–79, 81, 86, 89, 122,
    147, 208, 258, 259
Solomon, 117–21
Timothy, 274, 276–277, 279, 283–284, 307
tower of Babel, 36
Ur, 43, 45, 67
Zechariah, prophet: 126, 155, 157–58, 221;
    priest: 5, 174, 189
Zerubbabel, 5, 155–56, 222